Garden Wildlife

Second edition

Written and illustrated by **Richard Lewington**
with bird illustrations by **Ian Lewington**
Introduction by **Ken Thompson**

To my daughter Alexandra

BLOOMSBURY WILDLIFE
Bloomsbury Publishing Plc
50 Bedford Square, London, WC1B 3DP, UK

First published in the United Kingdom 2008
This edition published 2019

A catalogue record for this book is available from the British Library

Library of Congress Cataloguing-in-Publication data has been applied for

ISBN: PB: 978-1-4729-6483-0; ePDF: 978-1-4729-6482-3; ePUB: 978-1-4729-6484-7

2 4 6 8 10 9 7 5 3 1

Designed by D & N Publishing, Baydon, Wiltshire
Printed and bound in India by Replika Press Pvt. Ltd.

To find out more about our authors and books visit www.bloomsbury.com and sign up for our newsletters

Contents

Preface to the second edition

The preparation of the first edition of this book took longer than expected, owing to the untimely death of Steve Hopkin, the original author, who was tragically killed in a car crash in May 2006, before the project had properly begun. Steve was a leading authority on many of the less well-known groups of invertebrates, and I hope, that in taking over as author, as well as illustrator, I have done justice to the animal life that shares our immediate environment, and which he was so looking forward to portraying in words.

Working on this book, and studying the wildlife in and around my garden, has made me aware of just what I've been missing, almost literally, on my own doorstep. I've also discovered how, over the years, wildlife adapts and evolves, resulting in the need for this updated and enhanced edition, which now includes common garden species that were rarities ten years ago. Whether we like it or not, we share our gardens with a huge number of creatures, and it should be remembered that despite a tiny minority that we occasionally clash with, we need them perhaps more than they need us.

Such is the diversity of life that surrounds us in our gardens, that it would have been impossible to complete this book without the help of many specialists, all of whom have been generous in sharing their knowledge, checking texts, finding and posting elusive specimens, and even in one case (SG), regularly dropping off subjects for portrayal, by bicycle, on his way through my village. Thanks, therefore, go to: Steve Gregory of the British Myriapod and Isopod Group; Dr Steve Head; Geraldine Holyoak; Darren Mann and Dr George McGavin (the latter formerly) of Oxford University Museum of Natural History; Sir David Attenborough; Robin Buxton; Peter Chandler; the late Professor Michael Majerus; John Partridge; Chris Raper; Tony Rayner; and the late Bob Saville. I should also like to thank Ken Thompson for his inspirational and thought-provoking Introduction.

One area of wildlife illustration I tend to avoid is bird illustration, for it is well known there is another Lewington, my brother Ian, who is far more accomplished than I at painting birds. I'm therefore delighted that for this edition he has added further to what I think should be regarded (even though I'm biased) as some of the finest portrayals of garden birds.

Many of the photographs in this book are by Richard Revels, and all are of outstanding quality. Thanks to him and the other photographers for enhancing the marvels of the wildlife garden.

The importance of design and editing is often underestimated, so I must thank Andrew and Anne Branson, who founded British Wildlife Publishing and were responsible for publishing the first edition, and Katy Roper of Bloomsbury Publishing for this edition, for their indefatigable patience and attention to detail.

Richard Lewington, April 2019

Introduction

A nation of gardeners

To an extent that seems unique in Europe, and perhaps in the world, the British are a nation of gardeners. Vast garden-free areas of terraced housing in industrial cities survive only in memory, and the bold post-war experiment in high-rise living is now widely acknowledged to have been a failure (no doubt partly because – as so often with mass housing in Britain – it was done on the cheap). For many Britons, the housing ideal remains the original 1930s Metro-land of steeply pitched roofs, mullioned windows, half-timbering and tall chimneys.

But the housing itself, desirable as it may have been, was only ever half the story. The British, even if they spent all day in an office in the city, always fancied themselves returning to what *Country Life* described as 'a rose-tinted view of the English countryside ... idyllic villages, vernacular buildings and already dying rural crafts ... a utopian never-never world of peace and plenty in a pre-industrial Britain'. Some of this utopia may have existed in the surrounding countryside, but if an Englishman's home was his castle, part of the appeal lay in the attached country estate, even if it was only a quarter of an acre. Here, the Lord of the Manor was the absolute ruler of a perfectly-manicured lawn, an equally perfect privet hedge, and maybe a shed or a greenhouse.

Time and fashion have moved on, and modern gardens display a bewildering array of styles, although a surprisingly high proportion still retain the basic formula of lawn surrounded by shrubs and herbaceous borders. Something else that hasn't changed is the sheer scale of the garden resource; around a quarter of the area of the average British city is private garden. But what certainly has changed is the context in which these gardens exist. Over much of lowland Britain, intensive agriculture (whether arable or pastoral) has swept away the countryside into which the original Metro-land expanded. Many hedgerows have gone, and the fields themselves contain only wheat or ryegrass, plus as few other weeds as modern science can manage. Wildlife has now been pushed back into odd, neglected corners, linear habitats such as road verges, railways and river banks, and the leftovers of mineral extraction such as disused quarries and gravel pits.

Garden wildlife

The impacts of the changes in the wider countryside on the relative importance of gardens and farmland for wildlife are well documented. Frogs and Hedgehogs are now both doing far better in gardens than they are in the wider countryside. In the arable prairie of eastern England, the Song Thrush is now virtually extinct outside gardens. You would think that recognition of the value of gardens for wildlife would by now be universal, but paradoxically many 'serious' naturalists remain a bit sniffy about garden wildlife. Gardens are home, they say, only to widespread and abundant species such as 'cabbage white' butterflies, sparrows and pigeons, and anyway, gardens (and their wildlife) aren't really 'wild'.

But in the last 10–20 years, a more enlightened attitude to gardens as wildlife habitats has begun to prevail, with people recognising that there never was much truth in those criticisms. The first simply isn't correct: as we shall see, there's plenty of rare, unusual and interesting wildlife in gardens if you bother to look for it. In any case, many formerly common species are now far from common. The second, more serious criticism is actually the opposite of the truth, and to see why, we need to take a broader look at the history of British wildlife and its habitats.

Almost the whole of Britain, apart from a few seashores and mountain tops, has been heavily modified by centuries of human activity, primarily farming. Indeed, those habitats now most prized by naturalists, such as lowland heath,

▲ Gardens are now one of the main habitats for the Hedgehog.

meadows and limestone pasture are entirely man-made. The rich wildlife of these habitats is a by-product of traditional, low-intensity farming. Even ancient broadleaved woodland, the habitat with the best claim to be 'undisturbed', is often far more interesting and diverse if managed by regular coppicing. Thus, there are few if any really 'wild' habitats remaining anywhere in Britain. But the story doesn't end there. None of the products of these wildlife-rich habitats, whether wool, charcoal or hay, pays enough for anyone to make a living these days, which is why modern, intensive (and wildlife-poor) farming has largely taken over. Where traditionally-managed wildlife-rich farmland persists today, it is because it is owned (or at least managed) by someone whose primary concern is the wildlife itself, rather than making money. Many, perhaps most, also have some form of statutory designation: national or local nature reserves, Sites of Special Scientific Interest, Special Protection Areas, Special Areas of Conservation, and so on. In other words, such places are even less wild today than they have ever been, with every detail of their management tailored to the requirements of particular rare, endangered or charismatic wildlife.

Against this background, to criticise gardens for their lack of 'wildness' is just comical. In truth, the wildlife of gardens is some of the most genuinely wild in the whole country. True, gardens are carefully managed, wholly artificial habitats, but then so is nearly everywhere else, and at least very few gardens are managed primarily with wildlife in mind. The rich wildlife of the average garden is an unintended by-product of gardening, an activity with quite different priorities (flowers, vegetables, recreation), just as it was once a by-product of agriculture.

I should add that not only has the context of the wildlife in gardens changed completely in the last 50 years, but so has the environmental context. Wider awareness of recycling, pollution, climate change and the health benefits (physical and psychological) of gardening has also led to changes in the behaviour of gardeners. Most garden-owners are now aware that gardens reduce the 'heat island' effect of cities and that gardens can strongly ameliorate the flooding caused by large areas of impermeable concrete and tarmac. There is a direct connection to gardening for wildlife here, for, as we shall see, the same things that improve the contribution of gardens to the sustainability of the physical environment (growing trees, composting) also improve gardens as wildlife habitats. Not that the battle is won – far too many homeowners are happy to pave over their front gardens to provide car parking – but that's a separate story.

How many species?

I mentioned earlier the 'rich wildlife' of the average garden, but even the keen wildlife gardener is probably unaware of just how rich. In fact, until not so long ago, everyone else was equally in the dark. The transformation in our understanding of garden wildlife can be traced to one remarkable woman: Jennifer Owen, who spent 30 years documenting the wildlife of her unremarkable

▲ Village gardens, showing a good range of shrubs and trees as well as lawns and flower borders. Research has shown that structural diversity, even in a small garden, is a key element in attracting a wide range of wildlife.

suburban garden in Leicester. Her findings are reported in a unique book, *Wildlife of a Garden*. As we shall see, the wildlife in Owen's garden turned out to be mind-bogglingly diverse, but if we start with the vertebrates, 'rich' isn't the first word that comes to mind: three different amphibians, and half a dozen mammals. She did manage about 50 different bird species, and there would be a few more if we include racing pigeons and escaped cage birds, but that's it; few urban gardeners are likely to see more.

Move down the size scale though, and things change dramatically. Owen recorded 1,997 different insects in her garden, plus 138 other invertebrates, over half of them spiders. In a few cases, she found a surprisingly high percentage of the total UK list in her garden: almost half the harvestmen, for example, and around a third of the butterflies, lacewings and hoverflies. Because she never even attempted to count or identify many groups of insects, the total number of species that turned up in Owen's garden is unknown, but it was almost certainly many thousands. The insect fauna of her garden is not dramatically inferior to that of Monks Wood Nature Reserve (despite the latter being over a thousand times larger), and for bees is actually larger, illustrating just how good gardens are for pollinators.

Owen's garden is not especially large and contains most of the things you would expect to find in a typical suburban garden: lawn, flowerbeds, herbaceous borders, deciduous and evergreen shrubs and trees, fruit bushes and an apple tree, a pond, a compost heap, greenhouse, paths and paving. Owen was perhaps less tidy than some gardeners, and she didn't use pesticides, although she was happy to use chemical fertilisers. In other words, her garden seems pretty 'average', although we don't know if it's exactly typical of British gardens, and whether the other 16 million are as good for wildlife, or worse, or maybe even better. The only large study of a wide range of gardens is the BUGS (Biodiversity in Urban Gardens in Sheffield) project, in which I and several colleagues looked at 61 gardens in Sheffield. For various reasons, the BUGS results cannot be compared directly with Owen's survey, since BUGS took place over a much shorter period and used a much more limited range of standardised sampling techniques. Nevertheless, BUGS confirmed that there wasn't anything very unusual about Owen's garden, and that most gardens are good for wildlife. BUGS found, for example, 276 species of beetles, 135 species of true bugs, 81 species of arachnids (spiders and harvestmen) and 55 species of craneflies. I don't know why, but for some reason it's that last statistic that always amazes me. Speaking as a mere botanist, I had no idea there were 55 different craneflies in the whole world, never mind in Sheffield gardens. I now know there are around 300 species in the British Isles, but I'm still astonished that we found so many of them. Bearing in mind that there are many other large families of flies, and a great many other groups of invertebrates, that we didn't even attempt to identify, you can begin to appreciate just how much (largely unnoticed) wildlife there is in gardens.

Soil dwellers

We'll look at why gardens are so good for wildlife later, and what we can do to make them even better, but first let's think about what all these animals are doing in our gardens. First of all, an observation: the most important animals in gardens are not necessarily the most diverse, and are often the least obvious. As we'll see, there's plenty of herbivory going on in gardens, but most plant material is eventually consumed not by herbivores, but by detritivores, i.e. consumers of dead material. In the BUGS project, we used three standard sampling methods: Malaise traps, designed to catch flying insects, and two which caught animals that live in and on the soil surface. One of these was pitfall trapping, which is simply using plastic coffee cups sunk into the ground to collect the animals that fall in, while the other was extracting animals from samples of 'litter', i.e. the layer of dead and partly-decayed plant material lying on the soil surface. In both cases, the catch was dominated by woodlice. Pitfall traps caught about as many woodlice as all other creatures combined, while litter samples contained more than twice as many woodlice as everything else together. The diversity of woodlice gives no clue to their importance; Owen found just eight species, and so did BUGS. Nor are their huge numbers obvious to casual inspection, since they hide during the day under stones or anywhere cool, dark and damp, and are only active at night. Some woodlice occasionally eat living plants, but overwhelmingly their diet consists of dead plant material, although they will also eat animal remains and dung. Abundant as woodlice are, however, they are far from the commonest detritivores in the garden. That position is occupied

▲ Woodlice, such as this Common Shiny Woodlouse looking rather like an extra from *Star Wars*, are one of the most numerous feeders of dead plant material.

by Collembola, or springtails, so called because of the springing organ under the abdomen that can be released to send the animal spinning through the air. Springtails are primitive wingless insects, and even the largest are very small. They are found in huge numbers in leaf litter, eating the litter itself and also feeding on the fungi that help to consume the litter. Because of their tiny size and huge numbers, Owen did not attempt to identify or even count them, and neither did BUGS.

After woodlice, the second-most abundant ground-dwelling animals caught by BUGS were slugs and snails. Despite some species having a deserved reputation as destroyers of living plants, most slugs and snails subsist largely on rotting vegetation, fungi, lichens and algae. Thus it's clear that the overwhelming majority of ground-dwelling animals in gardens are predominantly detritivores, and that's without even mentioning millipedes or earthworms, arguably the most important of all consumers of dead plants. This huge abundance is a testament to the prime importance of the food chain with dead, rather than living, plants as its base. Few gardeners are aware of this, because most of the animals involved are small, subterranean, nocturnal, or all three. All these animals also support a wide range of predators, including mites, beetles, centipedes, spiders, frogs, Hedgehogs and birds. As in the rest of the garden, most *individual* animals consume plants (alive or dead), but most *species* are predators.

Herbivores

Of course, as gardeners are all too well aware, many animals eat living plants too. But even here a lot of the damage takes place out of sight, below ground. Many soil-dwellers are indiscriminate consumers of dead plants, fungi and living fine roots – in fact, any organic matter that happens to come their way. Others, however, are more specialised consumers of plant roots. Familiar examples are the larvae of craneflies (leatherjackets), click beetles (wireworms), various noctuid moths (cutworms), and, of course, the dreaded Vine Weevil.

Above or below ground, the majority of herbivores fall into one of two broad classes: chewers and suckers. Naturally, chewers cause the most obvious damage, often leaving clear signs of their activity in the form of holes in leaves. Among the insects, the three major groups of chewers, each with species regarded as pests by most gardeners, are beetles, sawflies and Lepidoptera (moths and butterflies). In many cases, the adults do not eat plants at all, and even if they do, it's usually the larvae (caterpillars) that do most damage, since this is the part of the life cycle that does most of the growing, so naturally it needs the most food. Herbivores have plenty of enemies, so defences against predators are many and various, including camouflage, irritant hairs, hiding inside a variety of cases, rolled leaves or silken tents, or simply tasting bad. If a caterpillar is brightly coloured, for example the Cinnabar moth on ragwort, that's a sure sign it does not taste good. Many larvae spend all or most of their lives concealed inside plant stems or seed heads; others have gone even further and live inside trees, living or dead. Wood is a very poor food, so such larvae develop only slowly, but their reward is protection from most (but not all) predators. One group of specialist wood feeders is the longhorn beetles, which are large, handsome beetles with long antennae. Most are quite rare, but the Wasp Beetle is not uncommon in gardens.

Other chewers have come up with lifestyles that vertebrates, by virtue of their large size, cannot hope to emulate. The larvae of around 500 British insects, mainly moths, beetles and flies, live inside leaves. Naturally, to do this you have to be small, and it's definitely a case of 'By their works ye shall know them'; the insects themselves are rarely seen, although the mines themselves are often conspicuous. Probably the most familiar example in gardens is the Holly Leaf Miner, although another is occasionally a pest of beetroot (both these are flies). Leaf-mining insects are generally fairly specific to particular plants or groups of plant, but that does not mean that alien plants do not have them. The Firethorn Leaf Miner, a small moth, was introduced into Essex some time in the 1980s and can now be found making obvious mines on the upper surface of pyracantha leaves throughout much of England and Wales. It seems only a matter of time before it colonises the whole of Britain. Other insects have hit on the idea of persuading the plant to provide them with food *and* a hiding place: these are the gall-formers. The pre-eminent group here, responsible for most familiar galls, including marble and spangle galls of oak and Robin's pincushion mainly on wild roses, are the gall wasps. Again, the actual insects are tiny and rarely seen, and many have complex life cycles, involving alternating sexual and parthenogenetic generations. The latter involves reproduction without sex, in which females produce exact copies of themselves. Insects, like everyone else, are always on the look-out for a free lunch, and some gall wasps (and other insects, including flies and moths) do not make their own galls, but lay their eggs in the galls formed by other species. This behaviour is not strictly parasitism, and such species are known technically as *inquilines*, although they may accidentally cause the death of the rightful owner.

Gall wasps provide some of the most striking examples of the power of natural selection. Although the gall itself provides significant protection against predators, gall wasp larvae are nevertheless targeted by a variety of enemies, including the inquilines already mentioned, parasitic wasps, birds and even rodents. In response, some gall wasps of oaks have persuaded the tree to make galls that secrete nectar, something oaks would never normally do. The nectar attracts ants, which then help to defend the galls against predators. Another defence is to make galls with thick, tough walls, but even this does not always work. Parasitic wasps that attack particularly tough galls have ovipositors toughened with manganese, while other parasites have got round the same problem by laying eggs in very young galls. The young parasite can live on the gall tissue itself for some time, only later turning its attention to the growing gall wasp larva.

Herbivores that suck plant fluids are almost all in a single order, the Hemiptera or true bugs. Bugs vary widely in appearance and are hugely diverse, with around 1,700 species in the British Isles, but all share mouthparts modified into a piercing tube, like a tiny hypodermic needle. Such mouthparts are equally good for sticking into animals, and many bugs are predators, but among the herbivores are probably the most abundant plant-eaters in the garden, the aphids. Aphids have many enemies, and one of their defences is to secrete honeydew, which attracts ants, which in turn help to protect the aphids against predators and parasites. Ants are not the only insects attracted to these hordes; careful observation of aphid colonies will reveal social wasps, several different kinds of flies and even bees collecting the sugary honeydew. Much of it, of course, also falls on cars and garden furniture, much to the annoyance of gardeners. Mostly, however, aphids have given up any serious attempt at defence, relying largely on safety in numbers. In spring and early summer aphids rapidly build up vast colonies by parthenogenesis, with winged sexual forms appearing later. Most have more than one host plant during the year, hence names like Peach-potato Aphid and Rose-grain Aphid. The Rose Aphid, the rose-growers *bête noire*, starts off on roses in spring but moves onto scabious and teasel in summer.

Not all bugs are as unattractive as aphids. Many shieldbugs are large, handsome insects, and good but rather erratic fliers. The Hawthorn Shieldbug,

▶ Aphids, such as these Lupin Aphids, are herbivores that feed by sucking sap through a tubular mouth-piece. They are able to reproduce parthenogenetically, sometimes having several young a day. Two of the aphids in the photograph have just given birth.

a glossy green and bronze bug, with distinctive pointed 'shoulders', was frequent in Jennifer Owen's garden, and it is in mine, too. The froghoppers (or spittle-bugs), another group of bugs, have developed two interesting defences against predators: the nymphs blow bubbles out of their backside and hide in the resulting froth (cuckoo spit), while the adults are capable of jumping prodigious distances.

Pollinators

Specialist pollinators are valued by most gardeners, and indeed (along with birds) are the main target of most 'wildlife gardening', although most gardeners draw the line at cabbage white butterflies. The line between pollinators and herbivores is sometimes blurred: leaf-cutter bees remove pieces of leaf to build their nests, and click beetles and chafers eat pollen, nectar and the flower itself (some insects that frequent flowers, e.g. soldier beetles, are actually predators). Such beetles offer an interesting insight into the early evolution of pollinating insects. Primitive insects, almost certainly beetles, began to visit primitive flowers to eat pollen and ovules (immature seeds), both of which are rich in protein and a much better food source than leaves. In wandering between flowers and between plants,

▲ A Common Carder Bee collecting nectar and pollen from lungwort. Bumblebees are important pollinators of garden plants.

these beetles were the first insect pollinators. Natural selection quickly favoured plants that attracted pollinators with colour, scent and nectar, a process that eventually led to the evolution of modern specialist insect pollinators – moths, butterflies and modern flies and bees.

Among these, bees are the most specialised of all, since all stages of the life cycle depend entirely on flowers for food. The bees most often noticed by gardeners are the largest – Western Honey Bees and bumblebees. Both are *social*, i.e. they build large communal nests, with a queen who lays the eggs and female workers that collect the pollen and nectar. Uniquely among social bees, Honey Bee nests (hives) persist from one year to the next. To get them through the winter, they store honey, a habit that makes them very useful to us. Honey Bees are common in gardens, and some of them may be wild, but most will be 'farmed' by beekeepers.

Bumblebees are also social, but their nests are strictly annual affairs, abandoned at the end of the summer. Only mated queens survive the winter, setting out to establish new nests in the spring. There are 24 species of bumblebee in the British Isles, and both Jennifer Owen and BUGS found that six species are common and almost ubiquitous in gardens (see page 158). Four of these look rather similar, with variations on the familiar stripy yellow, black and white jerseys, and indeed two (*Bombus terrestris* and *B. lucorum*) are so similar that you need to be an expert to tell them apart. A fifth (*B. lapidarius*) is black with a red bottom, while the sixth and commonest (*B. pascuorum*) is slightly smaller, and a rather tawny colour all over. Both Owen's study and the BUGS project – and the first edition of this guide – were too early to record the Tree Bumblebee *B. hypnorum*, which was first found in the New Forest in 2001, remaining relatively scattered until at least 2009. Since then, this European bee has spread rapidly and is now one of the commonest bumblebees in British gardens. As its name suggests, the Tree Bumblebee nests in holes in trees and it is particularly fond of nestboxes provided for birds. These nesting habits are so different from those of any native bee that there is no reason to expect the Tree Bumblebee to compete with them – it is just an interesting and useful addition to our fauna. Like all bumblebees, *B. hypnorum* is a useful pollinator and completely harmless, as long as you leave it alone.

One of the rewards of getting to know your bumblebees is that you begin to notice that they have distinct flower preferences. For example, *Bombus terrestris* and *B. lucorum* both have relatively short tongues and prefer rather short, open flowers, although they will also 'rob' nectar from long-throated flowers, such as honeysuckle, by biting a hole in the flower. In my garden, I notice that the flowers of most runner bean and *Abelia* flowers have had such holes bitten in the base. In contrast, *B. hortorum* has a long tongue and is one of the commonest pollinators of deep flowers such as honeysuckle and delphiniums. *B. lapidarius* is extremely fond of massed small flowers such as knapweed – in my garden, for example, it's by far the commonest visitor to chives. Every gardener knows you need to grow lots of flowers to attract bumblebees, but few are aware of their nesting requirements. Some, including *B. terrestris* (hence the name), nest in holes in the ground (frequently using old mouse holes), while others, such as *B. pascuorum*, nest on the soil surface. Nests are commoner in gardens than most people realise, but they often remain undiscovered, though gardeners soon notice when a nestbox intended for birds is taken over by Tree Bumblebees.

More abundant than bumblebees in terms of numbers of species, but much less so in terms of numbers of individuals (ten times less in the BUGS study), are solitary bees. Nearly all are much smaller than bumblebees, so many gardeners do not notice them, but they are useful pollinators. As the name suggests, they live solitary lives, single females making small nests in holes in the ground, in hollow plant stems, dead wood or masonry. It's possible that, abundant as they are in gardens, numbers of all bees are limited by availability of nest sites, so it's worth trying to increase the number of sites (see later).

Both the other major pollinators – hoverflies, and moths and butterflies – have larval stages that do not depend on flowers. Moth and butterfly larvae (caterpillars) are plant-eaters, and we have looked at them already. Hoverflies are extremely abundant in gardens, confirming once more just how good gardens are for pollinators; in the BUGS study, hoverflies were the second-most abundant group of flying insects, after parasitoid wasps. Adult hoverflies eat nectar and pollen, but their larvae are quite varied in their habits. Some live in dung, decaying matter or water, eating rotting plants, many eat aphids, and one (the Large Narcissus Fly) is a minor pest of garden bulbs. Although many are important aphid predators, the legless, maggot-like larvae of hoverflies probably go unnoticed (or if noticed, unrecognised) by most gardeners. All adult hoverflies are bee and wasp mimics, despite being quite harmless. The technical term for this kind of mimicry, where a harmless animal 'cheats' by resembling a toxic or dangerous one, is Batesian mimicry. In practice, hoverflies are easily distinguished from bees and wasps by their short antennae.

Predators

Most of the larger animals in gardens are predators: Moles, Common Frogs, newts, Slow-worms, Hedgehogs, Foxes, bats and many birds. This, in itself, is one reason for appreciating all the smaller wildlife in your garden – even if you don't like creepy-crawlies themselves, most of them eventually end up as a meal for something larger. In addition, however, there is a host of smaller predators in gardens, many of them among the garden's most charismatic inhabitants. Personally, I think dragonflies alone are sufficient justification for digging a pond. Superb, acrobatic fliers with huge eyes, dragonflies (and their smaller relatives, damselflies) snatch their prey out of the air and then find a convenient leaf to rest on while consuming it at their leisure. Fearsome as adult dragonflies are, their aquatic nymphs are even more frightening, taking anything and everything up to the size of small fish. Other large aquatic predators include diving beetles, backswimmers and pondskaters. The last two are true bugs, and the bugs and beetles are also both major predators on land. Most ground beetles (carabids)

▲ A charismatic garden predator: a Spotted Flycatcher with a Swallow-tailed Moth.

and rove beetles (staphylinids) are predators, with the largest members of both, the Violet Ground Beetle and the Devil's Coach-horse, instantly recognisable even to the least observant gardener. Both are nocturnal predators of slugs, among other things. Many other beetles (and their larvae) are also important predators, and the larvae of ladybirds will be familiar to most gardeners. Most bug species are herbivores, but several are common and important predators. The Common Flower Bug, a useful predator of aphids and red spider mites, was extremely abundant in Jennifer Owen's garden, and in mine, and probably is in yours as well. Note that all the larger predatory bugs can (and will) pierce human skin if handled. Hardly life-threatening, but an unpleasant surprise if you're not expecting it.

At least some members of many other insect orders are predators, for example, lacewings and several types of flies. Large, bristly robberflies snatch other insects from the air or pluck them off leaves. Unfortunately, some flies (e.g. mosquitoes, midges and horse-flies) have taken to attacking mammals, including man. Even some bush-crickets (close relatives of grasshoppers) are carnivores, and not far away, in Europe, there are more exotic predators, including mantids and ant-lions. Indeed, ant-lions – rarely seen in Britain until relatively recently – are now spreading across suitable sandy habitats in south-east England.

However, the third great group of insect predators in British gardens are the wasps, which, like bees, come in social and solitary varieties. Also like bees, it's the larger, social species we mainly notice, although there are far more species of solitary wasps. Social wasps are regarded as an unpleasant nuisance by many gardeners, but they really are important predators, particularly of other insects. They also make large and elaborate nests from paper, and workers can often be seen scraping the raw material from fences and sheds. Some of the larger solitary wasps are quite similar to social wasps in appearance, but the majority are smaller and less brightly coloured. Most adult wasps make do with some pollen and a sip of nectar, but they catch other invertebrates to feed to their young. Social wasps are completely omnivorous, but solitary wasps tend to specialise on caterpillars, beetles, moths, flies, aphids, spiders, bugs or even other wasps. A nest in a hollow plant stem, dead wood or in the ground is stocked with paralysed prey and then an egg laid on top. Species that nest in the ground prefer undisturbed, sandy soil, which is uncommon in gardens, so most species in gardens nest in holes in plants. Some wasps are *kleptoparasites* (literally, parasites by theft) and lay their eggs in the nests of other solitary bees or wasps. The young parasite eats the rightful owner and then, to add insult to injury, usually its stored food as well. One example, the brilliantly metallic ruby-tailed wasps, are quite common in gardens.

Varied and abundant as insect predators are, there are other kinds of important garden predators, including spiders and centipedes. I get the impression that most gardeners' tolerance of creepy-crawlies goes down as the number of legs goes up, which puts centipedes at the bottom of the list (even if they don't all have 100 legs!). Centipedes hunt insects, spiders and worms, mostly at night. A quick rummage in the compost heap will soon turn up the common brown centipede, *Lithobius forficatus*, with 15 pairs of legs. Large ones will bite humans, but the bite is not dangerous. Other longer and more sinuous centipedes in the genera *Stigmatogaster* and *Geophilus* are common in soil.

From Shelob in *Lord of The Rings* to the famous scene in *Dr No*, spiders are always the bad guys, so I'm not going to try to persuade the arachnophobes among you to like spiders. But please try to remember that virtually all are completely harmless, and that they (along with their relatives, the harvestmen) are among the most diverse and numerous predators in every garden. Jennifer Owen found 91 species of spiders and harvestmen, and BUGS found 81 species. However, we really have no idea how many individual spiders there might be in an average garden. BUGS caught quite large numbers of spiders in pitfall traps

► Spiders, such as this Garden Spider, are important predators of a wide range of insects.

and litter samples, and a few in Malaise traps (a trap that looks a bit like a tent with no sides, designed to catch flying insects). But most garden spiders are not ground dwellers, and, of course, none of them fly, so BUGS sampled spiders very inefficiently. To show just how inefficiently, we didn't even record the Garden Spider in my garden, even though I know it's very common. The most abundant spiders in gardens are the lyniphiids (money spiders), most of which build a horizontal sheet web (often with a scaffold of threads above it) in shrubs or grass. Look at your garden on a misty autumn morning to appreciate just how plentiful these spiders really are.

I said I was not going to try to persuade you to like spiders, but I defy you to dislike Common Zebra Spiders, with their banks of enormous forward-facing eyes like car headlamps. They're common everywhere, on sunny walls and fences. Another spider that southern gardeners should look out for is the Flower Crab Spider, which lurks in flowers, waiting to pounce on unwary visiting bees, flies and butterflies. As its name suggests, it has a strongly crab-like appearance, but its most remarkable feature is the ability to change colour to match the flower it lives in – anything from white to yellow or pale green.

Parasitoids

Some insects have discovered ways of making a living that simply do not exist – perhaps fortunately – among vertebrates. The predators we've just been talking about kill their prey (obviously), and a single predator usually kills several prey during its lifetime. Parasites, on the other hand, rarely kill their hosts, and a single host may support many parasites. For example, around a quarter of the world's human population is infected by one species or another of nematode worm parasites (roundworms). Roundworms generally don't kill you, they just make you ill. Many insects, usually called *parasitoids*, have adopted a lifestyle that combines elements of both predators and parasites. Parasitoids usually develop inside their hosts (like a parasite), but the host is always killed (like a predator). Adult parasitoids search for their prey, often the eggs, larvae or pupae of other insects, then lay one or more eggs on, or more often in, the host. The young parasitoid develops inside the host, consuming it entirely apart from the skin, then pupates and eventually emerges as a new adult.

This sounds simple, but some of the biology involved is awesome (not to mention gruesome) in its complexity. Hosts have all kinds of mechanisms to defend themselves against parasitoids, including attempting to seal off (encapsulate) the parasitoid. Devious ways round this include laying eggs directly in the host brain, where the immune system cannot get at it, and the mother parasitoid injecting viruses that disable the host's immune system. Keeping the host alive, at least for the time being, is also a priority, and most parasitoids are careful to eat only non-essential organs first, such as body fat and reproductive organs. In other cases, specialised cells called teratocytes emerge from the egg along with the embryo. The teratocytes absorb food from the host and the parasitoid feeds on them rather than on the host itself, thus prolonging its life.

▲ This leggy ichneumon wasp is a parasitoid that lays its eggs directly into its victim, which then plays host to the developing larva.

Amazingly, some parasitoids are even hyper-parasites, attacking other parasitoids. Most parasitoids are wasps, although quite a few flies have adopted this lifestyle. A few are large insects, and those that attack hosts hidden deep inside plant stems may have fearsome-looking egg-laying ovipositors, but most are small and rather inconspicuous. Indeed, the smallest of all insects are parasitoids. If you're observant, you will often see parasitoid wasps quartering the vegetation, their long antennae constantly probing the way ahead, clearly searching for prey. If you're lucky, you may see tiny parasitoids working their way through a colony of aphids, pausing briefly to lay a single egg in each one. If you look carefully at an aphid colony, you will often see parasitised 'mummified' aphids. All parasitoids are quite harmless to humans, and indeed this way of life simply does not exist among large animals. The genius of the makers of the film *Alien* was to realise how frightening it would be if creatures existed that combined large size, the jaws and predatory instincts of a dragonfly nymph, and the life cycle of a parasitoid wasp.

Individual parasitoids are fascinating enough, but what makes them really remarkable is their abundance and almost unbelievable diversity. Parasitoid wasps were by far the most abundant flying insects caught during the BUGS project (many more than all other bees and wasps combined). However, although we counted them, we made no effort at identification. Jennifer Owen, on the other hand, was extremely fortunate to have a collaborator who was an expert on one large family of parasitoid wasps, the Ichneumonidae, and was prepared to spend three years (1972–74) identifying her Malaise trap samples (a heroic task!). Astonishingly, 529 species of ichneumonids were recorded in her garden, of which 15 were new records for Britain and four were completely new to science. Moreover, this is far from the whole story, since 1973 added 129 species not caught in 1972, and 1974 added a further 74 species not caught in either of the first two years. The implication is plain: if identification had continued, more species (perhaps many more) would have been found. Another pointer in the same direction is that Owen regularly collected larvae of moths and hoverflies and raised them to maturity, in order to identify the species (identifying the larvae themselves is virtually impossible). Sometimes the larvae raised were parasitised, and she found 20 species of ichneumons in this way, four of which were *not* among the 529 species caught in the Malaise trap. Finally, it's worth repeating that all these species belong to just one family of parasitoid wasps, albeit probably the largest. There are several other families.

Parasitoid wasps may be an extreme example, but they exemplify just how much wildlife there is in the average garden, most of it completely unnoticed. Much wildlife gardening advice, it seems to me, is rather misguided, for two quite different reasons. First, most advice encourages gardeners to concentrate only on large, obvious, brightly-coloured and generally 'desirable' wildlife. There's a lot more to garden wildlife than birds, bees and butterflies, and the rewards for the patient, observant gardener are enormous. Second, 'obvious' wildlife often has quite obvious requirements; few gardeners need telling to grow lots of flowers for pollinators or to buy a bird-feeder (although, having bought one, most gardeners do seem to need reminding to actually use it). Even here, however, I think there are other things gardeners could do that are not quite so obvious (see next section).

▲ Newly emerged parasitoid wasp larvae feeding on a noctuid moth caterpillar.

Gardening for wildlife

▲ An attractive garden with a nectar-rich flower border which, as well as providing colour for the gardener, is ideal for butterflies and bees.

Now that we've encountered some of the wildlife in our gardens, what can we do to attract even more? Well, first of all, here are a few things you *don't* need to do. Recall that all the wildlife I've just described (and more) was found in Jennifer Owen's garden. Recall also that she made few concessions to wildlife gardening beyond abstaining from pesticides and not being obsessively tidy. In other words, carry on doing exactly what you are doing already and a wealth of wildlife will be perfectly happy in your garden. Above all, there is no need to try to recreate any particular 'wild' habitat. The semi-natural habitats that we value for their wildlife, such as lowland heath, old meadows, chalk grassland and ancient woodland, are the product of centuries of coppicing, flooding, burning and grazing. You couldn't recreate them if you tried, and, what's more, they aren't in any objective way 'better' for wildlife than the average garden, they're just different.

Nor should you lose much sleep over the size or location of your garden. Not only can you do nothing about either, BUGS showed that they really don't matter. Small town gardens are just as good for wildlife as large, suburban gardens. You may find this surprising, but believe me, there are good biological reasons for not finding it surprising at all.

Start at the bottom

Since so much garden wildlife depends ultimately on dead plants, it follows that you simply can't have too much dead stuff in your garden. Lots of soil organic matter will encourage the myriad of animals that consume it, and the many other animals that eat them, right up to birds and Hedgehogs. Moreover, a soil rich in organic matter will be more permeable to water, less easily damaged by heavy rain, and more moisture-retentive. Given that climate change promises both more floods and droughts, the best thing you can do to future-proof your garden is keep your soil well covered with mulch or growing plants, and make and use as much compost as you can. The fact that all this will be good for wildlife too is just a bonus. Your compost heap itself will also make a good home for wildlife, especially if you have an open, wooden bin rather than one of the enclosed, plastic kinds. BUGS showed clearly that gardens with compost heaps had more beetles, which is hardly surprising, since compost is prime beetle habitat, especially for predatory staphylinids. If you're lucky, your heap may attract larger wildlife such as Slow-worms or even Grass Snakes. Mice nest in my compost heap, and although I know some gardeners would see that as a problem, I don't.

Don't forget dead wood, either. The larvae of many insects, especially beetles, depend on dead wood, and it's a resource in short supply in the average garden. A pile of logs, partly buried in a shady spot, will attract many species – maybe even Stag Beetles if you live in southern Britain. Even better, if you can manage it, is a dead tree stump (the bigger the better), since many insects prefer standing dead wood. If tree stumps aren't your idea of attractive garden furniture, they can easily be disguised with honeysuckle or clematis.

Native and alien plants

Much has been written about the relative virtues of native and alien plants for native wildlife in gardens. On the face of it, it looks like an open-and-shut case that native plants are better for native animals. The Sheffield BUGS project found rather little support for this idea, but admittedly it wasn't really designed to answer that particular question.

Much better evidence comes from the Royal Horticultural Society's (RHS's) Plants for Bugs project, which involved filling plots with plants of three levels of 'nativeness' (genuine natives, northern hemisphere 'near natives' and southern hemisphere 'exotics') and then capturing, counting and identifying the invertebrates that turned up. The first report from the study looked at pollinators and concluded that it does not matter a great deal whether you grow natives or not. Most gardeners, familiar with how happy pollinators are to visit foreign plants such as buddleia, asters and lavender, will not be surprised by that result.

A more recent paper reported the results of all the animals hoovered up by a 'Vortis' suction sampler: beetles, flies, bugs, spiders, springtails and wasps, among others. The spiders, wasps and some of the other insects are predators, but many of those captured eat plants. And because many plant-eating insects are quite picky about their diet, this is where you might expect to find the closest

▲ A garden with a display of coneflowers and marigolds, none of which are native species, but from a wildlife point of view this is not essential.

dependence on native plants – essentially, if the plant they eat isn't there, you're not likely to find them. By far the largest group of insects caught are those that eat dead plants (detritivores – mostly springtails). This large group apparently did care to some extent about plant origin, preferring native plants, but the exotics were a very close second, with near-natives third. For the insects that eat living plants, natives were favoured, followed by near-natives and exotics in that order. But the difference between the three kinds of plants was not large – plenty of wildlife was supported by all three. The other consistent message, whatever the origin of the plants, was that more is better: the bigger the volume of vegetation, the more insects there are of nearly every kind. This is essentially the same message that emerged from the BUGS project: having lots of plants is more important than where those plants come from.

Trees, trees and more trees

The most consistent result to emerge from BUGS was the value of trees, large shrubs and hedges. Essentially, large woody plants provide a large volume of vegetation, which in turn translates into more plant-eating animals, and ultimately more predators. Among the more important predators are birds, many of which depend on caterpillars, spiders and aphids to feed their young. Great Tits routinely raise fewer young in gardens than they do in woodland (their natural habitat), because most gardens simply don't provide enough insects for them. Exactly which trees you grow isn't very important, but willow, birch, hawthorn, apple and rowan are all good choices for a small garden. Note that there are native and alien species of all four, but the wildlife in your garden won't notice the difference. I should warn you that holes will appear in the leaves of your trees, but you should learn to regard these as a sign of your success as a wildlife gardener. If such manifestations of herbivory distress you, just make sure you don't look up.

As well as providing more food and more physical space for wildlife, note that trees also contribute to soil organic matter and the damp shade favoured by many soil animals. A tree is also the perfect place to hang a bird-feeder and nail a bird box.

Grass

Lawns are not completely useless for wildlife, but they are not very good either. Long grass, on the other hand, is a different story altogether. And please note that I am *not* trying to persuade you to grow a 'wildflower meadow', despite them having become almost a compulsory accessory for the fashion-conscious wildlife gardener. Most garden soils are too fertile for a really successful meadow, and anyway they really are a hopelessly inefficient way of growing flowers. The easiest

▲ A less 'tidy' area of long vegetation and a woodpile in your garden will provide a new dimension for wildlife, perhaps even attracting species such as Stag Beetles and Meadow Brown butterflies to breed.

place to grow lots of flowers (and thus please your local pollinators) is in a mixed herbaceous/shrub border. No, I want to persuade you to grow some long grass for its own sake. I mentioned earlier that Jennifer Own had no truck with conventional wildlife gardening, and one manifestation of this was that she had no meadow, or anything like it. As a result, despite recording 68 species of moths breeding in her garden, she never had any success persuading grass-feeding species to breed. And no grass-feeding butterflies either, despite there being plenty of both. So, rather than growing nettles in the (almost certainly vain) hope of persuading Small Tortoiseshells or Red Admirals to breed, you would be much better off cultivating a patch of long grass. Meadow Brown and Speckled Wood butterflies breed in my long grass every year, and probably grass-feeding moths as well. Long grass also provides habitat for grasshoppers, nesting sites for surface-nesting bumblebees (including *Bombus pascuorum*, the commonest garden species), and places for moths and frogs to hide. Elephant Hawk-moths and Large Yellow Underwings hide in my long grass during the day, and I'm sure they're only the more obvious ones.

Those of you determined to grow some wildflowers in your grass will find that the high soil fertility typical of gardens is your big enemy. Cutting your patch of long grass every year and removing the cut material will slowly reduce the fertility of the soil beneath. You could also try sowing the hemi-parasite yellow rattle, which will have a similar effect. Eventually, once the grass looks a bit undernourished, try some of the more robust wildflowers, such as knapweed, meadow crane's-bill and field scabious. Introduce plants, rather than seeds; if they are happy and your grass is thin enough, they will soon self-seed.

Ponds

It more or less goes without saying that a pond adds a whole new dimension to garden wildlife. Frogs, newts and dragonflies may visit your garden whether you have a pond or not, but of course they won't stay and breed unless you have a pond. Animals such as birds and Foxes will visit the pond to drink, and other animals with aquatic larval stages (e.g. many flies) will also benefit.

However, for the gardener who is keen actually to see the wildlife in his or her garden, a pond's chief advantage is the unrivalled opportunity to get up close and personal with your garden wildlife. Looking for much of the less obvious wildlife in the rest of the garden can sometimes be a frustrating business – you know it's out there somewhere, but where exactly? Ponds don't have this problem, since the diving beetles, backswimmers, pondskaters and tadpoles are right there, under your nose. Certainly, there's nothing quite like a pond for introducing children to garden wildlife. If you're lucky, one summer morning you may even see a dragonfly larva crawl from the water and the adult insect emerge.

Although bigger and deeper ponds will attract more wildlife, size and depth are not crucial, so you should be able to fit a pond into even a small garden. It helps to choose an open, sunny spot, and at least one shallow sloping side is highly desirable (failing that, be sure to include a ramp with good grip to allow animals to climb in and out), and don't add any fish. Lots of vegetation is good for wildlife –

▲ A garden pond will provide a home for a rich variety of wildlife, as well as endless interest for you.

submerged plants will keep the water oxygenated, floating plants will keep the water dark and cool, which will stop algae growing and keep the water clear, while emergent plants are essential if you are to persuade dragonflies to breed.

Gadgets

Surveys consistently reveal that many gardeners would willingly do more to attract wildlife, if only they knew how. There's plenty of advice available, but most of it tells you what you already know: dig a pond, grow more flowers, put up a bird box. Ignorance about the needs of most less-obvious garden wildlife has left the way open for the wildlife gardening industry to sell you a variety of wood and plastic objects that are (allegedly) just the thing your local Hedgehogs/butterflies/ladybirds/bees are looking for. You'll probably find a whole section of your local garden centre devoted to these things, and even organisations that ought to know better (e.g. the National Trust) sell some of them. But do any of them work? And are they worth buying even if they do?

Some simply do not work. BUGS tried two different bumblebee nesting box designs for three years in many different gardens, and even tried to fool bees into thinking they were actually old mouse holes by putting used mouse bedding in them. The results were clear – no takers in any garden in any year. Hole-nesting bumblebees nest in my garden every year, usually in a hole in a dry stone retaining wall, while *Bombus pascuorum* nests in my long grass. In the absence of such a wall, any pile of old rocks, logs or bricks is worth a try.

▲ Some of the gadgets that definitely do work. Bird-feeders with Greenfinches, Goldfinches and Siskins.

Some gadgets work but can hardly be described as value for money. BUGS found that nests for solitary bees work very well, and attract far more than just bees, but why pay £10 or £20 for something you could make yourself in five minutes? Drill some holes in any old piece of wood, or fill an old tin can with paper straws, lengths of old bamboo cane or old hollow plant stems, and fix it somewhere sunny. Many other gadgets, including houses for butterflies, ladybirds and lacewings, simply don't work, and none of the Hedgehog boxes in a small trial by *Which? Gardening* in 2010 were found to be occupied. You'd be far better off making sure your garden has the sorts of opportunities insects and other animals would naturally use to nest or overwinter: hollow plant stems, heaps of dead leaves, holes in dead wood, dense vegetation, ivy, log piles and the loose bark of dead trees. Spare a thought, too, for the poor invertebrates that offer no commercial opportunities at all and therefore don't even appear in the catalogue. So far as I can tell, no-one has yet figured out how to make an honest buck out of spiders, grasshoppers or – heaven forbid – ants. As for the unattractive crew that really power the garden ecosystem, such as earthworms, springtails and woodlice … well, enough said.

Of course, bird boxes and feeders do work, as millions of gardeners will testify, but don't think that's *all* the birds in your garden need. Peanuts and sunflower seeds are all very well, but even birds that are quite happy with seeds and other scraps in the winter (e.g. Blue Tits, House Sparrows and Chaffinches) need insects during the breeding season. Young sparrows eat aphids, leafhoppers, beetles, flies, spiders, ants and caterpillars, and studies have shown that the more of these there are around, the more young sparrows survive. Since all garden wildlife is ultimately fuelled by plants, both dead and alive, there's no mystery about how to ensure your garden has lots of sparrow-food: cover the ground with as many different plants as you can, don't be too quick to tidy up fallen leaves or cut down dead plants, and grow plenty of shrubs, climbers and even trees if you have room. These will also provide nesting opportunities for those garden birds (the majority) that don't use nestboxes.

Beyond the garden

You should also think about how your gardening affects wildlife in the wider world. Peat represents one of the planet's great stores of organic carbon, but once it's dug up and turned into potting compost, it is soon oxidised and returned to the atmosphere as carbon dioxide. Peat bogs also support diverse communities of animals and plants, many of which live nowhere else. And although peat grows, it does so very slowly, so effectively it is a non-renewable resource.

The wildlife-conscious gardener should therefore avoid using peat or peat-based compost. Some peat-free alternatives have a reputation for being not very good, or at least not performing very consistently. Mostly this is because many contain a high proportion of green waste, which is cheap but very variable, and has several undesirable properties. Look out instead for brands based on composted bark, wood fibre and coir; such products may be more expensive but are worth the extra cost.

Hands off

▲ The Emperor dragonfly is one of the impressive predatory insects that may breed in garden ponds.

In the modern world, we have got used to being in complete control of our environment, both at home and at work. It's easy to try to extend this control into the garden, and of course part of the pleasure of gardening is 'taming the wilderness' and bending nature to our will. Indeed, so far as the plants in your garden are concerned, your control is limited only by the amount of time you are prepared to spend weeding, dead-heading, staking and pruning. But don't forget that the wildlife in your garden really is wild, with its own interests and priorities. It's tempting to divide wildlife into those you like and those you do not, and to try to encourage the former and discourage the latter. But this is possible only in the broadest terms, for example growing plants that slugs don't like will reduce slug damage, while growing more flowers will attract more pollinators. Any more direct interference is likely simply to demonstrate just how interrelated everything is in your garden, and that for every action, there is an equal and opposite reaction. Gardening writer Val Bourne recounts how, in a previous career in horticultural research, one of her jobs was to produce thriving crops of aphids on glasshouse crops for research purposes. Her foolproof method for doing so was to spray with a non-systemic insecticide, close the windows and wait; two weeks later a bumper crop of aphids was guaranteed. The spray killed most aphids, but a few lurking in nooks and crannies always survived. Predators were present in smaller numbers anyway, but being much more active than the aphids, they all came into contact with the spray and were killed, allowing the surviving aphids to prosper unchecked.

Some gardeners mistakenly believe that Magpies and Sparrowhawks are responsible for the recent decline of some songbirds, and one or two have even taken to shooting Magpies. Not only does this have no effect at all on the Magpie population, but there is not the slightest evidence to implicate Magpies in the decline of songbirds. To take an example from my own garden, I occasionally see a Heron taking a frog from my small garden pond. My reaction, like yours no doubt, depends on how I happen to feel that day about the relative merits of Herons and frogs. Naturally, I feel a bit protective about 'my' frogs, but Herons are wildlife as well, and they have to eat; am I only happy if they do this out of my sight? One year, huge numbers of frogs filled my small pond with frog spawn as usual, but I never saw more than a few tadpoles, and even they soon disappeared. Later, at least 25 Blue (Southern) Hawker dragonflies emerged from the pond. Suddenly everything became clear – it takes a lot of tadpoles to feed that many hungry dragonfly larvae. Clearly, it's impossible to compare the relative value of frogs and dragonflies; I enjoy watching both, and I just hope a few tadpoles survive most years.

The lesson is that all the wildlife in our gardens is connected in more ways than we realise, and that any attempt to interfere probably will not work, and may even have the opposite of the desired effect. To a large extent, gardening for wildlife is not about what you buy, what you plant, or even what you do; it's an attitude to the whole of gardening. Resolve to take an interest in the wildlife in your garden, quietly to watch it at work, to accept that even 'pests' have their uses, and you're a wildlife gardener – even if you have no ambition to own a wildflower meadow and you never buy anything from the wildlife gardening catalogue.

Identification guide to garden wildlife

Small Tortoiseshell feeding on buddleia.

How to use this section

▲ More than meets the eye. A cluster of ladybirds, including three 7-spot Ladybirds, three 2-spot Ladybirds and a Pine Ladybird.

Selecting the species

When compiling a list of species typically encountered in gardens, the selection is inevitably subjective and depends on a number of factors. Included in the following identification part of this guide is a wide cross-section of garden wildlife one may well encounter, even though the number of species in some groups, such as the ichneumon wasps or springtails, could have been increased ten-fold, and still not be fully covered. Many species within these groups, however, are very small and similar, and, hopefully, the inclusion of a larger proportion of the more popular and showy groups, such as the butterflies, which are given a generous amount of space, with around a third of all species included, will be understood.

The location of the garden, both geographically and in relation to the surrounding countryside, influences its wildlife. For example, living as I do in central England, the Red Kite, which is a predictable, almost daily visitor above my garden, and the regular occurrence in my moth trap of the Four-spotted and Webb's Wainscot moths, are pleasing arrivals, but not appropriate for inclusion in a book on typical garden wildlife. There will, therefore, undoubtedly be some omissions, particularly among the larger invertebrate families, but hopefully nothing the reader will find too serious. A list of further reading at the end of the guide includes some books that will enable some of the groups to be explored in more depth.

Beyond the familiar

This guide, in covering such a wide range of subjects, from deer to mites, aims to familiarise the reader with the diversity of life that surrounds us, and to create a greater understanding and interest, particularly in some of the less popular animal groups. As someone who has always been interested in a wide range of natural history subjects, I'm often surprised at how little some naturalists know about subjects even quite closely related to their own specialist interests. Moth enthusiasts, for example, are often unable to identify, even to the correct order, insects that appear in their moth traps at night, many of which may be even more abundant than the moths they are recording.

Naming the creatures

Although the variety of life even in a small garden can appear bewildering, there is a universally accepted way of naming all life-forms. This discipline, known as taxonomy, divides up the natural world into understandable groupings. So, for example, a 7-spot Ladybird belongs to the phylum Arthropoda (meaning 'jointed foot'), the class Insecta, order Coleoptera (meaning 'sheath wing'), the family Coccinellidae (meaning 'little red sphere'), genus *Coccinella* and has the species name *septempunctata* ('seven spots'). These names, based on a combination of Latin and Greek, are universally understood throughout the scientific world. The genus and specific names are always written in italics, with the genus name starting with a capital letter, followed by the specific name, always written in lower case.

Though often difficult to remember and sometimes off-putting to the newcomer to natural history, they may be descriptive of either the appearance or behaviour of the species, and their origins and meanings are often fascinating. For example, in the case of the Brimstone butterfly, *Gonepteryx rhamni*, the generic name means *gonia* = angle *pterux* = wing, and the specific name *rhamni* refers to the larval foodplant, buckthorns (*Rhamnus*). These scientific names have been used throughout the book, but, wherever widely accepted common or vernacular names exist, these too have been used, and to make unfamiliar species more accessible, these have been given priority. The convention we have followed here is to give the common name of species initial capitals, e.g. Song Thrush for *Turdus philomelos*, but have used lower case for generic or family names e.g. thrushes. For plants, we have used lower case for the common names throughout, for ease of use.

Arrangement and size

The animal life described and illustrated in the following pages is divided, for convenience, into two groups, the vertebrates and the invertebrates. The former group, containing the mammals, birds, reptiles and amphibians, appears first, and most are illustrated smaller than life size; their dimensions are shown in the accompanying text opposite the illustrations.

The insects, which include the majority of the invertebrates described, are arranged broadly according to accepted conventions, with more primitive groups first (although some smaller insect orders have been grouped together for convenience). The actual size of the invertebrates, which range from life-size up to ×35, appear on the plates, next to the illustrations. These illustrations, which have all been painted from actual specimens, have mostly been drawn to scale, although, because of the wide variation in sizes, this has not always been possible.

Some guides provide the use of keys in order to help the reader identify the animals described. However, it was felt that as the guide covers so many different orders and families that this would not be workable. One of the best methods to arrive at an identification is simply to look through the colour plates until you have found an illustration that most closely approximates to the creature you are trying to identify. Careful cross-referencing to the text and other related animals illustrated will then allow you to refine your identification. Do bear in mind, however, that for some groups there are many species that look similar, and that the species described and illustrated will only be an example. The abbreviations used in the species accounts are as follows: L = length; WS = wingspan.

Mammals

Hedgehog *Erinaceus europaeus*
L22–27cm This familiar inhabitant of parks, gardens and hedgerows is welcomed by everyone, especially gardeners, as it is a formidable hunter of many destructive creatures such as some slugs and larvae. It is an omnivore, however, and as well as eating fruit and fungi it also occasionally feeds on some more beneficial creatures, including frogs, birds' eggs and nestlings. The Hedgehog is mainly nocturnal and is often detected at night by its loud snuffling, and in the daytime by the distinctive oily, black, sausage-shaped droppings found on lawns. Females build large nests, and litters are produced between May and October. At birth, the tiny, helpless young lack spines, but by the time they are adults they have several thousand. Those born later in the year need to reach a body weight of at least 450g, and ideally 600g, to survive hibernation. Winter is spent intermittently in a hibernaculum made from grass, dry leaves and moss, hidden in a hedge bottom, compost or bonfire heap. **Distribution** Common throughout mainland Britain and Ireland, but has declined drastically in the past few decades. The tidying-up and fencing of gardens, the removal of hedgerows in the wider countryside and the increasing use of pesticides have all contributed to the Hedgehog's decline, and fewer Hedgehogs occur where Badgers, the principal natural predator, are common.

Common Shrew *Sorex araneus*
L8.5–14cm The Common Shrew is seldom seen, even though it is widespread and highly active among dense vegetation, by day and night, throughout the year. Much of its time is spent bustling along runways in search of food, as it has to eat the equivalent of its own body weight each day in order to survive. It will eat almost any invertebrate, but tends to avoid millipedes. Territorial confrontations usually result in a frenzy of high-pitched squeaking, which is often the best way of confirming shrews' presence. Young are born from April onwards. The hectic, non-stop lifestyle often results in high mortality, and shrews typically live for only 12–18 months. In urban areas, many shrews are killed by cats but are not eaten, probably because of the unpleasant odour exuded by glands on the flanks. **Distribution** Widespread, but not found in Ireland. **Similar species** The **Pygmy Shrew** *Sorex minutus* is smaller and paler, and lacks the light brown band along the flanks.

Mole *Talpa europaea*
L11–16cm Common and active by day and night, throughout the year, Moles live a solitary, subterranean life and, although the young emerge to disperse and adults sometimes forage above ground, they are rarely seen. The black, velvety fur, which can lie forwards or backwards, and the powerful, shovel-like forelegs allow the Mole to move easily in both directions along its burrows. The most obvious evidence of the presence of Moles are molehills, produced from soil excavated from burrows. These are most often seen in meadows and woodland, but are less welcome in gardens. Most active time is spent hunting, mainly for earthworms, but many other invertebrates are eaten. The helpless, naked young are born in April or May, and are self-sufficient at six weeks. Mortality is high, however, and the average life-span is only three years. **Distribution** Occurs throughout Britain, but absent from Ireland, Isle of Man and most Scottish islands.

Common Pipistrelle *Pipistrellus pipistrellus*
WS 20–24cm This is the smallest and commonest bat in Britain, and is the one most often seen flying at dusk around human habitation. There are, in fact, three distinct 'pipistrelle' species – Common *P. pipistrellus*, Nathusius' *P. nathusii* and Soprano *P. pygmaeus* – although they are only easily separable by their echolocation calls. They are most abundant during the summer months, when large numbers of insects are on the wing; each bat may eat up to 3,000 insects in a single night. Pipistrelles may also forage on mild winter evenings, providing the temperature rises above 8°C. Summer nursery roosts are mainly on south-facing, outer parts of buildings, behind cladding, fascias and tiles, whereas winters are spent mainly in roof spaces and cavities in houses. Although their wingspan may exceed 20cm, adults weigh only 5g – less than a 2p coin – which, by the end of hibernation, may have dropped to 3.75g. **Distribution** Found throughout the British Isles, where it and other species of bat are fully protected. **Similar species** The less common **Serotine Bat** *Eptesicus serotinus* is another house-dwelling species, confined to southern England and Wales. It is larger, darker and slower on the wing.

Brown Long-eared Bat *Plecotus auritus*
WS 23–28cm This medium-sized bat is easily identified, even in flight, by its long ears, which almost equal the length of the body. These enable it to differentiate between insects and the vegetation on which the insects feed, and, combined with agile flight, allow prey to be plucked from foliage or from the ground, a feat that few other bats can achieve. This ability, however, makes them vulnerable to cat predation in urban areas. They are most active between April and October. The young are born in the summer, each female producing only one baby a year. Winter roosts are often in cool attics in buildings, where the ideal temperature remains around 0°C, although hollow trees may be used. During hibernation and when resting the ears are folded back, resembling a ram's horns. **Distribution** Found throughout Britain and Ireland, but scarcer further north. **Similar species** The **Grey Long-eared Bat** *Plecotus austriacus* was recognised as a separate species only in the 1960s. Only rarely found in southern England, it has slightly darker, greyish fur, but is very difficult to distinguish from its common relative.

droppings
Hedgehog
Common Shrew
Mole
Common Pipistrelle
Brown Long-eared Bat

Fox *Vulpes vulpes*
L80–110cm About 150,000 Foxes live in urban areas, taking opportunistic advantage of large gardens in which to hunt birds, rodents and invertebrates, as well as scavenging on human rubbish and fruit. They also benefit from being fed by people, who enjoy the sight of town Foxes. Even the most densely populated cities have waste ground, railway embankments and overgrown gardens with tangled vegetation and rubbish where Foxes can breed. One of their less welcome traits, however, is the pungent smell left from scent marking, and droppings are often left in prominent, open places. These can be distinguished from those of dogs by the presence of fur, bits of bone and insect remains, and often have a twisted, pointed end. Mating, which can be a noisy affair, takes place mostly in January and the young are born after 52 days' gestation; they leave their home territory in autumn. Although adults may live for up to eight or nine years, mortality can be high and a life expectancy of three years is more usual. In urban areas up to 100,000 Foxes may be killed each year. **Distribution** Common and widespread throughout Britain and Ireland.

Rabbit *Oryctolagus cuniculus*
L35–50cm First introduced for their flesh and fur in the 12th century, Rabbits originate from the Mediterranean and are now well established in Britain. Following the introduction of myxomatosis in 1953 the population dropped to less than 1%, but numbers gradually recovered. However, in the last 20 years the population has declined drastically, by about 60%, due mainly to Viral Haemorrhagic Disease. Rabbits live communally in a warren, a system of underground tunnels, and although active mainly at dusk and after dark, will feed in the daytime if undisturbed. Nesting burrows are dug in spring and the helpless young are born mainly between February and August. Food includes a wide range of grasses and herbs, as well as saplings and bark, with damage often caused in cultivated areas. **Habitat and distribution** Often venturing from the surrounding countryside into gardens, parks and allotments, Rabbits occur in most habitats throughout Britain and Ireland. **Similar species** The **Brown Hare** *Lepus europaeus* is larger and more angular, with longer ears and legs; it is much less likely to visit gardens.

Badger *Meles meles*
L80–95cm Rural gardens surrounded by well-vegetated, wooded countryside may be visited by Badgers, whose striking black-and-white mask make them perhaps the most recognisable British mammal. Mainly active from dusk until dawn, they are rarely seen, but obvious signs of their presence may be the unwelcome excavations on lawns, where they forage for earthworms. These form a large part of a diverse diet, which includes other invertebrates, birds' eggs, voles and, more often in the autumn, nuts, fruit and seeds. Most young are born in January or February. **Distribution** Found throughout Britain and Ireland, the highest populations being in the mild, south-west of England.

Grey Squirrel *Sciurus carolinensis*
L42–55cm First introduced into Britain from North America in the 1870s, the Grey Squirrel, although attractive and agile, is an unwelcome alien and a serious pest that damages forest and orchard trees by stripping bark to get at the sappy tissue. Its introduction also coincided with the decline of the native Red Squirrel, making it even more unpopular. More robust than its native cousin, the Grey lacks the conspicuous ear tufts, and, although it has reddish flanks, it is mainly silvery-grey. Melanic and albino specimens occasionally occur. It is mainly vegetarian, but occasionally insects, birds' eggs and even nestlings are taken. Bird-tables are also regularly visited, and many devices have been developed to deter squirrels. Young are born in a drey, an untidy football-sized nest made from twigs and leaves, often lodged high in the fork of a tree. **Distribution** Throughout England and Wales, parts of lowland Scotland and central Ireland. **Similar species** The nocturnal **Edible Dormouse** *Glis glis* is smaller, with a more pointed face and large dark eyes. It may enter gardens and even houses in the winter, sometimes causing considerable damage. It is found only in the Chilterns, within a 50 sq mile area around Tring, where it was introduced in 1902.

Red Squirrel *Sciurus vulgaris*
L32–44cm Britain's only native squirrel. In the summer, the Red Squirrel has a warm chestnut-brown coat, white belly, pale tail and sparsely tufted ears. In the winter, the coat becomes greyish-brown, the tail darkens and the ear tufts become longer and thicker. Occasionally, melanic or albino individuals occur. Active and agile, the Red Squirrel spends most of its time in treetops, though its presence is most noticeable when it has fed on the ground, where piles of discarded pine cone scales and cores may be found. The diet also consists of acorns, hazel nuts, beech masts and fungi. Usually quite shy, Red Squirrels are most easily seen during the breeding season, which occurs between January and March, and again from June until September, when mating chases take place and a single female may be pursued by as many as 30 males. The nest (or drey) is built close to the tree trunk, at least 3m above the ground. It is spherical, about 30cm in diameter, and is constructed of twigs and lined with grass, moss and shredded bark. Litter size varies from one to eight and the young leave the nest at about ten weeks of age. **Habitat and distribution** Mostly found in mature Scots pine woodland but sometimes visit gardens. Found mainly in Scotland, northern England, north Wales, East Anglia and parts of Ireland, with isolated populations on the Isle of Wight and Brownsea Island.

dropping

track

Fox

Rabbit

tracks

Badger

Grey Squirrel

Red Squirrel

Muntjac *Muntiacus reevesi*
L90–110cm This is the smallest deer found in Britain, and has spread from Woburn Park, in Bedfordshire, since its introduction in 1901. Often seen in car headlights as it crosses roads, it is also active in the daytime, and may visit gardens in rural areas. Its distinctive, sharp bark often reveals its presence. About the size of a Labrador dog, with a hunched appearance, it has a deep chestnut-brown coat that becomes duller in winter. Bucks have backward-pointing horns and upper canine teeth that form tusks, and when alarmed both sexes raise their tails to reveal a brilliant white undersurface. In gardens, they browse on herbs and seedlings, and will remove the bark from small trees and shrubs. Occurring mainly in deciduous or mixed woodland with dense understorey, in severe weather they sometimes seek shelter in garden sheds or outbuildings. Young can be born at any time of the year, and Muntjacs may live for up to 13 years. **Distribution** Their range has slowly expanded throughout much of Britain; recently introduced into Ireland.

Roe Deer *Capreolus capreolus*
L100–135cm Rather larger than the Muntjac but still the smallest native deer, the Roe Deer sometimes visits larger gardens. It has an orange-brown summer coat, which turns greyish brown in winter, the pale patch on the rump becoming more conspicuous. Both sexes have a black nose and moustache, and bucks have antlers, each with three forward- and backward-facing points. Capable of jumping quite high fences, they may cause damage to garden shrubs, including roses, particularly in spring. Roe Deer droppings are approximately 10–14mm × 7–10mm, often rounded at one end and pointed at the other – very similar to those of sheep, goats and other species of deer. Young are born in May and June and remain with their mother until the following year. **Distribution** Mainly in northern and southern England, East Anglia and Scotland; recently recorded from Ireland.

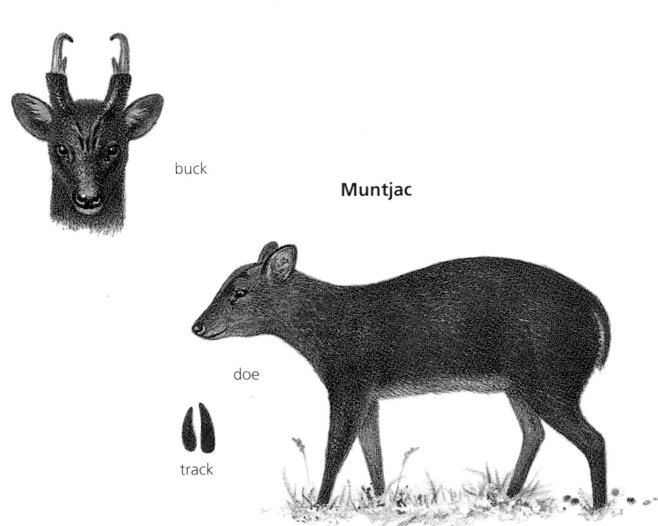
buck
Muntjac
doe
track

buck
Roe Deer
doe
track

House Mouse *Mus musculus*
L14–19cm Perhaps our most successful and adaptable mammal. More often associated with indoors, the House Mouse also frequents gardens and hedgerows, particularly in summer. The coat is a greasy, brownish grey, and gives off an unpleasant odour, absent in other mice, and the black, smelly droppings found in cupboards and larders are often the first sign of its presence. Although it is omnivorous, grains are the preferred diet. Mice will gnaw any material to wear down their teeth, often causing damage in the home. Their reproductive rate is the reason for their success – each female can produce up to 50 young a year. These are born in a nest made from grass and leaves, although paper, string and other man-made materials may be included. The main breeding season is from March to October, but indoors it may be continuous. Cats, owls and rats are all predators but man is by far the main controller, setting traps and poisonous baits to reduce numbers, but never completely eradicating them. **Distribution** Ubiquitous throughout Britain and Ireland, including most inhabited islands. **Similar species** The **Wood Mouse** has larger ears and eyes, a longer tail and a warm-brown coat.

Wood or **Long-tailed Field Mouse** *Apodemus sylvaticus*
L17–22.5cm The warm-brown coat, long tail and larger eyes and ears distinguish the Wood Mouse from the House Mouse. It is equally as common around human habitation, especially in autumn when it enters sheds and outbuildings. Here, it can damage stored fruit, and is also unpopular in the garden, where bulbs and newly-sown seedlings may be eaten. Mainly nocturnal, Wood Mice are agile climbers and forage for food in trees and bushes. In late spring, when fewer seeds and fruits are around, invertebrates, including snails and insects and their larvae, are an important part of their diet. Young are born continuously throughout the summer in an underground chamber, but mortality is high for those born in spring, and few adults survive for more than 18 months. **Distribution** Widespread in a wide variety of habitats throughout Britain and Ireland.

Yellow-necked Mouse *Apodemus flavicollis*
L18–26cm This is similar to the Wood Mouse but is larger, with a yellow patch forming a collar on the chest. The colour of the coat on the upper parts is also richer, with a more clearly defined border between this and the white underparts. Its preferred diet comprises seeds and fruit from trees and shrubs, but it will also eat invertebrates. Gardens close to deciduous woodlands are more likely to be visited by this species. In the autumn and winter, houses and outbuildings provide shelter during colder periods. Breeding success in spring is greater than that of the Wood Mouse, although the survival rate in winter is poor, and populations decline by the following spring. **Distribution** Found mainly in the south-east, south and west of England, and eastern Wales, with scattered records in other parts.

Bank Vole *Myodes glareolus*
L12.5–18cm This distinctive vole, with its chestnut-coloured fur and comparatively long tail, is the commonest species occurring in gardens and allotments, where it may cause damage to seeds, bulbs and roots, as well as the soft bark of young trees and shrubs. It travels along a network of runways under rough grass and vegetation, as well as through burrows below ground, and during summer months is most active at night. Up to five broods, each averaging four young, may be produced each season, which normally lasts from April until September. Droppings are usually dark brown to black, but greenish in summer. **Distribution** Widely distributed throughout the British mainland, and discovered in south-west Ireland in the 1960s. **Similar species Field Vole** (see below). Voles differ from mice in having a more rounded head and body, smaller eyes and ears, and a shorter tail.

Field or **Short-tailed Vole** *Microtus agrestis*
L10–18cm Less often found in gardens than the Bank Vole, this species is slightly larger, with brownish-grey fur and a shorter tail. It may cause some damage to cultivated plants but prefers fairly tall, unkempt grassy places that border larger gardens. Its green, oval droppings can be found along its runways. Its breeding habits are similar to those of the Bank Vole, with several broods produced each year. Young voles are able to breed at six weeks of age, and in some years populations may reach plague proportions, causing much damage. However, stress caused by over-crowding reduces breeding success and numbers soon drop. **Distribution** Found throughout the British mainland, but absent from Ireland.

Brown Rat *Rattus norvegicus*
L38–52cm This unpopular garden visitor, often associated with sewers and rubbish tips, is thought to have been introduced into Britain from Asia in the 18th century. It has now spread to most parts of the world. Although mainly nocturnal, when predators are few and populations are high individuals can become quite bold in the daytime, climbing trees and feeding on bird-tables with some agility. Grains are the preferred food, and large populations build up around farms, but Brown Rats are omnivorous, and capable of eating almost anything organic. Warm compost heaps often attract breeding females, and in mild winters young may be born throughout the year. Up to five litters a year are produced, giving females the potential to produce 55 offspring in a season, each capable of reproducing themselves when just two months old. Tell-tale signs of rats are pathways made along fences and under sheds, smeared with grease from the fur; also, their dark, tapered, cylindrical droppings. **Distribution** Common throughout Britain and Ireland, especially around man-made habitats, less frequent on high ground.

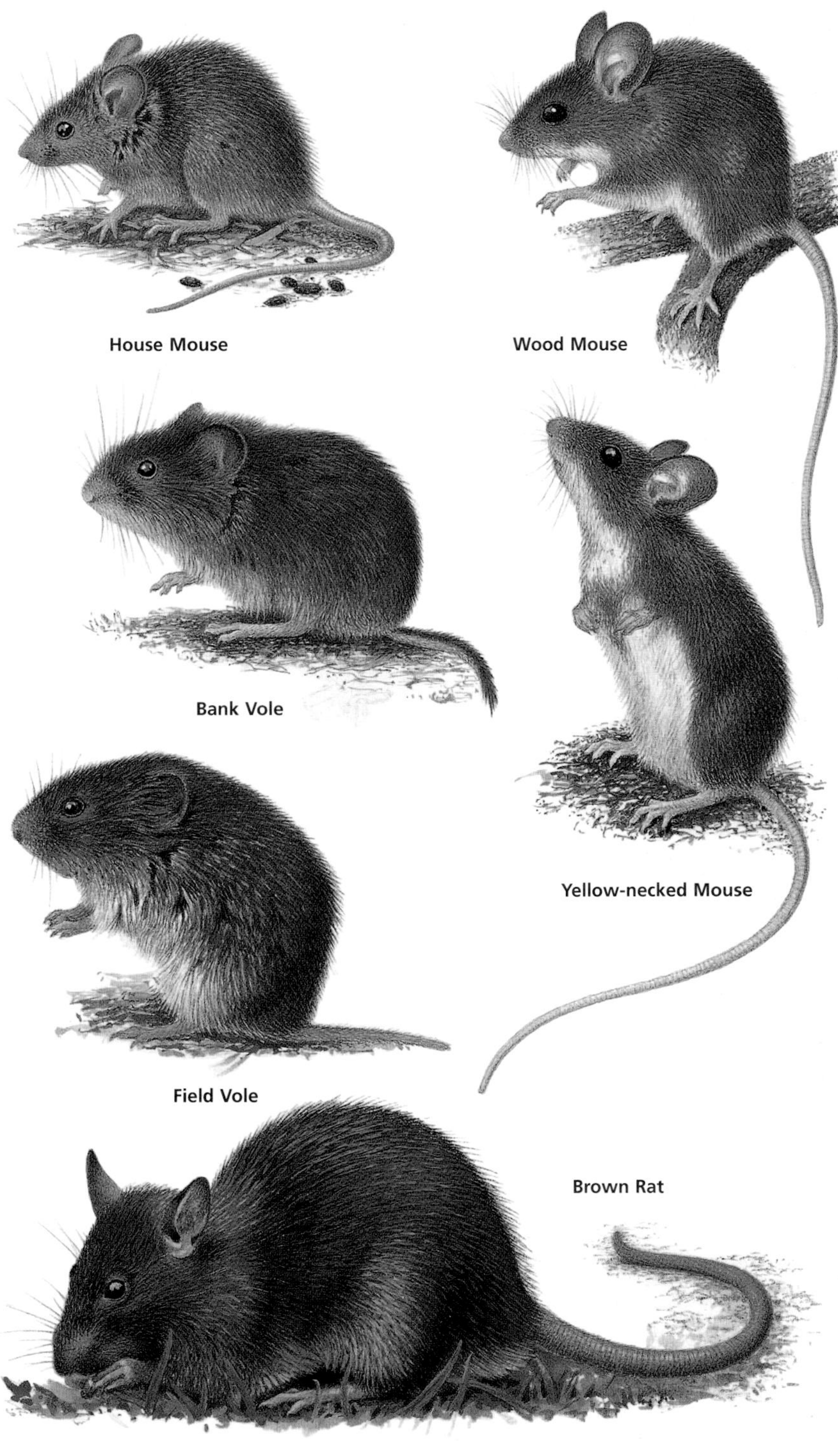

House Mouse

Wood Mouse

Bank Vole

Yellow-necked Mouse

Field Vole

Brown Rat

Birds

▲ Starlings feeding at a garden bird-table.

Most people enjoy birds visiting their gardens and delight in helping them, especially through the winter months, by feeding table scraps, bird seed and peanuts, for there are few species that are unwelcome or cause damage. For the majority of people, even those with just a passing interest in wildlife, birds are the most popular of wildlife subjects and attract far more attention than any other group. From the smallest gardens in city centres to large rural gardens containing mature trees, birds will appear, to take advantage of food, nesting sites and shelter. The garden is a good place for the novice bird enthusiast to learn the more familiar species, and for more experienced birdwatchers to keep records of visiting birds and their behaviour. For organisations such as the British Trust for Ornithology (BTO), which runs the Garden BirdWatch (GBW), and the Royal Society for the Protection of Birds (RSPB), which runs the Big Garden Birdwatch, these records and observations contribute important information on fluctuations in populations. Over the years, a wider overall picture of the surrounding environment continues to emerge from the findings.

Gardens with a good variety of trees and shrubs will add to the diversity of bird life, providing nesting and roosting sites, as well as places where males can proclaim their territories from prominent perches, and keep a look-out for predators. Other denser vegetation will provide nesting places for more secretive birds such as Dunnock or Blackcap, and dead trees, fallen branches and rotting logs are all also beneficial, if space allows. In the autumn and winter months, berries from native trees and shrubs such as hawthorn and ivy are invaluable food sources, when visitors from Scandinavia such as Redwing and Fieldfare join our resident thrushes to exploit the berry crop. However, many non-native ornamental plants such as cotoneaster and pyracantha are also beneficial, and rowans sometimes attract small flocks of exotic-looking Waxwings.

Lawns, especially if they are not too heavily manicured and are allowed to become more interesting, with plant species other than grasses, can be popular hunting grounds for birds such as Starlings, Blackbirds and thrushes, which all help to keep down invertebrates such as leather-jackets; those lawns that have not been too heavily treated with fertilisers and chemicals should have plenty of earthworms. Larger birds, like the plump Woodpigeon, also forage on lawns, and the Green Woodpecker, which specialises in probing for ants in the turf with its long, barbed tongue, may also appear. A more familiar relative and frequent garden visitor is the Great Spotted Woodpecker, which visits from the surrounding countryside, attacking peanut-containers and, less popularly, nestboxes, in search of nestling tits if it can get to them.

The locality and the countryside surrounding the garden will have an influence on the birds that visit, and some that are not typically garden birds, such as the Hawfinch or Lesser Spotted Woodpecker, may visit if the garden has suitable parkland, old orchards or woodland nearby. Similarly, a garden on the edge of a downland village could have Yellowhammer or Red-legged Partridge venturing in. With increasing pressures on the wider countryside, often from quite sudden changes in agricultural practices, building development and road construction, gardens have become increasingly important as feeding and breeding refuges for birds. In recent years, the planting of winter wheat, usually in September, has resulted in fewer stubble fields containing spilt seeds and arable weeds, which provide food for finches and buntings throughout the harshest winter months. Areas of set-aside (a scheme that was abolished in 2008), where land was allowed to lie fallow, undoubtedly helped, although usually only temporarily, and often coming to an abrupt end with the spraying of herbicides. The overall reduction in the availability of food on farmland in winter, and the tidying up of spillages around farms, are thought to be some of the reasons for the recent decline of several of our familiar farmland birds. This includes the 70% decline in House Sparrow numbers, although other factors, such as the lack of nesting places on houses and the removal of cover in gardens, have contributed to the decline.

While some species traditionally regarded as farmland birds have declined, unable to adapt to changes, some have altered their behaviour and now rely increasingly on the way that we manage our gardens for their survival. The Reed Bunting, which is now much less common, and the Siskin are more frequent on bird-feeders, especially in the late winter months, due possibly to a lack of food in the wider countryside. Recently, the Goldfinch, which has a penchant for sunflower and nyger seeds, has been appearing much more regularly in gardens.

In addition to winter feeding, regular feeding in gardens throughout the year, or at least into early summer (avoiding whole peanuts and bread) has become the recommended norm. As a result, a much wider range of food is now available, including live food such as mealworms and waxworms. This extra feeding has helped populations of birds such as the Greenfinch, which is maintained by food put out in gardens in April and May, when natural food is at its lowest.

▼ A Song Thrush with a snail on a garden lawn.

Nestboxes

Why provide nestboxes?

With pressure on suitable nesting sites for birds in the wider countryside, gardens are becoming increasingly important, indeed vital, for the breeding fortunes of some species, and it is now as important to provide nestboxes in gardens as it is to help birds through the winter by feeding. The majority of birds nest in trees and shrubs, or amongst climbing plants, such as ivy and honeysuckle, but birds such as Blue Tits, Great Tits, House Sparrows and Starlings nest in holes and crevices, either in trees or buildings, and these too are becoming increasingly scarce. The general tidying-up in gardens, the removal of dead trees and branches, and the reduction of nooks and crannies in modern buildings, also make it harder for birds to find suitable nesting sites.

▲ A family of Great Tits in a nestbox.

Designs

Although bird nestboxes range in size from those suitable for birds as small as Blue Tits up to the size of a Tawny Owl, there are two designs that cover the majority of cavity-nesting species in gardens. By far the most frequently used box is the familiar tit or hole entrance box, which, depending on the size of the box and the opening, can be adapted to suit a variety of species. The other type, the open-fronted box, is of a similar design except that instead of a hole, the top half of the front is cut away.

Hole entrance box

Suitable for:
Blue Tit/Coal Tit 25mm (hole diameter)
Great Tit 28mm
House Sparrow/Nuthatch 32mm
Starling 45mm
Jackdaw 150mm

Typical hole entrance nestbox.

Open-fronted box

Suitable for: Wren, Robin, Spotted Flycatcher, Pied Wagtail

Specialist nestbox for a Treecreeper, with the entrance at the side.

Open-fronted nestbox. The panel at the front should be high enough to retain the nest.

Location

Positioning the nestbox is important, with several factors to be considered. Avoid direct sunlight and prevailing wind and rain, and to prevent disturbance by other birds position the box away from bird-feeders. A height of between 1.5m and 5m above ground level should be chosen. Remember, there are more than 9 million cats in Britain, which are by far the most abundant predators and account for the death of most birds in gardens. So, to prevent ambush, choose a place, perhaps a wall or fence, where feeding adults, or young birds leaving the nest, will be safe. Nestboxes are best sited in the winter months, but any time of year will do, as boxes may also be used by birds as roosts and, even if they are not occupied for years, other animals such as small mammals, bees and moths may make use of them.

Construction

Commercially-made nestboxes are often expensive and over-elaborate, sometimes incorporating a feeding table and several perches, as well as luxury accommodation. As mentioned, feeding and breeding areas should be clearly separated from each other, so these constructions are best avoided. There is also great satisfaction to be gained from making and positioning one's own purpose-built, DIY nestbox, especially when the first occupants take charge. Nestboxes don't need to be precision made, and can be constructed from scrap wood such as from old palettes, and fixed together with galvanised nails, or screws. Holes should be drilled in the bottom unless the joints are rough enough to allow for drainage. The sloping roof can be hinged with a rubber flap, for easy access, as boxes should be cleaned out annually. Wood preservative to prolong life should only be used on the outside. Several other specialist designs for birds such as Treecreepers (see above), House Martins, Swifts and larger birds such as Tawny Owls and Kestrels, are also available. All of these, and many others, are detailed in the BTO guide, *Nestboxes: Your Complete Guide* (Cromack 2018).

Bird-feeders

Feeding the birds

Over the years there have been conflicting opinions about when, and what, to feed garden birds, and whether, in addition to the pleasure we get, feeding has any long-term benefits for the birds themselves. More recently, the consensus is that rather than just feeding in the winter, all-year-round feeding is beneficial, even though 'in times aplenty' birds will choose natural food before resorting to artificial feeding. Should you choose to feed all year, avoid offering bread and large table scraps when young birds are around, and peanuts should always be held in mesh containers, never supplied whole. It is also important when feeding birds, either throughout the year or just through the winter months, not to suddenly stop feeding. If you are going away, or plan to discontinue all-year-round feeding, gradually reduce the amount of food you put out, so the birds can begin to look elsewhere for provisions.

Some of the same principles that apply to the positioning of nestboxes also apply to the siting of bird-feeders. Siting the feeder in a quiet, open place, but within reasonable distance from foliage, may give birds refuge from attack from Sparrowhawks or cats. Cleanliness of bird-feeders is also important, and to prevent Salmonella and other diseases, in both the winter and summer months, regular cleaning of surfaces and feeders with mild detergent is essential.

Finally, before embarking on buying elaborate feeders, which may cost around £40 and reach as long as 120cm, also consider growing suitable berry, fruit and seed-bearing plants, which may well attract birds that are unimpressed by man-made designs and offerings.

Feeder designs and food

Apart from the simple platform bird-table, the two most popular feeder designs are the traditional wire-mesh peanut-feeder, and the plastic tubular seed-feeder. Peanuts are best supplied in wire-mesh holders to prevent young birds from swallowing them whole, and to prevent squirrel attack. Even then, if they are not made from hardened wire, they may be damaged. A variety of designs built to deter squirrels is now available. If squirrels are not a problem, peanuts in plastic-mesh containers can prove popular, and in recent decades, Siskins have learnt the attraction of peanuts in red-mesh feeders.

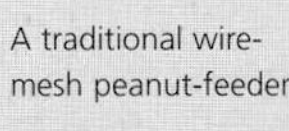

A traditional wire-mesh peanut-feeder.

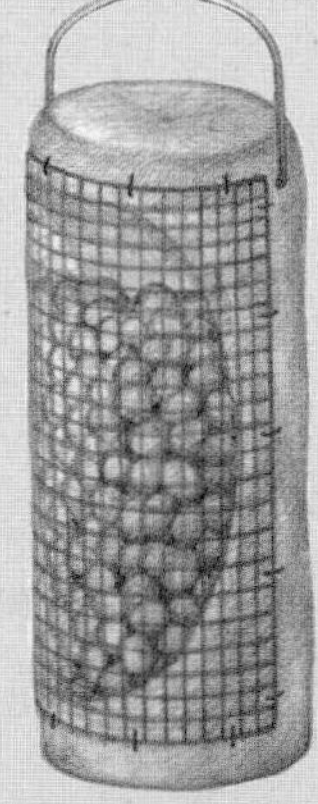

A plastic tubular seed-feeder.

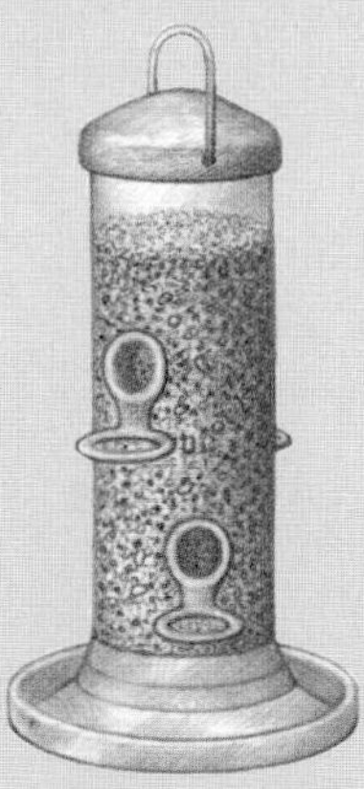

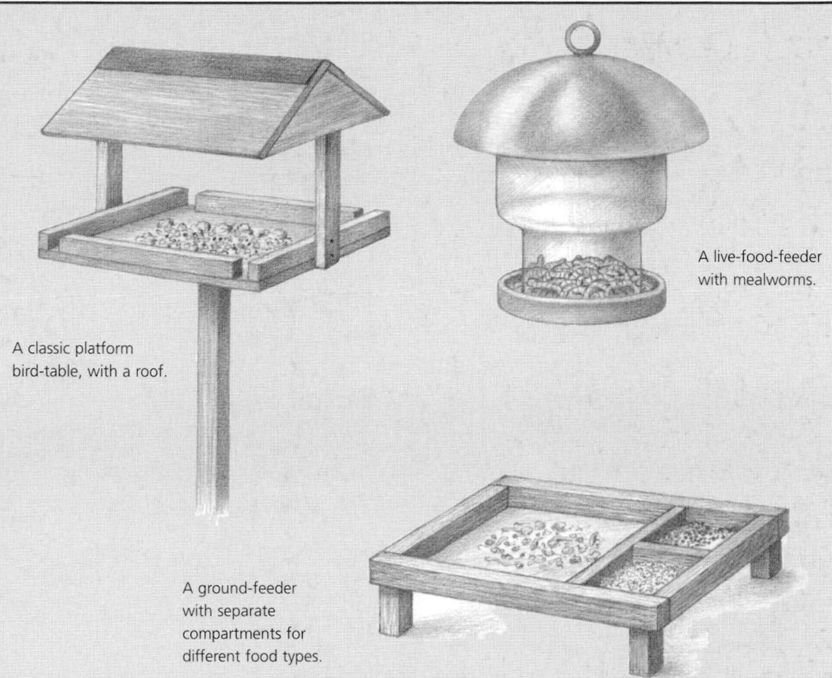

A classic platform bird-table, with a roof.

A live-food-feeder with mealworms.

A ground-feeder with separate compartments for different food types.

A huge array of seeds to appeal to a variety of birds is now available, via a multi-million-pound bird-food industry, and many plastic seed-feeders have been designed to contain not only seeds, but many other offerings.

Peanuts now only account for around 15% of wild bird food, but are attractive to many species, including Nuthatch and Great Spotted Woodpecker. Care should be taken to buy from reputable suppliers, so as to avoid peanuts contaminated with aflatoxin, a mould which can be harmful to birds.

Mixed seeds are perhaps the most popular food, coming in a variety of blends, formulated to suit different dispensing methods, including table, container or ground-feeders.

Sunflower seeds are high-energy food; the black seeds are more popular, and have higher oil content than the striped variety, but are more expensive.

Sunflower hearts are more expensive still, as they lack the external husk which makes up half the weight, but they contain the highest calorie content of all.

Nyger seeds have a high oil content and are especially attractive to Goldfinches and other finches, but they need a special feeder with small holes, or a catching tray.

Live food Mealworms and waxworms are available as high-protein food for Robins, Pied Wagtails and Wrens, and also for sparrows to feed to their young.

Suet and fat are supplied as high-energy bars or cakes, containing seeds, berries and crushed insects; they can either be suspended from feeders or placed on the ground.

Water As well as feeding the birds, supplying fresh water for drinking and bathing is essential.

Hygiene

Both water containers and feeders should be cleaned regularly with mild detergent and thoroughly rinsed, to protect from harmful bacteria.

Grey Heron *Ardea cinerea*

L85–100cm A large, stately, grey, black and white bird with long legs and a pointed, dagger-shaped bill, the Grey Heron is often seen waiting motionless by the waterside or in fields. Its flight is slow and flapping, with its legs outstretched behind, and its call is a distinctive harsh 'kraank', usually made whilst in flight. Herons often visit gardens with ponds, particularly ornamental ponds stocked with fish, though their diet also includes amphibians, small mammals, birds and insects. Breeding takes place early in the year, usually between February and May, and the huge twiggy nests, usually containing three or four eggs, are built in tall trees, or occasionally in reedbeds, in colonies known as heronries. These usually have 10–30 nests but occasionally 100 or more are recorded. **Habitat and distribution** Found throughout Britain and Ireland, in many habitats, often away from water.

Woodpigeon *Columba palumbus*

L38–45cm A plump bird, with a mostly light blue-grey plumage and conspicuous white wing and neck flashes, the latter being absent in juveniles. It is a strong flier, often taking off with a loud clattering of wings, and produces a similar wing-clapping sound during its undulating display flight. Its call is often confused with that of the Collared Dove, but is less monotonous, and is made up of five rather than three syllables, with a stress on the second. It lays two white eggs in a strong platform nest made from twigs and sticks, built in trees and tall bushes. Pigeons and doves are unique in producing crop milk, a high-protein liquid fed to the young. This is produced from vegetable matter. The growing of agricultural crops throughout much of the year has increased the breeding success of Woodpigeons and has led to a population explosion, with flocks of many thousands of birds being found in some parts of the country. **Habitat and distribution** This is mainly a farmland bird, but it often comes into gardens and may become quite tame, foraging on lawns, bird-tables and in the vegetable patch, where it may do considerable damage to brassicas. Found throughout the country, with numbers increased by immigrants in winter. **Similar species** The **Stock Dove** is smaller and stockier; it lacks the white neck and wing markings, and has two black dashes at the base of each wing.

Stock Dove *Columba oenas*

L33cm Similar in many respects to the Woodpigeon, the Stock Dove is a much shyer bird, which is less likely to visit gardens. Smaller, with a shorter tail, its plumage is darker blue-grey with an iridescent patch on the neck and it lacks any white neck or wing flashes. The wings have two black dashes and in flight the trailing edges show dark margins. The main difference between the two species is their diet, the Stock Dove having a more slender bill suited to seed-eating, unlike the more varied, often destructive, diet of the Woodpigeon. Stock Dove nests are built in holes in trees and buildings but sometimes holes in the ground are used. Two white eggs are laid in up to four broods from April until August. Its song is a monotonous 'ooo-wooo'. Amber-listed as a species of conservation concern, there are about 260,000 territories in the UK; 5% the number of Woodpigeon pairs. **Habitat and distribution** Mainly found along woodland edges, parkland, farmland and coastal regions but also larger gardens, throughout most of Britain and Ireland, apart from remote uplands.

Collared Dove *Streptopelia decaocto*

L30–34cm The Collared Dove is more elegantly built than the Woodpigeon, which is often found in its company. It has a quicker, more manoeuvrable flight, and pairs are often seen dashing through gardens in close formation. It has buff-coloured plumage, often with a subtle pinkish tinge, and a characteristic black half collar and dark tips to the wings. Juveniles are paler than adults and lack the well-defined collar. Much of its time is spent on rooftops or in trees, when the repetitive 'coo-cooo-co' call, which is sometimes mistaken for that of a Cuckoo, can become irritating. Breeding starts in March, with five broods or more produced throughout the year. The two white eggs are laid on a flimsy platform nest, made from fine twigs and built in trees, particularly conifers, or on buildings. **Habitat and distribution** Occurs mostly near habitation, in parks, gardens and around agricultural buildings. A regular visitor to bird-tables and farmyards, where it feeds on spilt grain and animal feed. Has colonised Britain and Ireland only in the last 60 years, and has become so successful in some places that it is regarded as a pest. However, in the past 10 years its population has declined slightly. **Similar species** The much rarer **Turtle Dove** *S. turtur* is slightly smaller but is similar in shape and in flight. It is more richly marked with orange-brown and has a conspicuous, white-banded tail. It is a shy summer visitor, and is sometimes seen in gardens in rural areas.

adult
juvenile
Grey Heron
juvenile
adult
Woodpigeon
adult
juvenile
adult
Stock Dove
Collared Dove

Ring-necked or **Rose-ringed Parakeet** *Psittacula krameri*

L40cm This invasive species, a native of sub-Saharan Africa and southern Asia, was first recorded after its release into Britain, in 1969. The parakeets' distinctive green colour, long pointed tail and wings, and loud squawking call, make their presence unmistakeable in parks and gardens, particularly in London, where they may cause damage to flowers, fruit and berries, as well as compete with other garden birds on bird-tables. At night, large roosts of several thousand birds may congregate. Females, which lack the neck-ring of the males, lay three or four eggs in natural cavities and nest-boxes from January to June. It seems, to date, they have had little effect on other hole-nesting species, but this could change as their population increases. Their nesting success is high, resulting in a gradual, overall increase in the population, sustained by increasingly warmer winters and artificial feeding in gardens. **Habitat and distribution** Found in parks and gardens in urban areas. Estimated by the RSPB to be around 8,600 pairs in the UK in 2012, the main concentration is in London and south-east England, but they have been recorded from every English county.

Tawny Owl *Strix aluco*

L36–41cm More often heard than seen, this is the owl responsible for the familiar 'to-wit to-wooo' call, although it also makes other eerie sounds in the night. Its large, dark, rounded form distinguishes it from other owls, most of which are less frequent in gardens. Its diet consists mainly of small mammals, but it will take birds and, less often, frogs and insects. By day, it usually rests, concealed amongst ivy, close to a tree trunk, but is sometimes discovered by small birds, which will harass it mercilessly. It is most active in autumn, when males proclaim their territories. Breeding begins early in the year, from about March. The nest is usually in a hole in a tree, although nestboxes are also used where natural holes are hard to come by. **Habitat and distribution** Occurs mainly in woodland, parks and large urban gardens, where mature trees provide shelter and nesting sites. Widely distributed, but absent from Ireland.

Sparrowhawk *Accipiter nisus*

L28–40cm This predator is usually seen either circling overhead, being mobbed by other birds, or dashing low across gardens in an ambush attack. The Sparrowhawk is best identified by its broad, rounded wings and comparatively long tail. The smaller male has a steely-grey back and rufous-barred underside, whereas the female, which may be up to 6cm longer, is greyish brown, with a white underside finely barred with brown. The size difference of the sexes also reflects prey preference, with males usually targeting tits, sparrows and finches, and females going for larger birds, such as starlings and thrushes. A shy, nervous bird that usually makes its nest away from human habitation, often on top of an old crow or pigeon nest. The female incubates the eggs. **Habitat and distribution** Pesticides and persecution resulted in a population crash in the late 1950s, but in more recent years the Sparrowhawk has become a familiar sight, especially in urban areas, and it is now widespread throughout Britain and Ireland. **Similar species** The **Kestrel** *Falco tinnunculus* is more streamlined, with longer, more pointed wings. Its flight is interspersed with hovering.

adult ♀
adult ♂
Ring-necked Parakeet
Tawny Owl
adult ♂
adult ♀
adult ♂
juvenile ♀
Sparrowhawk

Green Woodpecker *Picus viridis*

L30–33cm Also known as the 'yaffle' for its loud, 'laughing' call, the exotic-looking Green Woodpecker is the largest and most colourful of our three woodpeckers. Males and females are similar in colour, with a crimson crown and a conspicuous greenish-yellow rump in flight, but the male also has a red flash in his moustache. Young birds are more heavily spotted and less brightly coloured than adults. An ungraceful but characterful bird, on the ground it moves with ungainly hops and on the wing its flight is heavy and undulating. It often visits lawns in rural gardens in search of ant nests. As well as a fondness for ants, it has a varied diet, including insect larvae and even nestlings; later in the year berries, fruits and nuts are also eaten. The nest is in a hole in decaying timber, usually excavated by both male and female. Up to seven white eggs are laid from late April. **Habitat and distribution** Mainly open deciduous woodland, parks and large gardens where there are mature trees. Found throughout England and Wales and has spread more recently into Scotland, but is absent from Ireland.

Great Spotted Woodpecker
Dendrocopos major

L22–24cm The most familiar woodpecker to visit gardens, the Great Spotted Woodpecker is regularly seen on bird-feeders, where whole families may arrive to feed on fat and peanuts. Often heard before it is seen, in spring the male drums loudly, often on a dead branch for maximum effect. The call is a sharp, far-carrying 'keck, keck'. The bold, white shoulder patches, most obvious in flight, distinguish it from the Lesser Spotted Woodpecker; the female lacks the red nape patch of the male and juveniles have a red crown. As with other woodpeckers, it has an undulating flight. Its diet consists mainly of larvae and invertebrates, chiselled out with the powerful beak and long tongue, but conifer seeds and nestlings may also be eaten. The nest hole is excavated by both sexes in either deciduous or coniferous trees, where up to six white eggs are laid. **Habitat and distribution** This is the commonest woodpecker and is found in all kinds of woodland, suburban parks, and gardens, where populations benefit from peanut-feeders. Seen all year round throughout Britain, though only a few pairs nest in Ireland.

Lesser Spotted Woodpecker
Dryobates minor

L14–16cm Similar in many ways to its larger relative, the Lesser Spotted Woodpecker is a much more elusive bird that occasionally visits orchards and gardens. About the size of a Chaffinch, with a short, pointed bill, the male has a red crest, but no other part of the plumage of either sex contains red. The territorial drumming of the male is more rapid, slightly longer and not quite so loud as the Great Spotted Woodpecker. The Lesser Spotted prefers to forage in crevices among smaller branches and twigs, feeding mainly on wood-boring larvae. The unlined nest chamber is often high on a horizontal bough, with its entrance on the underside. Four to six eggs are laid from April until June. **Habitat and distribution** Deciduous woodland, old orchards and parkland. Declining and red-listed as a bird of conservation concern. Occurs in England and Wales, absent from Ireland and Scotland.

Nuthatch *Sitta europaea*

L13–14.5cm A typical bird of mature, deciduous woodlands and parks, the Nuthatch is similar in its behaviour to the unrelated woodpeckers, but is far more agile, being able to move quickly in all directions, including headfirst down tree trunks, in search of insects, larvae, seeds and nuts. It has a distinctive, stocky build with a long, pointed bill, prominent eye stripe, and orange-buff flanks that are slightly darker in the male. High in the topmost branches of mature trees, its distinctive shrill 'tuit tuit' call and loud tapping of seeds often give its presence away. Breeding is in a cavity of a tree, or sometimes in a nestbox, but it is unique among British birds in using mud to reduce the size of the entrance hole and to smooth out irregularities inside. Up to nine eggs are laid on a layer of leaves and bark, in a single brood, and both parents help to rear the young. **Habitat and distribution** Mature oak and beech woods, open parkland and large gardens, where it may be a regular, assertive visitor to bird-feeders. Widespread in England and Wales, less frequent in the north-east and Scotland, absent from Ireland.

Treecreeper *Certhia familiaris*

L12–13cm This inconspicuous, mouse-like little bird has a slender, down-curved beak, used for extracting invertebrates from crevices in bark, and a sharp, stiff tail. Its characteristic feeding behaviour often starts from the base of a tree, from where it jerks its way up the trunk, finally descending with a deeply undulating flight to the base of the next tree to repeat the process. It nests behind loose bark or in a tree-trunk cavity, where a single clutch of five eggs is laid in April and May. Juveniles lack the contrast of the adults and have a fluffy, scaly appearance. The high-pitched trilling song is mostly heard in spring, when pairs display and chase each other in spirals around tree trunks. **Habitat and distribution** Found mainly in deciduous woodland, parks and gardens. In winter, hollows in trunks of large wellingtonia trees are often used as roosting sites. Fairly common throughout Britain and Ireland.

adult ♂
adult ♀
adult ♀
juvenile ♂
Green Woodpecker
adult ♀
adult ♂
adult ♀
juvenile
juvenile ♂
adult ♂
adult ♀
adult ♀
Lesser Spotted Woodpecker
Treecreeper
Great Spotted Woodpecker
Nuthatch

Swift *Apus apus*
L16–18cm The long, sickle-shaped wings and streamlined, torpedo-shaped body of the Swift reflect a life spent mostly feeding, sleeping and even mating in the air. Newly-fledged young may be airborne for much of their first two years before alighting to breed. Its shape and sombre colour, relieved only by a slightly lighter throat, tell it apart from the Swallow and House Martin, which occur in similar places. Swifts are usually associated with high summer, when excited flocks scream through towns and villages. The first birds arrive in Britain from central Africa in early May, and are gone by the end of August. Strictly insectivorous, individuals may fly hundreds of miles in a day, collecting aerial plankton, which is held in a bulging throat pouch. The nest is made in a crevice under eaves, usually in older buildings, and two or three long, white eggs are laid in a single brood. **Habitat and distribution** Usually around habitation but ranges far and wide. Found throughout Britain and Ireland, but is scarcer further north.

House Martin *Delichon urbicum*
L12–14cm The arrival of the first House Martins from Africa begins in early April and continues into June. They stay well into October in warm years. Although lacking the mobility and turn of speed of the Swallow or Swift, the House Martin also spends most of its time in the air, its short tail, white rump and clearly contrasting markings making it conspicuous, even at great heights. This gregarious bird breeds colonially, large numbers often congregating on telephone wires, especially before their southerly migration in autumn. The nest, constructed from beakfuls of mud collected from the edges of ponds and muddy puddles, is situated under the eaves of often quite modern houses. It is a neat, rounded structure with a small entrance slit at the top, and is lined with feathers and grass. A clutch of four or five eggs is laid, with up to three broods a year produced. Around the nest site, House Martins make a contented, budgerigar-like twittering. **Habitat and distribution** Found mostly near habitation, including new housing estates, throughout Britain and Ireland. It has suffered an overall decline in numbers, but has shown a slight increase in recent years. **Similar species** The **Sand Martin** *Riparia riparia* is smaller, dull greyish brown above, white below, with a dark breast band, and lacks a white rump. Usually found near water.

Swallow *Hirundo rustica*
L17–22cm The harbinger of summer, the first Swallows arrive in Britain in early April from their wintering grounds in South Africa, taking about five weeks to complete the 5,000 mile journey. This graceful bird, with its characteristic long, forked tail and russet-coloured chin, spends much of its time in the air, acrobatically catching insects or swooping low over ponds to drink, landing occasionally to gather mud for its nest. The female is slightly duller than the male and has shorter tail streamers, which in juveniles are even shorter. The open, cup-shaped nest is constructed from mud and straw, and built under cover, often in a barn or old shed with open access. Four or five eggs are laid, and in good summers three broods may be reared. **Habitat and distribution** Open country, around farms, villages and cultivated places, often near water. Occurs throughout Britain and Ireland.

Waxwing *Bombycilla garrulus*
L18cm Flocks of this handsome, crested visitor, which takes its name from the waxy red tips to the inner flight feathers, arrive in Britain and Ireland from Scandinavia and Russia in late autumn to take advantage of our winter berry crop. It is the size and build of a Starling, with a unique combination of an overall pinkish-buff colour, black eye-stripe and yellow tip to the tail. Small groups are most likely in suburban gardens, parks and supermarket car parks, where they feed on the berries of rowans, cotoneaster, pyracantha and other berry-bearing ornamental trees. Its flight is swift and direct, and the contact call is a distinctive, high-pitched trilling. **Habitat and distribution** Found mainly in hedgerows and suburban habitats. An irregular visitor; in some years, large 'irruptions' occur, when many thousands arrive, but by the end of April they will have departed for their breeding grounds.

Starling *Sturnus vulgaris*
L20–22cm The Starling is still a common bird in towns and cities, where tens of thousands may congregate in huge flocks prior to roosting. However, its population has declined drastically by 66% in the last 40 years, and it is now red-listed as a bird of conservation concern. The first impression is of a black bird but, close to, the plumage is a beautiful, glossy, iridescent green and purple, with white tips to the feathers, particularly intense in the winter. The breeding male has a pale blue flush to the base of the bill, which in the female is pink. Juveniles have a dull, greyish-brown plumage, with a pale chin. It is a noisy, restless bird with a jaunty walk, quite unlike the measured hops and runs of a Blackbird. The Starling can be a greedy bully on the bird-table. Although it may cause damage to fruit, particularly cherries, it is mostly beneficial in gardens, seeking out leatherjackets, chafer grubs and other damaging invertebrates on lawns. Although not a melodic songster, the Starling is an expert mimic of other birds, and of man-made sounds such as telephone ringtones. It lays up to six sky-blue eggs in holes in trees and man-made cavities, usually raising two broods a year. **Habitat and distribution** Suburbs and farmland throughout Britain and Ireland.

juvenile
adults
adults
juvenile
House Martin
Swift
juvenile
adults
juvenile
Swallow
first
winter
Waxwing
adult
adult
winter
moulting
juvenile
adult
summer
adult
winter
juvenile
Starling

Robin *Erithacus rubecula*

L12.5–15cm Primarily a woodland species, the Robin has adapted to an urban existence and is now Britain's best-loved and most familiar garden bird, often becoming tame enough to be fed by hand. Despite its friendliness to gardeners, the male is quarrelsome and battles with rival males that enter his territory. Courtship is in January and nest-building begins in late February and March, when six or more pale orange-brown speckled eggs are laid in a cup nest, made from leaves and moss, and lined with hair. Robins are well known for siting their nests in strange places, such as flowerpots and in the pockets of jackets hanging in sheds, but usually the nest is secreted away amongst ivy or in an open-fronted nestbox. Up to three broods a year may be reared. The red breast and face of the adult is unmistakable, but juveniles have a less distinctive, softly speckled, brown plumage. Apart from late summer, when moulting occurs, the male sings a thin melodious song, which sometimes continues into the night where there is street lighting, sometimes causing confusion with the song of the Nightingale. When alarmed, Robins make a sharp 'tic-tic' call. **Habitat and distribution** Resident and common in woodlands, parks and gardens throughout Britain and Ireland. Although the population is gradually increasing, mortality is high, and only one in six birds survives the first year, with domestic cats killing about a million Robins a year.

Dunnock *Prunella modularis*

L14–15cm A shy, unobtrusive bird, sometimes called the Hedge Sparrow, the Dunnock is not a sparrow at all, but an accentor, and is more often seen on the ground, feeding mouse-like on scraps beneath bird-feeders, or scuttling low down amongst bushes and shrubs. Unlike the House Sparrow, it has a fine, insectivorous bill, with warm-brown plumage, streaked with black, and a grey head and neck. Sexes are similar, and in the breeding season the female may live with two males, the subordinate helping the dominant male to protect the territory. The neat cup-shaped nest is made in thick vegetation by the male and female, constructed from twigs and roots, and lined with hair, wool and moss. Two broods are normally reared, and the four or five brilliant sky-blue eggs are incubated by the female, although both sexes, including occasionally the subordinate male, help rear the young. The song of the Dunnock is loud, melodious and rambling, similar to, but not as explosive as, that of the Wren. **Habitat and distribution** Found in almost any well-vegetated habitat. A common resident, widespread throughout Britain and Ireland, and more conspicuous in gardens in the winter.

Wren *Troglodytes troglodytes*

L9–10cm Apart from the Goldcrest, the Wren is the smallest British bird. It is a plump, perky little bird with a cocked tail and mouse-like movements. Its well-camouflaged plumage and secretive behaviour mean it often goes unnoticed in gardens. However, its small size is made up for by the shrill, explosive territorial song and angry 'tic-tic-tic' alarm call. The male builds several domed nests from moss and dried grass, hidden in nooks and crannies. One of these is selected by the female, who lines it and lays up to 12 eggs; she is then deserted by the male, who goes on to set up further females in other nests. The Wren rarely visits bird-tables as its diet is made up almost entirely of insects, spiders and other invertebrates. This means that in severe weather populations crash, through lack of food. However, with large broods, numbers soon build, and following mild weather it again becomes Britain's most numerous breeding bird. In hard weather, roosts of up to 40 individuals may huddle together for warmth in nestboxes. **Habitat and distribution** Common all year round in a wide range of habitats, and found throughout Britain and Ireland.

Pied Wagtail *Motacilla alba*

L17–19cm This distinctive and active bird is often seen on rooftops and in gardens, leaping and dashing jerkily across lawns in pursuit of insects, constantly wagging its long tail. The contrasting black, grey and white plumage is unique to British and Irish Pied Wagtails. The Continental race, the White Wagtail, a scarce passage migrant in spring and autumn, has a light grey back with a black bib. Juveniles of both races lack contrast, are brownish grey and are difficult to tell apart. The untidy nest is usually found in a crevice in a rocky bank or wall, but it may be built in odd places such as in farm machinery, old abandoned cars or in woodpiles. Five or six greyish-brown speckled eggs are laid, the female producing a second brood, leaving the male to rear those of the first. The deep, undulating flight and the 'tizzick' call are distinctive. Large flocks often congregate prior to roosting. This usually occurs in reedbeds or bushes, but more recently, railway stations, city shopping centres and other warmer urban environments are being used, especially in winter. **Habitat and distribution** Prefers open places. Present throughout the year in all regions; in autumn, some birds migrate south but many remain in Britain and Ireland. Winter is often spent near reservoir edges, on river banks and in gardens with ponds, where the insect life is richer.

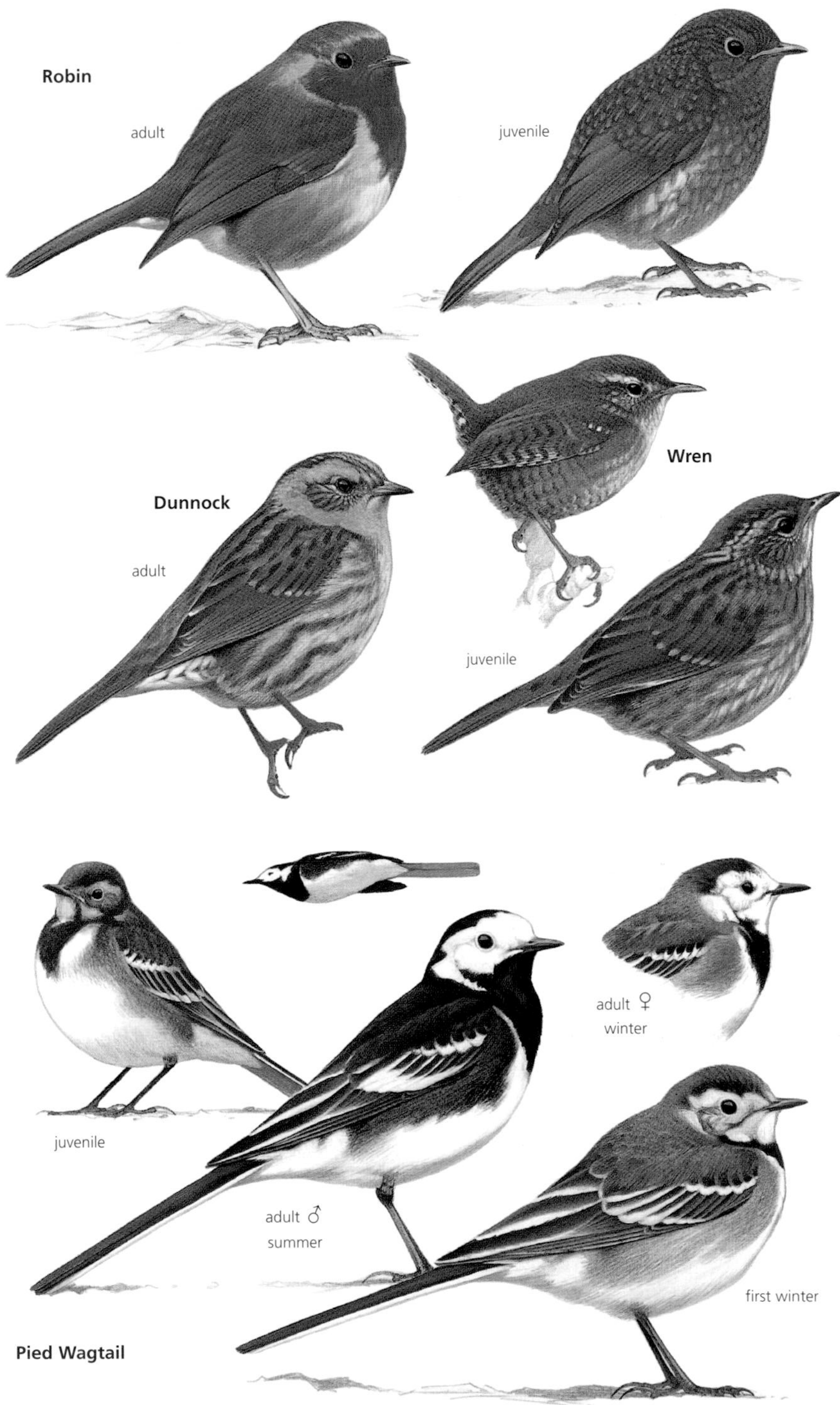
Robin
adult
juvenile
Wren
Dunnock
adult
juvenile
adult ♀
winter
juvenile
adult ♂
summer
first winter
Pied Wagtail

Mistle Thrush *Turdus viscivorus*
L26–28cm The largest of all the thrushes, the Mistle Thrush is an assertive, upright bird, more wary than the familiar Song Thrush, and associated with parks and playing fields rather than small gardens. Its plumage is greyer, with bolder, rounded spots on the breast, and in flight the undersides of the wings and the tips of the outer tail feathers are white. It is often seen singing its melodious, plaintive song, high in a bare treetop on blustery winter days, hence the alternative name, Stormcock. The Mistle Thrush breeds in late February, constructing a nest from grass and mud, often quite high up in the fork of a tree. Up to six attractively mottled eggs are laid, and the nest is fiercely protected, sometimes against much larger birds. The flight is long and undulating, with brief wing-closing, often accompanied by a loud rattling call. Worms and insects are eaten in pastures and lawns, and berries and fallen fruit are aggressively guarded from other thrushes in winter. **Habitat and distribution** Parks, cemeteries and recreation grounds, but also larger, more mature gardens with trees. Found throughout Britain and Ireland but less widespread in the north.

Song Thrush *Turdus philomelos*
L21–23cm The clear, musical, flute-like song of the Song Thrush, with notes and phrases repeated several times over, is one of the most easily recognised of garden bird songs. It is often performed from rooftops and aerials in towns and villages. The warm-brown upper plumage and breast streaked with smaller, arrow-shaped spots differentiate it from the larger Mistle Thrush, and in flight the undersides of the wings are pale orange-buff. The cup-shaped nest, made from grass and moss and smoothly lined with mud, resembles half an empty coconut shell. The female lays four or five beautiful blue eggs, finely spotted with black, with two or three broods each year. Worms and larvae comprise most of the diet in spring, followed by caterpillars and fruit, and in autumn snails are a favourite, being hammered on a rock, the well-known 'thrush's anvil' (see page 199), to get at the fleshy body. **Habitat and distribution** Common in a variety of wooded and suburban habitats, and widely distributed. Has suffered a serious decline in the farmed countryside, and the reduction of suitable feeding habitats has resulted in high mortality of young in the first year of life, but there appears to have been some recovery in recent years.

Blackbird *Turdus merula*
L24–28cm Originally a bird of woodland edges and glades, the Blackbird has adapted to man-made habitats, and has become one of Britain's most well-known and loved birds. The smart black male, with his orange bill and eye-ring, starts to proclaim his territory in February by posturing to other males, and by producing what is often regarded as the most beautiful and melodious song of any British bird. Females and juveniles are rufous-brown, the latter having paler flecks on the upperside, whereas first-year males have a patchwork of black and brown feathers, and a dark bill. Breeding starts in early March, and the nest, made from twigs and mud, and lined with grasses, is usually built in shrubs and vegetation but sometimes on the ground or in buildings. Up to six dull, greenish speckled eggs are laid, with as many as four broods in a season. In winter, Britain's Blackbird population is boosted to about 15 million by large numbers of birds migrating from Scandinavia and the Continent, these often forming into groups to squabble over fallen fruit and berries in gardens. As well as its beautiful song, it has a harsh clucking alarm call and a high-pitched 'seee' call. **Habitat and distribution** The Blackbird is regarded as the most common garden bird, and is found in virtually every habitat throughout the country.

Redwing *Turdus iliacus*
L19–23cm This small thrush, about the size of a Song Thrush, arrives in Britain from Scandinavia and Siberia from late September. Often the first sign of its arrival is the thin 'seep' contact call, usually heard on clear autumnal nights. Flocks often fly in the company of Fieldfares, both species coming to exploit the winter berry and fruit crop. In flight, the Redwing appears dumpy, rather like a Starling, but seen close-up, its bold eye-stripe and russet flanks distinguish it from the similar Song Thrush. Most of the autumn and early winter is spent in fields and hedgerows, but when the weather is harsh and snow covers the fields, Redwings visit gardens and compete for food with other thrushes. **Habitat and distribution** Towns, gardens and open farmland. Most winter-visiting birds depart in March and April, but a few dozen are resident and breed in hedgerows and large gardens in northern Scotland.

Fieldfare *Turdus pilaris*
L23–27cm Almost equal in size to the Mistle Thrush and similar in character, the Fieldfare usually reaches Britain from Scandinavia in early October, often in mixed flocks with Redwings. Its plumage is a rich mix of chestnut-brown on the back, grey on the head and rump, which is most noticeable in flight, and an ochreous, spotted breast fading to white on the belly. Fieldfares fly in unmistakable, ragged, open groups, continually communicating with a harsh chattering call. The diet consists mainly of grubs and invertebrates, but these are usually scarcer by the time the birds arrive in Britain, and hedgerow berries and fruits become the main food as winter deepens. As food in the wider countryside becomes scarcer, gardens with fallen fruit are visited, and territories are aggressively guarded from other smaller thrushes. **Habitat and distribution** Widely distributed, mainly in fields and hedgerows, moving into parks and gardens as the winter hardens. They return to their breeding grounds in early spring, although a few pairs breed in the far north of Britain.

juvenile
juvenile
adult
adult
Song Thrush
Mistle Thrush
adult ♂
first winter ♂
Blackbird
adult ♀
juvenile
Redwing
Fieldfare

Spotted Flycatcher *Muscicapa striata*
L13–15cm This long-distance migrant reaches Britain in late April, after its journey from wintering grounds in South Africa. A subtle, brownish-grey bird, with a streaked breast; juveniles have paler spotting on the head and back. But the Spotted Flycatcher is more easily identified by its behaviour than its appearance. Often perching upright on a conspicuous branch or overhead wire, it darts and swoops acrobatically to catch airborne insects, returning to the same perch time and again. The neat nest is made from grasses and moss, lined with hair and cobwebs. It is often built against an ivy-covered tree trunk, or on a ledge in an old wall, although open-fronted nestboxes are also used. Four or five red-brown speckled eggs are laid. Up to two broods are reared, and the birds return to Africa around September. **Habitat and distribution** Mainly found in woodland edges and openings but equally at home in town parks and mature gardens. Found throughout Britain and Ireland, but has declined drastically in recent years and is red-listed as a bird of conservation concern.

Chiffchaff *Phylloscopus collybita*
L10–12cm The repetitive 'chiff-chaff' song of this olive-brown warbler gives it its name and helps differentiate it from similar species, especially the Willow Warbler, which occurs in the same habitats. Of the two, the Chiffchaff's plumage is slightly duller, with a less clearly defined eye-stripe, and its legs are dark blackish-brown, rather than pale orange-brown. Migrants first start arriving from the Mediterranean or Africa early in March, and stay until late summer. However, with milder winters, increasing numbers are remaining in Britain throughout the year. The cosy domed nest, with an entrance in the side, is made from leaves, grass and moss, and lined with feathers. It is usually built above ground level in shrubby undergrowth, and two broods are often produced, each typically containing six eggs. The Chiffchaff is an insectivorous bird, but in the late summer it will eat berries, and individuals that remain throughout the winter sometimes visit bird-tables for fatty scraps. **Habitat and distribution** Found in all places where shrubby undergrowth and taller trees grow, including damp, overgrown gardens. Found throughout Britain and Ireland, but less common in the treeless far north. **Similar species** The **Willow Warbler** *P. trochilus* is best distinguished by its clear, liquid, descending song, and by the features described above. It sometimes visits gardens and is probably our most widely distributed summer visitor.

Goldcrest *Regulus regulus*
L8–9.5cm This is Britain's smallest bird. The high-pitched 'zee-zee-zee' song of the Goldcrest is often the first sign of its presence, as most of its time is spent searching for invertebrates deep in the foliage of conifer trees, often high up. The well-camouflaged, olive-green plumage is broken by the lemon-yellow crest, bordered with black; this can be erected during courtship, but is absent in juvenile birds. The tiny, neat nest is made from moss, lichens and cobwebs, and is suspended from a branch. Breeding starts in April, and typically six to eight eggs are laid, in two broods lasting until August. Populations fluctuate according to the weather, crashing in severe winters and flourishing after mild ones. Surprisingly for such a small bird, often quite large numbers of Continental birds arrive in the autumn to take advantage of our slightly milder weather. **Habitat and distribution** Found mainly in coniferous woodland, less common in deciduous woodland and a regular visitor to parks and gardens with ornamental conifers. Occurs throughout most of Britain and Ireland except the Fens and Scottish Highlands. **Similar species** The rare **Firecrest** *R. ignicapillus* has a dark eye-stripe with a white stripe above, and bronze-coloured shoulders.

Blackcap *Sylvia atricapilla*
L13–15cm The male Blackcap is one of the more easily recognised of the warblers, and has a beautiful melodious song, although this can be confused by the inexperienced with that of the plainer **Garden Warbler** *Sylvia borin*, or even the **Nightingale** *Luscinia megarynchos*. The female and juvenile also have caps, but they are chestnut-brown. Most Blackcaps arrive from the Mediterranean and Africa in April, but birds heard singing in March are probably those of an increasing number from central Europe that spend the winter in Britain, often visiting bird-tables for scraps. The nest is a neat cup made from grasses and rootlets, lined with moss and hair, usually 30cm or more above ground, often in a bramble patch or thicket, with trees and shrubs nearby. Four to six eggs are laid, and in the south two broods are produced. The Blackcap's diet consists mainly of insects and other invertebrates, but later in the year various fruits, including blackberries and elderberries, are eaten. **Habitat and distribution** A bird of woodlands, well-grown hedges and copses, it is also found in larger, overgrown gardens, where thick bramble patches provide nesting sites. Widespread in the summer months, but distribution is more restricted to the south in winter. **Similar species** The **Marsh Tit** *Poecile palustris* is similarly marked, but is slightly smaller and has distinctive white cheeks and a black bib. It occasionally comes into gardens in the winter, when it may visit the bird-table.

juvenile
adult
Spotted Flycatcher
spring
juvenile
Chiffchaff
adult
Goldcrest
autumn
adult ♀
adult ♂
Blackcap

Blue Tit *Cyanistes caeruleus*
L11–12cm Everyone with a bird-table and peanut-feeder in the garden will have been visited by Blue Tits, the best known of all the colourful winter acrobats, that go on to occupy garden nestboxes in the spring. Males and females are alike and juveniles are paler, with yellowish cheeks. Winter visitors from the Continent are brighter than resident birds. They are mainly insectivorous, and breeding is synchronised to the huge numbers of Winter Moth caterpillars that appear in spring, when the insatiable appetite of the young is at its peak; a single brood may eat about 12,000 caterpillars. The female makes a cosy nest of moss, feathers, hair and cobwebs, either in a nestbox or in a crevice in a tree or wall. Here, in early April, she puts 'all her eggs in one basket' and lays up to 12 eggs in a single brood, although in gardens, where food is less abundant than in woodland, usually only six or seven eggs are laid. There is only an occasional second brood. Mortality is high at 90% with, on average, only one fledgling surviving the first year. Later in the year, when invertebrates are scarcer, the Blue Tit depends more on nuts, seeds and fat at the bird-table. At this time, it is most numerous in gardens, and becomes the second-most common garden bird after the Blackbird. It has a wide range of clear, high-pitched calls, most commonly 'tse-tse-tse-tsuu'. **Habitat and distribution** A common, mainly woodland, bird, but found in many other habitats throughout the year. Widely distributed throughout Britain and Ireland, with about 3.5 million breeding pairs.

Great Tit *Parus major*
L13.5–15cm This is the largest and most aggressive of the tits and is an agile acrobat on the bird-feeder. The sexes can be separated by the central belly stripe, which in the male is broad and black, and in the female is narrow, uneven and paler; juveniles are altogether paler, with yellow cheeks. Breeding begins in late March, and as well as nestboxes, natural holes in trees and walls (and even mailboxes!) are used as nesting sites. As an omnivore, the Great Tit eats a wide range of food, including vegetable matter, but its main diet, especially in the summer, is caterpillars foraged from the foliage of deciduous trees. It has a wide vocabulary, the most familiar in spring being a loud 'tsee-saw-tsee-saw'. In winter, mixed flocks of tits, Nuthatches and finches roam woodlands, parks and gardens, foraging for food and taking advantage of a greater number of eyes looking out for predators. **Habitat and distribution** Found in woodland, parks and gardens with plenty of vegetation. Occurs throughout Britain and Ireland.

Coal Tit *Periparus ater*
L10–11.5cm The smallest of the true tits, the Coal Tit has a dumpy, greyish-buff body and a striking black-and-white head. It lacks the bright colours of commoner garden tits, although some races, particularly those autumn visitors from the Continent and juveniles, have a slightly yellowish tinge. The white patch on the nape is diagnostic. The slender bill is ideal for probing into conifer cones for insects, which reflects the Coal Tit's preference for coniferous woodland. Its diet is mainly insects, but seeds and fruit are also eaten. It is energetic and fast-moving when foraging, frequently flying to and from bird-tables to hoard food in nearby crevices. When concealed in a treetop, it can be identified by its distinctive, repetitive 'teechu-teechu-teechu' song. The nest is made from moss, hair and fur, built in a crevice, often low down in a tree or wall, or in a nestbox, where a clutch of seven to 12 eggs is laid. An occasional second brood is reared in good summers. **Habitat and distribution** Prefers mainly coniferous woods but is found in all types of woodland, parks and gardens throughout the country.

Long-tailed Tit *Aegithalos caudatus*
L12–14cm Without its tail, the Long-tailed Tit, which is not a true tit, would easily be the smallest of all the British tits. They are most often seen in active parties of up to 20 birds, following each other, skipping from tree to tree in ones or twos, and making contact with a high-pitched 'sree-sree-sree' call. They sometimes visit gardens to feed on peanuts and fat balls. The adult plumage is pink, white and black, quite unlike that of the juvenile, which is much duller and has a shorter tail. In mid-summer, both start a long moult, and by October they appear indistinguishable. Breeding starts early in the year, at the beginning of March, and the nest is a masterpiece that takes up to a month to build. The beautiful dome-shaped nest is made from moss, hair and cobwebs, covered with lichens and lined with around 2,000 soft feathers. It is usually positioned in a thorny shrub or, less often, quite high up in the fork of a tree. Here, up to 12 eggs are laid, well insulated from bad weather. Both parents, often aided by other non-breeding individuals, feed the young. In winter, groups of Long-tailed Tits huddle together for warmth, but mortality can be high and in severe weather, when insect food is scarce, the population may crash by up to 80%. **Habitat and distribution** Woodland fringes, clearings, along hedgerows, in parks and gardens. Widespread, except for the far north and west of Scotland.

adult
juvenile
adult
Blue Tit
adult
adult ♂
adult ♀
Great Tit
juvenile
white patch on nape
adult
Coal Tit
juvenile
adult
Long-tailed Tit
juvenile

Jay *Garrulus glandarius*
L32–36cm The Jay, the most colourful member of the crow family, is a shy woodland bird that sometimes visits parks and large gardens. It is unmistakable, especially in flight, with its conspicuous white rump and harsh, shrieking call. It has pinkish-brown plumage, a finely spotted black-and-white crest and beautiful silvery-blue patches on each wing. The Jay is well known for hoarding acorns in the winter, with a single bird scattering up to 2,000, this being the most important method of oak-tree propagation. Sweet chestnuts, beech masts and pine seeds are also eaten, as well as fruit, eggs, nestlings and invertebrates. Built in thick vegetation, the nest is made from sticks and twigs, thickly lined with rootlets. Four to six eggs are usually laid in a single brood. **Habitat and distribution** Deciduous and coniferous woodland, parks and gardens with mature trees. Resident throughout Britain and Ireland as far north as southern Scotland; in winter the population may be boosted by birds from the Continent.

Magpie *Pica pica*
L40–50cm An inquisitive and opportunistic member of the crow family, the Magpie is a striking bird with its pied plumage glistening iridescent purple and green in the sunlight. In recent years, the increase in Magpie numbers has gained it an undeserved, villainous reputation as a garden predator, being blamed for the demise of familiar songbirds, even though domestic cats still kill far more small birds than Magpies. In the winter months, flocks of chattering, squabbling non-breeders maraud through gardens like mischievous youths, in contrast to established pairs, which are far less obtrusive in their behaviour. The large, untidy, domed nest is constructed in a thick thorn hedge or high in a tree, from sticks and twigs, and lined with mud and a layer of fine grasses and roots. Up to ten greenish-grey blotched eggs are laid in a single brood in April. By June or July the dumpy, short-tailed young are ready to leave the nest. **Habitat and distribution** Found in a wide variety of habitats. In recent decades the Magpie has adapted to urban life, including large cities, following a reduction in persecution. Occurs throughout the British Isles, except north-west Scotland.

Jackdaw *Coloeus monedula*
L31–34cm The smallest of the three common black 'crows', the Jackdaw can be distinguished by its slate-grey cheeks and nape, short bill and silvery-white eyes. In flight it can show great agility, often mixing with flocks of Rooks, but its smaller size, faster wingbeats and sharp 'chack-chack' call are characteristic. Jackdaws mate for life, and pairs are typically seen perching on rooftops or chimney stacks, the latter being sometimes chosen as nesting sites, although colonies may be established in holes in trees or derelict buildings. The nest is made from twigs, lined with grass and wool, and four to six pale blue, blotched eggs are laid in April and May, and incubated by the female. Their omnivorous diet includes invertebrates, fruit, small nestlings and rodents, as well as waste from rubbish tips. **Habitat and distribution** Commonly found in towns and cities, as well as more rural places around farms, villages and churches. Occurs throughout the British Isles, except the Scottish Highlands.

Rook *Corvus frugilegus*
L43–48cm Flocks of Rooks, the most sociable of the crow family, are most frequently seen foraging in pastures where, as well as eating harmful grubs, they may also cause damage to root crops and cereals. They are equally conspicuous at their communal nest sites, 'rookeries', particularly as they prepare for nesting in February and March, when the trees are still bare. At this time of year, the nasal 'kaah-kaah' call of the Rook is at its most intense, and in Scotland, where some colonies contain over 1,000 pairs, the noise can be deafening. Adult Rooks can be distinguished from Carrion Crows by their glossier plumage and more pointed bill, which is surrounded by pale, bare skin; this area is dark in juveniles, which also have the shaggy 'trousers' of the adults. **Habitat and distribution** Not a regular garden visitor, but Rooks may come into village gardens that are surrounded by fields and open farmland. Found throughout Britain and Ireland, except for the far north-west of Scotland.

Carrion Crow *Corvus corone*
L45–49cm Although non-breeding and small family groups of Carrion Crows may be seen after the breeding season and in winter roosts, this is a wary bird that usually appears singly or in pairs. Individual males often proclaim their territories from treetops, with a harsh 'krark-krark-krark' call. The plain black plumage lacks the glossy sheen and pale grey bill base of the Rook, and in flight the tail is square-ended rather than wedge-shaped. The nest is made from twigs and grass, usually positioned high up in the fork of an isolated tree, giving a good all-round view. The four or five eggs are usually laid in mid April and are incubated by the female, who is fed by the male. The diet is opportunistic and wide ranging, and although it includes invertebrate pest species, the Carrion Crow's fondness for eggs, especially those of game birds, and carrion, such as lamb corpses, has made it unpopular among farmers. **Habitat and distribution** A farmland bird that ventures into larger gardens, particularly in late spring and early summer. Found throughout Britain, but in Ireland and north-western Scotland it is replaced by the grey-and-black **Hooded Crow** *C. cornix*, which was, until recently, regarded as a race of the Carrion Crow.

Jay
Magpie
Jackdaw
wedge-shaped tail
juvenile
square-ended tail
adult
Rook
Carrion Crow

House Sparrow *Passer domesticus*
L14–16cm Closely associated with human habitation and once regarded as an agricultural pest, the House Sparrow in Britain has suffered a dramatic decline of more than 70% over the last 40 years, with a population now of around 5 million, and is now red-listed as a species of conservation concern. The male is distinctive, with a grey crown and nape, a rich chestnut-brown back and a black bib, the size of which indicates his dominance over other males. Females and juveniles are drabber and a nondescript, brownish grey, streaked with black above and greyish white below. An opportunistic omnivore, the House Sparrow will eat almost anything, including seedlings and flowers, with a particular liking for yellow, nectar-bearing spring flowers such as crocuses and primulas, making it unpopular among gardeners. It is a social bird that nests in colonies. Territorial males try to attract females by posturing and repeating their monotonous 'chirrup' call close to the nest site. This may be under eaves, in a wall cavity or, less often, scruffy dome-shaped nests are made from dried grass and straw amongst dense ivy or in hawthorn bushes. Usually four or five eggs are laid, between March and August, in up to four broods, which are incubated by both sexes. **Habitat and distribution** Most common around dwellings in towns, villages and agricultural buildings, where they form winter flocks with finches and buntings. Widely distributed throughout Britain and Ireland; most common in south-east England, but it has disappeared from many places. Possible causes for the decline include fewer weedy stubble fields in which to forage, as well as fewer suitable nesting sites in modern houses, and the garden 'make-over', which tidies up undergrowth and wilder areas where the House Sparrow can feed and shelter. **Similar species** The **Tree Sparrow** *P. montanus*, the country cousin of the House Sparrow, is shyer and far less common in gardens. It is best distinguished by the dark cheek spot and smaller black bib, which are present in both sexes.

Chaffinch *Fringilla coelebs*
L14–16cm This is Britain's commonest finch and, after the Wren, our second-most common breeding bird. The male Chaffinch is easily recognised and is often seen searching for dropped seeds and crumbs beneath the bird-feeder or under bushes. As well as his distinctive 'pink-pink' call, in the breeding season the male sings a bright, trilling territorial song, usually from a conspicuous perch. The female is more sombrely coloured, although like the male she has characteristic double white wing bars and a greenish rump. The neat nest, usually blended into the fork of a tree or shrub, is built in April or early May, from moss, roots and lichens, lined with fur and feathers. Usually only a single brood is produced, containing four or five eggs, which are pale blue with darker, purplish-brown spots. The Chaffinch's diet is varied, consisting mainly of invertebrates in spring and summer, but in winter, flocks including large numbers of Continental birds forage for seeds on the ground throughout the countryside. **Habitat and distribution** Primarily a woodland bird, but found in many habitats and frequent in gardens. Distributed throughout Britain and Ireland, with large numbers of birds arriving from Scandinavia in the autumn.

Brambling *Fringilla montifringilla*
L14–16cm An irregular winter visitor to Britain from Scandinavia, the Brambling may sometimes be seen in mixed flocks with other finches and buntings, often in the company of its close relative, the Chaffinch. The mottled, rusty-buff plumage resembles that of the Chaffinch, but the white wing bars are less prominent, and in flight the main distinguishing feature is a conspicuous white rump. The female is duller, with a pale grey head and nape, which is absent in juveniles. The flight call is a short 'keep-keep'. **Habitat and distribution** Up to a million birds may arrive in a good year; they are found mainly in beech woodlands from mid-September until April, but when the beech mast is exhausted they occur on farmland and in gardens, where they feed on weed seeds, grain and at bird-feeders. They are thinly distributed throughout Britain and Ireland, becoming scarcer in the far west and north. Has occasionally bred in the north.

♂
adult ♂
winter
adult ♂
summer
House Sparrow
adult ♀
greenish rump
♂
adult ♂
winter
adult ♂
summer
Chaffinch
adult ♀
white rump
♂
adult ♂
winter
adult ♂
summer
Brambling
adult ♀
winter

Bullfinch *Pyrrhula pyrrhula*
L14–16.5cm Unfortunately, this shy, handsome finch has a liking for the tender flowers and leaf buds of many fruit and ornamental trees and shrubs, especially those of apple, pear, plum, cherries and forsythia, making it unpopular with gardeners and fruit growers. The male has a beautiful rose-coloured breast, contrasting strikingly with the black head and bib. The white rump is conspicuous in both sexes as they fly away. The female is otherwise much duller, giving her greater camouflage as she incubates the eggs. She builds her nest from fine twigs, lined with hair and rootlets, in dense bushes. Four or five eggs are usually laid, with up to three broods in a season. At first, the young are fed on small insects and other invertebrates but the diet gradually changes, and by the time they fledge, seeds form the major part of their diet. From early December the Bullfinch turns its attention to buds, using its stout bill to crush the outer husks and eating up to 30 buds a minute. As small groups forage along hedgerows, they maintain contact with a plaintive 'peeu-peeu' call. **Habitat and distribution** Occurs in well-vegetated places, including woodlands, hedgerows and scrub, mainly visiting gardens and orchards in the winter and spring. At this time of year, netting is best used to protect fruit and ornamental trees. Widely distributed, but has declined recently as a result of the removal of tall, dense hedgerows, and is now amber-listed as a species of conservation concern.

Greenfinch *Chloris chloris*
L14–16cm The male of this common garden visitor has an attractive moss-green plumage, with bright yellow patches on the wings and tail. The female and juveniles, by contrast, are much duller and are often mistaken for House Sparrows, although both usually have a faint greenish tint and juveniles are lightly streaked with brown. In spring, the male can be seen performing his display flight, launching himself from a perch and circling with a butterfly-like flapping over his territory. A variety of calls are made from perches and in flight, including Canary-like trills and the familiar nasal 'dweeez'. The nest is made from twigs, moss and rootlets, lined with hair and wool; it is well concealed in vegetation, with ornamental conifers often favoured in gardens. Four to six eggs are laid from May onwards, and up to three broods are reared until September. The young are fed on insects at first, but the diet soon progresses to seeds. In autumn, large flocks of Greenfinches mix with other finches and buntings, feeding on weed seeds and grain in stubble fields and on waste ground. Gardens are also visited, and by April and May, when food in the countryside is exhausted, bird-table feeding of sunflower and nyger seeds and peanuts can make a major contribution at a time when many birds die from starvation. **Habitat and distribution** Widespread and common in many habitats throughout Britain, but more vulnerable in recent years because of the growing of winter wheat and the 'tidying up' of the countryside.

Lesser Redpoll *Acanthis cabaret*
L11.5–12.5cm A small finch, often found in mixed flocks with Goldfinch and Siskin, the Lesser Redpoll is most often seen in gardens in mid-to-late winter, where it favours nyger and other finer seeds at the bird-table. Often overlooked, it has a warm streaky-brown plumage but close inspection reveals the diagnostic crimson forehead and black chin. A breeding species in Scotland, northern England and Wales, during the winter months birds move south, often in large numbers known as 'invasions'. The nest is built in birch woods and young conifer plantations; there may be two broods, each containing four or five eggs. Birds often congregate at the tops of birch, alder or conifer trees and can be detected by their metallic twittering calls. They have a buoyant, undulating flight, typical of finches. **Habitat and distribution** The Lesser Redpoll breeds in woodland, but also visit gardens. Its fortunes have fluctuated in the last 50 years and although it is now more frequently seen in gardens, generally speaking it is of conservation concern and is now red-listed. **Similar species** The **Common Redpoll** *A. flammea* and **Arctic Redpoll** *A. hornemanni* are very similar, though they are much less likely to occur in gardens. Both are slightly larger and appear rather cooler in colour, though, because of variability, some specimens are impossible to identify.

adult ♀
Bullfinch
adult ♂
adult ♂
adult ♀
juvenile
adult ♂
Greenfinch
adult ♀
adult ♂
juvenile
first winter ♂
Lesser Redpoll
♂

Goldfinch *Carduelis carduelis*

L11.5–13cm The collective name 'a charm of Goldfinches' describes perfectly this pretty little finch, which has become more common in gardens in recent years following a decline in the 1970s and 1980s. Now, twice as many visit gardens as 20 years ago, possibly as a result of a decline in natural food but also because of their fondness for sunflower hearts and nyger seed in bird-feeders. Adults of both sexes are similar and unmistakable. Juveniles are dull greyish brown, with fine streaks, and lack the striking head pattern of the adults, but do have the yellow wing bars. The fine, pointed bill allows Goldfinches to exploit the seeds of flowers such as dandelion and groundsel, and they are well known for their acrobatics on thistles, burdock and teasels. The beautiful nest is sited in the outer branches of trees and bushes and is built from moss, lichens, grass and hair, bound with spiders' webs and warmly lined with fur and down from plants and seeds. Five or six eggs are usually laid, in up to three broods lasting into September. The cheerful song of the Goldfinch is a canary-like twittering, and in flight the contact call is a metallic 'tickalick-tickalick'. **Habitat and distribution** Found in a variety of habitats, its distribution has gradually spread northwards into Scotland.

Siskin *Spinus spinus*

L11.5–12.5cm An infrequent winter visitor to gardens in the south, the Siskin is one of the smallest finches, resembling a small, brightly-marked Greenfinch. The female is duller and lacks the black cap of the male, but shares the yellow-and-black streaked plumage, bright yellow wing bars and forked tail. Juveniles are greyish buff and more heavily streaked. An agile bird, often seen feeding in the tops of birch and alder trees. In the last 50 years or so, Siskins have also developed a fondness for peanuts, particularly those suspended in red net bags, but only, it seems, in the late winter months. Resident birds breed mainly in coniferous areas of Scotland, Ireland and, more irregularly, in parts of Wales and England. In autumn, these birds move away from their breeding grounds and forage for food with Siskins from the Continent. The neat nest is made high up in the outer foliage of a conifer tree, where three to five eggs are laid in April, in one or two broods. The call is a shrill 'tseew', with a varied twittering jingle in the breeding season. **Habitat and distribution** Breeds mainly in coniferous woods, less often in mixed woodlands, but moves further afield in autumn and winter. Found throughout Britain; birds visiting gardens outside the autumn and winter months are likely to be resident breeders.

Reed Bunting *Emberiza schoeniclus*

L14–15.5cm With a reduction in its wetland habitats, the Reed Bunting has suffered a decline, although in recent years it has managed to adapt to drier places and in the colder winter months it occurs regularly in gardens, on and beneath bird-feeders. Easily passed by as a House Sparrow, the plumage, especially that of the female, is far less striking in winter than in the breeding season, but even so, the head pattern, streaky plumage and white outer tail feathers are diagnostic. **Habitat and distribution** Breeds in reedbeds, damp scrub, young conifer plantations, and cereal and oilseed-rape fields. In autumn and winter, mixes with other buntings and finches, feeding in stubble on weed seeds or spilled grain; most likely to visit gardens in hard weather in late winter. Widely distributed, but absent from the far north of Scotland. It has been in decline since the 1970s and is amber-listed as a species of conservation concern.

adult ♂
Goldfinch
adult ♂
adult
♀
juvenile
adult ♂
Siskin
adult ♂
juvenile
adult ♀
♂
adult ♂
summer
adult ♂
winter
Reed Bunting
adult ♀ winter

Reptiles

Common or **Viviparous Lizard**
Zootoca vivipara
L12–18cm Lizards are sun-loving animals and are often seen warming themselves in sunshine on logs or stones. The sexes are similar, and although there is great variation in colour and markings, the male tends to be darker and more strongly marked than the female and has an orange-red belly, heavily spotted with black. In the female, the belly is yellow or greyish, with little spotting, and she also lacks the male's bulge at the base of the tail. Mating begins after hibernation, in April and May, and following skirmishes with rivals the male grabs the female in his jaws and mates, with little courtship involved. This reptile is also known as the Viviparous Lizard, meaning it gives birth to living young. However, this is not entirely accurate as the young are born in a thin membrane from which they quickly break free. One female may produce up to 15 young, which are a dark, bronze colour at first, developing their paler markings as they mature. Full maturity is reached in two and three years, respectively, for males and females.

Hunting takes place when the lizard's body has warmed sufficiently, and a variety of invertebrates, in particular soft-bodied larvae and spiders, are preferred. The Common Lizard is itself preyed upon, especially when young, but like all lizards it has the ability to shed its tail to distract predators as it makes its escape. It is then able to regenerate a new but stumpier tail. **Habitat and distribution** Widely distributed throughout Britain and the only reptile to occur in Ireland. It is found in many habitats, including gardens and allotments with open, undisturbed, south-facing areas.

Slow-worm *Anguis fragilis*
L35–50cm Despite its smooth, polished, worm-like appearance, the Slow-worm is a legless lizard and a highly beneficial garden inhabitant. Its colour ranges from a light greyish brown to deep bronze or copper, but whereas the colour of the male is uniform, the female has a dark belly, often with longitudinal stripes and flecks running along the back and sides. Males have proportionately larger heads than females, and some have a number of blue spots on their bodies.

Slow-worms are less often seen basking than Common Lizards, but may sometimes be found on warm grassy tussocks after hibernation, and in July and August, when females bask before giving birth. Small sheets of corrugated iron or pieces of carpet, placed in the sun, will also attract Slow-worms, giving them warmth and protection. Mating takes place between April and June, and the female gives birth to between ten and 20 young, which break through an enclosing membrane soon after birth. The slender, newly-hatched young are about 75mm long, and are yellow, with a black dorsal line and belly. Maturity is reached by the age of three years in males and four or five years in females, and some individuals live to over 50 years.

In the daytime, Slow-worms hide beneath logs, in crevices in the soil and in leaf litter or compost heaps, emerging at night to feed on a wide range of invertebrates. Worms and insects are included in the diet, but the Slow-worm's preference for snails and slugs, especially the Field Slug *Deroceras reticulatum,* a serious pest species, make it most welcome in gardens and allotments. Despite its ability, like other lizards, to shed its tail to avoid predation, the Slow-worm has many enemies, and in gardens Hedgehogs, Foxes and cats may kill them, while the young may be taken by birds, frogs and toads. **Habitat and distribution** Numbers are in decline but the species is widespread, being most common in the west and south-west of Britain but absent from Ireland.

Grass Snake *Natrix helvetica*
L80–170cm This large, non-venomous snake sometimes visits gardens to hunt around ponds or to lay its eggs in the warmth of a compost heap. Its colour varies little and is usually a shade of olive-green or brown, spotted with black, and with a prominent yellow collar bordered with black, giving rise to its other name of Ringed Snake. The sexes are similar, although females grow larger than males and may exceed 1.5m.

After a lengthy courtship and mating, which takes place in April and May, the female seeks the warmth of manure or compost heaps, or a pile of decaying leaves and grass. Here, she constructs a chamber and lays up to 40 eggs; several females may choose the same place to lay, forming collections of several hundred eggs. The white eggs are 25–30mm long, moist and shiny at first but later sticking together and becoming matt as they dry. The young hatch in August and September, appearing as tiny, dark adults. At this stage, they feed on slugs, worms and tadpoles, but by the time they are fully grown, frogs are the main diet. Other amphibians and reptiles, as well as small mammals and birds, are also taken. Hedgehogs and Badgers will eat Grass Snakes and the young are vulnerable to many other predators. The Grass Snake has a variety of defence mechanisms, however, to escape predation, including inflating itself and hissing threateningly, discharging a foul-smelling fluid and feigning death. Humans also misguidedly kill snakes, although it should be remembered that all British reptiles are fully protected. **Habitat and distribution** Found throughout England and Wales but becoming scarcer; absent from Scotland and Ireland.

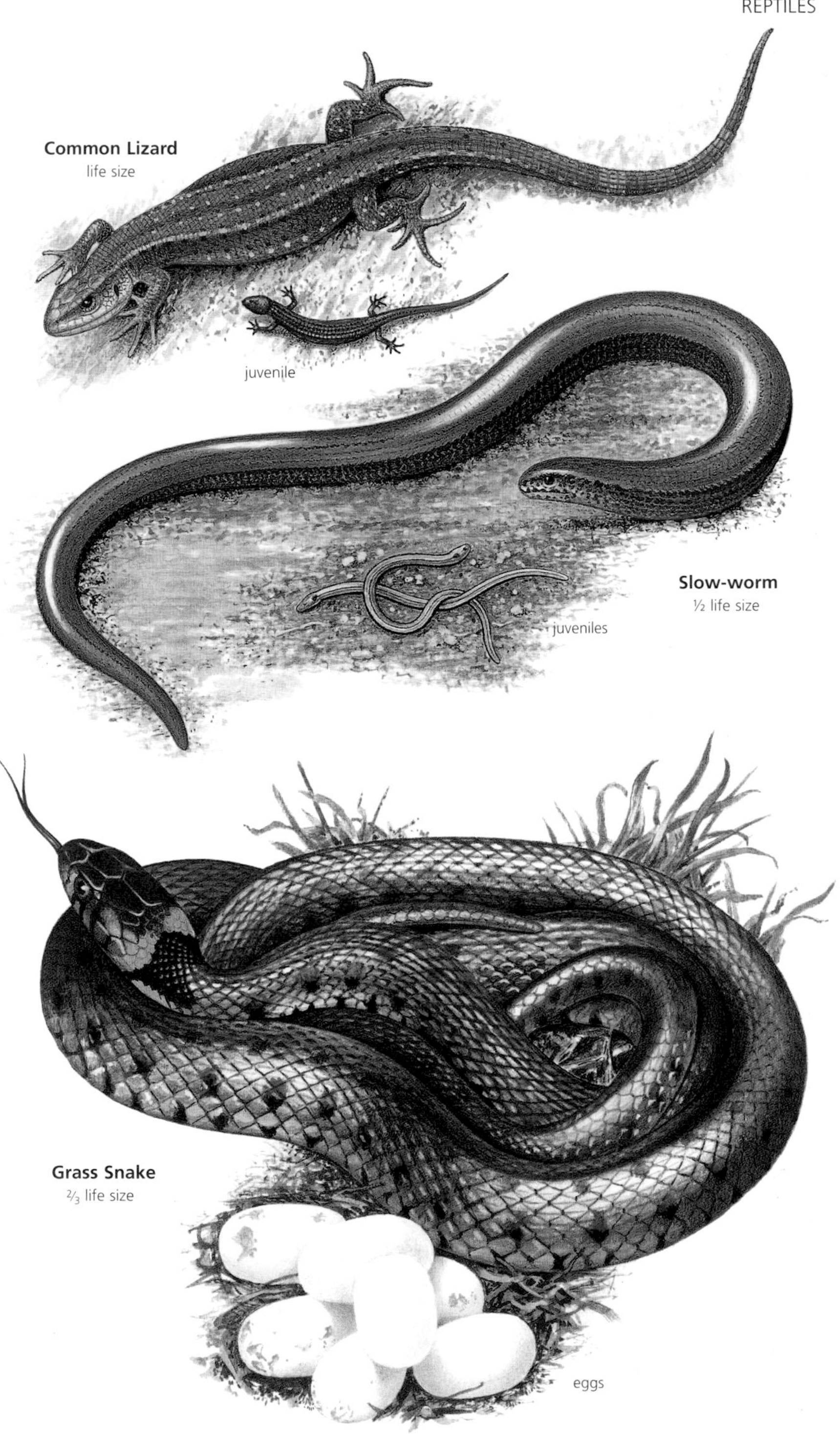
Common Lizard
life size
juvenile
Slow-worm
½ life size
juveniles
Grass Snake
⅔ life size
eggs

Amphibians

Common Frog *Rana temporaria*
L up to 9.5cm The Common Frog is our most familiar amphibian and in recent years, as wetland habitats have declined, it has become even more dependent on garden ponds for its survival. Variable in colour, the smooth, damp skin may be yellow, olive, pink or grey, blotched and marbled with black, brick-red or brown, the most constant marking being the dark, triangular temporal patch behind the eye, containing the ear-drum. From this patch, a prominent fold runs along each side of the body. Sexes are similar, although the male is less stoutly built than the female and has a pad on his first finger, which becomes swollen in the breeding season and is used for gripping the female in the mating embrace, or 'amplexus'.

Breeding takes place after hibernation, usually in February and March, when large numbers may congregate and make the water 'boil' as males croak and grapple for females. During mating, which can last for up to 24 hours, the male fertilises the eggs as they are laid, with, depending on size, each female laying up to 4,000 eggs. The eggs sink at first, but then swell and rise to the surface to form a continuous mass of spawn. Having absorbed its egg yolk, the developing tadpole, which at first is black and then brown speckled with gold, starts to feed independently on algae. By the fifth week, limbs begin to develop. At ten to 12 weeks the metamorphosis into a tiny frog is complete, and the young leave the water in May or June.

Frogs are very beneficial in the garden as snails form a major part of their diet, but many other pests and invertebrates are also eaten. Capable of breathing through their skin, frogs usually hibernate in mud and debris at the bottom of ponds or around their margins, although some spend the winter in shelters away from water. This begins in autumn, but in mild winters some frogs may emerge from hibernation. In recent years, Ranavirus, a disease also known as 'redleg', has affected populations, and transferring frogs, tadpoles or their spawn between ponds is now discouraged. **Distribution** Found throughout Britain, with more widely scattered records for Ireland.

Common Toad *Bufo bufo*
L up to 10cm Apart from during the breeding season, toads are usually encountered either foraging at night or hiding under rocks in the daytime. They are generally clumsier than frogs, and run and crawl, rather than hop. They also differ physically in several ways. The skin is uneven and warty, and is usually some shade of brown, mottled with darker blotches. The eyes have narrow, horizontal pupils and behind them are two large paratoid glands, which contain poisonous toxins. Ants and certain species of beetle are the preferred food but many pest species and some beneficial creatures, such as worms, young amphibians and reptiles, are also eaten.

After emerging from hibernation and migrating, often in large numbers, to their breeding ground, mating takes place, usually between February and April. The eggs are fertilised as the male embraces the female limpet-like, in amplexus, and the long strings of eggs are laid among waterweed, in deeper parts of the pond than are used by frogs. Metamorphosis is completed in ten to 15 weeks, according to the temperature, and the young usually leave the water in June. Hibernation begins in autumn, either singly or in groups, in a dry rockery, a hole in a bank or under a shed, sometimes far from the breeding ground. Full maturity is reached at the age of five or six years, but in captivity toads may reach 50 years of age. In recent years, Chytridiomycosis, a fungal disease that causes lethargy and skin shedding in amphibians, has been found in Common Toads. **Distribution** Widely distributed throughout Britain but absent from Ireland.

Smooth or **Common Newt**
Lissotriton vulgaris
L up to 11cm This is the commonest and most widespread of the three newt species found in Britain, and the only species found in Ireland. The breeding male has a wavy crest running the length of his body and tail, and is olive-brown, boldly spotted with black, and with a bright orange belly. The female is similar, although more sombre in her colours and markings, but lacks the male's wavy crest. Mating occurs after hibernation, in March and April, when the male performs his elaborate courtship, crossing in front of the female and posing dramatically, with his tail folded double and trembling urgently. After fertilisation, the female lays separately up to 300 eggs, each wrapped in the leaf of an aquatic plant. The tadpole differs from those of toads and frogs in having external gills for breathing. It completes its metamorphosis in about 15 weeks, leaving the water in July and August. Most adults also leave the water at about this time, when their skin becomes drier and duller, and the male loses his crest (although the sexes can still be distinguished). From now and throughout the winter, young and adults live in damp crevices or beneath logs and stones, emerging at night to feed on invertebrates. **Distribution** Widespread and common throughout much of England, scarcer in Wales and Scotland, and the only newt found in Ireland. **Similar species** **Palmate Newt** *L. helveticus* The breeding male lacks the wavy crest, but females, apart from being slightly greener and having an unspotted throat, are almost identical. Mainly occurs on higher ground, heaths and moors, and is much rarer in gardens. **Great Crested** or **Warty Newt** *Triturus cristatus* is much larger and darker, reaching 17cm. It is a protected species, which occurs only rarely in gardens.

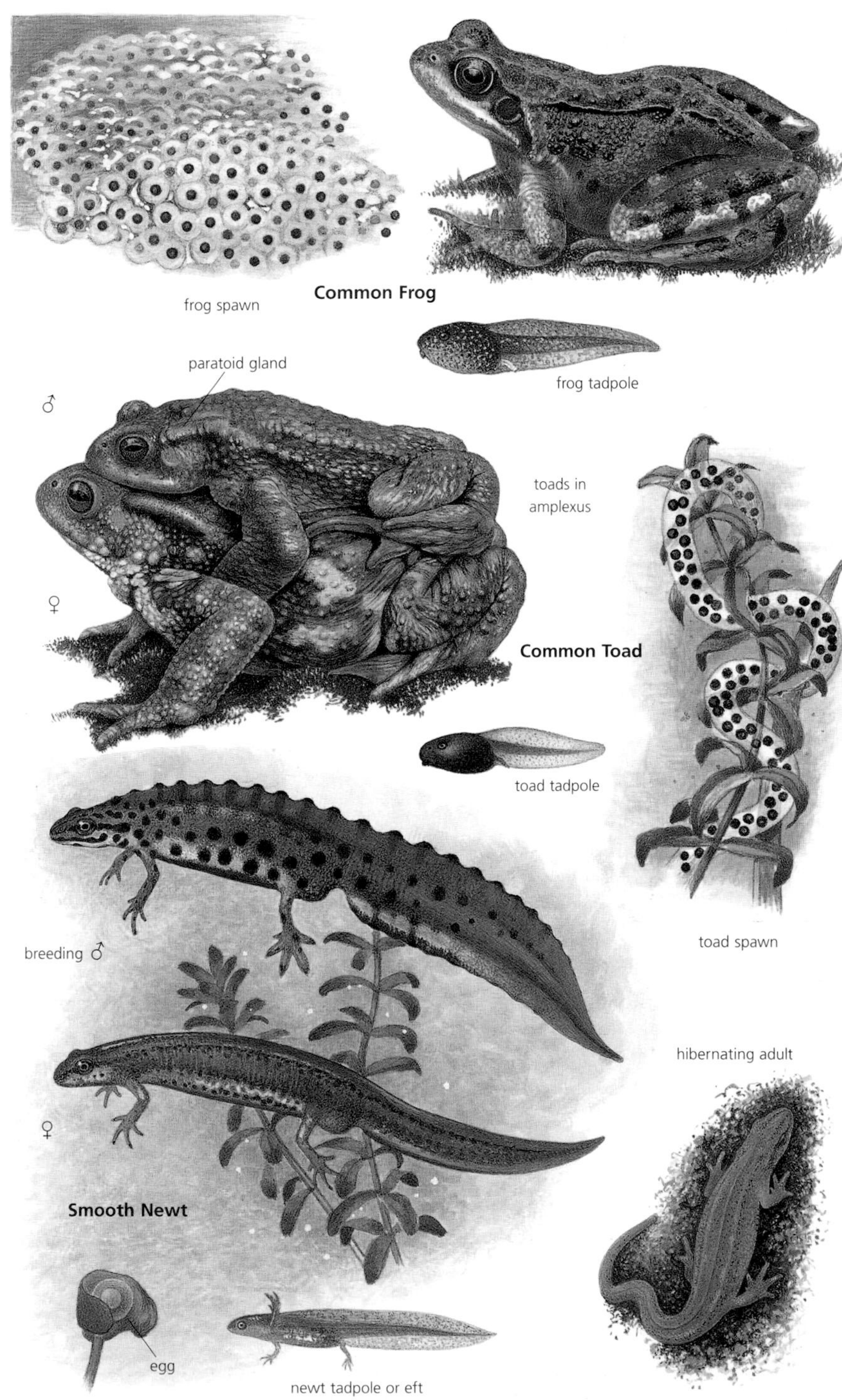
frog spawn
Common Frog
frog tadpole
paratoid gland
♂
toads in
amplexus
♀
Common Toad
toad tadpole
toad spawn
breeding ♂
hibernating adult
♀
Smooth Newt
egg
newt tadpole or eft

Mayflies Ephemeroptera

Despite their name, mayflies appear throughout the summer months, with adults living, without feeding, anything from less than a day to up to a week. They fly by day or by night, and males are most often seen dancing up and down in large mating swarms near water. Most of their life cycle is spent below water, where the nymphs (see page 208) feed on animal or vegetable matter. On emergence from the nymphal stage, the dull-winged adult mayfly, known to anglers as the 'dun', is unique among insects in having an extra moult, when a much shinier insect, the 'spinner', appears.

Drake Mackerel *Ephemera vulgata*
Males of this large, four-winged mayfly, with its three tails, can sometimes be seen in huge numbers performing their mating dance. These displays, which may rise to 6m, are usually seen close to lakes and slow-moving water, between May and July. Here, the female lays her eggs by dipping her abdomen into the surface of the water. The resulting nymphs live for up to three years, burrowing in mud and feeding on vegetable matter. **Habitat and distribution** Found near still or slow-moving muddy habitats, from May onwards, throughout the summer. Common in central and southern England and Wales.

Pond Olive *Cloeon dipterum*
The Pond Olive is a small, two-winged and two-tailed mayfly, whose males have divided eyes, forming a turret on top of the head. An unusual feature of this species is that, unlike most mayflies, the eggs hatch immediately after being washed off the tip of the female's abdomen at the water's surface. These nymphs are free-swimming and are frequently found when pond-dipping. **Habitat and distribution** Widespread and often abundant from May to November. Breeds in still and slow-moving water, and may be found in even the tiniest of ponds.

Dragonflies and damselflies Odonata

This ancient group of insects, which dates back 300 million years, are masters of the air, being able to hover and even fly backwards in their search for prey. Despite the size and appearance of some dragonflies, they are completely harmless to man and should be welcomed into gardens, as both the adults and larvae are ferocious predators of many insect pests. Mating pairs can be seen flying in tandem on warm days, pausing to lay eggs among water plants or allowing the eggs to be washed from the tip of the female's abdomen, although some females lay their eggs unaccompanied. The larvae (see page 208) are aquatic and, depending on the species, spend from one to five years developing, feeding on invertebrates and even small fish. When fully grown, the larva crawls from the water and clings to vegetation. Its skin then splits and the adult emerges, leaving the empty skin, or exuvia, behind. Damselflies differ from dragonflies by their more slender bodies and equal-sized wings, which are normally held together above their abdomens.

Large Red Damselfly *Pyrrhosoma nymphula*
The first damselfly to appear in spring, this species is the largest that occurs regularly in gardens. The sexes are similar, although the female is stouter and has more black on the abdomen. Eggs are laid among submerged vegetation while the male and female are in tandem. The larva takes two years to complete its life cycle. **Habitat and distribution** Widespread throughout, near ponds and slow-moving water, from late April to August.

Blue-tailed Damselfly *Ischnura elegans*
The commonest of all the damselflies, the male is easily recognised by his bright blue 'tail'. The tail of the female may also be blue but there are several colour forms, which are duller and less conspicuous. Egg-laying takes place without the male in tandem, the female cutting a slit in submerged surface vegetation to conceal her eggs. The larval stage lasts a year in the south, but may be up to two years further north. **Habitat and distribution** Found around ponds, lakes and rivers throughout Britain and Ireland, from May to September.

Azure Damselfly *Coenagrion puella*
Distinguished from other 'blue' damselflies by the 'U'-shaped mark on the male's second abdominal segment, and the narrow, lyre-shaped stripes on the thorax. The female is usually black and green, but in some specimens the green is replaced with blue. Viewed from the side, both sexes have two short, black bars on the thorax. Eggs are laid on surface vegetation, nearly always in tandem, with the male often standing upright, without support. **Habitat and distribution** A common garden damselfly found in the summer months throughout Britain and Ireland, except in northern Scotland.

Common Blue Damselfly
Enallagma cyathigerum
The male Common Blue Damselfly can be identified from other 'blue' damselflies by the mushroom-shaped black mark on the second abdominal segment, and the broad blue stripes on the front of the thorax, a feature shared with the female. She is more robust, blacker and the ground-colour varies from blue to dull green. Viewed from the side, both sexes have a single short, black bar on the thorax. Egg-laying sometimes takes place with the female completely submerged, either with or without the male in tandem. **Habitat and distribution** Often abundant, throughout the British Isles. Found in a variety of habitats, including gardens, from May to September. Often found some distance from water.

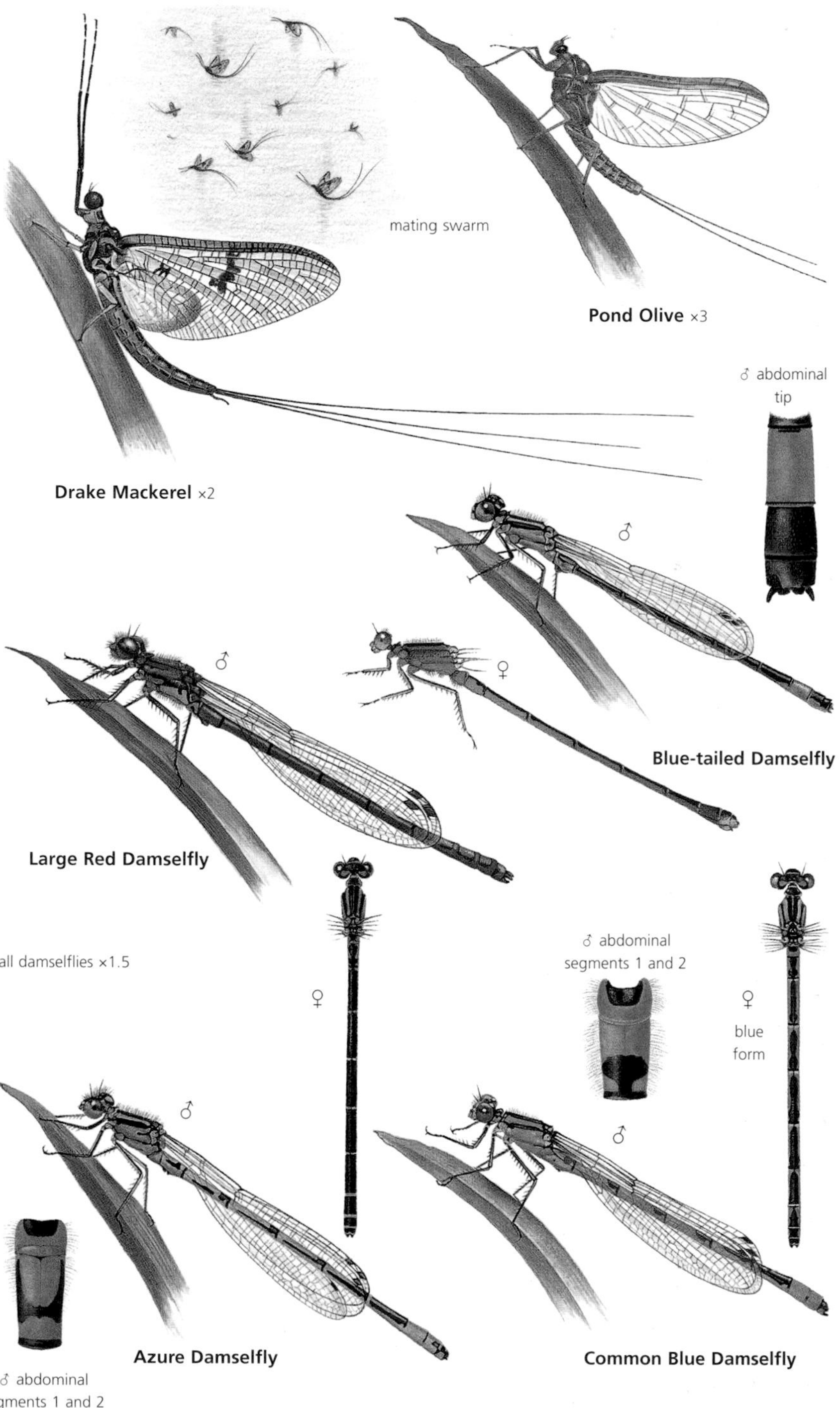
mating swarm
Pond Olive ×3
♂ abdominal tip
Drake Mackerel ×2
♂
♂
♀
Blue-tailed Damselfly
Large Red Damselfly
all damselflies ×1.5
♀
♂ abdominal segments 1 and 2
♀
blue form
♂
♂
Azure Damselfly
Common Blue Damselfly
♂ abdominal segments 1 and 2

Hawkers

Hawkers are mostly large, strong-flying dragonflies that get their name from their habit of restlessly patrolling back and forth, 'hawking' for insects along woodland rides and over gardens and ponds. In very hot weather and at night they rest, hanging in trees and bushes, but sometimes continue to fly at dusk or even after dark, when they may be caught in moth traps. Their torpedo-shaped larvae are voracious inhabitants of still and slow-moving water, feeding on a variety of invertebrates and even tadpoles and small fish. The aquatic stage may last for up to four seasons.

Southern Hawker *Aeshna cyanea*

The most frequent of the large hawker dragonflies to visit gardens, the Southern Hawker can appear quite tame, the female especially, inspecting possible egg-laying sites around ponds and often settling on onlookers, probing with the tip of her abdomen into shoes and clothing. The handsome male is boldly marked with blue, green and black, while the female is green and dark brown. Both are easily identified by the two broad, apple-green stripes on the front of the thorax. The flight period is from June until October. After mating the female lays her eggs alone, in vegetation in and around the water's edge. The larva hatches the following spring, and may live for three seasons. When fully grown, the larva crawls from the water at night and the adult dragonfly emerges, leaving its empty skin, the exuvia, attached to a stem. The best way to find out which species are present in a garden pond is to inspect the vegetation surrounding the pond as early in the morning as possible; you can then more easily identify the newly-emerged adults before the sun has warmed them into action. **Habitat and distribution** The Southern Hawker is common around woodland and garden ponds, the females often laying their eggs in small, stagnant ponds. Distributed throughout England and Wales, with isolated populations in Scotland.

Brown Hawker *Aeshna grandis*

A large and conspicuous dragonfly, immediately identified by its amber-coloured wings, and often seen hawking along tall hedgerows and in gardens, well away from water. The sexes are similar, but the male has a narrower 'waisted' abdomen, with blue spots along the sides. The flight period is from June into October and the life cycle is similar to that of the Southern Hawker. The well-camouflaged larva, which feeds mainly on midge and other aquatic invertebrate larvae, takes from two to four years to reach maturity. **Habitat and distribution** Often seen away from water, but breeds in lakes, slow-flowing rivers, and park and garden ponds. Found in the lowlands of central, southern and south-east England and most of Ireland, but absent from south-west England, Scotland and most of Wales.

Migrant Hawker *Aeshna mixta*

This species has become increasingly common in recent years and is readily identified from other hawkers by its smaller size and habit of hawking swiftly, often in large numbers, around tall trees and shrubs, occasionally soaring high into the air. The female is mostly brown, with yellow abdominal spots; the male is more boldly marked with dark brown and blue. Both have a distinctive, yellow, elongated triangular mark behind the wing bases, at the base of the abdomen, but the reduced stripes on the top of the thorax distinguish the Migrant from the Southern Hawker. The life cycle is similar to that of other hawkers. The female usually lays her eggs in the stems of aquatic plants, although she may sometimes be observed away from water, curving her abdomen into the base of trees and shrubs. Adults appear later in the year than other hawkers, flying from late July and sometimes continuing into late November. **Habitat and distribution** Occurs around all types of still and slow-flowing water, including garden ponds, except where the soil is acidic. Its range is expanding northwards, but it is currently found in much of lowland England, Wales and south-east Ireland.

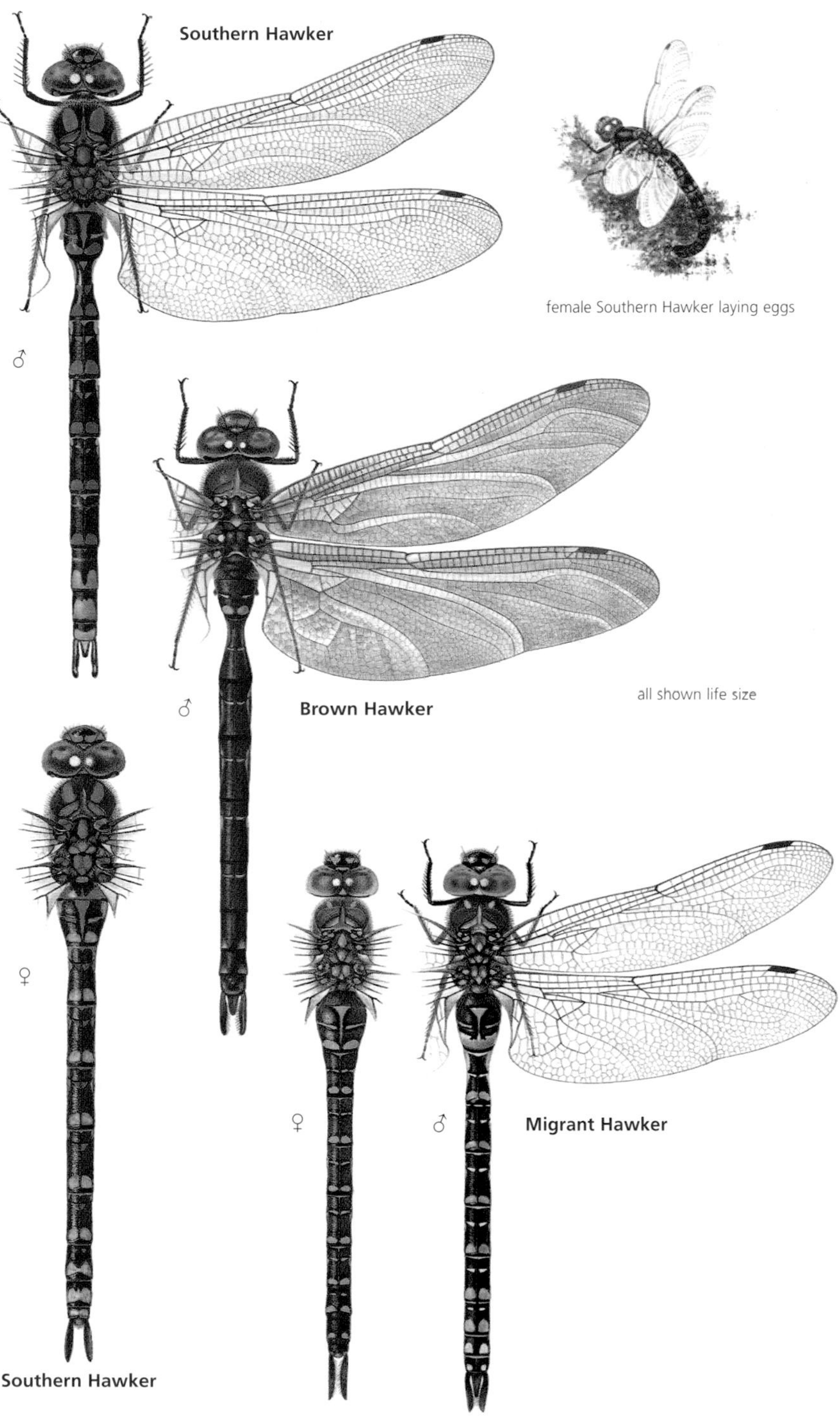

female Southern Hawker laying eggs

all shown life size

Common Darter *Sympetrum striolatum*
The male of this very common dragonfly is most often seen perching on vegetation, darting out to catch insects or to inspect other males entering his territory, returning to the same perch time and again. Later in the year, in warmer weather, both sexes perch high up on posts and in tree branches, often away from water. Immatures of both sexes are yellowish brown, but as they age the female becomes olive-green and the male develops an orange-red abdomen. During mating the pair fly in tandem to a suitable egg-laying site, and as the male holds the female they dip repeatedly as the eggs are released; occasionally, the female lays her eggs unaccompanied by the male. The larvae take a year to mature and adults start to appear from mid-June and, in good years, can be seen as late as mid-November, often being the last dragonfly of the year to be seen. **Habitat and distribution** One of the commonest British dragonflies, found throughout Britain and Ireland, near many kinds of ponds, lakes and rivers and also well away from water. Migrants from the Continent boost our populations in the summer.

Emperor *Anax imperator*
Britain's largest and most impressive dragonfly, the male is most often seen majestically patrolling lakes and ponds in summer. His distinctive sky-blue and black abdomen, held in a slight downward curve in flight, and plain green thorax contrast with the more robust, predominantly dull green female. She is more often seen unaccompanied, following a brief mating, flying or hovering low over the water's surface, pausing to settle on vegetation and curving her abdomen below the surface to lay her eggs in aquatic plants. These hatch after three weeks, and when fully grown, after one or two years, the well-camouflaged greenish-brown larva is a voracious predator mainly of invertebrates but also of tadpoles and small fish. Newly-emerged Emperors spend the first few weeks of life away from water, returning when they are mature to set up territories and to breed. The flight period is from early June to late August, with individuals living on average for about a month. **Habitat and distribution** Found mainly near lakes, gravel pits and slow-moving rivers, but females will sometimes breed in quite small garden ponds. Most common in southern England, becoming scarcer further north, but its range is expanding northwards, and it has recently colonised south-east Ireland.

Broad-bodied Chaser *Libellula depressa*
The robust male Broad-bodied Chaser can sometimes be seen perching for long periods on emergent vegetation, aggressively defending his garden pond territory from other males. Newly-emerged individuals of both sexes are olive-yellow; in the female this darkens to greenish brown and the male develops a powdery blue-grey abdomen. Both have yellow spots along the sides of the abdomen and conspicuous dark patches at the base of the wings. After mating, the male watches over the female, guarding her as she dips the tip of her abdomen into the water to wash off the eggs. These hatch after a few weeks and the larvae take up to three years to develop, spending most of the time submerged in plant debris at the bottom of the pond. The flight period lasts from mid May until August. **Habitat and distribution** Occurs near well-vegetated ponds and lakes, but is also quick to colonise newly dug garden ponds. Mainly found in central and southern England and Wales; absent from Scotland and Ireland. **Similar species** Several other species of chaser resemble the Broad-bodied Chaser but only the **Four-spotted Chaser** *L. quadrimaculata* is likely to occur in gardens. It is slimmer and has four conspicuous dark spots on the wings, and is found throughout Britain and Ireland.

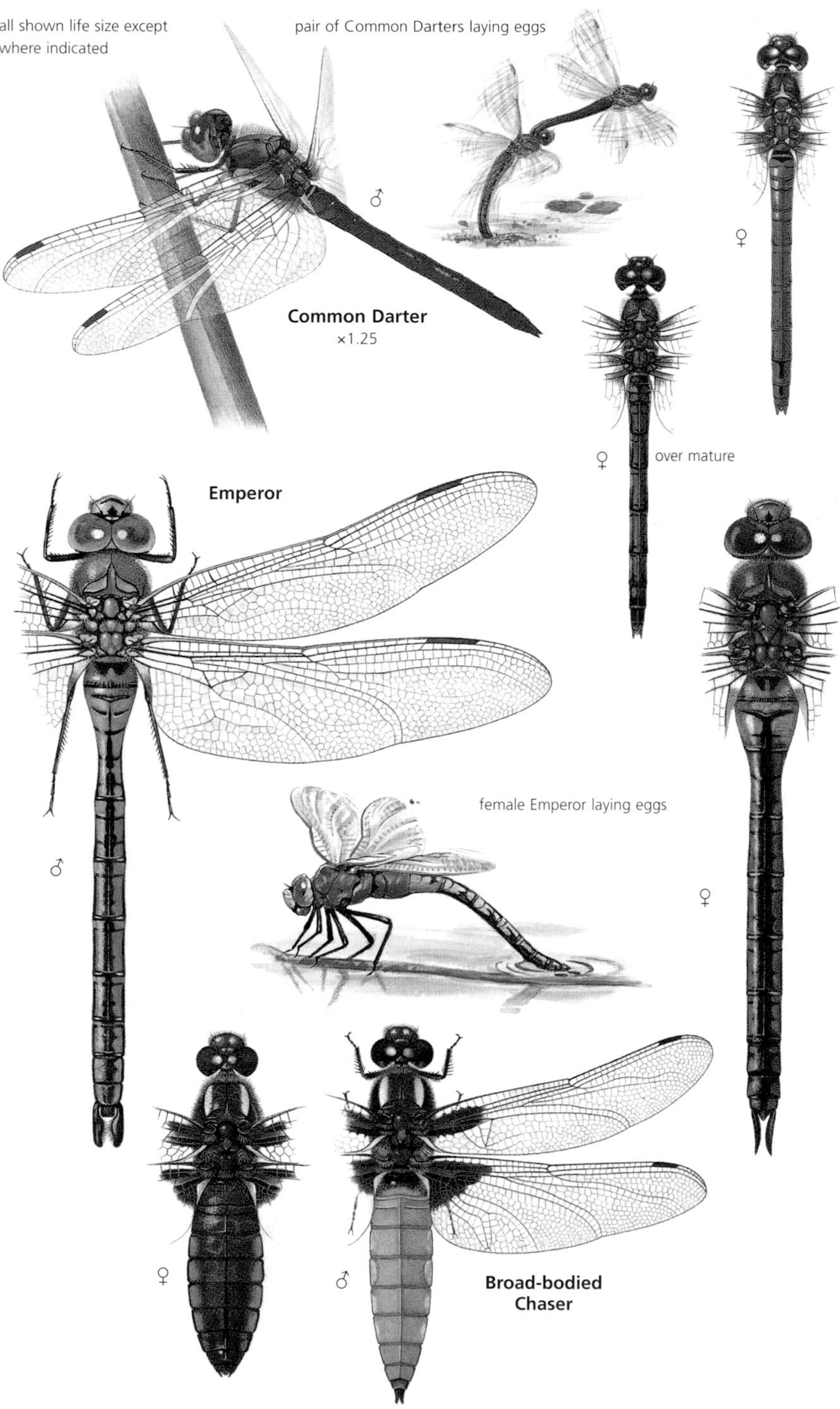
all shown life size except where indicated
pair of Common Darters laying eggs
♂
Common Darter
×1.25
♀
♀
over mature
Emperor
♂
female Emperor laying eggs
♀
♀
♂
Broad-bodied Chaser

Bush-crickets, grasshopper and earwigs
Orthoptera and Dermaptera

Speckled Bush-cricket
Leptophyes punctatissima
A long-legged, flightless bush-cricket, with a beautifully camouflaged green body, minutely speckled with dark spots. Both sexes have tiny, saddle-like wings, browner in the male. The female has a broad, curved ovipositor. Eggs are laid in crevices in bark, where they remain until the following May. On hatching, the nymphs, which resemble green capsid bugs, live and feed on the foliage of various plants such as bramble, nettles and honeysuckle. Maturity is reached in August and adults live until November. The male makes a faint, high-pitched chirp every few seconds, and adults sometimes enter houses by crawling up vegetation on walls. Quite common in gardens and rough herbage, throughout England, Wales, south-west Scotland and parts of Ireland.

Oak Bush-cricket *Meconema thalassinum*
A delicate, pale green bush-cricket, with a yellow line along the back. The female has a long, curved ovipositor and the male two long, pincer-like cerci at the tip of the abdomen. Eggs are laid in crevices in bark. These hatch the following June and, after several moults, nymphs reach maturity in July. Adults survive into November, living in trees, shrubs and hedgerows, and feeding on invertebrates. They are mainly active at night and can often be found on walls and ceilings, having flown in through lighted windows. Unlike other bush-crickets, the male produces a rapid but quiet burst of sound by drumming one of his hind legs on a leaf. Common in well-vegetated places, including gardens, throughout central and southern England and Wales. **Similar species** In the last 50 years, the **Southern Oak Bush-cricket** *M. meridionale* has spread northwards from southern Europe, possibly aided by hitching a ride on motor vehicles, and was recorded for the first time in gardens in southern England in 2001. It resembles the Oak Bush-cricket, but has reduced flaps rather than fully functional wings.

Dark Bush-cricket *Pholidoptera griseoaptera*
The female is generally paler than the male, varying in colour from light to dark brown, but the most distinctive feature of both sexes is the bright yellow underside of the abdomen. The forewings are reduced to tiny pads, almost absent in the female, and although much time is spent concealed amongst bramble patches, nettles and other scrubby vegetation, adults may be seen sunning themselves on foliage. They have an omnivorous diet of leaves, flowers and pollen, as well as small invertebrates. Eggs are laid in crevices in bark and hatch the following April. The small nymphs gain some protection from their spider-like appearance, and after several moults become fully-grown in July or August, surviving well into November in mild autumns. The song of the male is a short, irregularly repeated 'psst-psst', and is a familiar sound on late summer evenings, often lasting through the night. This is one of the commonest bush-crickets in the south of England but becomes more local further north.

Field Grasshopper *Chorthippus brunneus*
Grasshoppers are associated with wild, grassy meadows and are not generally regarded as garden insects, as they tend to avoid neatly trimmed lawns. However, the Field Grasshopper is a common species and a most able flier in hot weather, often colonising wasteland, roadside verges, allotments and larger, more natural gardens. It varies greatly in colour, from buff, pink or purple to almost black, with mottled or striped markings. Its long wings reach beyond the hind knees, and the best distinguishing feature is the densely hairy underside of the thorax. The song of the male is a series of short, sharp, half-second chirps. Eggs are laid in a pod, a cell made from hardened froth mixed with soil particles. The nymphs hatch in late spring and reach maturity in June, the adults lasting into November. The commonest grasshopper in urban habitats, often on derelict or disturbed ground. Abundant in central and southern England and Wales; also found in Scotland and Ireland.

Lesser Earwig *Labia minor*
This is the smallest European earwig and, although quite common, because of its size it is seldom seen. It is more plainly coloured than the Common Earwig, and its scurrying movements give it the appearance of a rove beetle or an ant. Active by day and night, it flies in the sunshine on warm days and is attracted to lighted windows and moth traps on sultry nights. It is mainly found in or around warm, moist compost or manure heaps, with a preference for horse manure. Here, the eggs are laid and guarded over by the female; breeding is continuous throughout the year. Widely distributed throughout Britain and Ireland, and far commoner than records suggest.

Common Earwig *Forficula auricularia*
A familiar and often maligned garden insect, whose omnivorous diet involves nibbling petals and tender leaves of garden flowers, as well as eating small insect pests such as aphids. After hibernation, when most males have died, the female lays her eggs in a chamber in the soil where she cares for the eggs and young until they are ready to disperse. She may then produce a second brood. As the nymphs grow they moult, to reveal a soft white skin which quickly darkens and hardens; maturity is reached in mid summer. Found in many habitats, especially around human habitation, and recorded from throughout Britain and Ireland.

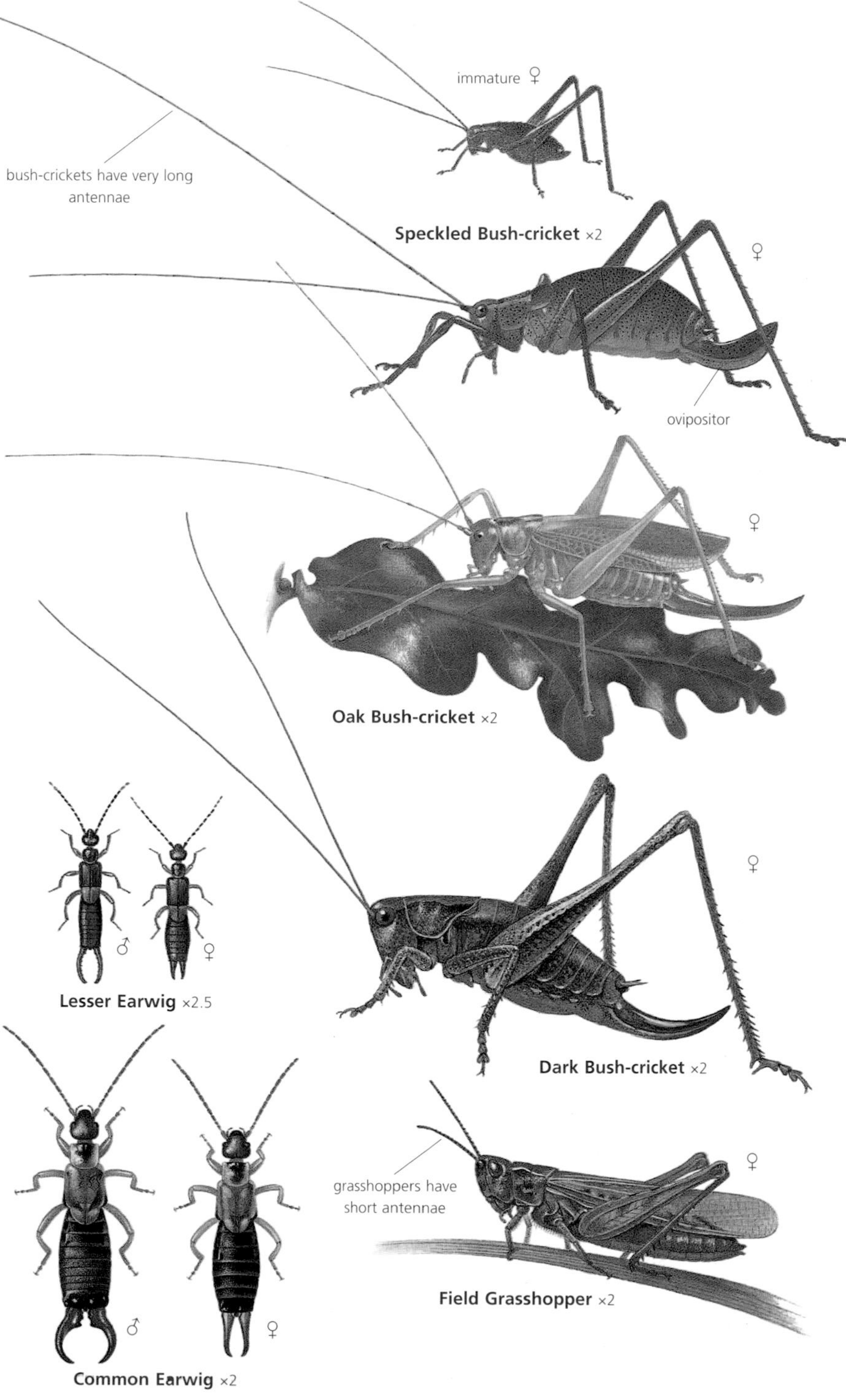

Speckled Bush-cricket ×2

Oak Bush-cricket ×2

Dark Bush-cricket ×2

Lesser Earwig ×2.5

Field Grasshopper ×2

Common Earwig ×2

True bugs Hemiptera

▲ A Parent Bug guarding its offspring.

Most non-entomologists tend to give all crawling and flying creatures the derogatory title of 'bugs', but true bugs in the insect world belong to the order Hemiptera, meaning 'half wing'. This refers to the forewings of many species, which are divided into a thickened basal half and a membranous outer half. In Britain, the Hemiptera comprise three groups, all of which are well represented in the garden. The first is the Heteroptera, the true bugs, which includes the shieldbugs, capsid bugs, assassin bugs and water bugs. The second group, the Auchenorrhyncha, includes the leafhoppers and froghoppers, and the third group, the Sternorrhyncha, includes the whiteflies, aphids and scale insects; these latter two sub-orders were previously grouped together as the Homoptera.

All bugs have an incomplete metamorphosis. Rather than having four distinct stages of egg, larva, pupa and adult, like butterflies or beetles, they have only three, although some, such as many aphids, have only two stages as the females give birth to nymphs. In most cases, however, the nymph hatches from the egg and grows continuously, shedding its skin until its final moult into an adult, missing out on the resting pupal stage; this is known as hemimetabolism. Virtually all bugs feed by injecting their tube-like beak, or rostrum, into plant or animal food and sucking up the juices, often producing enzymes that break down the cells. Of the bugs frequently encountered in Britain, some of the larger species such as the Fly Bug and Common Backswimmer, which is often captured by pond dippers, can pierce human skin, giving a painful bite if carelessly handled.

The Heteroptera contains many of our largest and most colourful bugs, most notably the shieldbugs, of which several species are found in gardens. They get their name from the shield-like scutellum, the triangular plate covering much of the body, and have obvious membranous wing tips. Some members of this diverse group, such as the Pied Shieldbug, are conspicuously marked with warning colours, while others, such as the Hawthorn Shieldbug, are beautifully camouflaged amongst foliage, although in the autumn the colours of those species that hibernate often become more sombre. As well as being cryptically camouflaged, some bugs are well known for giving off pungent odours to deter predators, as the name of one of the commonest, the Green Stinkbug, suggests.

Their diets vary, depending on the species, and while most feed on the sap from fruit, berries and foliage, others are carnivorous, feeding on caterpillars and other soft-bodied invertebrates, some of which are harmful to garden plants. Others have a mixed diet of plant and animal matter. Capsid bugs, the largest family of Heteropterans, are generally elongated bugs with soft bodies and long spindly legs. They are mainly sap suckers and some species that occur in gardens occasionally cause damage to garden plants, but others are omnivorous and eat pests such as red spider mites. In other families beneficial species include the damsel bugs and the Fly Bug, which are highly predatory.

The froghoppers and leafhoppers, along with the aphids and their relatives, are herbivorous and use enzymes to break down plant cells when feeding on stems and leaves. Most species of froghopper are buff or brown and rely on their cryptic markings for protection, but if alarmed they leap, using their powerful hindlegs to escape predation. One colourful exception, often found in gardens, is the Red-and-black Froghopper, which relies on its warning coloration for protection. All froghopper nymphs are soft, immobile creatures that produce a unique method of defence. They make froth from their rear end that surrounds them and, as well as concealing them, also prevents desiccation. This conspicuous method of protection is the familiar 'cuckoo spit' often seen attached to many garden plants. The frothy mass may cause slight distortion to plants, but is otherwise harmless.

Although they are mostly much smaller and less robust than froghoppers, the leafhoppers appear in far greater numbers in gardens, with some species causing problems by transmitting viral diseases to cultivated plants. When disturbed, they often fly a short distance and then return to the foliage. Most visible damage takes the form of mottling or speckling on the leaf surface, but only a few species cause significant damage.

The Sternorrhyncha contains some of the most troublesome and notorious pests in the garden, including aphids, whiteflies, jumping plant lice and scale insects. They often appear in enormous numbers and can reproduce at an astonishing rate, taking advantage of and spreading rapidly through cultivated crops. Aphids attract more attention from gardeners and the agrochemical industry than any other pests for, as well as damaging plants by feeding on juices and blocking the sap flow, they also carry many viruses. Several hundred species occur in Britain. Some, such as the Peach-potato Aphid, feed on many plant species and can be a vector to more than 100 viruses, whereas others are host specific or have two alternating host plants, one woody and one herbaceous. Their powers of reproduction are tremendous, either laying eggs or giving birth to live young which, themselves, are capable of reproducing, without mating, in about a week. Some species exude a waxy powder or, in the case of the Woolly Aphid, tufts of waxy threads for their protection, but this does not prevent the majority of aphids forming a major food source for many vertebrates and invertebrates. Most notable amongst the latter are lacewings and ladybirds, together with many predatory bugs. However, some insects, such as various species of ant, actively protect aphids and in return are allowed to feed on their sweet, sugary secretions, which often speckle cars parked beneath trees. Insectivorous and omnivorous birds eat large numbers, and if these natural predators are encouraged in the garden, the need for chemical controls should be reduced.

Hawthorn Shieldbug
Acanthosoma haemorrhoidale
This beautiful red and green herbivorous shieldbug is found on many trees and shrubs, well camouflaged amongst the foliage and berries of hawthorn, its principal foodplant. The female lays batches of about 24 eggs on the underside of leaves. Hibernation is spent in crevices or grass tussocks and the adults reappear in spring. Sometimes flies at night and is attracted to light. Found widely throughout Britain and Ireland.

Parent Bug *Elasmucha grisea*
So-called because the female shows maternal care, protecting groups of up to 30 eggs and the young nymphs from parasites and parasitoid attack. Most frequent from late August to October; adults hibernate in leaf litter. Found mainly on birch, throughout much of Britain and Ireland.

Juniper Shieldbug *Cyphostethus tristriatus*
The Juniper Shieldbug was once restricted to wild juniper but is now found in gardens on cypress and ornamental junipers. Adults appear after hibernation in March and produce one generation lasting into autumn. Occurs mainly in the south and Midlands but its distribution is expanding.

Red-Legged or **Forest Shieldbug**
Pentatoma rufipes
Easily recognised by its distinctive shape and the bright yellow tip to the scutellum. Found on most native trees, particularly oaks, where it feeds on sap as well as invertebrates. Batches of 12 or so eggs are laid on leaves; the nymphs hibernate and reach maturity the following July. Occurs in gardens and orchards throughout Britain and Ireland.

Common Green Shieldbug
Palomena prasina
Found in many well-vegetated habitats, particularly on hazel bushes. The female lays batches of around 100 eggs on leaves in mid-summer, and the nymphs reach maturity in September. Females are generally larger than males; the bright green adults become bronze-red before entering hibernation, the green colour returning just before emergence in spring. Also know as the Green Stinkbug from the odours secreted from glands when disturbed. Widespread.

Sloe or **Hairy Shieldbug** *Dolycoris baccarum*
Poorly named, as this rather hairy bug is rarely seen on sloe, but is frequent in rough, herbaceous vegetation. Eggs are laid in batches on leaves in mid-summer, and the nymphs reach maturity from mid-August. Adults hibernate, re-emerging in spring. Widely distributed but less common in the north.

Pied Shieldbug *Tritomegas (Sehirus) bicolor*
A small but conspicuous bug found commonly amongst low vegetation, especially white deadnettle. The female digs a cavity in the soil and lays a batch of about 45 eggs which she protects, along with the newly emerged young for the first few days of their lives. Two generations may occur in favourable years, the adults hibernating either beneath moss or several centimetres below ground. Common in the south but scarcer further north and west.

Bishop's Mitre Shieldbug *Aelia acuminata*
Common in rough, dry, grassy vegetation, where the female lays two rows of six or seven eggs on grass blades in June. Adults hibernate in grass tussocks and emerge the following April or May. Occurs from Wales and the Midlands southwards.

Dock Bug *Coreus marginatus*
A large, conspicuous bug often seen resting, or mating tail to tail, on the foliage of docks, sorrels and rhubarb, where the female lays groups of large brown eggs. Older nymphs feed on the seeds of the foodplant before hibernating in late autumn; they mature the following spring. More common in southern Britain and Ireland, absent from the north.

Hawthorn Shieldbug ×2

Parent Bug ×2

Juniper Shieldbug ×2

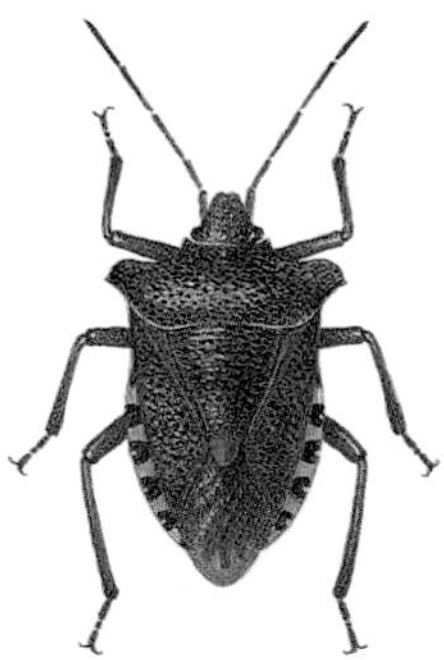

Red-legged Shieldbug ×2

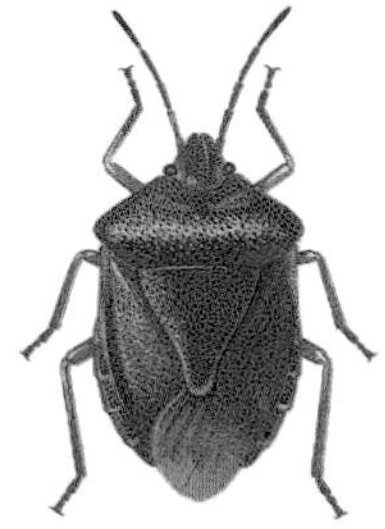

Common Green Shieldbug ×2

Sloe Shieldbug ×2

Pied Shieldbug ×3

Bishop's Mitre Shieldbug ×2

Dock Bug ×2

Cinnamon Bug *Corizus hyoscyami*
The striking red and black warning coloration of this slightly hairy bug makes it conspicuous amongst vegetation in gardens. Adults appear from hibernation in April and produce nymphs in August and September. These are buff-coloured with darker speckling, and after reaching maturity they go into hibernation in September and October. Until recently it was restricted to coastal regions of southern England and Wales, but it is now found throughout England, Wales and parts of Ireland.

Common Flower Bug *Anthocoris nemorum*
A beneficial garden bug, which feeds on many small insect pests, such as aphids, whiteflies and Red Spider Mites. Adults hibernate behind bark or in leaf litter until early spring, when they emerge to hunt in low vegetation and on trees and shrubs. Abundant and widespread throughout Britain and Ireland.

Hot-bed Bug *Xylocoris galactinus*
As its name suggests, this small, predatory bug is found in warm places, such as compost and manure heaps, where it hunts mites and other soft-bodied creatures. It breeds throughout the year and is widely distributed in all parts of Britain and Ireland.

Nettle Ground Bug *Heterogaster urticae*
This bug lives and feeds on nettles, with many often congregating to mate on plants growing in sunny situations. Eggs are laid on the ground or low down on the stems of nettles, and the nymphs reach maturity in September. Hibernation often takes place gregariously in crevices behind bark. Common in the south, recently recorded from Scotland but absent from Ireland.

Spear Thistle Lacebug *Tingis cardui*
Named after the delicate, lace-like appearance of the forewings and pronotum (the shield-like covering of the thorax). This bug is a plant feeder, the adults hibernating then emerging in spring to lay their eggs on the leaves of spear thistle. Found throughout Britain and Ireland.

Common Damsel Bug *Nabis rugosus*
The commonest of several similar, highly predacious bugs that live in dry grasslands where, well-camouflaged amongst grasses, they help to control invertebrate populations. Brachypterous forms, with reduced wings, sometimes occur. Maturity is reached in August and adults hibernate until the following spring. Common in all parts of Britain and Ireland.

Fly Bug *Reduvius personatus*
Adults of this species of assassin bug fly at night and are often attracted to lighted windows. The nymphs conceal themselves with dust particles, and both adults and young prey on small invertebrates. This bug can give a painful bite if carelessly handled. Found mainly in and around buildings, in central and southern England.

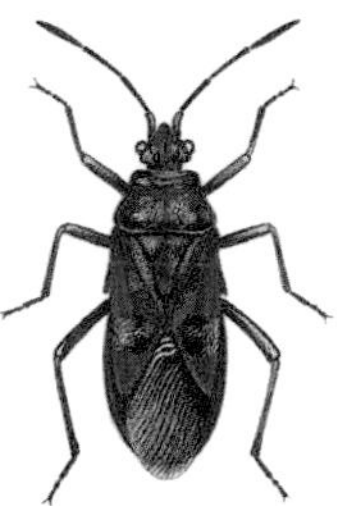
Cinnamon Bug ×3

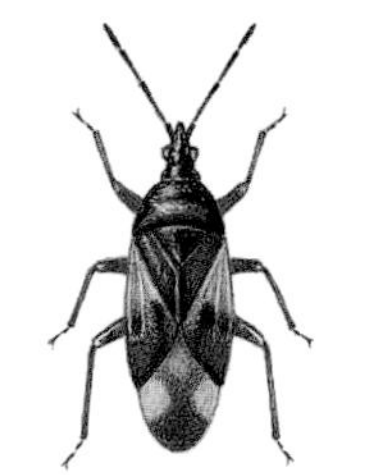
Common Flower Bug ×6

Hot-bed Bug ×6

Nettle Ground Bug ×3

Spear Thistle Lacebug ×6

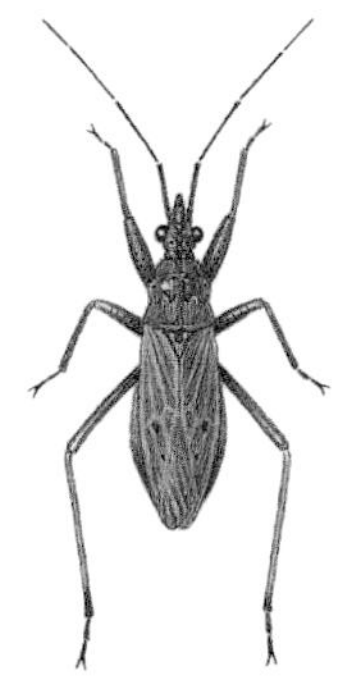
Common Damsel Bug ×3

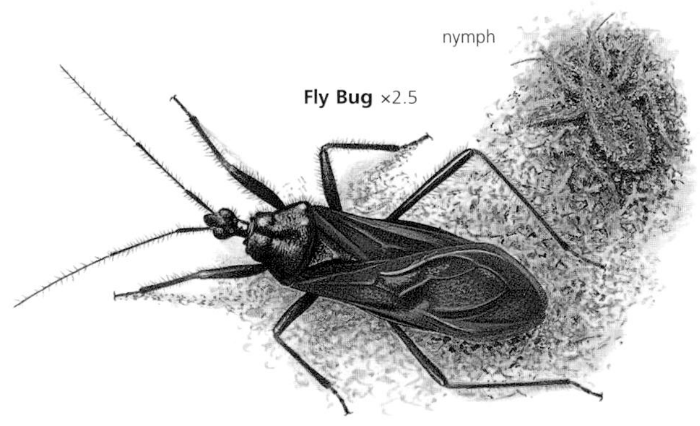

Fly Bug ×2.5

Oak Capsid *Harpocera thoracica*
One of several capsid bugs found commonly on oaks, this bug shows a distinct difference between the sexes. Eggs laid in early summer hatch the following spring and the nymphs feed on young leaves and catkins, developing rapidly into adulthood by late May. Adults live only for a short period after mating and egg-laying, and are attracted to light at night. Widespread throughout Britain and Ireland.

Black-kneed Capsid
Blepharidopterus angulatus
Adults and nymphs can be distinguished from most other green capsid bugs by their black 'knees' and the yellow triangular scutellum. Found on many deciduous trees, it is regarded as a major predator of Red Spider Mite on fruit trees. Estimates suggest a single female can destroy up to 3,000 mites in her lifetime. Overwintered eggs hatch the following spring and maturity is reached in late June. Widespread in all parts of Britain; also recorded in Ireland.

Tarnished Plant Bug *Lygus rugulipennis*
This bug sometimes causes damage to ornamental plants, soft fruit and potatoes, but also feeds on many naturally occurring herbaceous plants. Adults hibernate in leaf litter and reappear in spring, when females lay their eggs in plant stems and buds. The nymphs, which are predominantly green, reach maturity in late July and give rise to a second generation in September. Adults are most abundant before hibernation in the autumn. Widespread throughout Britain; also recorded in Ireland.

Lucerne Bug *Adelphocoris lineolatus*
One of many green capsid bugs, distinguished by the pale patches at the tips of the thickened part of the forewings. Found mainly on vetches and clovers, it occasionally causes damage to chrysanthemums, and in the USA is a pest of lucerne. Eggs are laid in plant stems, where they overwinter, hatching the following May, with only one generation a year. Maturity is reached in July. Common and widespread in many parts of Britain and Ireland.

Common Green Capsid *Lygocoris pabulinus*
This capsid is abundant on a variety of plants. Up to 200 eggs can be laid by a single female on woody plants such as apple, cherry, currant and plum. They hatch the following April and after a few weeks the nymphs move to herbaceous plants such as nettles, thistles and docks, but are also found on soft fruit, potatoes and ornamental plants, where they can cause damage. Maturing in June, they produce a second generation of adults, which return to lay eggs on the woody host plants in the autumn. Common throughout Britain and Ireland.

Capsid bug *Heterotoma planicornis*
Immediately recognised by the enlarged, hairy second segment of the antennae and pale green legs, this bug and its reddish nymphs feed on small invertebrates, as well as tender buds and unripe fruits. It is often common on nettles and in rough vegetation. Widespread, but most abundant in southern England. Absent from Scotland.

Capsid bug *Phytocoris tiliae*
This variable and beautifully camouflaged species is found on many deciduous trees, particularly oak. It also often occurs on apple trees, where it is a valuable predator of Red Spider Mite and on the eggs of the Codling Moth. The nymphs, which hatch in early summer, reach maturity in a few weeks and the adults continue into late October. Common throughout Britain and Ireland.

Water Measurer *Hydrometra stagnorum*
A delicate, predatory water bug which slowly patrols pond margins, detecting prey such as daphnia and mosquito larvae by their vibrations, and then spearing them through the surface film. It also feeds on dead or distressed insects on the surface. Adults overwinter, appearing in spring to mate and lay eggs. These are laid singly, attached at an angle to plant stems at water level. Fairly common throughout Britain and Ireland.

Common Pondskater *Gerris lacustris*
Commonly seen skating jerkily across the surface of garden ponds, investigating any movement that may be a meal. Its forelegs are used to grab prey, which is then jabbed with the beak. The middle legs act as the oars, and the hindlegs as a rudder. Forms range from those with reduced, bud-like wings to those with wings fully formed. After hibernating on land, the adults become active in spring and return to the water to mate and lay eggs. The following generation matures in mid-summer and gives rise to a second generation of adults by mid-August. Found virtually everywhere, and is probably the most widespread British bug.

Common Backswimmer *Notonecta glauca*
This voracious predator, often seen hanging motionless, upside down beneath the surface of the water, renewing its air supply, can inflict a painful bite on the careless pond dipper! Adults fly, and are one of the first colonisers of newly dug ponds. They mate in the winter and spring months, and by June the small, pale nymphs are often the pond's most abundant and active inhabitants. They have one generation a year. Widespread and common, although other species occur in different water types.

Lesser water boatman *Sigara dorsalis*
Lesser water boatman *Corixa punctata*
These two common bugs belong to a large, confusing family that contains many similar species. They swim with less vigour than the Backswimmer and are mainly herbivorous. Adults overwinter and are active from January. Males produce an audible 'song' during courtship, made by rubbing the forelegs along the side of the head. Both are widely distributed throughout Britain and Ireland.

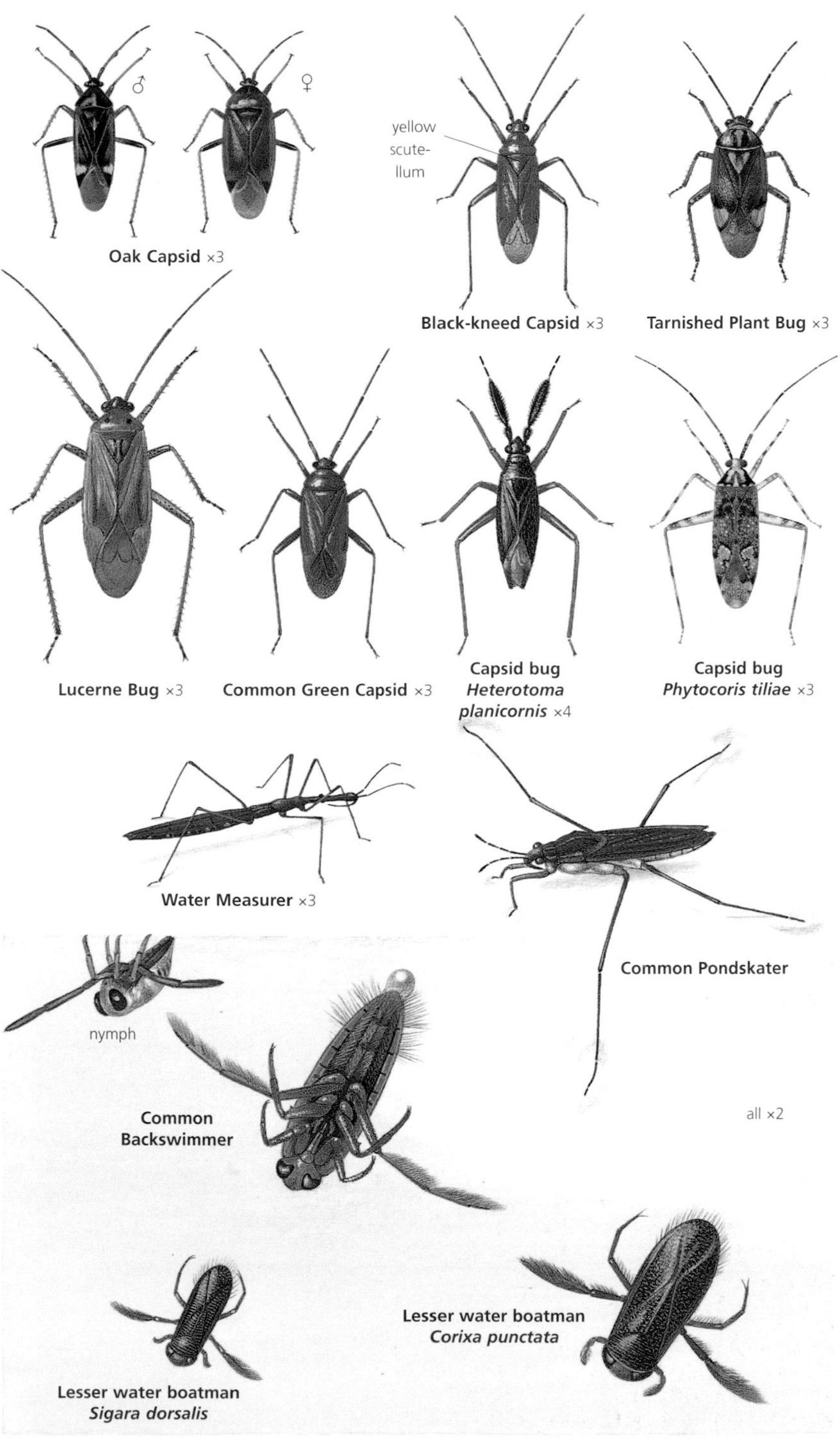

Oak Capsid ×3

Black-kneed Capsid ×3

Tarnished Plant Bug ×3

Lucerne Bug ×3

Common Green Capsid ×3

Capsid bug ***Heterotoma planicornis*** ×4

Capsid bug ***Phytocoris tiliae*** ×3

Water Measurer ×3

Common Pondskater

Common Backswimmer

Lesser water boatman ***Corixa punctata***

Lesser water boatman ***Sigara dorsalis***

Red-and-black Froghopper
Cercopis vulnerata
The bold colours warn predators of this bug's noxious taste. Conspicuous in rough vegetation, they can leap a considerable distance if alarmed. Nymphs overwinter underground and feed in spring on root sap, surrounded by a mass of froth. Adults occur from April to August. Found mainly in wilder gardens, more frequent in the south. Absent from Scotland and Ireland.

Common Froghopper *Philaenus spumarius*
The nymphs of this variable species produce the well-known 'cuckoo spit', found along hedgerows and, in herbaceous borders, on plants such as sorrel, lavender and rosemary. Eggs laid on plants in the autumn hatch in early spring. Young nymphs climb tender stems and produce a froth by mixing air with a secretion from their rear end. Adults are found from June to November. This is the most common and widespread froghopper.

Potato Leafhopper *Eupteryx aurata*
Leafhoppers jump and fly actively in the sunshine. This species, along with several others, is found on potatoes and is frequent in gardens and allotments, but causes little damage. Also occurs commonly on many other plants, from spring to autumn.

Rhododendron Leafhopper
Graphocephala fennahi
This large, attractive leafhopper lays its eggs on the flower buds of rhododendrons, which sometimes leads to bud blast, a fungal pathogen. Eggs overwinter and hatch in spring, and the nymphs feed on the undersides of the leaves until they reach maturity in July. Restricted to central and southern Britain.

Leafhopper *Kybos populi*
One of many small, green leafhoppers, readily disturbed from trees and shrubs. This species occurs throughout England in the summer months, on poplars and aspen. They cause little damage, and are preyed upon by large numbers of invertebrates.

Jumping plant louse or **sucker** *Psylla* sp.
Several species are found in gardens, feeding on plants as diverse as apple, bay laurel and box. They resemble aphids but are more active and can jump as well as fly. The nymphs also secrete sticky honeydew and woolly wax. They can cause leaves to shrivel and drop, and those occurring on fruit trees may cause a reduction in crop yield.

Black Bean Aphid or **Blackfly** *Aphis fabae*
The best known of several similar black aphids found on garden plants. Huge numbers of both winged and wingless forms appear from May to July on a variety of plants, most noticeably on beans. There are two generations, and in September the winged females migrate to lay their eggs on spindle, which overwinter until the following spring. On hatching, colonies disperse and return to the summer host plants to repeat the cycle. Large numbers are eaten by predators and are killed in adverse weather. Widespread in Britain and Ireland.

Peach-potato Aphid *Myzus persicae*
Occurs in pink as well as the more usual pale green form, and is a vector to about 100 plant viruses, although it does not occur in huge colonies like some species. Eggs overwinter on peaches and nectarines, giving rise to winged forms in the spring which cause leaf-curl; they then migrate to a wide variety of ornamental plants and vegetables. Adults can survive mild winters. Widespread in Britain and Ireland.

Woolly Aphid or **American Blight**
Eriosoma lanigerum
The purplish-brown bodies of Woolly Aphids are hidden beneath white, fluffy wax, which infests the base of new growth, and cracks in the bark of apple, hawthorn, cotoneaster and other shrubs. Wingless females overwinter in crevices in bark or on roots and give rise to several generations, including some winged, which disperse to form new colonies. Accidentally introduced from America over 200 years ago, the species is now widespread.

Rose Aphid or **Greenfly** *Macrosiphum rosae*
Either pink or green in colour, and distinguished by the black 'knees' and tubular cornicles at the rear of the abdomen. It appears on roses along with similar species of aphid in spring; later in the year, winged forms migrate to scabious and teasel. Adults can continue through mild winters. Widespread.

Cabbage Whitefly *Aleyrodes proletella*
This and the similar Greenhouse Whitefly can appear in clouds on their respective host plants. Found mainly on cabbages and other brassicas in gardens and allotments, eggs are laid in curves or circles on the underside of leaves. Nymphs and adults have a coating of mealy wax and secrete honeydew, which often attracts sooty moulds, making the leaves discoloured and sticky. Distribution cosmopolitan.

Horse Chestnut Scale *Pulvinaria regalis*
Female scale insects are protected by a scale-like waxy secretion and are hardly recognisable as insects. Reproduction is mostly parthenogenetic, as the tiny winged males rarely occur, the eggs being laid under a white mass of waxy fibres. Introduced to Britain in the 1960s and has spread to the north of England and Wales; now found on many tree species.

Brown Soft Scale *Coccus hesperidum*
The yellowish-brown female is up to 4mm long and can be found on many ornamental plants. Reproduction is parthenogenetic. Each female lays up to 250 eggs and the young nymphs are wind dispersed. Tiny parasitic wasps are commercially available as biological control agents. Distribution cosmopolitan.

Citrus Mealy Bug *Planococcus citri*
These sap-sucking insects, originating from warmer regions, have become established pests in greenhouses in temperate regions. The females are wingless and are covered in a powdery wax, which also protects the eggs; the males are winged. Distribution cosmopolitan.

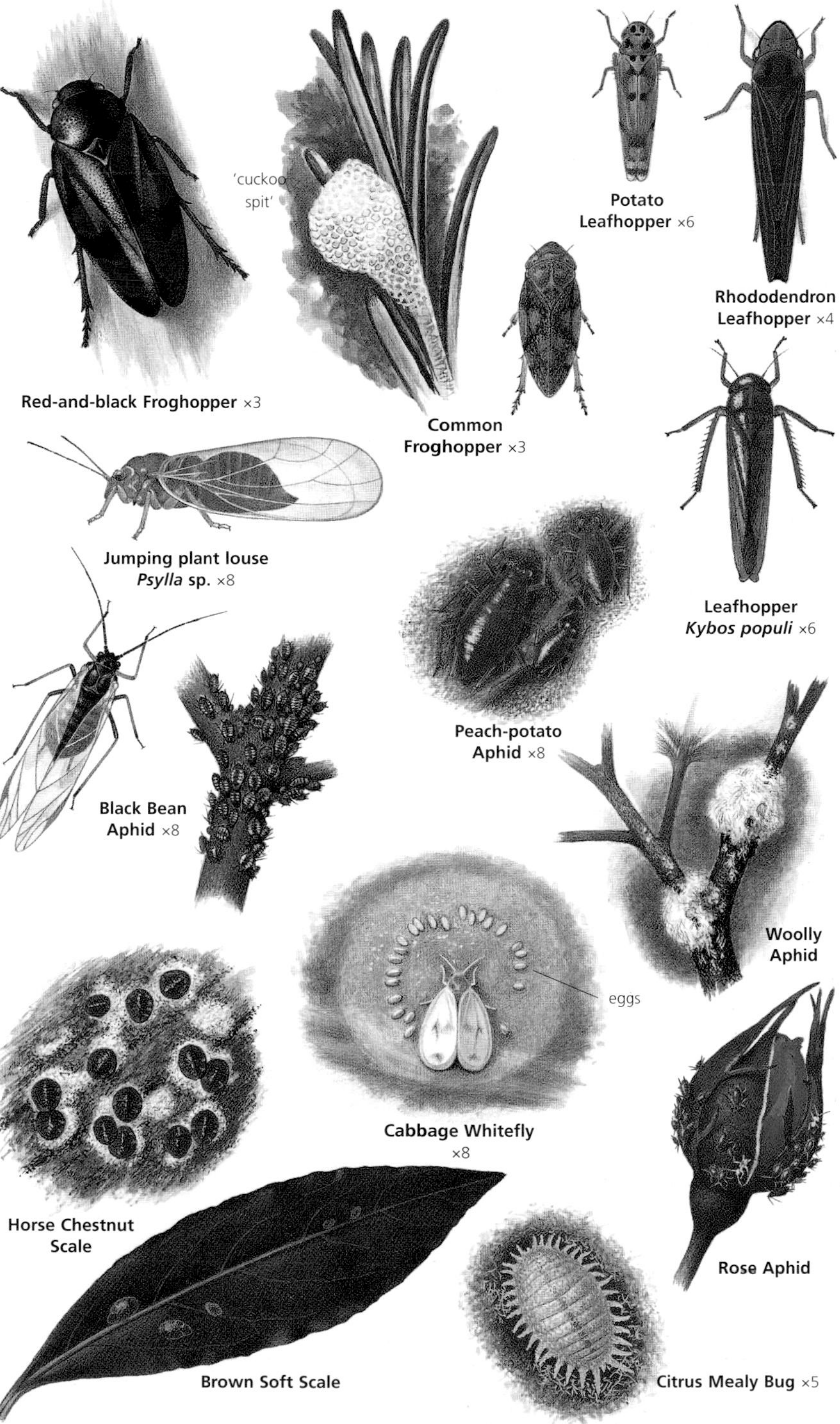

Red-and-black Froghopper ×3

Common Froghopper ×3

Potato Leafhopper ×6

Rhododendron Leafhopper ×4

Leafhopper *Kybos populi* ×6

Jumping plant louse *Psylla* sp. ×8

Peach-potato Aphid ×8

Black Bean Aphid ×8

Woolly Aphid

Cabbage Whitefly ×8

Horse Chestnut Scale

Rose Aphid

Brown Soft Scale

Citrus Mealy Bug ×5

Two-pronged Bristle-tail or **Diplura**
Campodea fragilis
One of about a dozen British species with body lengths up to 5mm. These primitive insects are related to the familiar indoor Silverfish. Diplurans are found in moist, humid places, such as compost heaps, leaf litter and amongst garden debris, but little is known of their life histories. *Campodea fragilis* is one of the commonest and most widespread.

Springtails Collembola

Springtails are the world's most abundant insects, often with in excess of 40,000 occurring in a square metre of leaf litter. They get their name from the forked springing organ, known as a furcula, held folded beneath the abdomen. When disturbed, this is flicked rapidly against the ground, projecting the insect into the air in a split second. In some species, however, this organ is absent. Found in virtually every terrestrial habitat, in gardens they are most often encountered when stones and logs are lifted and they leap, spinning in all directions to avoid danger. Springtails feed mainly on fungi, pollen grains and organic detritus, and play an important role in gardens as nutrient recyclers. About 250 species occur in Britain, ranging in size from 0.5mm to 6mm.

Springtail *Orchesella villosa*
One of our largest and hairiest species, reaching 5mm. Its body pigment varies from yellowish brown to dull olive green. In older specimens, the dense hairs often wear off. Widespread, very common in the south but becoming scarcer further north.

Springtail *Orchesella cincta*
Reaching about 4mm, this species is readily identified by the pale central band on the abdomen. Found under logs and stones, and in leaf litter. Common and widespread in gardens and hedgerows throughout Britain and Ireland.

Springtail *Podura aquatica*
A stocky, blue-grey springtail, with short legs and antennae, reaching about 2mm in length. It is sometimes found in large congregations on the surface of puddles, ponds and streams. Widespread and locally common, but possibly declining, due to its vulnerability to pesticides.

Springtail *Pogonognathellus longicornis*
One of the largest British springtails, with a body length up to 6mm. It has a shiny, scaly appearance, and when disturbed rolls its long antennae into coils, making it easily identified. In older specimens the dark grey scales often become worn, giving a yellow-blotched appearance. Found in compost heaps and leaf litter, widespread and very common in gardens throughout Britain and Ireland.

Barkflies Psocoptera

These insects, formerly known as barklice, are the outdoor relatives of the tiny, soft-bodied booklice, which feed on microscopic moulds and mildews in damp houses. Unrelated to true lice, they live on the bark and foliage of various deciduous and coniferous trees, where they feed on fungi, algae and lichens. Some species have two pairs of well-marked wings, others are wingless. Although seldom observed, they occur in every well-vegetated garden. There is a dedicated UK Barkfly Recording Scheme; 68 British species have been recorded.

Barkfly *Ectopsocus briggsi*
A small barkfly, with a distinctly banded abdomen. The female, which sometimes occurs with reduced wings, rendering it flightless, lays small batches of white, pearl-like eggs on leaves. Found at all times of the year on the foliage of trees and shrubs. Both this species and *Graphopsocus cruciatus* are the only tree-living barkflies to overwinter as adults, usually in evergreens. Common and widely distributed throughout Britain and Ireland.

Picture-winged barkfly
Graphopsocus cruciatus
This distinctive and easily recognised barkfly, with boldly marked wings, is one of the commonest species to occur in gardens, and is found on a variety trees and shrubs. Common and widespread throughout Britain and Ireland.

Picture-winged barkfly *Philotarsus parviceps*
Often common on the foliage and twigs of fruit trees in gardens and orchards, the distinctly patterned wings are less heavily marked than those of the closely related but much scarcer *P. picicornis*. Common and widespread throughout Britain and Ireland.

Thrips Thysanoptera

These tiny, slender insects, often known as thunder flies from their habit of swarming in warm, thundery weather, are often encountered indoors, where they have the annoying habit of hibernating behind the glass of framed pictures. They usually have two pairs of narrow wings, which are fringed with long, fine hairs, giving a feather-like appearance, but in some species the wings are absent. Although some are carnivorous, most species rasp or suck sap. When they occur in large numbers, damage, which is characterised by a silvery mottling of the leaves, is sometimes caused to garden plants.

Grain Thrips *Limothrips cerealium*
A pest of cereal crops such as wheat, oats and maize, the Grain Thrips is also found on several species of wild grasses. Females are brown or black, reaching a length of just under 2mm, and occur throughout the year as they hibernate through the winter. The smaller, wingless males live in the summer months only. Most eggs are laid in June and July, and the resulting females swarm on warm days in August, prior to hibernation, often causing an irritating tickling when they land on exposed skin. Found in many parts of the world.

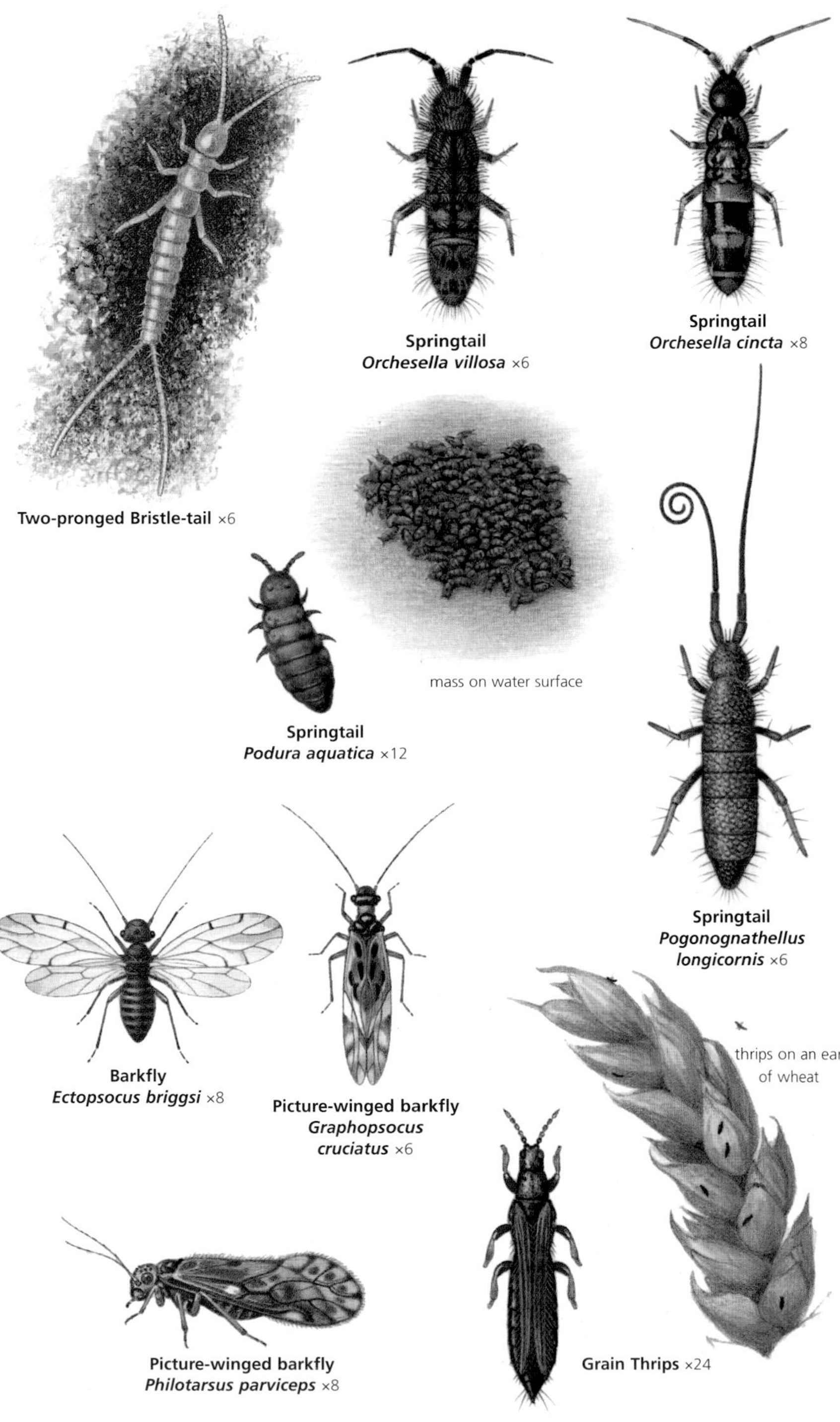

Two-pronged Bristle-tail ×6

Springtail
Orchesella villosa ×6

Springtail
Orchesella cincta ×8

Springtail
Podura aquatica ×12

Springtail
Pogonognathellus longicornis ×6

Barkfly
Ectopsocus briggsi ×8

Picture-winged barkfly
Graphopsocus cruciatus ×6

Picture-winged barkfly
Philotarsus parviceps ×8

Grain Thrips ×24

Lacewings Neuroptera

Green lacewing *Chrysoperla carnea*
The commonest of 14 or so green lacewings and the only one that hibernates as an adult, often indoors, having turned pale pink in the autumn. Adults and larvae are voracious predators of aphids and other small invertebrates. When young, the larvae gain protection by attaching skins and debris left over from meals to spines on their bodies. Up to 500 eggs are laid singly or in groups at the tips of delicate stalks on the underside of leaves. When fully grown, after having eaten several hundred aphids, the larva pupates in a cocoon in debris near the ground. Active mainly at night and often attracted to lighted windows. **Habitat and distribution** Found in gardens and other well-vegetated habitats, throughout Britain and Ireland.

Brown lacewing *Hemerobius humulinus*
Generally smaller and more inconspicuous than the green lacewings, this is one of about 30 related species. Eggs are laid directly on plants; adults and larvae feed on aphids, mites, scale insects and other pest species. Unlike the green lacewings, the larvae lack warts and spines and do not decorate themselves with debris. **Habitat and distribution** Widespread, occurring in gardens from spring until autumn.

Lacewing *Conwentzia psociformis*
A tiny, powdery-white lacewing, often mistaken for a whitefly but with wings held more steeply roofed. This beneficial garden predator is found on the foliage of trees, especially oaks, and shrubs, where it feeds on aphids, whiteflies, scale insects and mites, including the notorious Glasshouse Red Spider Mite. The larva pupates in a rounded silken cocoon on the underside of leaves, and adults are active from April until the autumn. **Habitat and distribution** Probably under recorded, most records are from the south-east, but it is found throughout England, Wales and parts of Ireland.

Scorpionflies Mecoptera

Scorpionfly *Panorpa germanica*
One of three widespread and similar species, found frequently in scrubby hedgerows and gardens. The male has conspicuous, scorpion-like genitalia and a long beak, but is quite harmless, and both sexes are easily observed as they search for mates and food amongst low, sunlit vegetation. The diet is varied, and in addition to nectar and fruit also includes small insects such as aphids, dead carrion, often insects caught in spiders' webs, and even bird droppings. The bristly larva lives mostly below ground and, although similar in form to a moth larva, has eight rather than five pairs of false legs. **Habitat and distribution** Found throughout Britain and southern Ireland, from May until August.

Alderflies Megaloptera

Alderfly *Sialis lutaria*
Usually seen clinging to waterside vegetation or flying clumsily in the sunshine, this is the commonest of our three species of alderfly. It lays neat batches of up to 500 eggs on leaves and stones and, on hatching, the larvae (see page 208) drop into the water and spend the autumn and winter feeding on small invertebrates in mud at the bottom of ponds and slow-moving water. **Habitat and distribution** Widely distributed. Adults are most common in May and June.

Caddisflies Trichoptera

Known to anglers as 'sedges', caddisflies are mostly active at dusk and at night, the adults being less familiar than the cases of the aquatic larvae. The name Trichoptera refers to the wings, which are densely covered in hairs. Most species rest with their wings held roofed over their backs. They lack a proboscis and instead lap up nectar or moisture from vegetation. The larvae fall into three categories – free-living, net-makers and case-makers – and it is the latter group, all of which are vegetarian, that are most often encountered in garden ponds. Pupation takes place inside the case. There are 198 British species.

Grouse Wing *Mystacides longicornis*
This and related species of 'long-horned caddisflies' have long antennae and resemble some long-horned micro-moths. This species has clearly banded markings, red eyes and distinctive palps, which are held out to the side of the head, a characteristic of all *Mystacides*. **Habitat and distribution** Common and widespread near still water, including garden ponds. Flies by day and night from May until June.

Cinnamon Sedge *Limnephilus rhombicus*
A member of the largest caddis family, the Lymnephilidae, containing 58 species, many of which have semi-translucent wings that are various shades of pale, yellowish brown. The larva, which is common in still and slow-moving water, makes its case from a variety of plant materials attached at right angles to the tube (see page 208). **Habitat and distribution** Widespread. Adults are found from May until September.

Large Cinnamon Sedge *Stenophylax vibex*
One of the largest caddisflies, with shiny, speckled orange-brown wings. Often attracted to artificial light, such as moth traps at night. Flies in late summer and autumn.

Mottled Sedge *Glyphotaelius pellucidus*
One of the most easily recognised species, with a scalloped outer edge to the attractive mottled wings, which are more boldly marked in the male than the female. The larva makes its broad, flat case from rounded pieces of overlapping vegetation. **Habitat and distribution** Widespread and common in small, well-vegetated ponds. Flies from May to October.

Speckled Peter *Agrypnia varia*
Cryptically marked, with attractively mottled and speckled wings, and an olive-green body. **Habitat and distribution** Widespread, and found in ponds, lakes and slow-moving water from July until September.

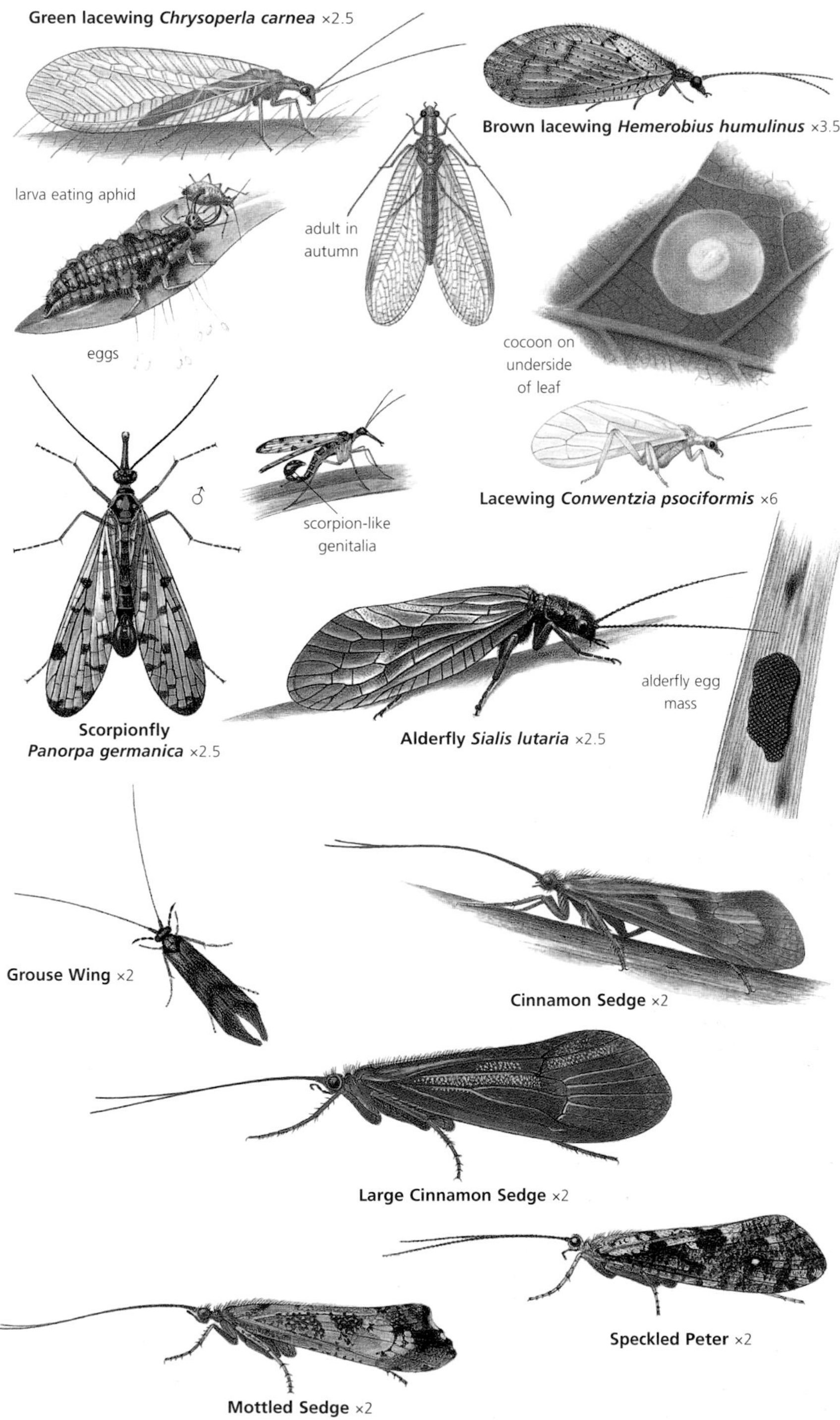

Green lacewing ***Chrysoperla carnea*** ×2.5

Brown lacewing ***Hemerobius humulinus*** ×3.5

Lacewing ***Conwentzia psociformis*** ×6

Scorpionfly ***Panorpa germanica*** ×2.5

Alderfly ***Sialis lutaria*** ×2.5

Grouse Wing ×2

Cinnamon Sedge ×2

Large Cinnamon Sedge ×2

Speckled Peter ×2

Mottled Sedge ×2

Butterflies and moths Lepidoptera

▲ A Red Admiral butterfly basking in the sun.

Butterflies and moths are the best loved and most thoroughly studied group of insects. Although the lepidoptera is not the largest order, with more than 2,500 British species, it receives the most attention, with the largest invertebrate charity in the world, Butterfly Conservation, dedicated to its well-being. Lepidoptera means 'scale wing', referring to the flattened, overlapping scales that give the wings a huge variety of colours and patterns. The division between butterflies and moths has no scientific basis, and distinguishing between the two groups is not always easy. However, butterflies always have clubbed antennae, whereas, apart from the burnet moths, which have curved, slightly swollen tips to theirs, most moth antennae are either feathery or simple and thread-like. Butterflies fly by day, but so too do many moths, many of which also rival the colours of butterflies.

Most lepidoptera feed on nectar and honeydew, which is sucked through a tubular proboscis. When not in use, this is held coiled beneath the head, although in some moths it is absent, or reduced and not used. Butterflies are closely associated with flowers on warm summer days, when gardens are brightened by their activities, and at dusk and at night the association is repeated by most moths, when far greater numbers visit and act as pollinators to a wide variety of cultivated flowers. Most caterpillars found on garden plants, apart from those of the 'cabbage white' butterflies, belong to moths. Few of these occur in large enough numbers to cause problems, but one or two species, such as the Cabbage Moth and related noctuids, commonly known as 'cutworms', may burrow into brassicas or eat through the stems of young plants.

Butterfly gardening has become a popular pastime in recent years. Now, a great variety of native and ornamental plants are grown to attract butterflies and many other insects. Of our 59 species of resident and regularly occurring butterflies, about a third are likely to appear in gardens. Many of these are our commoner, less habitat-specific species, such as the Peacock and Red Admiral, which are among the most beautiful and spectacular. The buddleia *Buddleia davidii,* often called the 'Butterfly Bush', is perhaps the most favoured nectar plant. Not only does it attract butterflies, moths and other insects for the copious amount of nectar it produces, but it is also host to the caterpillars of around two dozen species of moth which feed on the foliage, the most spectacular of these being the caterpillar of the Mullein moth, which usually feeds on wild and cultivated mulleins. Among other plants grown to encourage butterflies are the ice plant *Sedum spectabile* (but not the sterile hybrid 'Autumn Joy'), Michaelmas daisies and aubretia, while in the herb garden marjoram, thyme and lavender will all attract plenty of summer species.

Many familiar species visit gardens from the surrounding countryside but few of these regularly stay to breed. The inclusion of some of the less attractive plants, such as common nettle, might encourage some egg-laying vanessids, and honesty, dame's-violet and other crucifers may attract the female Orange-tip and Green-veined White. However, their two relatives, the 'cabbage whites', are less welcome and occasionally cause damage in the vegetable garden. Later in the year, less obvious food sources help certain species to build up their reserves in preparation for migration or hibernation. The Red Admiral, Comma and Peacock benefit from rotting fruit left on the ground, often appearing tipsy from the effects of fermentation, and ivy is an essential nectar source for butterflies and many other insects preparing for hibernation.

Moths

Moths are the often neglected relatives of the butterflies, but they are not dull, they don't live in wallets and only one or two species feed on clothes. They are amongst the most colourful, diverse and abundant creatures to visit gardens, and it is only because most fly by night that they create less interest than butterflies. They are generally divided into two groups, the micro-moths and macro-moths, but this division, like that between butterflies and moths, is an artificial split of convenience. Each group is made up from certain families, which, as their names suggest, are either smaller or larger moths. There are about twice as many 'micros' than 'macros', many of them difficult to identify, and, confusingly, some species are larger than some macro-moths.

Of the macro-moths that frequent gardens, the spectacular hawk-moths are well represented, with the Poplar Hawk-moth and Elephant Hawk-moth being common and widespread. Perhaps the most colourful family is the tiger moths, many of which display warning colours. The two largest families of macro-moths are the noctuids, which include the infamous cutworms, and the geometrids, meaning 'ground measurers', named after the looping action of the caterpillars. Both these families have a large number of species, many of them cryptically camouflaged, rendering them invisible by day.

▲ A Hummingbird Hawk-moth feeding on buddleia.

Few people realise the abundance of moths that visit our gardens at night, far outnumbering the butterflies that visit by day. Typically, a mercury vapour moth trap, run in an average garden in July, might catch 500 to 1,000 individuals, and many 'mothers' as they are often known, contribute valuable records and information before releasing their catches the following day. This is a fascinating and useful pastime that even the less mobile naturalist, who cannot easily venture into more remote countryside, can enjoy.

Butterflies

Small Skipper *Thymelicus sylvestris*
This is an inconspicuous, golden-brown butterfly with a rapid, buzzing flight. The male Small Skipper has a short black line on each forewing, the sex-brand, which is absent in the female. Both have orange-brown under-tips to the antennae. Adults are fond of nectar from a variety of flowers, and the female lays her eggs in the sheaths of Yorkshire-fog or creeping soft-grass. Occurs in a single brood from June until August. **Habitat and distribution** An occasional garden visitor, especially where colonies breed on nearby grassy roadside verges and disturbed ground. Found commonly throughout central and southern England and Wales, with an expanding range recently reaching Scotland. **Similar species** The **Essex Skipper** *T. lineola* is very similar but has ink-black under-tips to the antennae. Found mostly south of a line from the Humber to the Severn estuary, but has recently been recorded from Scotland and County Wexford in Ireland.

Large Skipper *Ochlodes sylvanus*
This is a more robust and boldly marked skipper, which often flies with the Small Skipper. The male frequently perches on sunlit vegetation guarding his territory from other males, while resting in characteristic skipper posture, with forewings raised and hindwings held flat. The female is similar but lacks the black sex-brand on the forewings. Eggs are laid singly, usually on the blades of cock's-foot grass, the main larval foodplant. Flies in a single brood from late May until the end of August. **Habitat and distribution** Prefers rough grassy places and sometimes visits garden flowers. Widespread throughout England and Wales, just reaching southern Scotland.

Small Copper *Lycaena phlaeas*
A brilliant, lively little butterfly that often settles on warm, sunny ground, where the aggressive male will set up territory and battle with any intruders, including other much larger insects. Although they live in small colonies, individuals sometimes wander and females may lay eggs on stunted dock or sorrel plants growing in gardens. First appears in April, and in hot summers may have up to four broods, lasting into November. **Habitat and distribution** Found in a variety of habitats, including brown-field sites, waste ground and gardens. Occurs throughout Britain and Ireland but there has been a decline in recent years.

Brown Argus *Aricia agestis*
Both sexes of this little butterfly resemble the female Common Blue, but can usually be distinguished by the complete absence of any blue on the upperside and the different arrangement of spots on the underside of the hindwing. The eggs are laid singly on the leaves of common rock-rose or crane's-bills. Flies from May until September in two broods. **Habitat and distribution** Mainly found on unimproved grassland, but waste ground, railway embankments and set-aside fields are also colonised. Individuals sometimes stray into gardens and have been observed egg-laying on cultivated varieties of rock-rose. Most frequent in southern and eastern England, but also found in the south-west and parts of Wales.

Common Blue *Polyommatus icarus*
The bright lilac-blue male Common Blue is often confused with the Holly Blue but the undersides are quite different. The female varies from being predominantly brown with a dusting of blue to nearly all blue, both colour forms having orange margins. There are usually two broods between May and October. **Habitat and distribution** A familiar butterfly where common bird's-foot-trefoil, clovers and black medick grow in grassy meadows. It will also colonise gardens, laying eggs in turf containing a mixture of herbs which include its larval foodplants. The most widely distributed blue, found throughout Britain and Ireland.

Holly Blue *Celastrina argiolus*
Most silvery-blue butterflies flying in parks and gardens, often around tall shrubs, are likely to be Holly Blues, as this butterfly is more frequent in villages and urban places than in the open countryside. It often settles with its wings closed, when its distinctive, finely spotted underside can be seen. It prefers to feed from honeydew exuded on leaves by aphids, rather than from flowers. In spring, eggs are laid singly on the flower buds of female holly bushes, but in summer mainly ivy is used, although dogwood, snowberry and pyracantha are also used. The caterpillar, which is quite easy to find, eats the buds, flowers and berries. The first blue to appear in spring, there are normally two broods between late March and September, but abundance varies from year to year. **Habitat and distribution** Parks, gardens and churchyards, especially those with an abundance of ivy; also in woodland and on shrubby hillsides. Its range is expanding; found throughout England and Wales, scarcer in the north and widely distributed in Ireland.

all shown life size
except where indicated
♂
♂
♀
♂ underside
♀
♂ underside
Small Skipper
Large Skipper
♂ and ♀ similar
underside
Small Copper
♂ and ♀ similar
twin
spots
underside
Brown Argus
♂
♂ underside
♀
♂
caterpillar ×1.5
♀ blue form
♂ underside
caterpillar feeding on
ivy buds ×1.5
♀ typical form
Common Blue
Holly Blue

Brimstone *Gonepteryx rhamni*
The Brimstone is a wanderer in the countryside, the sulphur-yellow male being one of the first butterflies to be seen in spring, emerging after hibernating concealed in a tangle of ivy or deep in a bramble patch for the past five months. After mating, these hibernators may live on until June, making them the longest-lived British butterfly. The less conspicuous female is similar in size and shape to the male but is greenish white and may be confused with the Large White. The hooked wings and absence of any black, however, should confirm identification. In spring, Brimstones favour yellow flowers such as dandelions, daffodils and primroses for nectar, but a wider range of flowers are sought in the summer and autumn, including thistles and knapweeds, and in gardens the flowers of runner beans, sweet peas and buddleias are favourites. During poor weather and at night the butterfly hangs beneath a leaf, and what was a conspicuous, eye-catching butterfly becomes a perfectly camouflaged yellowing leaf. Alder buckthorn and buckthorn planted in gardens soon attract the attention of females, who lay their eggs singly on buds and young leaves. The green caterpillar rests perfectly concealed on the upper midrib of a leaf, but can be detected by the leaf damage it causes. **Habitat and distribution** Occurs in a wide range of habitats, including downland, woodland rides and roadside verges, as well as gardens in urban areas. It is widespread and common in England and Wales, with an expanding range, but is scarcer in the west. It has a scattered distribution in Ireland, where it is mainly found on limestone soils in the west.

Cabbage whites

The Large White and Small White (see page 106) are known collectively as 'cabbage whites', but although they resemble one another, their biology is quite different and their early stages are distinct. The caterpillars of the Large White live gregariously and are far more destructive, although the Small White is usually the most abundant species. The best way to protect crops from their attention is with fine fruit-netting laid over the plants, or by picking the eggs and caterpillars from the leaves. When removing eggs, care should be taken not to destroy the similar egg batches laid by ladybirds. These are usually laid in smaller groups, are brighter yellow, and lack the vertical keels.

Large White *Pieris brassicae*
Unpopular with serious vegetable growers, the gregarious caterpillars of the Large White can cause considerable damage in the vegetable garden. Nevertheless, the adult female especially, with her chalky-white wings and bold black markings, is an attractive butterfly, often mixing with more colourful species on buddleias and hebes in mid-summer. The male is similar, although a little smaller, and lacks the spots and streaks on the upper side of the forewings. Most often seen around human habitation, the Large White has taken advantage of commercially- and domestically-grown crucifers, with a particular attraction to brassicas. Each year, the population is boosted by immigrants from the Continent, which occasionally arrive in huge numbers, although these influxes rarely have any long-lasting effect on overall numbers and probably result in an increase of natural predators. One of these is the tiny parasitoid wasp *Cotesia glomerata* (see page 150), which lays its eggs in the caterpillar. These hatch and the wasp grubs feed internally until they themselves are ready for pupation. They then emerge through the host's skin and make conspicuous yellow cocoons around the shrivelled corpse. The female Large White lays batches of up to 100 eggs, usually on the underside of brassica leaves but will also lay on nasturtiums, which some people plant to distract them from more valuable crops. The eggs hatch after about ten days and the smelly caterpillars, which contain mustard oils to deter predators, live in voracious groups, moving on as they make the leaves ragged. When fully grown, the caterpillars wander off and pupate, often on a wall, fence or shed, and the chrysalis of the final brood of the year remains here for the winter. On a few occasions, caterpillars have been recorded throughout the winter months. The first adults hatch in April, and in long hot summers three broods may hatch, lasting into October. **Habitat and distribution** Ubiquitous, found almost everywhere except the highest mountains, being most frequent on farmland, gardens and allotments. **Similar species Small White** (see page 106).

all shown life size except where indicated

Small White *Pieris rapae*
The solitary caterpillars of this very common white butterfly, which has benefited from the widespread growing of brassicas, are usually less damaging than those of the Large White but are equally unpopular with gardeners. The female butterfly is more heavily marked with black than the male, which may lack all markings other than dark wing tips, but at rest the sexes are hard to separate. The yellow skittle-shaped eggs are laid singly on the underside of leaves of brassicas, crucifers and nasturtiums in gardens, but also on wild crucifers such as garlic mustard and charlock away from cultivation. The velvety green caterpillar is cryptically coloured and relies on this, rather than on distasteful mustard oils, for its protection. It has a faint yellow dorsal line down its back and a row of yellow spots along the sides. Pupation may take place on the foodplant or on walls and tree trunks. The colour of the chrysalis varies, depending on the background. The Small White is often the first butterfly of the year to emerge from its chrysalis, appearing in late March in warm springs. Two, occasionally three, broods are produced, lasting into October, with numbers, boosted by immigrants, peaking in early August. **Habitat and distribution** Occurs in almost any habitat except high mountains, but most frequent in gardens, allotments and farmland. **Similar species** The **Large White** *Pieris brassicae* is usually bigger, with blacker, heavier markings; the male always lacks the black central spot on the upperside of the forewings. The **Green-veined White** *P. napi* has a black dusting running in from the margins on the upperside and grey-green scales bordering the veins on the underside.

Green-veined White *Pieris napi*
Closely related and similar in many ways to the Small White, the caterpillars of this attractive butterfly do very little damage to garden plants, although eggs are sometimes laid on cultivated crucifers such as aubretia, alyssums and horse radish. Adult butterflies also visit many garden flowers for nectar, lavenders being a particular favourite. It is most easily distinguished from other whites by the delicate grey-green dusting of scales along the veins on the underside, although these may be quite faint in some specimens. On the upperside, the forewings have dark scales running in along the veins from near the margins. The caterpillar resembles that of the Small White but it lacks the faint yellow dorsal line and has a row of yellow-ringed black spots (spiracles) along the sides. **Habitat and distribution** A common garden visitor but also found in many habitats in the wider countryside, including damp lanes, woodland rides and meadows, as well as the upland moorlands of Wales and Scotland, but less often on dry downland. The most widely distributed of any butterfly, found throughout Britain and Ireland. **Similar species** **Small White** (see left).

Orange-tip *Anthocharis cardamines*
For many butterfly enthusiasts, the sight of the first male Orange-tip is a sign that spring has arrived. This leisurely wanderer of the countryside patrols lanes and meadows and is a frequent garden visitor, the male often pausing to feed from flowers during his search for a female. She may be mistaken for a Small White as she lacks the bright orange tips of the male, but the underside reveals a beautiful marbled green and black pattern, rendering both sexes almost invisible when they rest on the flowerheads of umbellifers. Eggs, which turn a bright orange after a few days, are laid on isolated plants of wild and cultivated crucifers, including honesty and dame's-violet, but only one or two eggs are laid on each plant, so no harm is caused. The well-camouflaged caterpillar rests and feeds mainly on the seedpods, but when young it may also eat other caterpillars it encounters. When fully grown it will sometimes eat the leaves, buds and flowers. The elegant, curved chrysalis is usually straw-coloured and remains hidden, attached to vegetation, for up to 11 months. **Habitat and distribution** Found in many habitats but prefers rather damp lanes and meadows, often near water. Common but never abundant, the Orange-tip has expanded its range in recent years, especially northwards, and occurs throughout Britain and Ireland. **Similar species** The male is distinctive, but from above the female may be confused with other whites; the bold black spot in the centre of the forewings, however, is diagnostic.

♂ first brood
grey wing tip
♀ first brood
all shown life size except where indicated
♂ first brood underside
caterpillar ×1.5
Small White
♂ first brood
♀ first brood
black dusting
♂ first brood underside
caterpillar ×1.5
Green-veined White
central black spot
♂
♀
underside
caterpillar ×1.5
Orange-tip

Vanessids

The following five species of butterfly, commonly known as vanessids, lay their eggs on common nettle, although some also lay on other plants. They all occur regularly in gardens, being particularly associated with the well-known nectar-bearing plants and shrubs grown to attract butterflies, such as buddleias, hebes, sedums and Michaelmas-daisies. Most can be encouraged to lay their eggs on nettles, which can be planted in containers to restrict their spread. These should ideally be positioned in a sunny, sheltered place, with various stages of growth, providing both fresh young leaves and taller, more mature plants.

Comma *Polygonia c-album*

The ragged, torn outline of the Comma makes it unmistakable when feeding or at rest, but on the wing its rapid, gliding flight resembles that of some of the rarer fritillaries. Its name comes from the conspicuous, silvery, comma-shaped mark on the underside of the hindwings and, although the sexes are similar, the underside of the female is a little plainer than that of the male. In warmer years, a proportion of the butterflies resulting from eggs laid in spring are of the brighter orange *hutchinsoni* form. Less common than its near, garden relatives, the Comma is one of the first butterflies to appear after hibernation in early spring, when males set up fiercely guarded territories. Commas feed from a variety of garden blooms, starting in spring with sallow catkins and dandelions, and later in the year from a range of garden favourites such as buddleias, hebes and sedums. In late autumn, Commas, along with Red Admirals, wasps and other insects preparing for hibernation, are attracted to rotting fruit. Eggs are laid singly on the upper edge of common nettle, hop and elm leaves, and in gardens currant is sometimes used as a foodplant. The attractive, fully-grown caterpillar rests exposed on the upper surface of a leaf, relying on its resemblance to a bird-dropping for protection. Two broods are produced each year; those from the second enter hibernation in October. **Habitat and distribution** A butterfly of open woodland rides, orchards and gardens. It was a rarity a century ago but its range has expanded enormously in the last few decades and it is now common in England and Wales, and has started to appear in Scotland, with a few scattered records from Ireland.

Peacock *Aglais io*

Recently voted Britain's favourite, no other butterfly has the startling eyespots of the Peacock, which is, fortunately, still a common butterfly, regularly appearing in gardens to feed from buddleias, sedums and Michaelmas-daisies. In contrast to the richly marked upperside, the underside is plain and dark, giving the hibernating butterfly excellent camouflage in shady woodpiles and sheds. The first Peacocks appear after hibernation in February, the male setting up his territory on warm sunlit ground, sparring with rival males until a female appears. Having mated, she seeks out a nettle patch growing in a sunny position, and lays a batch of several hundred eggs on the underside of a leaf. The caterpillars hatch after two weeks and are gregarious, living in a silken web until they are fully grown after about a month. They then disperse and the black, spiny caterpillars, speckled with white spots, seek a sheltered place in which to pupate. Only one generation a year is produced, numbers reaching a peak in August. In late summer the Peacock starts to build up its reserves for the winter, and enters hibernation in September. One of the longest-lived British butterflies, those hatching from the chrysalis in July can live until the following May or June. If alarmed when resting, the Peacock may flash open its wings to expose its staring eyes and produce a hissing sound by rubbing its wings together. **Habitat and distribution** Found in many habitats wherever nettles grow in abundance, from downland and woodland rides to disturbed brownfield sites. Common in Britain and Ireland, with a range expanding northwards.

all shown life size
except where indicated
♂ underside
♀ underside
Comma
caterpillar ×1.5
underside
Peacock
caterpillar ×1.5

Small Tortoiseshell *Aglais urticae*
This is the most common of the vanessid butterflies, and although abundance fluctuates greatly from year to year, it is often one of the first butterflies to be seen in March after hibernation. The chequered orange-and-black markings are distinctive, but those less well acquainted with butterflies may confuse it with the Red Admiral. The sexes are alike and there is little individual variation, although in the cooler north some specimens may be a little darker. The dusky underside resembles that of close relatives, but the contrast between the inner and outer parts of the hindwing is diagnostic. The male is territorial and spirals high into the sky with rival males until a female passes by. She is then pursued relentlessly, and after mating lays a large batch of eggs on the underside of a young nettle leaf. The variable yellow-and-black caterpillars are gregarious and conspicuous, living together in dark clusters in untidy webs, moving on to fresh nettles as they grow. When fully grown, at about a month old, they separate and live alone before pupation; this takes place in a sheltered position, often suspended under a windowsill. Butterflies produced from eggs laid in spring emerge from the chrysalis after 12 days, producing a second brood in the south, but in Scotland only one brood appears. **Habitat and distribution** Found throughout Britain and Ireland, from sea level to mountaintops, including gardens where marigolds, buddeias, Michaelmas-daisies and other cultivated flowers are visited for nectar, and where nettles grow abundantly.

Red Admiral *Vanessa atalanta*
In recent years, the Red Admiral has been one of the most common of the colourful vanessid butterflies to appear in gardens and, although each year its fortunes depend on immigrants from the south, there is evidence that in southern England increasing numbers of butterflies are able to survive the winter. Recent surveys have discovered that even the eggs and caterpillars are capable of surviving the winter months. The main influx from the south occurs in late May and June, these visitors laying their eggs as they move north, to produce a generation that continues into the autumn, when a partial re-migration takes place. The sexes are similar and unmistakable from above, but at rest, with the forewings obscured by the hindwings, the underside of the Red Admiral is like other related species. A pale yellowish blotch on the top margin of the hindwing, however, is diagnostic. The green eggs are laid singly on common nettle leaves, and the caterpillar lives a solitary life concealed inside a tent-like structure made from leaves spun together with silk. As it grows, new shelters are made, and when fully grown the final conspicuous structure is used for pupation. The colour of the caterpillar varies, from the more usual yellowish grey, to black with yellow dashes along the sides. **Habitat and distribution** Found in many habitats, including gardens and orchards where nettles grow and where adults can feed from nectar-rich flowers and rotting fruit. Numbers vary from year to year, and in good years the Red Admiral can occur anywhere in the British Isles.

Painted Lady *Vanessa cardui*
One of the world's most widely distributed migratory butterflies, in some years the Painted Lady appears in Britain in huge numbers from southern Europe and North Africa, followed by years when it is rarely seen at all. It is an elegant, showy butterfly, that when freshly emerged has a rosy hue to its wings. The sexes are similar, the underside being more intricately marked than in any other British butterfly. It visits a variety of garden flowers, often in the company of other vanessids, and is far more frequent later in the year, when the offspring of earlier migrants have emerged. The main food-plants for the caterpillar are various thistles, but mallows, common nettle and viper's-bugloss are also used. The eggs are laid singly and the caterpillar resembles, and has similar habits to, that of the Red Admiral, leading a solitary life in a shelter of leaves spun together with silk. It is more slender, however, with a narrow, broken yellow line along its sides. Several generations may be produced each year, with sightings peaking in August and lasting into November. Unlike the Red Admiral, there is no re-migration south, and although there have been odd records of Painted Ladies surviving the winter, most perish. **Habitat and distribution** Found in many habitats, including agricultural land, brownfield sites, towns and villages, where there are plenty of thistles. Abundance varies from year to year, depending on conditions in southern Europe, and in good years, the most recent being 2009, it can appear anywhere, even on the most remote islands of the north.

all shown life size
except where indicated

Satyrids (Browns)

The caterpillars of all the satyrids feed on various wild grasses, and so benefit from gardens that are not too intensively manicured. Sunny corners and semi-shaded places allowed to become overgrown with grasses may well attract egg-laying females of several species.

Wall *Lasiommata megera*
A butterfly of warm, dry places, where it basks on the ground or on walls, with wings half open. The fortunes of the Wall have changed in the past 35 years and it has become much less common, especially in central and southern England and Wales. The female is like the male (illustrated), but is usually a little larger and lacks the black sex-brand across each forewing. When resting on the ground, with forewings concealed, the Wall is one of our best-camouflaged butterflies. Eggs are laid singly, in dry sheltered places, on blades of grasses such as cock's-foot, tor-grass and Yorkshire-fog, and the caterpillar of the final brood overwinters, feeding occasionally on mild nights. Up to three broods are produced, between April and October. **Habitat and distribution** Found along sheltered sunny lanes and paths, disused railway lines and on downland slopes, sometimes visiting gardens. More frequent in milder coastal regions, less common in central England but with a slight expansion in its northern distribution.

Speckled Wood *Parage aegeria*
Although the Speckled Wood sometimes visits flowers and rotting fruit in the autumn, in summer it more often feeds on the honeydew of aphids from the surface of leaves, for this is primarily a woodland butterfly whose male likes to bask on dappled, sunlit vegetation. From here, he attacks other males that enter his territory, spiralling high into the treetops then descending back to his perch. The female has larger cream spots than the male, but in later broods these are reduced in both sexes, giving them a darker appearance. Eggs are laid on various grasses, including cock's-foot and false brome, and a unique aspect of the life cycle is the overwintering stage, which can be passed either as a caterpillar or chrysalis. Up to three broods fly from March until October. **Habitat and distribution** Mainly woodland glades and edges but also in lanes and gardens with a scattering of trees, shrubs and tall grasses. Having declined in the first half of the 20th century, its range has expanded enormously and it is now common from the Midlands southwards, in Wales, Ireland and parts of Scotland.

Ringlet *Aphantopus hyperantus*
The darkest and plainest of all the 'brown' butterflies that visit gardens, the underside of the Ringlet nevertheless reveals the beautiful eye ringlets after which it is named. These are usually brighter in the female, who is also paler and slightly larger. She drops her eggs amongst coarser grasses growing in semi-shaded, often damp places, and the sluggish buff-coloured caterpillars feed intermittently throughout the winter until the following spring, producing a single brood from June until August. **Habitat and distribution** Prefers damp woodland glades and scrubby, overgrown sites where the soil is heavy and vegetation lush, occasionally visiting gardens. Found throughout southern England, Wales, Ireland and parts of Scotland, but absent from parts of north-west England and northern Scotland.

Gatekeeper *Pyronia tithonus*
This bright little butterfly, sometimes called the Hedge Brown, is a lover of flowery hedgerows and grassy lanes bathed in sunlight, where it spends much time feeding on brambles, common fleabane and ragworts, and in gardens marjoram is a great favourite. The female differs from the male (illustrated) in being slightly larger and in lacking the broad, black sex-brand across the forewings. Both sexes have twin-pupilled eye-spots on the forewings. Eggs are either laid or dropped amongst grasses, including cock's-foot, timothy and common couch. After hibernation, the pale green or ochreous caterpillar feeds at night until fully grown, when it pupates amongst dried vegetation. Only one brood is produced, from late June until the end of August. **Habitat and distribution** Warm, sheltered places along hedgerows, lanes, scrubby bramble patches and wilder gardens. Common in the south and expanding its range northwards into County Durham. In Ireland it is restricted to the southern and eastern coastal regions.

Meadow Brown *Maniola jurtina*
The Meadow Brown is our most abundant British butterfly, occurring in huge colonies on downland. It is also found in many other flowery habitats, and often wanders into gardens, where it can become established if conditions are right. The sexes differ, the female being larger and brighter than the male, but both have the single-pupilled eyespot on the forewing. Its flight in tall, wild grasses is erratic but leisurely, and although it prefers warm, sunny days it will also fly in dull, overcast weather. The female lays or drops her eggs amongst grasses, and after hibernation the hairy green caterpillar feeds at night until the following May. Only one brood occurs, lasting from early June until late September. **Habitat and distribution** Found in any unimproved, flowery habitats, including waste ground and roadsides in towns and cities. Widely distributed throughout Britain and Ireland, absent only from Shetland and high mountaintops.

all shown slightly smaller than life size

Wall

Speckled Wood

Ringlet

Gatekeeper

Meadow Brown

Moths

Micro-moths

Green Long-horn *Adela reaumurella*
Males of this long-horn can be seen swarming around trees in bright sunshine in May and June. The female, which has much shorter antennae, lays eggs on low vegetation and the young larvae drop to the ground and feed on leaf litter from within a case made of leaf fragments. Common throughout.

Firethorn Leaf Miner
Phyllonorycter leucographella
The larvae of this tiny moth create blister-like mines on the leaves of firethorn and occasionally other trees and shrubs, causing the leaves to distort and curl. The adult moth occurs in several broods from April until October. First recorded in Great Britain in 1989, this species is now common throughout England and Wales but has also spread to Scotland and Ireland.

Orchard Ermine *Yponomeuta padella*
One of eight similar species. The larvae can cause much damage to cultivated *Prunus* trees in gardens and orchards. They live gregariously in webs, which they extend as the branches are defoliated, finally pupating inside the web. Flies in July and August; widely distributed and abundant in the south.

Large Fruit-tree Tortrix *Archips podana*
A typically bell-shaped tortrix, this variable species is often seen in gardens, flying around shrubs in the sunshine. The green larva lives in a shelter made from spun leaves or flowers; it causes damage to fruit trees, but feeds on a huge range of other trees and shrubs. Flies from late June to early August; widely distributed but more common in the south.

Light Brown Apple Moth *Epiphyas postvittana*
This variable tortrix often has a distinctive 'V'-shaped marking when resting. Often found in gardens on *Euonymus*, and frequently disturbed from shrubs by day. The yellowish-green larva feeds on a wide range of wild and cultivated plants. Flies from May to October in two broods. Indigenous to Australia, it was first recorded in Cornwall 80 years ago and has quickly spread northwards.

Green Oak Tortrix *Tortrix viridana*
The larvae are sometimes responsible for completely defoliating mature oak trees, but are an important food for young birds in spring. They feed on several other tree species and can often be seen dangling from foliage on a silken thread. Flies from June to August and is found wherever oak trees grow.

Codling Moth *Cydia pomonella*
A notorious pest of apples, the larvae burrow into the core. Flies from June to August and occasionally again in the autumn. Found mainly in gardens and orchards throughout Britain and Ireland, but scarcer further north.

Twenty-plume or **Many-plumed Moth**
Alucita hexadactyla
Not a true plume moth, it can often be found resting indoors on walls, where it hibernates as an adult and emerges to breed the following spring. It has become common in town gardens due to the planting of honeysuckle; the pinkish larvae feed on the buds, flowers and pollen. Widely distributed.

Grass-veneer *Crambus pascuella*
Grass-veneer *Agriphila tristella*
These are two of the commonest of 40 or so species of grass-moth that are often disturbed by day from rough, grassy places. They appear bigger in flight than at rest, when they virtually disappear, head downwards, on a grass stem. The larvae probably feed on pith, low down in the stems of various grasses. The former flies from June to August, the latter from July to September; both are common and widespread throughout Britain and Ireland.

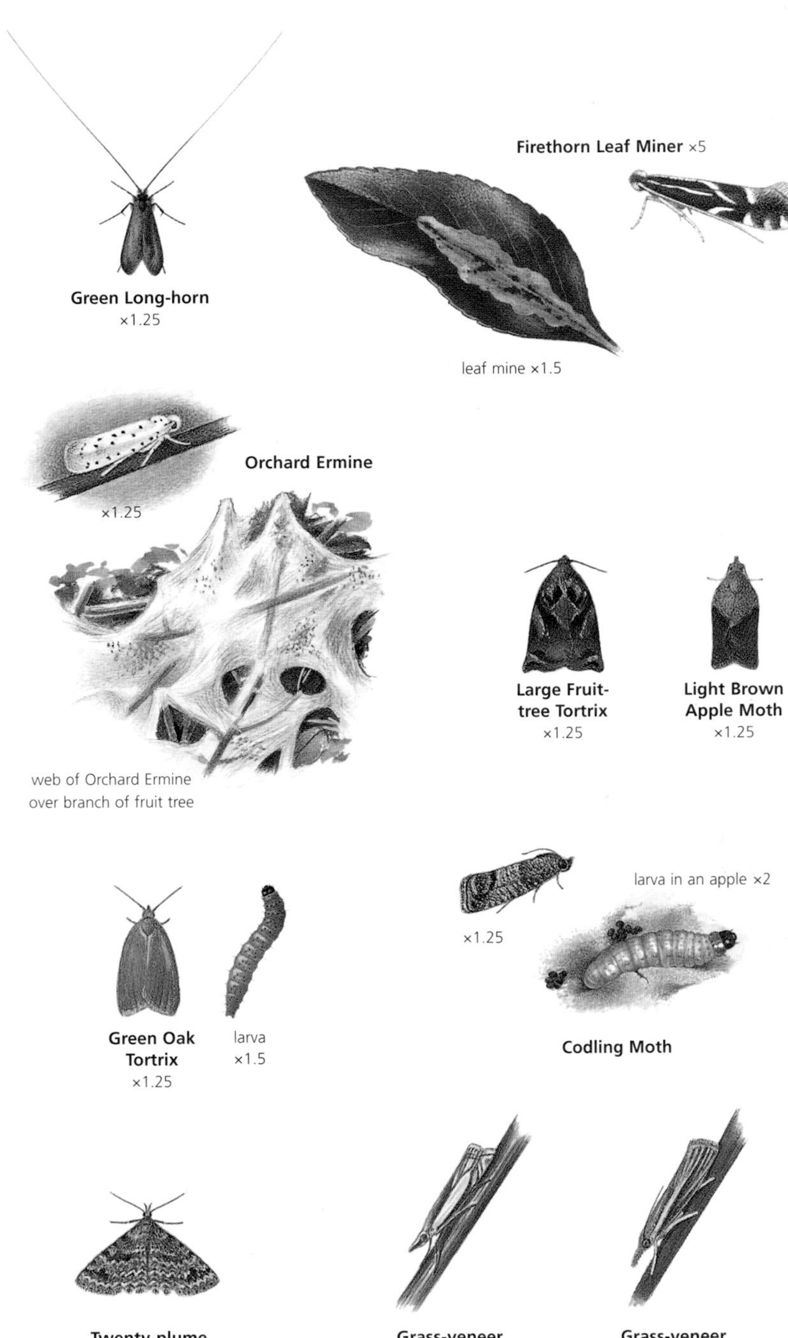

Firethorn Leaf Miner ×5
Green Long-horn
×1.25
leaf mine ×1.5
Orchard Ermine
×1.25
web of Orchard Ermine
over branch of fruit tree
Large Fruit-
tree Tortrix
×1.25
Light Brown
Apple Moth
×1.25
larva in an apple ×2
×1.25
Green Oak
Tortrix
×1.25
larva
×1.5
Codling Moth
Twenty-plume
×1.25
Grass-veneer
Crambus pascuella
×1.25
Grass-veneer
Agriphila tristella
×1.25

Garden Pebble *Evergestis forficalis*
The larvae sometimes cause considerable damage to brassicas in gardens and allotments, and less often to turnip and horse-radish, often ruining cabbages by burrowing right into the heart. Flies from May to September in two broods. Found throughout Britain and Ireland; most common around human habitation.

Small Magpie *Anania hortulata*
A conspicuous micro-moth, which flies at dusk and at night but is also easily disturbed from vegetation by day. The larva is green with a dark stripe along its back and a dark head. It lives concealed in a rolled leaf of common nettle and pupates in late spring after hibernation. The Small Magpie adult flies from May to September. Common in gardens, hedgerows and waste ground, it is widely distributed and abundant in the south but more local in the north.

Mother of Pearl *Pleuroptya ruralis*
One of the largest micro-moths, the Mother of Pearl, like the Small Magpie, is often seen when disturbed from vegetation by day. The larva is plain, shiny green, and lives in rolled leaves of common nettle and sometimes elm trees, pupating in late spring after hibernation. The Mother of Pearl adult flies from June to October. Common in gardens, woodland and waste ground, it is widely distributed throughout Britain and Ireland.

Mint Moth *Pyrausta aurata*
This distinctive little moth flies at night, but is most often seen flying in the sunshine around garden mints or marjoram, the larval foodplants. Flies from May to August in two broods, and has a scattered distribution throughout most of Britain.

Gold Triangle *Hypsopygia costalis*
An unmistakable pyralid, sometimes found indoors, whose larvae eat dry vegetation. Flies in July and August and is fairly common in gardens and farmland in southern England.

Wax Moth *Galleria mellonella*
The female is usually plainer and larger than the male. Often mistaken for a macro moth, they are found mainly around beehives. The larvae feed on the honeycomb, making destructive, silk-lined galleries through the wax. Flies from June to October, in two broods. It is widespread but has become much less common.

Bee Moth *Aphomia sociella*
The sexes are distinct, the male being smaller and more brightly marked. Larvae feed on the combs and detritus in the nests of bumblebees and wasps, mainly those above ground such as those built in bird nestboxes. Flies from June to August; widespread and common in most of Britain and Ireland.

White Plume *Pterophorus pentadactyla*
The pure white wings are split into five feathery plumes, only two of which are visible at rest. Sometimes disturbed by day from hedgerows and gardens where convolvulus, the larval foodplant, grows. The larva, which is green and clothed in long white hairs, hibernates when small. Flies in June and July and occasionally again in September.

Common Plume *Emmelina monodactyla*
The Common Plume can be easily identified by its distinctive resting posture, with tightly rolled wings forming a cross shape. By day it can be found resting on walls and windows and may be disturbed from vegetation; at night it visits a variety of flowers and is often attracted to light. The green hairy larva feeds mainly on various kinds of bindweed. Adults hibernate and have been recorded in every month of the year. The commonest of 45 species of plume moths occurring in Britain, it is widespread but more local in Scotland.

all shown ×1.25
except where indicated

Garden Pebble

larva in nettle leaf
×1.5

Small Magpie

Mother of Pearl

Mint Moth

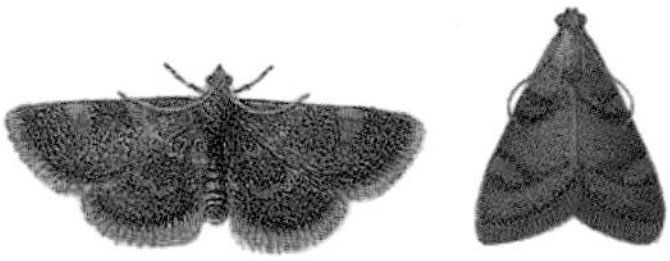

Gold Triangle

Wax Moth

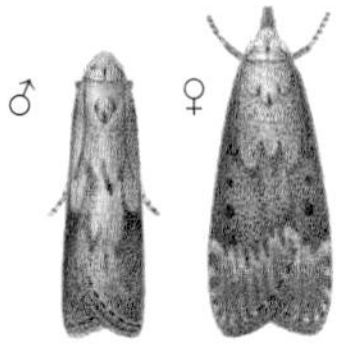

♂ ♀

Bee Moth

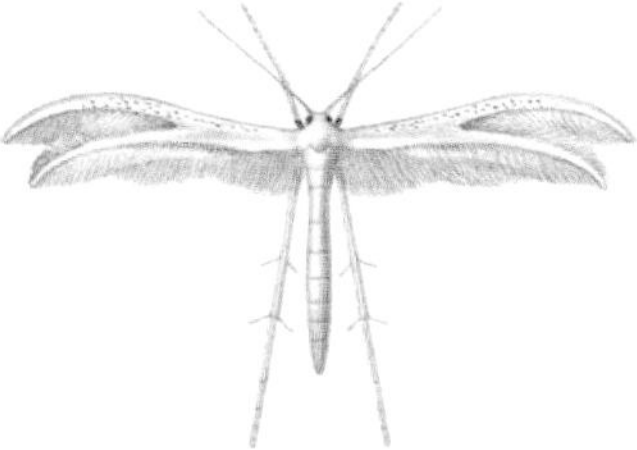

White Plume

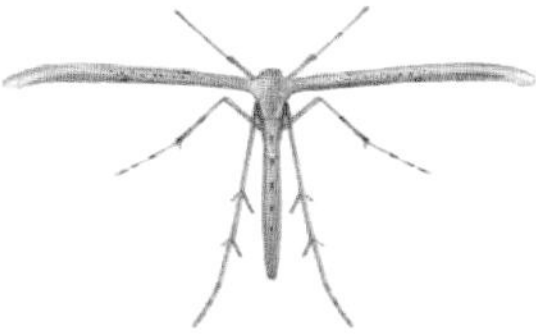

Common Plume

Swift moths and Leopard Moth

Swift moths are primitive moths, with three of the five British species occurring regularly in gardens. The adults have reduced tongues, making them incapable of feeding, and very short antennae. Females drop their tiny black eggs in flight, over grassy herbage. The off-white, grub-like larvae, with shiny orange-brown heads, feed on the roots of grasses and herbs, taking from one to two years to complete their growth. Two species may cause some damage to cultivated plants in gardens and allotments.

Orange Swift *Triodia sylvina*
The male is generally a shade of orange-buff, with irregular bands, while the female is usually larger, duller, and may appear very plain. However, both sexes are variable in size and markings. The larva is a root feeder but is unlikely to cause damage in the garden. Flies in July and August and is found throughout Britain, but is scarcer in the north and absent from Ireland.

Ghost Moth *Hepialus humuli*
Males of the silvery-white Ghost Moth attract mates by releasing pheromones while performing their ghost-like rising and falling dance over grassland at dusk. The female is larger than the male, with a golden ground-colour which can be paler in northern specimens. Northern males are creamy white, with faint markings similar to those of the female. The eggs are dropped among grasses and herbs, and larvae live for up to two years, feeding on roots, tubers and corms, sometimes causing considerable damage to flowers and vegetables. In suitable habitats, it is estimated that up to 50,000 larvae can be sustained in an acre. Flies from June until August and occurs throughout all of Britain and Ireland.

Common Swift *Korscheltellus lupulina*
The root-feeding larvae of this species, the commonest of the swifts, may cause some damage in cultivated places. The male's markings vary, from lines of bold white bands to specimens with unmarked, plain greyish-brown forewings. Females are larger and plainer. The slender, cream-coloured larva burrows through the soil, feeding for up to two years on the roots of grasses, weeds and cultivated plants. It pupates in the soil in spring and adults emerge after a month in one generation from May until July. Found throughout Britain; common in the south, scarcer further north and in Ireland.

Leopard Moth *Zuezera pyrina*
A distinctive moth, with spotted wings that appear worn and transparent near the tips, and a long abdomen which, especially in the female, projects well beyond the wing tips. The larva feeds for up to three years inside the outer branches of various deciduous trees, including garden species such as apple, cherry, black currant and lilac, often causing the terminal leaves to wilt. It pupates in a larval chamber and adults fly from late June until August. Quite common in gardens, parks and orchards throughout most of England and Wales; absent from Scotland and Ireland.

Clearwing moths

Despite being sun-loving, day-flying moths, clearwings are seldom seen and their presence is more often detected by old exit holes and empty pupal cases protruding from host plants. When newly emerged, the wings are covered in scales; most of these are lost after the first flight, giving some species a wasp-like appearance.

Currant Clearwing *Synanthedon tipuliformis*
An inconspicuous little moth with a rapid flight, most likely to be seen on sunny afternoons when the female is mainly active, laying her eggs on red currant and black currant bushes. The dull white larva lives for a year, tunnelling through the stems of the foodplant, causing minor damage. Dormant throughout the winter, it resumes feeding in spring and pupates concealed within the stem. Flies from May until July. Widespread but local, it has become rarer in recent decades as fewer currants are grown.

Red-belted Clearwing
Synanthedon myopaeformis
Most likely to be seen flying above and around apple trees on sunny afternoons, or resting on the trunks in the evening. Eggs are laid on the bark of cultivated apple trees, but pear, almond, rowan and hawthorn are also used. The larva feeds on the inner bark, where it pupates after a year, sometimes giving its presence away by leaving piles of fine, reddish droppings in crevices. The same mature trees can be used for many years, and old emergence holes and protruding empty pupal cases may be evident. Flies from mid-June until August. Widespread from the Midlands southwards.

Hornet Moth *Sesia apiformis*
The largest clearwing, which relies on its resemblance to the Hornet for protection. It is most likely to be seen on a tree trunk in the early morning, soon after having emerged. Mating takes place on the trunk and by mid-morning the female disperses to lay her eggs at the base of the trunks of black-poplar and its cultivated hybrids. The larva lives for up to three years, tunnelling low down in the wood and roots, and trees that are used repeatedly are sometimes killed as a result. Pupation is in a cocoon under the surface of the bark, and in mid-June empty pupal cases and emergence holes may be conspicuous around the base of the trunks. The flight period lasts well into July. Distribution is mainly in southern and eastern England and parts of Wales and Ireland.

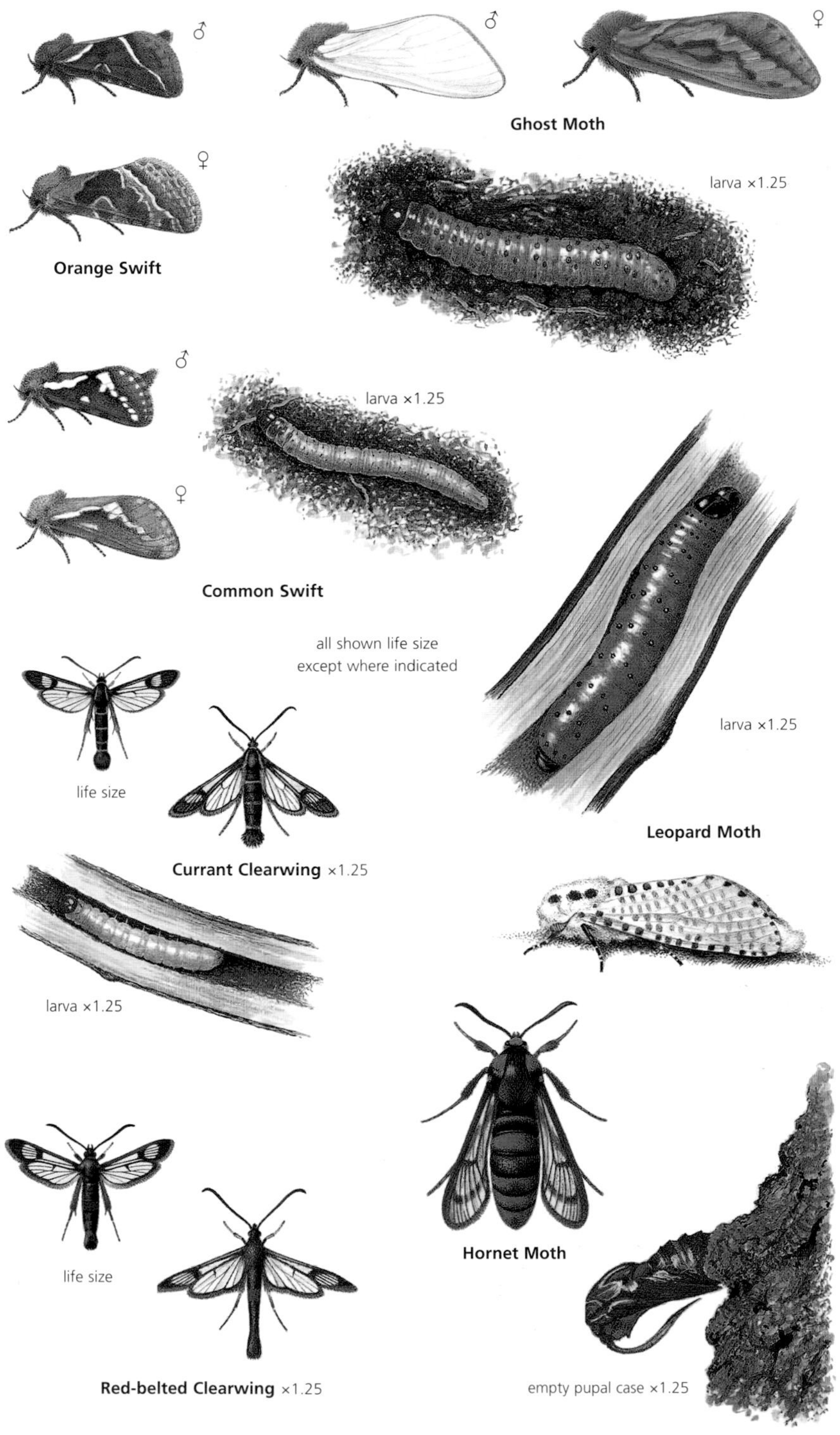

♂
♂
♀
Ghost Moth
♀
larva ×1.25
Orange Swift
♂
larva ×1.25
♀
Common Swift
all shown life size
except where indicated
larva ×1.25
life size
Leopard Moth
Currant Clearwing ×1.25
larva ×1.25
Hornet Moth
life size
Red-belted Clearwing ×1.25
empty pupal case ×1.25

Eggars and hook-tips

Pebble Hook-tip *Drepana falcataria*
When resting, the unusual hooked wings, with their 'pebble'-shaped central mark, give the Pebble Hook-tip the 'unmoth-like' appearance of a dead birch leaf. The sexes are similar, but specimens from Scotland have a paler ground-colour and darker markings. Eggs are laid on the underside of birch and alder leaves, and the larvae have modified rear legs which are not used and form a raised, blunt point. Pupation is in a cocoon spun between leaves, and the moths fly in two broods, in May and June, and in August and September. Widespread in Britain, with thinly scattered records from Ireland.

Lackey *Malacosoma neustria*
Like other eggars, the variably-coloured Lackey has a characteristic resting posture, with the hindwings showing in front of the forewings. The female, which is larger than the male, lays her eggs in a band around a twig of the foodplant, which includes many trees and shrubs, and especially in gardens, apple, cherry, hawthorn and plum. The most conspicuous part of the life cycle is the early larval stage, when groups of gregarious larvae cluster together on the foodplant on a communal web. Flies in July and August. Common in the south.

December Moth *Poecilocampa populi*
A handsome moth unlikely to be confused with other species since it flies from October, through the winter into January. The larger female lays her eggs on the bark of various deciduous trees. The eggs overwinter and the larvae feed from April until June, pupating in a cocoon on or below the ground. Common in parks and gardens throughout Britain and Ireland.

Hawk-moths

Hawk-moths are the most striking and enigmatic of all the moth families. There are 18 British species, including nine immigrants, that range in size from 'bee-hawks' to Britain's largest moth, the Death's-head Hawk-moth, whose larvae are sometimes found on potato leaves. Their flight is strong and manoeuvrable, and at rest most hold their wings in an elegant, delta-winged posture. Some species have exceptionally long tongues for probing deep into tubular flowers, whilst others have short tongues and are incapable of feeding. The larvae are smooth and cylindrical, often with eye-spots or stripes, and all except one, the Small Elephant Hawk-moth, have a long, curved tail horn.

Privet Hawk-moth *Sphinx ligustri*
This is one of the largest of our resident moths, and the one whose larvae were frequently collected by boys on their way to school in the days when privet hedges were neglected and allowed to grow wild. The forewings of the Privet Hawk-moth are brown, streaked with grey and black, and the moth relies on its camouflage for protection when resting on a tree trunk. However, if disturbed it raises its forewings to display its pink-and-black-banded hindwings and abdomen as a warning to predators that it may be distasteful, even though this is not the case with most hawk-moths. It flies after dark and feeds from a variety of flowers. The eggs are laid singly or in small groups on the leaves of wild and garden privet, but the larva also eats ash, lilac, snowberry and honeysuckle. The feeding damage done to leaves, and droppings on paths, are often noticed before the larva is seen, as it hangs, sphinx-like, at rest concealed amongst the leaves. The shiny chestnut-brown pupa is formed in August or September, in a chamber up to 15cm below ground, where it remains throughout the winter until the following June or July. Still common, although less so in parks and gardens since the tidying and trimming of privet hedges. Found throughout England and Wales, but more common in the south, with few records from Scotland.

Hummingbird Hawk-moth
Macroglossum stellatarum
Reports of a small hummingbirds seen feeding from garden flowers invariably turn out to be the Hummingbird Hawk-moth, as this active, sun-loving insect has similar habits, probing from flower to flower with a whirring blur of wings and a discernable hum. It also flies in dull weather and at night, constantly searching for nectar, which can be from flowers growing almost anywhere, from desolate cliff-tops to window boxes high on city centre flats. Nearly all the moths seen in Britain are migrants from southern Europe and Africa, which begin to arrive in spring, but in more recent decades, like other migrant insects such as the Red Admiral butterfly, more individuals are able to survive our increasingly milder winters, particularly in the south-west. Eggs are laid mostly on bedstraws and red valerian and the larvae grow quickly, with two or more broods produced between April and September. Hibernation takes place in crevices, sheds and unheated rooms, with clothing or curtains sometimes chosen as the resting place. Numbers vary from year to year, but in good years individuals can occur anywhere in the country.

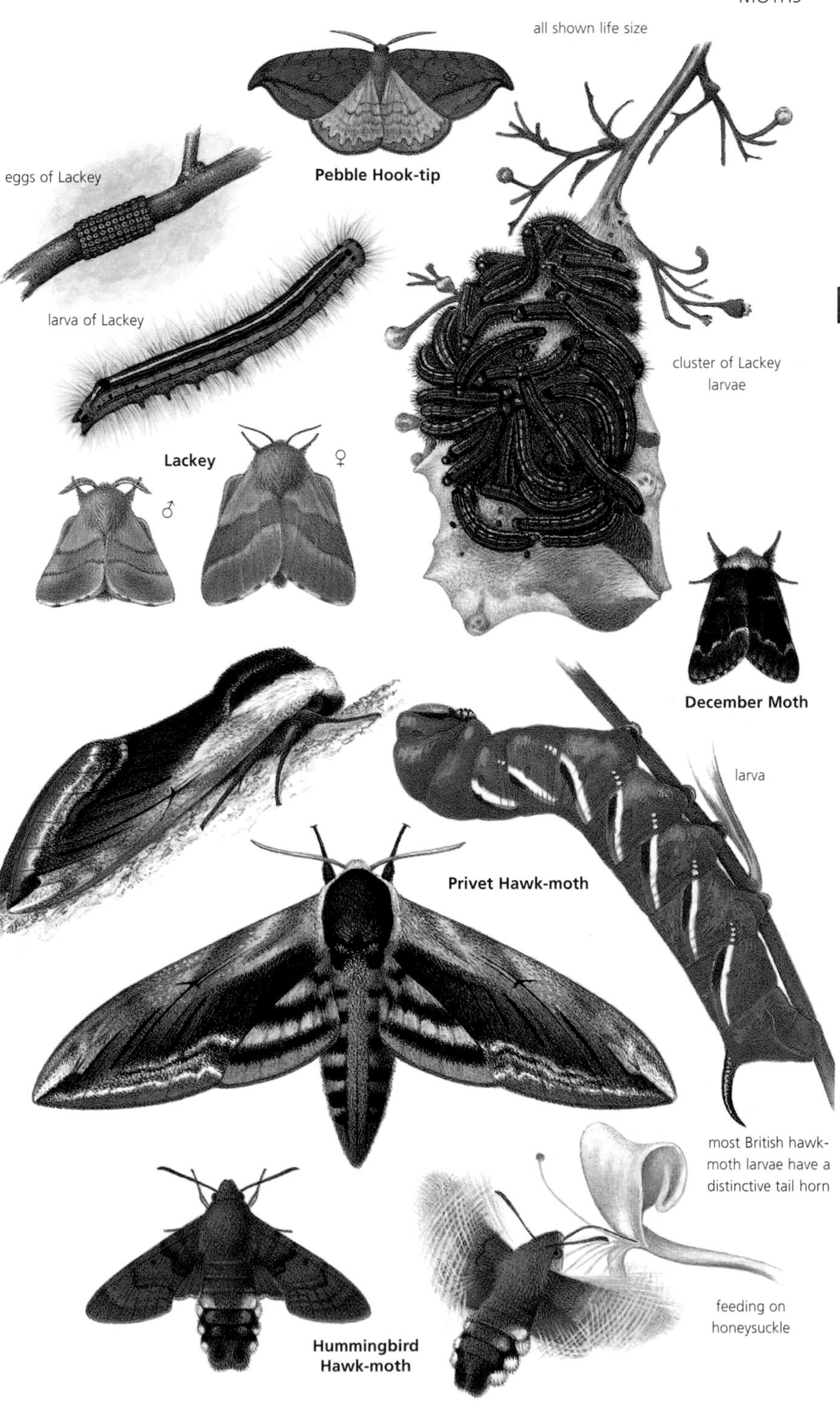
all shown life size
Pebble Hook-tip
eggs of Lackey
larva of Lackey
cluster of Lackey larvae
Lackey
♂
♀
December Moth
larva
Privet Hawk-moth
most British hawk-moth larvae have a distinctive tail horn
feeding on honeysuckle
Hummingbird Hawk-moth

Elephant Hawk-moth *Deilephila elpenor*
This beautiful and distinctive moth rests concealed in vegetation by day and only becomes active after sunset, when it visits a variety of garden flowers such as honeysuckle, valerians and buddleias. It gets its name from the larva, which has an elephant-like 'trunk' that can be retracted and puffed out when alarmed, creating a startling, snake-like appearance. The larva, which may be green or brown with four conspicuous eye-spots, is familiar to gardeners as it is often found eating garden fuchsias and bog-bean, as well as the more usual willowherbs and bedstraws. Sometimes found feeding on willowherb or bog-bean growing in ponds, it can withstand immersion, and is capable of wriggling some distance to the safety of the bank. Pupation is in a cocoon on the ground, amongst leaf litter and detritus, and the pupa overwinters until the following May, when the first moths emerge, flying until July. Occasionally a small second brood appears in August. Common throughout England, Wales and Ireland, expanding its range northwards, but scarcer in Scotland.

The following three closely related hawk-moths have cryptically marked forewings with scalloped margins, which, in the Eyed Hawk-moth especially, conceal brightly marked hindwings. The adults have reduced tongues and are unable to feed. The similar-looking larvae are greenish blue with pale stripes.

Lime Hawk-moth *Mimas tiliae*
One of the most variable of the hawk-moths; the sexes also differ, the female being more khaki-brown, whereas the male is greener, usually with greater contrast to the markings. In some specimens these markings may be reduced to a single spot, with the ground-colour orange-brown, yellow or green. A frequent moth in towns and cities where avenues of lime trees are commonplace. The Lime Hawk-moth can sometimes be found at rest on tree trunks or fence posts in the daytime, when it can resemble a withered leaf or piece of twisted bark. The bright green-and-yellow-striped larva is best distinguished by its pale blue tail, beneath which is a cluster of yellowish-red tubercles. When fully grown it descends to the ground and can often be found wandering in search of a suitable place to pupate; to assist its concealment it turns a dull greyish brown before burrowing just below the surface to pupate. Only one brood is produced, flying from May until early July. Common in southern Britain and has spread to northern England and Ireland, but is absent from west Wales and Scotland.

Eyed Hawk-moth *Smerinthus ocellata*
At rest, the beautiful cryptic shades on the forewings of the Eyed Hawk-moth provide perfect camouflage on the gnarled trunks of old willow or apple trees, but can give way to a startling display when the moth is disturbed. From a contorted piece of bark it turns into a staring predator, its abdomen turning into a nose or beak, capable of frightening any insectivorous bird. The larva is pale blue-green, with white stripes and a distinctive blue horn. Its main foodplants are willows and sallows, but in gardens and orchards some species of *Prunus* and apple trees are also used, particularly the large-leaved apple varieties. When fully grown, the larva turns a dirty yellow and wanders some distance from its foodplant to pupate a few centimetres below ground. The pupal stage lasts until the following May, when moths start to emerge, continuing until July; occasionally, a partial second brood occurs in August and September. Quite common along streams, river banks, lanes and damp woodland where willows grow, and in towns and gardens with well-established orchards. Widely distributed in England, Wales and Ireland, but local in the north of England and absent from Scotland.

Poplar Hawk-moth *Laothoe populi*
This is the most common and widely distributed hawk-moth, a cryptically marked species with a distinctive resting posture, its hindwings projecting in front of the forewings. The ash-grey, scalloped wings are marbled with darker bands and often have an attractive purple tinge, although some specimens, especially some females, may have a pinkish-buff ground-colour. The hindwings have a rusty patch, which is obscured by the forewings when the moth is at rest but is flashed when disturbed. Although the markings of the sexes may be similar, the male can be identified by the slender, upward-curving abdomen. Adult Poplar Hawk-moths do not feed, but are active from dusk and their heavy whirring flight often leads them to lighted windows after dark. The female lays her eggs on willows and poplars, including aspen and sallow, and when it is not eating, the stocky larva hangs concealed amongst the foliage. Its colour changes to a dirty green before pupation, which takes place a few centimetres below the surface, near the trunks of the foodplant, where it passes winter. The adults appear from mid May until August, and sometimes in a smaller second brood in August and September. Found commonly throughout Britain and Ireland.

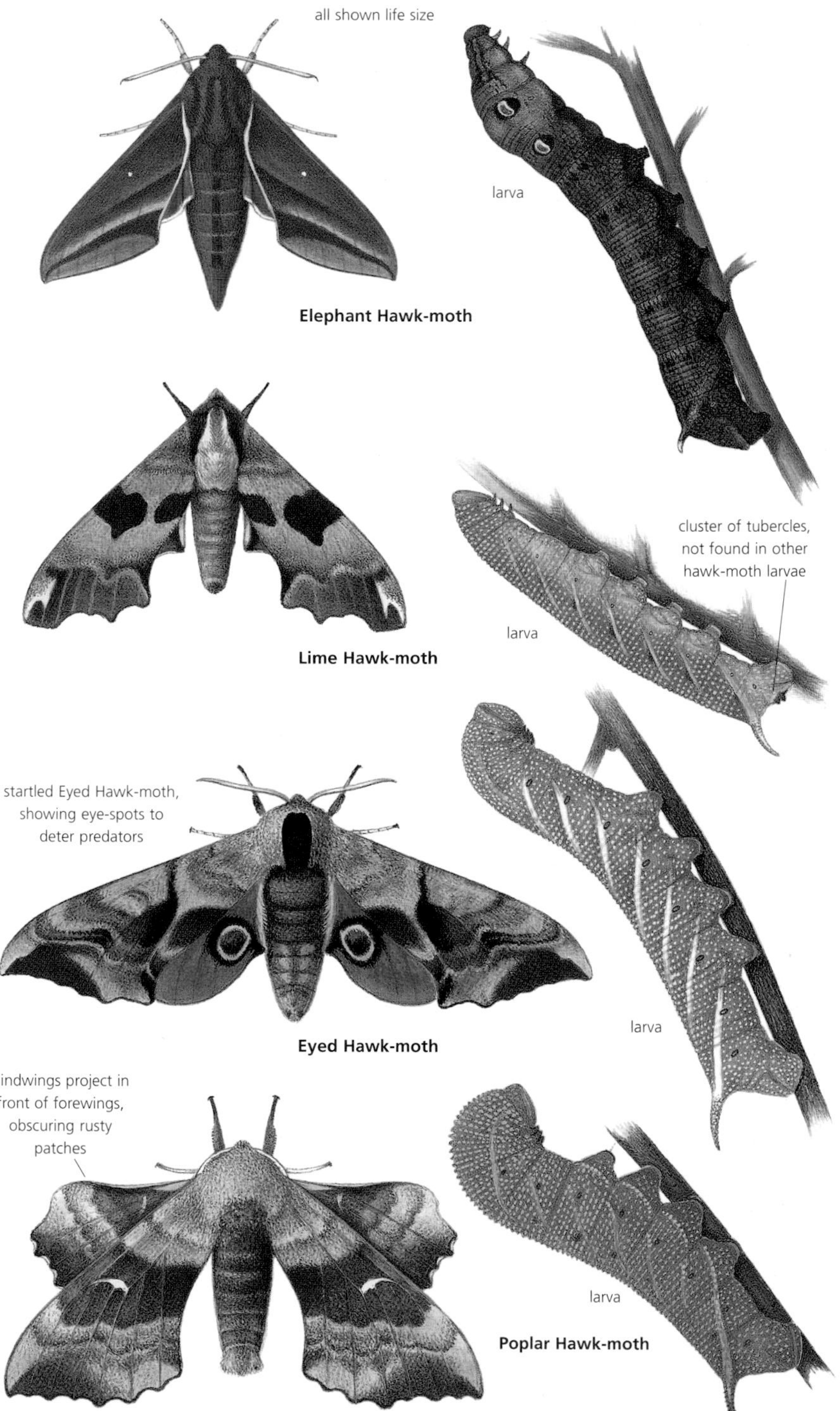

Elephant Hawk-moth

Lime Hawk-moth

Eyed Hawk-moth

Poplar Hawk-moth

Geometrid moths

Small Dusty Wave *Idaea seriata*
This tiny wave is often found on walls inside houses, and may be mistaken for one of the pug moths as it has a similar resting posture. The larva eats ivy and herbaceous weeds such as dandelion and docks. It occurs throughout England and parts of Wales and Scotland, flying in two broods between June and September.

Riband Wave *Idaea aversata*
The markings on this large wave vary considerably, with the outer two lines often forming a dark band. The larva, which hibernates when small, feeds on a wide range of herbaceous plants such as docks, chickweed and dandelion. One or two broods occur, from June until October; found throughout Britain and Ireland.

Blood-vein *Timandra comae*
The strong 'blood-vein' line that runs through the wings of this common moth help disrupt its shape, giving it protection when at rest. Eggs are laid on various low-growing herbs, especially docks, common sorrel and knotgrass, growing in well-vegetated, often damp habitats. Flies between May and November in up to three broods. Fairly common throughout England and Wales, but rare in Scotland and Ireland.

Garden Carpet *Xanthorhoe fluctuata*
Perhaps the most common geometrid moth in gardens and allotments, often found by day on walls and tree trunks. The Garden Carpet is distinctively marked, although some specimens, especially those in the north, appear quite dark. The larva feeds on both wild and cultivated members of the cabbage family. Flies in up to three broods in the south, two in the north, the flight period lasting from April until October.

Yellow Shell *Camptogramma bilineata*
This varies from pale yellow with slightly darker wavy lines to specimens that are very dark, the latter mostly found in the north and west. Often disturbed by day and less often attracted to light than many other geometrids. Larval foodplants include bedstraws, docks, chickweed and various other low-growing herbs. Flies from June until August. Common throughout Britain and Ireland in many habitats.

Common Carpet *Epirrhoe alternata*
Another frequent carpet moth, often disturbed in the daytime and regularly attracted to lighted windows at night. The larval foodplants are various bedstraws, especially cleavers, which is common on waste ground and in gardens. Flies in one or two broods from May until September. Common and widely distributed in most parts of Britain and Ireland.

Winter Moth *Operophtera brumata*
An abundant moth, whose larvae are the most important food source for many insectivorous birds in spring. The flightless, virtually wingless female emerges from her cocoon in October and uses pheromones to attract a mate. The male is conspicuous by torchlight, as the pair mate in leafless branches of virtually any deciduous tree and also some conifers, and in deepest winter, males are often seen flying weakly in car headlights. The eggs are laid in and around leaf buds and remain dormant until spring, when huge numbers of larvae often emerge to feed, sometimes causing considerable damage in orchards. Common and widely distributed throughout Britain and Ireland.

Lime-speck Pug *Eupithecia centaureata*
The Lime-speck Pug is the most distinctive of a confusing group of about 50 species of pug moths. It gains protection by mimicking a bird-dropping, allowing it to rest openly on leaves, walls or tree trunks. The larva feeds on many low-growing plants, including ragworts, yarrow, mugwort and Michaelmas-daisies. Flies in two overlapping broods between April and October. Widespread.

Common Pug *Eupithecia vulgata*
A variable species often difficult to separate from other pugs, but usually with a white, wavy outer-line, ending in a spot in the corner of the forewing. The larva feeds on the foliage of many trees, shrubs and low-growing herbage. Flies in one or two broods between May and August. Common throughout Britain and Ireland.

Magpie *Abraxas grossulariata*
One of very few poisonous geometrid moths, with distinctive warning colours that are also displayed in the larva and pupa. The Magpie moth has become much less common in recent years, due possibly to an increase in the use of insecticides to protect currant and gooseberry bushes in gardens and allotments. The larva also feeds on many other trees and shrubs, building a loose cocoon amongst leaves where the pupa is formed. Flies from June until August in a single brood. Widely distributed and still fairly common, although there has been a 70% decline in the past 50 years.

all shown life size except where indicated

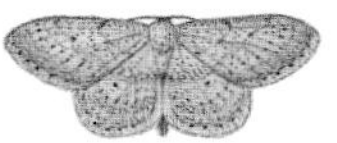

Small Dusty Wave

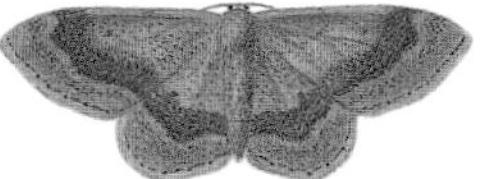

Riband Wave

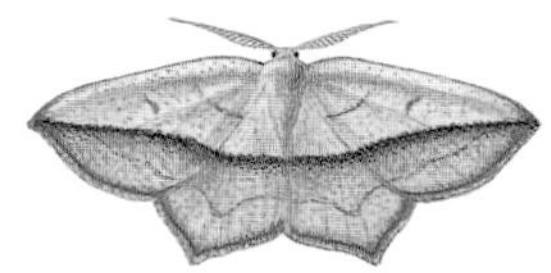

larva × 1.5

Blood-vein

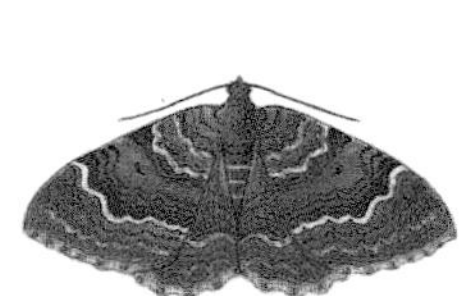

Garden Carpet

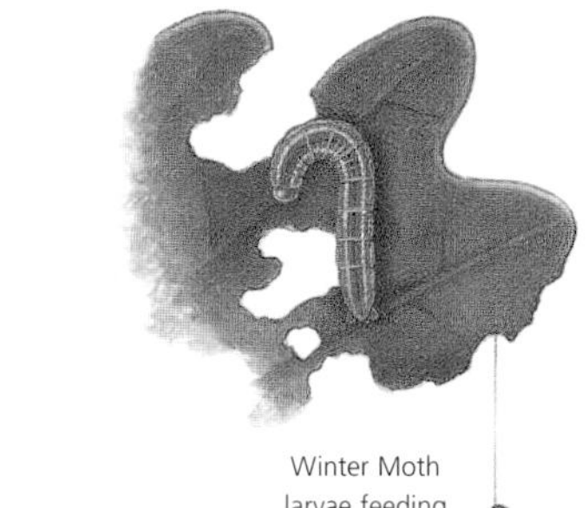

Winter Moth larvae feeding on oak

Yellow Shell

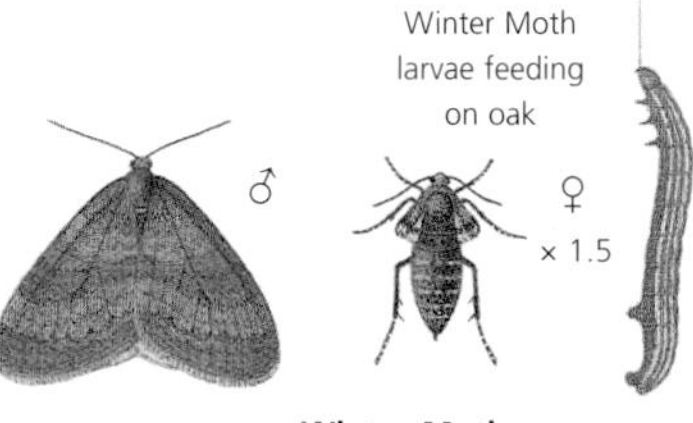

Winter Moth

Common Carpet

Lime-speck Pug

Magpie

Common Pug

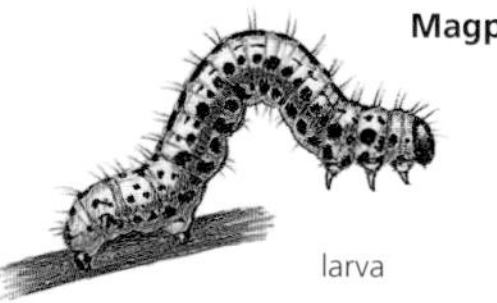

larva

Brimstone Moth *Opisthograptis luteolata*
The Brimstone is a familiar, brightly coloured moth, which emerges at dusk and is often attracted to lighted windows in the summer. The larva, which has a conspicuous hump on its back, feeds on many deciduous trees and shrubs, including hawthorn, blackthorn and rowan. Flies in up to three broods, from April until October. Common and widely distributed, and found in a variety of habitats, including gardens and hedgerows.

Swallow-tailed Moth *Ourapteryx sambucaria*
The distinctive pointed wings, with two short hindwing 'tails', are pale lemon-yellow at first but fade to a creamy white in older specimens. The slender larva feeds on many trees and shrubs, including some that are common in gardens, such as hawthorn, elder, horse-chestnut and ivy. Flies from June until August in a single brood, but individuals sometimes appear in October. Common in parks, gardens and scrub, and widely distributed throughout Britain and Ireland.

Pale Brindled Beauty *Phigalia pilosaria*
One of several geometrids that rest by day on tree trunks and which have melanic forms adapted to life in polluted industrial areas. The Pale Brindled Beauty is also typical of other winter-flying geometrids in having a spider-like wingless female. The eggs are laid on hawthorn, birches, oaks, lime, apple and many other deciduous trees, and the warty larva feeds at night, resting amongst twigs and foliage by day. Flies from January until March, in a single brood. Common in woodlands, parks and gardens throughout England, Scotland and Wales, but more local in Ireland.

Peppered Moth *Biston betularia*
This moth occurs in three named forms, with intermediates between all three also occurring regularly. The typical form is white, peppered with black, and is mostly found in unpolluted places where the air is clean and tree trunks are covered in lichens. The extreme melanic form *carbonaria* is dark sooty-brown, with two white spots either side of the thorax, and is more frequent in polluted industrial areas where trees have few lichens, and the trunks are stained black with soot. The first melanic specimens started to appear 150 years ago, but in the last 60 years, as pollution from coal-based industry has declined, the proportion of the *carbonaria* form of the Peppered Moth has also declined. The larva has a distinctive notched head, and feeds on a wide range of trees and shrubs. Flies from May until August, in many habitats throughout Britain and Ireland.

Mottled Umber *Erannis defoliaria*
The male Mottled Umber varies from creamy white with broad, ragged brown bands, to plain brick-red, speckled with darker brown. The female, which resembles a spotted spider, is wingless, and releases pheromones while clinging to leafless twigs on winter nights. The eggs hatch in spring and the distinctive larvae, which feed on many deciduous trees, are sometimes responsible for defoliating fruit trees, hence the specific name *defoliaria*. Males fly from dusk, between October and January, and are often found at rest around lighted windows at night. Found in many habitats, including woodlands, scrub and gardens throughout Britain and Ireland.

Willow Beauty *Peribatodes rhomboidaria*
This well-camouflaged geometrid moth also has a sooty-brown melanic form, which is more numerous and better concealed in polluted industrial areas. It is one of several similar, closely related species, the main distinguishing feature being the two central lines on the forewings which meet and form a dark blotch on the trailing edge. By day, moths may be found at rest on tree trunks and fence posts, and at night they visit various flowers for nectar. Eggs are laid on many trees and shrubs, including hawthorn, privet, ivy and yew, and the young, twig-like larvae hibernate and resume feeding in spring. One or two broods appear between June and October. Found commonly in many habitats, including city parks and gardens throughout Britain and Ireland.

Common Emerald *Hemithea aestivaria*
Of the ten or so species of emerald moth, the Common Emerald is the one most often seen in parks and gardens, and is distinguished by the chequered wing fringes and single, sharp point on the rear edge of the hindwing. It flies from dusk, and after dark the female lays her eggs on mugwort, where the young larvae feed before hibernation, after which they move to feed on various trees and shrubs such as birch and hawthorn. A single generation flies in June and July. Widespread, but absent from most of Scotland.

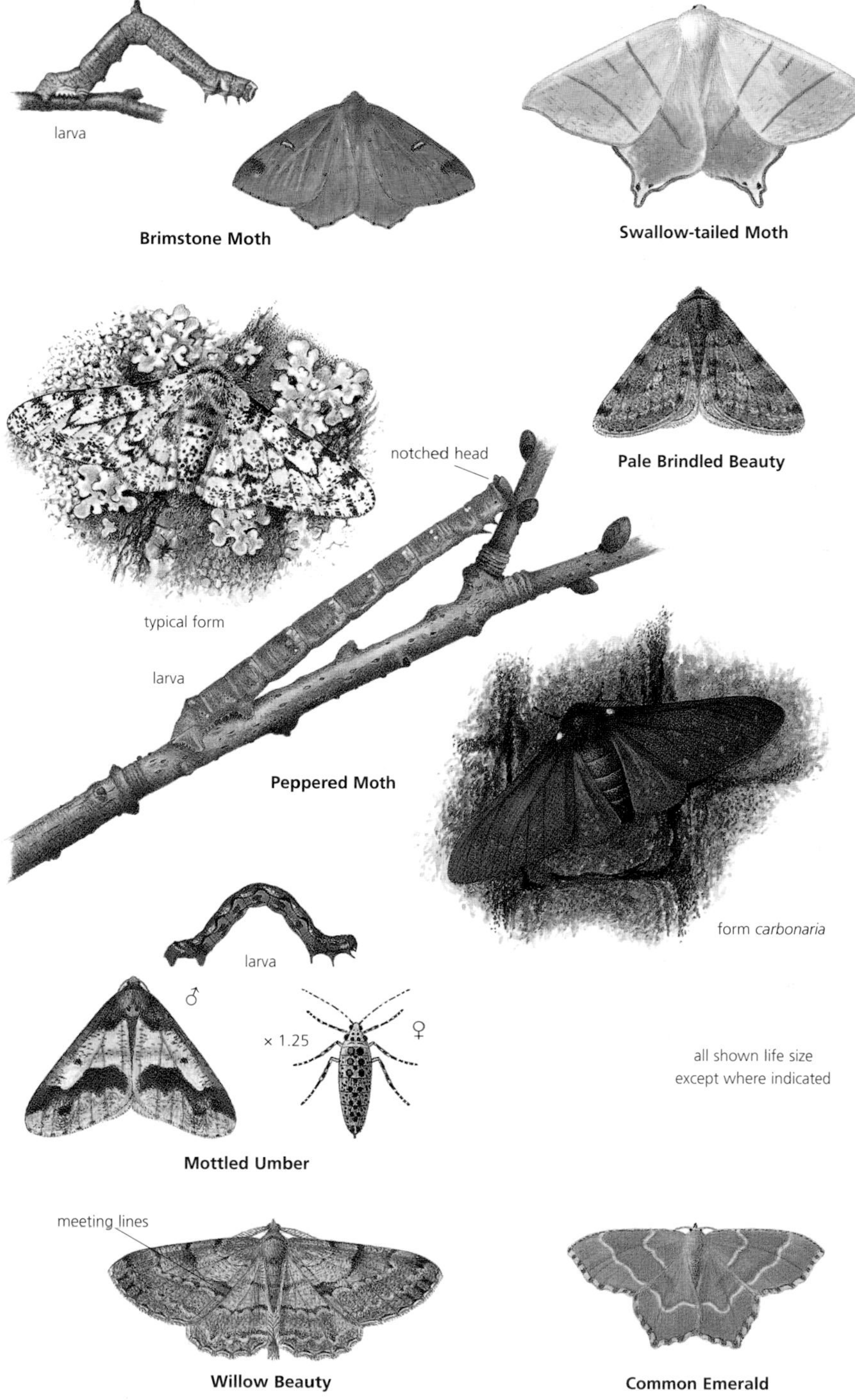
larva
Brimstone Moth
Swallow-tailed Moth
Pale Brindled Beauty
notched head
typical form
larva
Peppered Moth
form *carbonaria*
larva
♂
× 1.25
♀
Mottled Umber
all shown life size
except where indicated
meeting lines
Willow Beauty
Common Emerald

Prominents

Puss Moth *Cerura vinula*
Its furry, cat-like appearance gives the Puss Moth its name and, although there is little variation, Scottish specimens are often slightly darker. The eggs are usually laid in pairs, on the leaves of willows and poplars, and the resulting larvae are remarkable, with a saddle-like pattern designed to disrupt the overall shape. When alarmed it rears up, exposing a 'face' at the front end, at the same time waving red filaments from the rear end, to deter enemies. When fully grown it turns a dull purple and makes a tough, well-camouflaged cocoon on a tree trunk, constructed from chewed bark. The moth emerges from a hole it makes after softening the cocoon; it flies from May to July in one brood. Widely distributed in many habitats throughout Britain and Ireland.

Swallow Prominent *Pheosia tremula*
Prominents are named after the tuft of scales on the trailing edge of the forewing that are prominent when the moth is at rest. The shiny green larvae of the Swallow Prominent eat poplars and willows; those of the first brood pupate amongst leaves, whereas those that overwinter pupate below ground. Flies from April to August, in two broods in the south but only one in the north. **Similar species** The **Lesser Swallow Prominent** *P. gnoma* is usually smaller, and the white streak running in from the trailing corner is short and wedge-shaped, rather than long and thin. Both species are widespread in Britain and Ireland but commoner in the south.

Coxcomb Prominent *Ptilodon capucina*
Resembling a withered leaf, the intensity of the ground-colour varies from light reddish brown to dark purplish brown, but the rear part of the crest in all forms is a pale creamy white. The mainly green larva has a curious display posture, in which it throws back its head and lifts its rear end to expose red legs and tubercles to deter predators. It feeds on a wide range of deciduous trees and shrubs, including oaks, birches, hawthorns, beech, rowan and hazel, and is widely distributed in many habitats, making it the commonest of Britain's prominents. Flies in two broods between April and September in the south, but only one in the north.

Buff-tip *Phalera bucephala*
The Buff-tip's resemblance to a freshly broken birch twig is one of the best examples of cryptic camouflage in moths. Apart from the female being larger, the sexes are alike. The eggs are laid in batches on the undersides of the leaves of many deciduous trees and shrubs, with a preference for oaks, birches, lime and sallows. The larvae live gregariously in conspicuous clusters, and can defoliate entire branches. They rely on their warning coloration, hairy bodies and an offensive smell to protect them from predators, and when nearly fully grown, live solitarily before pupating in a chamber below ground. The winter is spent as a pupa and the moths emerge in a single brood from May to July. Found commonly throughout Britain and Ireland but more local in Scotland.

Tussocks and allies

Herald *Scoliopteryx libatrix*
This beautiful moth can be seen feeding from ivy flowers and over-ripe berries on autumn nights, prior to hibernating communally in caves, hollow trees and cool outbuildings. The eggs are laid on willows and poplars, and the slender green larva feeds concealed in the foliage from May to August. In the south, larvae may feed up quickly and produce a summer brood; otherwise, moths emerge from August and live until the following June. Plentiful throughout Britain and Ireland but more local in Scotland.

Snout *Hypena proboscidalis*
The commonest of several related species that take their name from the elongated, snout-like palps. The colour and size of the Snout varies, specimens from the second brood often being smaller and darker. It is frequently disturbed from vegetation by day, and at night visits garden flowers for nectar. The larva feeds on common nettle. The pupa is formed in a cocoon spun among leaves, with larvae from the second brood overwintering. Common throughout Britain and Ireland in many habitats where nettles abound.

Yellow-tail *Euproctis similis*
The virtually unmarked, pure white wings of the Yellow-tail resemble a small breast feather, but when disturbed by a potential predator the bright golden tail is suddenly erected, warning that this is an unpalatable species. The female, which is larger than the male and lacks the small brown spots on the forewings, uses the yellow hairs from the tip of her abdomen to protect the egg batch, which is usually placed on a leaf or twig of the foodplant. Hawthorn, blackthorn and oaks are favoured, but a wide range of deciduous trees and shrubs are used. The larvae are gregarious when young, but after hibernation they live singly, and because of their bright warning coloration are commonly encountered in gardens. Flies in July and August, although a few individuals sometimes appear in the autumn. Common in southern England but more local in Ireland and southern Scotland.

Vapourer *Orgyia antiqua*
The orange-brown male Vapourer is active by day and night and may be mistaken for a butterfly as he flies wildly around trees in the sunshine, searching for the flightless female who looks like a small, furry barrel of eggs. All her life is spent on the cocoon from which she emerged, even mating and laying her eggs there. The egg batch remains throughout the winter, and the hairy, newly-hatched larvae are dispersed, aided by air currents, to a wide variety of native and ornamental trees and shrubs, some of which may be entirely defoliated. A common moth found throughout Britain, particularly in town and city parks, and in gardens. Somewhat local in Ireland.

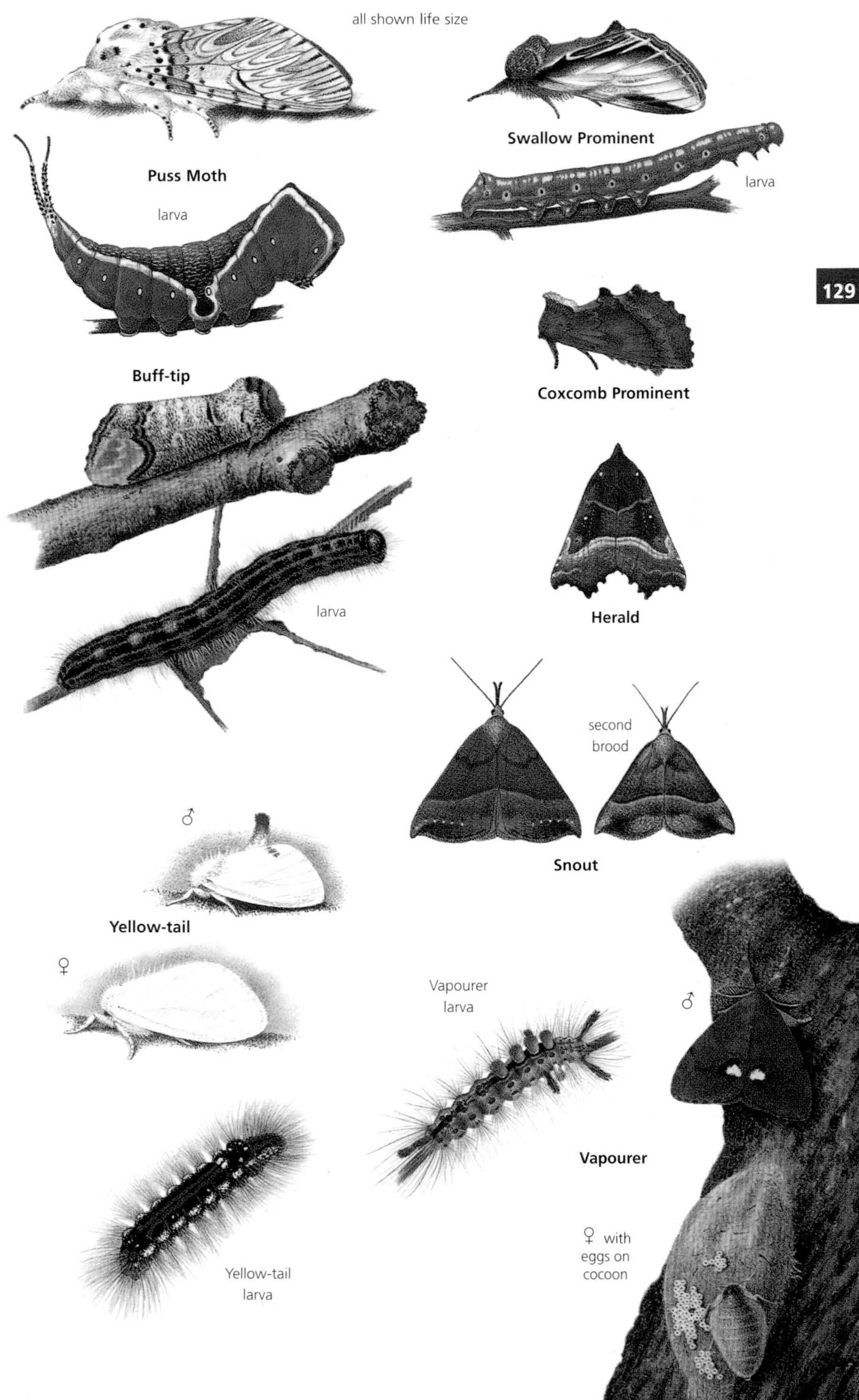
all shown life size
Swallow Prominent
larva
Puss Moth
larva
Buff-tip
larva
Coxcomb Prominent
Herald
second
brood
Snout
♂
Yellow-tail
♀
Vapourer
larva
♂
Vapourer
Yellow-tail
larva
♀ with
eggs on
cocoon

Pale Tussock *Calliteara pubibunda*
The male Pale Tussock is ash-grey, marked with darker lines and bands. Although the female is larger and paler, both are easily recognised by the furry forelegs, which are stretched out in front when resting. Darker melanic forms are becoming increasingly common in southern Britain. The hairy larva may be greenish or yellow, with dense toothbrush-like tussocks along the back and black bands between segments. It feeds from a wide variety of trees and shrubs, including hop, giving rise to the local name 'Hop-dog' in the south-east. One brood flies in May and June. Common and well distributed throughout most of Britain and Ireland, but rare in Scotland.

Tigers and allies

Some of the most beautiful moths belong to this group. They are characterised by their bright, warning coloration, particularly on the hindwings, and many of their larvae are hairy or distasteful to predators.

Buff Ermine *Spilosoma lutea*
The typical form of this variable moth has black dots forming an almost straight, inverted 'V' across the forewings, but in its extreme form is marked with vertical black striations. The female is paler than the male and similar to the White Ermine; this resemblance probably gives it some protection, as the White Ermine is an unpalatable species that predators avoid. The larva is hairy, with cream blotches along the sides, and is frequently found crawling or basking in the sun. It feeds on many low-growing herbaceous plants, including nettles, dandelions and docks, but also higher up on woody species such as honeysuckle and birches. Pupation is in a cocoon formed among leaf debris on the ground. Flies from May to July in a single brood. Common and widely distributed throughout most of Britain and Ireland, more local in the far north-east.

White Ermine *Spilosoma lubricipeda*
Probably the commonest of all the ermines and tigers, although in the past 50 years it has declined in abundance. Its ground-colour ranges from white or buff to ochreous brown in extreme cases, especially in specimens from Scotland and Ireland. Some forms resemble the Buff Ermine, but the spots, which vary in number, are more randomly scattered and lack the distinctive inverted 'V'. The abdomen is brightly marked yellow and black. They can be found openly at rest on vegetation, protected from predators by their warning coloration which indicates they are unpalatable. The eggs are laid in batches on the underside of the leaves of many low-growing plants, and the dark, hairy larva is commonly seen sunning itself or crawling quickly along the ground, as its specific name *lubricipeda*, meaning 'slippery foot', suggests. The pupa passes winter on the ground, in a silken cocoon mixed with larval hairs. Flies from May to July. Widespread throughout Britain but has become less common, local in Scotland.

Muslin Moth *Diaphora mendica*
The male Muslin Moth has distinctive smoky-grey wings, whereas those of the female are translucent silky white. In Ireland, males are creamy white, but all have a similar pattern of black spots and lack any yellow on the abdomen. The female is unusual in that she is active in the sunshine and may also be disturbed from undergrowth. The eggs are laid in rows on many common, low-growing plants such as docks, plantains and chickweeds, and the fully grown larva pupates in a cocoon made from silk mixed with its own hairs. Flies from May to June in one brood. Widespread and common in the south but more local in Scotland and Ireland.

Ruby Tiger *Phragmatobia fuliginosa*
The Ruby Tiger is less flamboyant than other tiger moths. It varies in brightness, and in the north it appears dark reddish brown, with smoky hindwings. This is the only tiger moth that has more than one brood a year in the south, and specimens from the first brood and those in the north frequently fly in the daytime. The larva feeds on a wide range of herbaceous plants such as docks, nettles and dandelions, and also on some woody plants. It also varies in colour from dark brown to buff or gingery brown, and may often be seen sunning itself in the daytime. Flies between April and September in two broods in the south and in a single brood from May to July in the far north. Widespread and common throughout Britain and Ireland.

Garden Tiger *Arctia caja*
The Garden Tiger is seldom seen, despite its flamboyant colours warning potential predators of its high toxicity. Its hairy, black-and-ginger larva, the 'woolly bear', is much more familiar, however, either spotted sunbathing or walking rapidly across paths prior to pupation. The young larva overwinters when small, becoming active again in the spring sunshine. When fully grown, the larva pupates on the ground amongst detritus, in a flimsy cocoon made from silk and hairs. A single brood appears in July and August, and the moth can be found in many habitats, including waste ground and overgrown gardens. The eggs are laid in batches on a wide range of herbaceous plants, including many weed species and cultivated plants. Still quite common throughout Britain and Ireland but has become much more infrequent in the last few decades, possibly as a result of increasingly mild winters and damp springs.

all shown life size
♀
♂
Pale Tussock
larva
Pale Tussock
♂
♀
larva
Buff Ermine
♂
♂
larva
White Ermine
♂
♀
larva
Muslin Moth
larva
Ruby Tiger
Garden Tiger
larva

Cinnabar *Tyria jacobaeae*
This familiar day-flying moth is equally well known in its larval stage, as the yellow-and-black-banded larvae feed conspicuously on the leaves of ragworts and, less often, on groundsel, in many cases reducing plants to skeletons. The moth has a weak, fluttering flight and is often disturbed from vegetation, but it gains protection from predators by toxins, which it obtains as a larva from the food-plant. The shiny brown pupa is formed in a loose cocoon just below ground, and lives through the winter until mid-May when the moth emerges; it flies in a single brood until August. Common and widespread throughout Britain and Ireland; more coastal above the Central Belt in Scotland.

Red Underwing *Catocala nupta*
A large, showy moth, occasionally seen feeding from buddleia in the sunshine, or resting, with its hindwings concealed, on walls or fences in the daytime, when it is readily disturbed. The larva feeds on willows and poplars and is well camouflaged by day, hiding in crevices on the bark of the foodplant. One brood appears from August to October. Well distributed in southern Britain; occasionally found as far north as southern Scotland. Recently recorded in Ireland.

Noctuid moths

This large and diverse family includes what most people regard as 'typical moths'. Many are various shades of brown and grey, giving them excellent camouflage amongst dead leaves and on tree trunks by day. Several of the larvae are pest species, commonly known as 'cutworms' from their habit of cutting through the stems of cultivated plants.

Burnished Brass *Diachrysia chrysitis*
The two metallic bands on the forewings may be joined or separated in this distinctive moth, and specimens of the second brood are often smaller. It is found in gardens, waste ground and open countryside where nettles and dead-nettles, the main larval foodplants, grow. Flies in June and July, and again in August and September in the south. Well distributed and common throughout.

Silver-Y *Autographa gamma*
The common and scientific names of this moth refer to the conspicuous silvery-white mark at the centre of each forewing. It flies by day as well as at night, and can be seen feeding and hovering around many garden flowers at dusk. The blue-green larva has reduced numbers of false legs, and feeds on many low-growing plants. Occurs in most habitats throughout Britain and Ireland, from May to September, but has been recorded in every month of the year. Common and often abundant, depending on immigration from the south, but rarely able to survive the British winter.

Grey Dagger *Acronicta psi*
This moth, and the almost identical Dark Dagger, can be separated only by microscopic examination, but their larvae are quite distinct. The larva of the Grey Dagger has a broad yellow band down the back (white and orange in the Dark Dagger), and a long black tubercle on the fourth segment. It feeds in gardens on many deciduous trees and shrubs, including roses, cotoneaster and fruit trees, although not in such densities as to cause much damage. Flies from May to July and sometimes in a second brood in autumn. Common in many habitats throughout Britain and Ireland.

Sycamore *Acronicta aceris*
A smart, ash-grey moth in its typical form; a darker grey form predominates in towns and cities. The spectacular larva, with its spiky orange tufts, can often be seen hurrying across paths, prior to pupation in a double silken cocoon, formed in a crevice. It feeds on several introduced species of tree, including horse-chestnut, sycamore and London plane, as well as field maple and oaks. Flies from June to August and is most common in urban habitats, mainly in the south-east of England.

Mullein *Cucullia verbasci*
The Mullein is rarely seen because of its bark-like, cryptic camouflage, but its larva has boldly marked warning colours, allowing it to feed openly on wild and cultivated mulleins, as well as on buddleia and figworts. Flies in parks, gardens and woodland rides, in a single brood in April and May, and is found in England south of Cumbria, and parts of Wales.

Angle Shades *Phlogophora meticulosa*
This common moth, whose unmistakable resemblance to a withered leaf means it is seldom seen, varies in colour from olive-green to reddish brown. Its larva, however, is frequently encountered among ground vegetation at any time of the year. It varies from bright green to buff-brown, according to surrounding vegetation, and feeds on many herbaceous plants, trees and shrubs. Moths visit flowers at night and are most common between May and October, but with numbers boosted by immigrants it has been recorded in every month of the year. Occurs throughout Britain and Ireland but is most frequent in the south.

all shown life size

Dark Arches *Apamea monoglypha*
This robust noctuid, whose ground-colour ranges from light brown to blackish, can be found on fence posts and walls by day, and at night often visits nectar-bearing plants in gardens. The ochreous, glossy larva lives in a chamber at the base of grasses, feeding on stems and roots and pupating below ground among grassy tussocks. Flies from June to August, and again in the autumn in the south. Common and widespread in many habitats, including gardens.

Common Rustic *Mesapamea secalis*
A very variable moth, whose most consistent feature is the white-outlined kidney mark on each forewing. The greenish larva feeds within stems of various grasses such as cock's-foot, and is sometimes a pest of cereal crops. Flies from July to August. Widely distributed, and abundant in many habitats throughout Britain and Ireland.

Blair's Shoulder-knot *Lithophane leautieri*
First recorded in 1951, Blair's Shoulder-knot has taken advantage of the popularity of conifers, such as the Leyland and Lawson's Cypress grown in gardens, allowing it to expand its range into Scotland and Ireland. Its narrow, soft-grey wings, finely etched with black, are held flat against the surface on which it rests; this, and its late flight period in October and November, make it readily identifiable. The larva is beautifully camouflaged amongst foliage, where it feeds on flowers and seeds from spring to July, pupating in the soil. Now widely distributed.

Dot Moth *Melanchra persicariae*
The Dot Moth is almost black when freshly emerged, with an obvious white 'dot' on each forewing. The larva may be green or brown, attractively marked along its length with darker scallops. It feeds on a wide range of herbaceous and woody plants, both cultivated and wild. The moth occurs in many varied habitats, in a single brood from June to August. A common garden moth in the south, which becomes increasingly scarce further north.

Cabbage Moth *Mamestra brassicae*
A drab greyish-brown moth with a kidney-shaped mark outlined in white on the forewings. The larva is more frequently encountered than the moth, as it is a serious pest of cultivated brassicas. It burrows into the heart of cabbages, leaving ragged holes and foul-smelling droppings; lettuces, onions and many other cultivated and wild plants are also eaten. When fully grown, it pupates in a cocoon in the soil. The main flight period is from May to October but it has been recorded in every month of the year. Very common in many habitats throughout Britain and Ireland, but scarcer in the north.

Common Wainscot *Mythimna pallens*
The most frequent of many straw-coloured noctuid moths that rely on their cryptic coloration for camouflage when resting in dried grasses and reeds. Individuals vary from the typical pale straw colour to reddish brown. The larva is a grass feeder and, like the moth, is ochreous-coloured and hard to see amongst grasses. Flies in the south from June until October, in two broods, and in the north in July and August, in one brood. Found in rough grassy places throughout most of Britain and Ireland.

Heart and Dart *Agrotis exclamationis*
As well as the heart and dart markings, the main distinguishing feature of this moth is the black collar, which is present in all colour forms. The fairly nondescript larva feeds on a variety of herbaceous plants. It overwinters fully grown and pupates in the following spring. It flies from May to August, reaching a peak in June or July when it becomes extremely common in gardens; occasionally a small second brood appears in September. Found abundantly throughout, but more local in the north.

Turnip Moth *Agrotis segetum*
One of several similar noctuid moths, ranging in colour from sandy brown to the commoner dark brown form. Males have pure white hindwings, which in the usually darker female are whitish grey. The larva is similar to that of the Heart and Dart. It lives below the surface and is one of the most serious crop pests in gardens and allotments, feeding on the roots of cabbage, turnip and carrots, as well as many herbaceous plants. It usually flies in two broods from May to October. Widespread in Britain and Ireland but more local in the far north; the resident population is boosted by immigrants.

Large Yellow Underwing *Noctua pronuba*
This common moth is often disturbed from low vegetation in gardens, flying rapidly for a short distance before disappearing into the undergrowth, when its bright yellow hindwings are concealed behind cryptically marked forewings, to confuse pursuing predators. The forewings are variably marked, although the stouter female is usually darker than the male. After dark it visits many nectar-bearing flowers, including buddleia and red valerian. Large batches of eggs are laid on many low-growing plants and grasses, and the green or brown larva feeds at night, sometimes causing damage to cultivated plants. The long flight period lasts from June until November, reaching a peak in August, when it is often the most abundant garden moth. Found throughout Britain and Ireland.

Setaceous Hebrew Character
Xestia c-nigrum
The distinctive, pale, 'V'-shaped marking on the forewings readily distinguishes this moth. The larva feeds at night on many plants, including nettles, chickweeds, groundsel and plantains, but is not a pest species. It has two broods in the south, between May and October, but is far more abundant in the second autumn brood; only one brood occurs in the north. Widespread throughout Britain and Ireland.

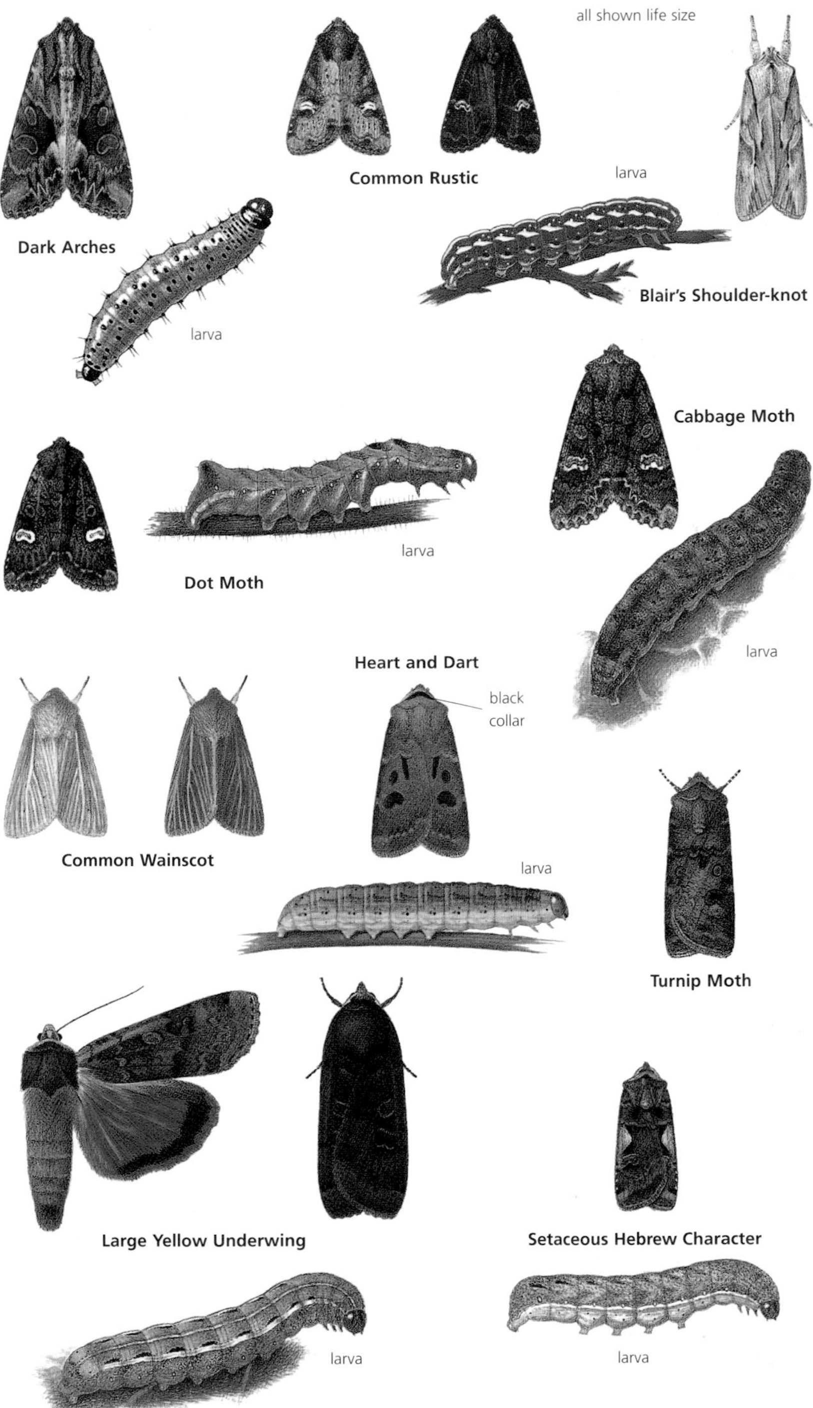
all shown life size
Dark Arches
larva
Common Rustic
larva
Blair's Shoulder-knot
Cabbage Moth
larva
Dot Moth
larva
Heart and Dart
black collar
larva
Common Wainscot
Turnip Moth
Large Yellow Underwing
larva
Setaceous Hebrew Character
larva

True flies Diptera

▲ Marmalade Hoverflies taking nectar at a thistle head.

This enormous group of insects, containing around 7,000 British species, is made up of many beneficial and some harmful species that affect our lives more than any other group. Diptera means 'two wings' and, unlike all other insects, most flies have one pair of well-developed, fully functional, membranous forewings, with the hindwings reduced to two tiny balancing organs called halteres. These help to control flight, giving tremendous manoeuvrability, allowing the fly to move in every direction, including landing upside down on the ceiling. Some species, especially parasites, lack wings altogether.

Some of the less endearing aspects of the lives of flies, particularly the various feeding habits of some adults and larvae, are often associated with disease, filth and agricultural problems. Most adults have one of two basic feeding methods: the first is by biting and sucking up liquids, as in the blood-sucking mosquitoes and horseflies, and the second is by licking and mopping, as in the Common House Fly, which also has the unpleasant habit of regurgitating over its food beforehand. Many species in the second category, however, such as the hoverflies, have more acceptable feeding methods, and are important flower pollinators as they imbibe nectar and pollen.

Fly larvae live in a wide range of habitats, and although they vary widely in appearance, they all lack the thoracic legs present in many other groups of insects. Best known amongst the aquatic species are the mosquitoes and non-biting midges, which are ubiquitous in all kinds of standing water. Muddy garden ponds also attract various hoverflies, including common drone flies and the yellow-and-black *Helophilus pendulus,* both of whose larvae live in sludge at the bottom. The drone fly larva is the 'rat-tailed maggot', which breathes with the aid of an extensible siphon that reaches to the surface of the water. More notorious are the dung and carrion feeders, which include the maggots of the bluebottles, greenbottles and flesh flies. These perform repulsive but nevertheless essential roles in breaking down decomposing organic matter, but their association with these habitats means the adults of several species are serious vectors of many bacterial and viral diseases. On the positive side, many larvae are beneficial as parasites of harmful pests, and are also important as decomposers, breaking down rotting wood and leaf litter. Species such as craneflies, whose larvae, leatherjackets, can become pests in lawns, often make up an important component in the diet of insectivorous and omnivorous birds such as Starlings and thrushes, whose young eat large numbers in the spring. They also form a part of the diet of small mammals and many invertebrates such as ground beetles and centipedes.

Of all the flies, some of the most attractive and easily recognised belong to the family Syrphidae, the hoverflies, which are associated with warm summer days when their humming flight is interspersed with visits to flowers for nectar and pollen. Many species are banded with yellow and black, and mimic wasps, both in looks and behaviour, and the drone fly is so-named from its resemblance to the male Honey Bee. Hoverfly larvae have diverse lives: some are aquatic, some live as scavengers in bees' nests, and many are well known as predators of aphids, and rank, alongside ladybirds and lacewings, as some of the most important friends of the gardener. However, less popular amongst gardeners are the larvae of a few species, notably the Large Narcissus Fly, which cause damage to the bulbs of various garden flowers. More than 280 species of hoverflies have been recorded in Britain.

Many small species of fly are abundant in gardens and can cause considerable damage in flower borders and the vegetable plot, even though the adults are rarely seen. The damage done by their early stages may be conspicuous, however, and is often the only indication of their presence. Perhaps the most notorious in the vegetable garden is the Carrot Fly, whose larvae burrow into

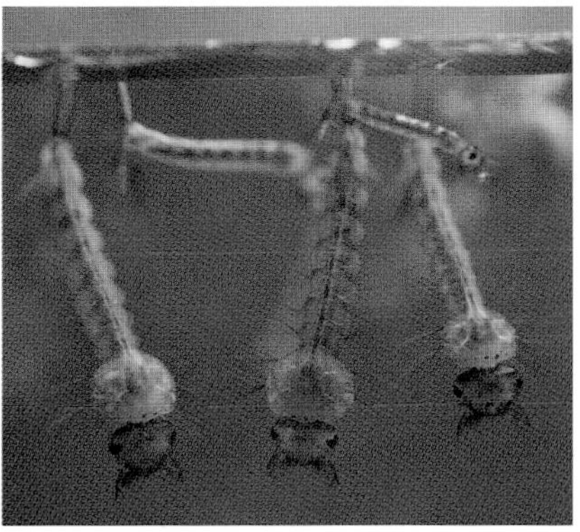

▲ Mosquito larvae hanging below the surface-film of water.

the developing roots not only of carrots but also parsnips and celery. Another celery pest with a different technique is the Celery Fly. Its larvae are leaf miners and tunnel into the leaves, creating semi-transparent, yellowish blotches.

Although a few species, such as the winter gnat, can be seen in swarms flying in the winter sunshine, most flies prefer warm sunshine. In the first months of the year, bluebottles, which, in the previous autumn mixed with the late vanessid butterflies on ivy flowers, are amongst the first insects to emerge from hibernation. They are soon accompanied by greenbottles and flesh flies, and by the time the first primroses and violets are in flower the delicate bee-fly is on the wing. Later, when hawthorn is in flower, large numbers of flies have appeared, one of the most conspicuous in late April being St Mark's Fly, which flies in lazy mating swarms, its rear legs hanging in flight. As the year progresses and the temperature rises, the abundance of flies increases and, in addition to those that fly by day and form a major part of the diet of insectivorous birds, many also fly at night. In gardens and elsewhere, thousands of these, along with many other insects, fall prey to bats, and other nocturnal predators such as spiders also take their toll of the night flyers. All these interconnections indicate that, apart from those few species that have a detrimental impact on our lives, the ecological benefits of true flies on the environment is incalculable.

Cranefly or **daddy-long-legs**
Tipula oleracea
Looking like giant mosquitoes, craneflies are most commonly seen trundling across lawns in the daytime or entering houses at night, attracted to light. However, they are quite harmless and, if captured, usually respond by shedding a leg or two. Their larvae, the well-known and destructive 'leatherjackets', feed on roots and stems of many garden plants, particularly in the spring, when they prefer damp soil. Lawns are often affected, and yellow patches may appear when larvae are abundant. Both adults and larvae form an important part of the diet of many garden birds. Adults are found throughout Britain and Ireland in the spring and summer, but are most common in May and June. **Similar species** *T. paludosa* is equally common but is browner and has proportionately shorter wings. It flies from June but is most common in August and September.

Cranefly *Limonia flavipes*
This is one of several species of cranefly with spotted wings held flat over the abdomen. Found commonly in woodland and well-vegetated places, including gardens, it is attracted to light at night, when it often bobs up and down while resting on walls. Adults are found throughout the year. Widely distributed.

Spotted Cranefly
Nephrotoma appendiculata
This common cranefly is often attracted by light into houses at night. It rests with its wings held flat, obscuring the brightly coloured abdomen. Eggs are laid in the soil, and the larvae can be destructive in the vegetable garden, feeding on roots and tubers of brassicas and potatoes, etc. Widely distributed. Frequent in gardens and allotments, and often found resting in lighted porches at night from May until September.

Winter gnat *Trichocera annulata*
Resembling a small cranefly, this is one of the few insects active on winter days, when mating swarms of males can be seen dancing up and down in the sunshine, even when snow is on the ground. The larvae feed on decaying vegetable matter and fungi. One of several similar species. Widespread; most common in the autumn and winter but found throughout the year.

Non-biting chironomid midge
Chironomus plumosus
This is one of the largest and most common of about 450 species of non-biting midges found in Britain. The male has feathery plumed antennae, and the wings of both sexes are held roofed over the abdomen. The female is plumper, and after being attracted to a mating swarm is soon grabbed by a male. The pair then leave the swarm and can be found mating on walls or surrounding vegetation. Eggs are laid in spiral strings, enclosed in transparent mucus and attached to vegetation in ponds, or on the inside of water butts. The young larva turns red after the first moult, and becomes the familiar bloodworm (see page 208), spending much of its life feeding on tiny organic particles from inside a tubular dwelling in the mud. It sometimes leaves its retreat and swims jerkily to the surface, when it becomes most vulnerable to predation. Bloodworms form an important part in the diet of many aquatic invertebrates and fishes. Common throughout, from April until September.

Spotted Mosquito *Culiseta annulata*
The female of this mosquito is probably responsible for most bites to humans, often piercing clothing and causing an allergic reaction and itchy swelling. It is our largest species, recognised by the white-and-brown-banded legs and the spotted wings, which are held flat over the striped abdomen. It breeds in many places, including garden ponds, polluted ditches and water butts, in sunny or shady spots, and is capable of breeding throughout the year.

Common Mosquito or **Gnat** *Culex pipiens*
The male Common Mosquito is harmless, and feeds only occasionally on nectar or honeydew. However, the species occurs in two forms: the *typical*, whose female feeds mainly from birds, and needs a blood meal before the eggs can develop, and the *molestus* form, whose female bites mostly humans, and does not need a blood meal for egg development. This form is also able to breed in tiny, restricted places and is active all year. Eggs are laid in floating rafts and the larvae are free-living, resting just below the surface and feeding on tiny organic particles (see page 208). They dive down and wriggle wildly if disturbed, but soon return to the surface. They pupate after about a week, and the comma-shaped pupa also hangs just under the surface until the emergence of the adult. Found virtually everywhere.

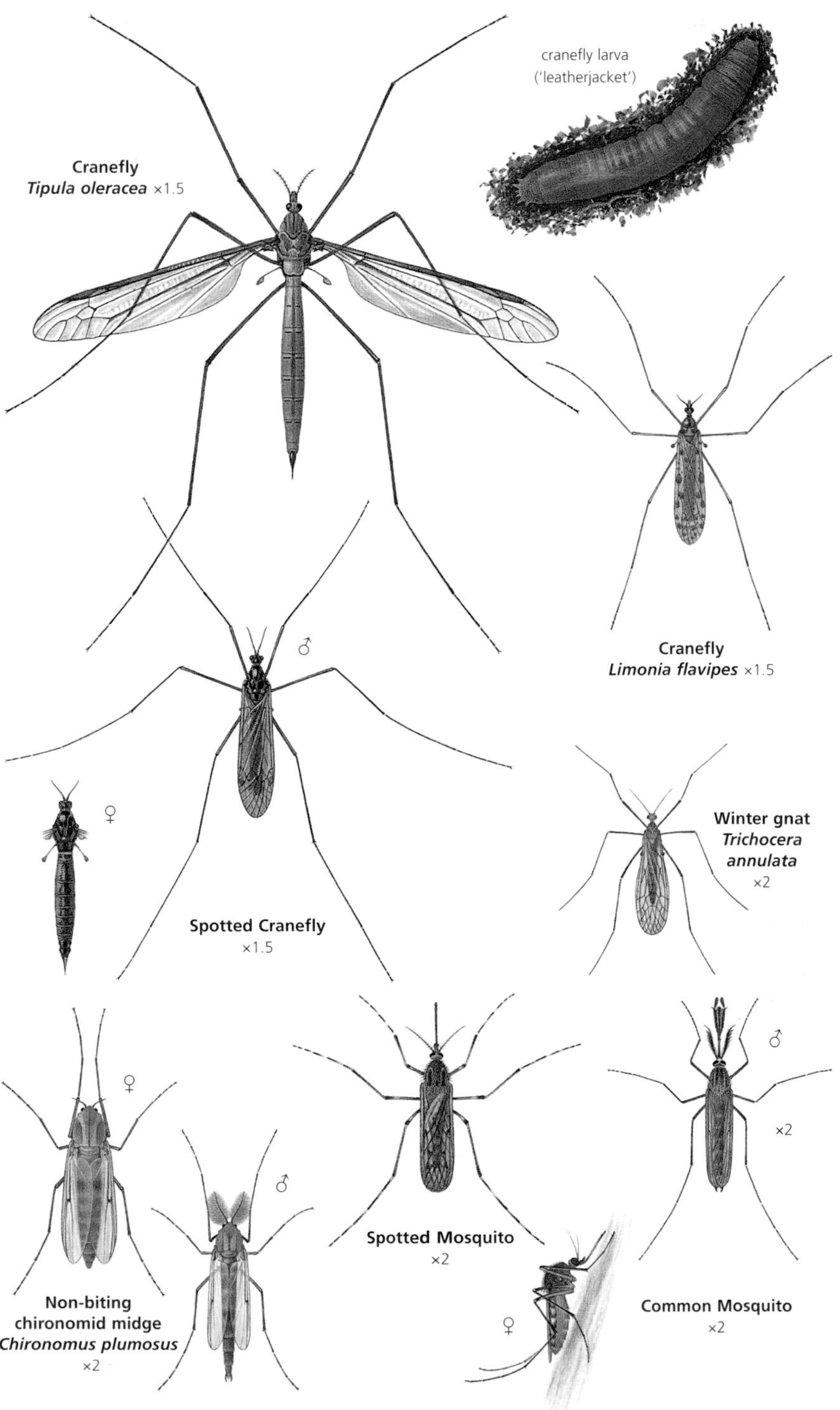

Cranefly
Tipula oleracea ×1.5

Cranefly
Limonia flavipes ×1.5

Spotted Cranefly
×1.5

Winter gnat
Trichocera annulata
×2

Non-biting chironomid midge
Chironomus plumosus
×2

Spotted Mosquito
×2

Common Mosquito
×2

Owl-midge or **moth-fly** *Psychoda surcoufi*
A distinctive member of a family of tiny, moth-like flies with hairy bodies and wings, which resemble some micro-moths. Often found in large numbers around drains, household refuse and in compost heaps, where they live and breed on decaying vegetation. Flies by day and at night, when many may be attracted to lighted windows. It appears to have become more widespread in recent years. More than 90 species of owl-midge have been recorded in Britain.

St Mark's Fly *Bibio marci*
Males, with their conspicuous dangling legs, are commonly seen flying sluggishly in mating swarms on warm sunny days. The female, which has much smaller eyes than the male, makes a tunnel in the soil and lays several hundred eggs in a chamber. She dies soon after, and her larvae feed gregariously on rootlets and organic matter in rich soil, leaf litter and compost heaps. Adults appear around St Mark's Day, on 25 April, and continue into June.

Bibionid fly *Bibio hortulanus*
This species is also common in gardens but is less gregarious than the closely related St Mark's Fly. The female has a chestnut-red thorax and abdomen, but the male is all-black. Often seen visiting flowers and resting on vegetation, on sunny days in June.

Downlooker Snipefly *Rhagio scolopaceus*
Named after its sudden, darting, snipe-like flight and its habit of often resting head down on a tree trunk. This day-flying predatory fly, with a tapered abdomen, catches airborne insects, while its larvae feed on the larvae of other invertebrates in the soil and leaf litter. Widely distributed; flies from May until August in well-vegetated habitats, including gardens. There are several similar species.

Soldierfly *Chloromyia formosa*
A metallic green and golden fly with a flattened body, tinged violet in the female. It has a sluggish flight and is more often seen resting on foliage in gardens. The larvae live in decomposing wood and damp leaf mould. Flies from May until August.

Cleg Fly *Haematopota pluvialis*
The commonest of four similar species, well known for the female's quiet approach and painful bite! After a meal of blood, she lays a large batch of eggs on vegetation, and the carnivorous larvae burrow into the soil and feed voraciously on other invertebrates. Widely distributed; most active on warm sultry days from May until October. **Similar species** The other very common and similar species, *H. crassicornis*, is more frequent in Scotland and the north.

Horsefly *Chrysops caecutiens*
A colourful fly with beautiful, iridescent purple and green eyes, whose female often inflicts a painful bite around the victim's neck or head, '*caecutiens*' meaning 'blinding', a reference to the effect of its bite. Eggs are laid on vegetation near water and the larvae live in mud and detritus. Flies from May until September. Found throughout Britain but absent from Ireland.

Dark-edged Bee-fly *Bombylius major*
The furry body and long, pointed proboscis suggest a stinging insect, but this is a harmless fly, often seen probing delicately into spring flowers such as primroses and violets, or hovering in the spring sunshine. Eggs are flicked out around the nest entrance of solitary bees, and the larvae find their way to the bee's larval cells. It is the commonest of nine bee-flies, and is found in sunny, sheltered places, from March until May.

Long-legged fly *Dolichopus ungulatus*
This, and related species, rest with their front end raised. They have elaborate courtship rituals and the males are noticeable by the large, ornate genitalia, held curved below the abdomen. They are often abundant near water and predate on small, soft-bodied invertebrates. The larvae live in wet mud, and are also carnivorous. Common in summer and autumn.

Robberfly *Leptogaster cylindrica*
This slender, cranefly-like predator flies slowly through long grass, picking off aphids and leaf-hoppers. Larvae live in leaf litter and rotting wood, feeding mainly on decomposing vegetation. Widely distributed, and flies from May until August.

Empid fly *Empis tessellata*
This is the largest member of the family, with a long, beak-like proboscis, and is often seen around hawthorn blossom where it feeds on nectar and on other flies. The larvae live in soil or rotting wood, but little is known of the life cycle. Common in many places, and flies from May until August.

Hoverflies

This is perhaps the most popular family of flies, associated with warm summer days, when their humming flight is interspersed with visits to flowers for nectar. Many species mimic wasps or bees, both in looks and behaviour. Most males have eyes that touch; those of the females are separated. The larvae have diverse lives, and many species are welcome in gardens as they are the most efficient of all aphid predators. Most species overwinter in the larval stage. More than 280 species of hoverfly live in Britain.

Hoverfly *Melanostoma scalare*
One of several similar, slender-bodied hoverflies, although the female is broader than the male. Flies low down in grassy habitats, the adults feeding on pollen from grasses and plantains, and the larvae on aphids. Widespread throughout Britain and Ireland, from April to November.

Common Hoverfly *Syrphus ribesii*
A common wasp-like species, that hovers with an audible hum and often visits cultivated flowers for nectar and pollen. Eggs are laid on vegetation and the fully-grown larva eats up to 50 aphids a day, finally pupating attached to a twig or leaf. It overwinters in the larval stage. Widespread; found in many habitats, including waste ground and gardens, and flies in several generations from March until October.

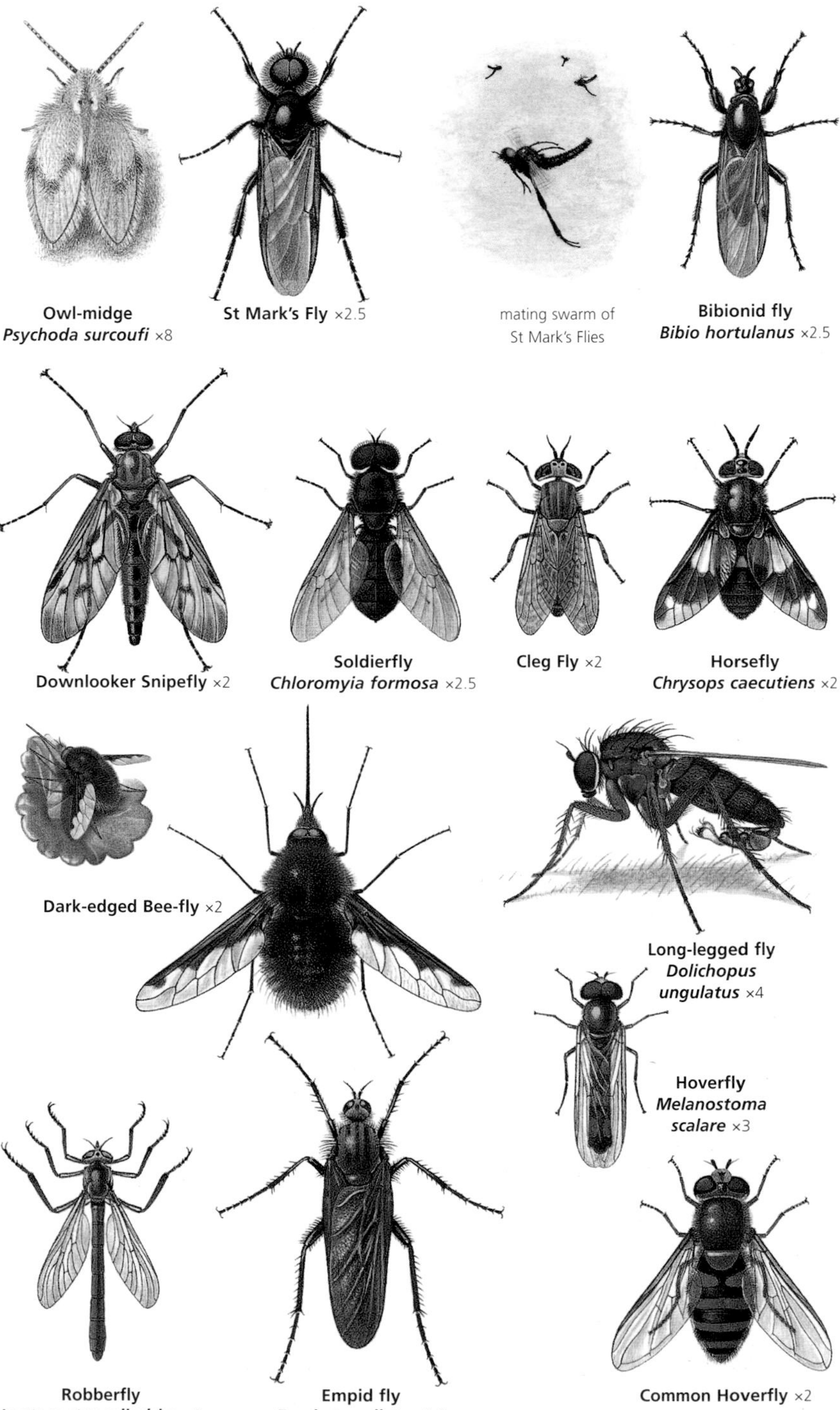

Owl-midge
Psychoda surcoufi ×8

St Mark's Fly ×2.5

mating swarm of
St Mark's Flies

Bibionid fly
Bibio hortulanus ×2.5

Downlooker Snipefly ×2

Soldierfly
Chloromyia formosa ×2.5

Cleg Fly ×2

Horsefly
Chrysops caecutiens ×2

Dark-edged Bee-fly ×2

Long-legged fly
Dolichopus ungulatus ×4

Hoverfly
Melanostoma scalare ×3

Robberfly
Leptogaster cylindrica ×2

Empid fly
Empis tessellata ×2.5

Common Hoverfly ×2

Hoverfly *Epistrophe eligans*
The yellow markings are confined to the front of the abdomen and are reduced to two triangles in the male, leaving the tail black. Often seen in gardens in spring, hovering in small groups around firethorn, hawthorn and blackthorn. The larvae feed on aphids in trees and shrubs. Flies from March until August, and is widespread in England and Wales, scarcer in the north, with few records from Scotland.

Hoverfly *Eupeodes luniger*
This migratory species varies in size and markings, but usually has three pairs of blunt yellow crescents on the abdomen. Numbers are boosted by migrants from southern Europe in the summer, when it can become very common in many places, including urban gardens. Flies from March until November throughout Britain and Ireland, and is particularly common in south-east England.

Marmalade Hoverfly *Episyrphus balteatus*
The two, double black bands on the abdomen are diagnostic of this very common species, whose numbers are sometimes boosted in the summer by huge numbers of migrants from southern Europe. They feed on and pollinate a wide range of wild and cultivated flowers, and the larvae eat aphids on many trees, herbs and vegetable crops. Adults appear in early spring, and this is the most abundant hoverfly that can hibernate as an adult. It is found throughout, but numbers can vary greatly.

Large Narcissus Fly or **Greater Bulb Fly** *Merodon equestris*
This hairy bumblebee mimic has several varieties, each resembling a different species of bee. After mating in spring, the female lays her eggs near bulbs of bluebells, daffodils and, less often, onions. The dirty-grey larvae burrow into bulbs, reducing them to a rotting mush. The species was thought to have been accidentally introduced with imported bulbs in the late 1800s, and is one of the very few pest species of hoverfly. Widely distributed, especially around habitation, but scarcer in the north, from May until August.

Hoverfly *Scaeva pyrastri*
The three pairs of forward-pointing white chevrons, and its large size, make this a distinctive species, often arriving from the south in mixed swarms with the Marmalade Hoverfly. Adults visit many flowers, with a preference for umbellifers, thistles and ragworts, and the larvae predate on aphids on ground-layer vegetation. Occurs in gardens and on waste ground throughout Britain and Ireland, but less common further north; numbers fluctuate greatly from year to year, but peak in July and August.

Hoverfly *Rhingia campestris*
A sluggish hoverfly, recognised by the orange abdomen with a black central line, and a long, beak-like proboscis, enabling it to probe deeply into flowers. It is often seen feeding from purple and pink blooms in spring, with two broods appearing between April and November. Eggs are laid on vegetation overhanging cowpats, and possibly other animal dung, and on hatching the larvae drop and live concealed in the cowpat, although adults are often seen well away from cattle. Found commonly throughout Britain and Ireland, but less abundant after hot, dry summers.

Great Pied Hoverfly *Volucella pellucens*
An unmistakable fly that often hovers in sunlit openings between trees and bushes, pausing to feed on flowers such as bramble and hogweed. The larvae live in the nests of Common and German Wasps, and several dozen can be found in a single nest. Found throughout Britain and Ireland in well-wooded habitats, from May until September.

Hoverfly *Helophilus pendulus*
This is the commonest of four related species that have a yellow and black striped thorax, distinguished by having the basal half of the hind tibia pale. They visit flowers and are conspicuous around garden ponds, where they buzz noisily, sunbathing and mating on the surface vegetation. The larvae live in sludgy ponds, rotting manure heaps and ditches, and are of the 'rat-tailed maggot' type. Occurs throughout the country, from April until October.

Drone fly *Eristalis pertinax*
This, and the similar *E. tenax*, gain some protection from their close resemblance to the male Honey Bee or drone. It is one of the few species that can be found throughout the year, and is commonly seen hovering motionless around garden shrubs, and visiting a wide range of flowers, including ivy, late in the year. The larva, the 'rat-tailed maggot' (see page 208), is off-white and grub-like, with a long, extendable, tubular tail, which it uses to reach to the surface of muddy, organically-rich or polluted water to breathe. Very common in many habitats throughout the country, especially farmyards and gardens.

Hoverfly *Volucella zonaria*
One of the largest and most impressive British hoverflies, whose rich chestnut, yellow and black markings mimic the Hornet, causing concern when it enters houses. The larvae live in the nests of Common and German Wasps. First established in the south 70 years ago, it has spread northwards, and often occurs on flowers in town and city gardens, from May until October.

Hoverfly *Volucella bombylans*
Various forms of this hairy hoverfly mimic certain species of bumblebee, particularly the Red-tailed and White-tailed Bumblebees. After mating in May, the female enters the underground nest of a bumblebee to lay her eggs. The young larvae drop to the bottom of the nest chamber and scavenge on dead bees and larvae, pupating in the autumn. Occurs throughout Britain and Ireland in well-vegetated flowery places, including urban gardens, from May until August.

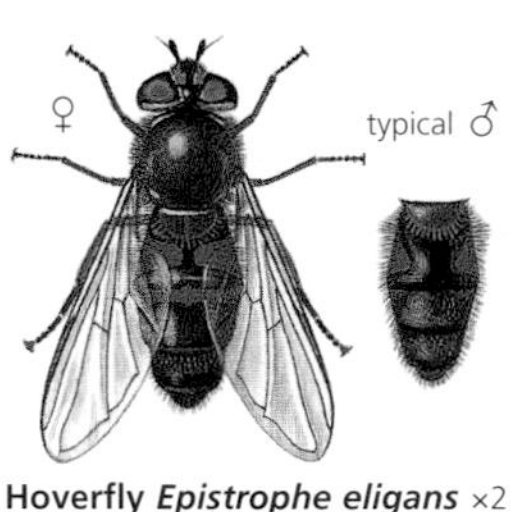

Hoverfly *Epistrophe eligans* ×2

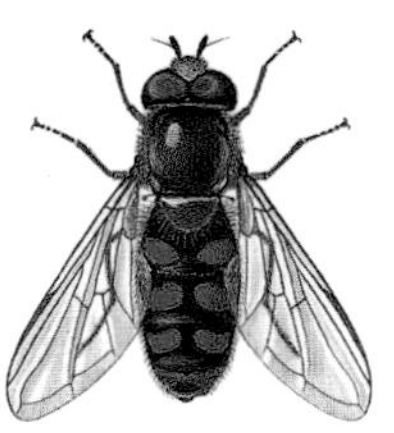

Hoverfly *Eupeodes luniger* ×2

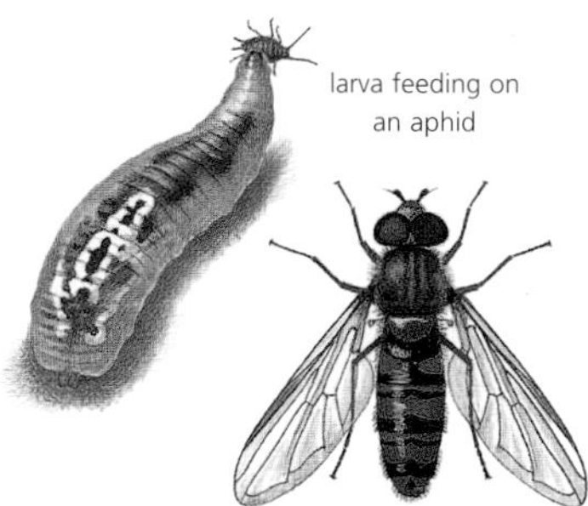

Marmalade Hoverfly ×2

Large Narcissus Fly ×2

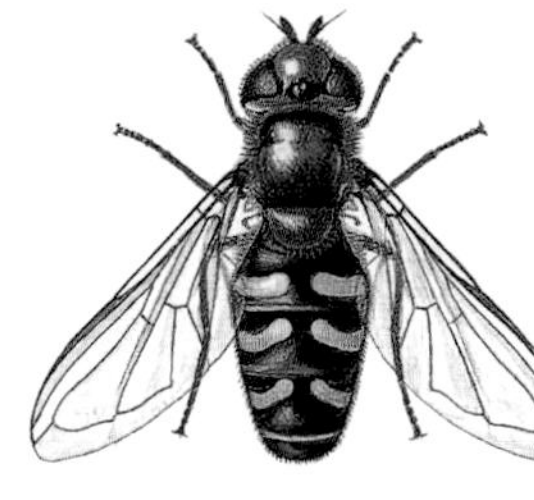

Hoverfly *Scaeva pyrastri* ×2

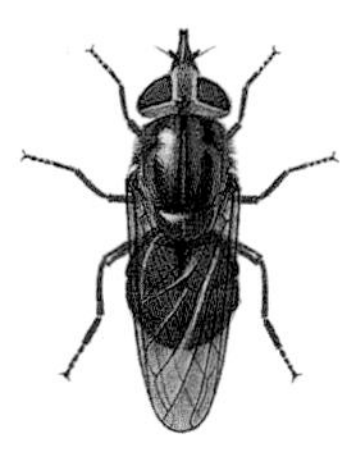

Hoverfly *Rhingia campestris* ×2

Great Pied Hoverfly ×2

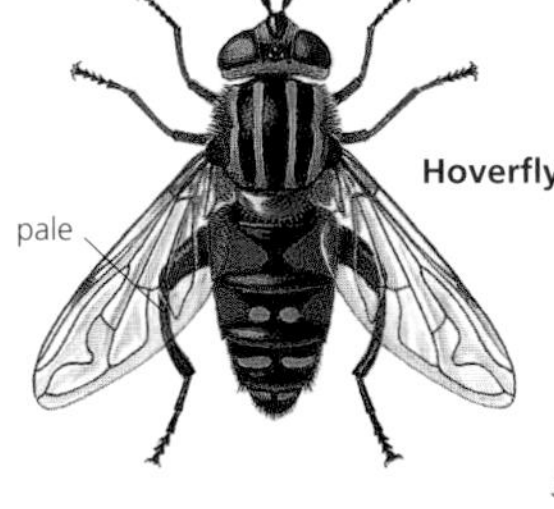

Hoverfly *Helophilus pendulus* ×2

Drone fly *Eristalis pertinax* ×2

Hoverfly *Volucella zonaria* ×2

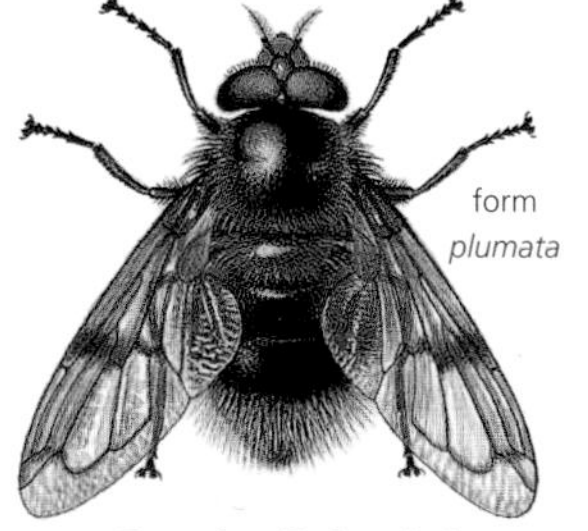

Hoverfly *Volucella bombylans* ×2

Thistle-stem Gall Fly *Urophora cardui*
Most species in the family Tephritidae have attractively patterned wing markings. The female Thistle-stem Gall Fly has a long ovipositor, used for laying eggs in the soft stems of creeping thistle. Four larvae usually develop, causing hard, bulbous galls and stunted leaves, most obvious in the winter. Occurs mainly in southern England and Wales, on waste ground and in overgrown gardens, from May until August.

Celery Fly *Euleia heraclei*
The larva of this fly mines the leaves of celery, parsnip and many wild umbellifers, causing the leaves to wither and die. Pupation occurs in the soil and adults fly from April until November, in several broods. Widespread and found in gardens, allotments and on waste ground.

Snail-killing fly *Tetanocera elata*
A sluggish fly, often seen resting on vegetation near ponds and in damp, marshy habitats. It is a beneficial garden insect as the larvae feed on gastropods, specialising in slugs, including pest species such as the Field Slug and Garden Slug. Common and widespread; flies from April until October.

Carrot Fly *Psila rosae*
This common and widespread fly is rarely seen, but the damage done to carrots, parsnips, parsley and celery by the creamy-white larvae is familiar to most gardeners. Eggs are first laid in the soil around the host plant in May and June. The larvae feed, often with their rear ends protruding from the root, and then pupate in the soil. A second brood appears in August and September.

Holly Leaf Miner *Phytomyza ilicis*
The familiar yellow and purple blotches on holly leaves, caused by the larvae of this fly, are present throughout the year, but cause no lasting damage to the tree. Eggs are laid on the underside of the mid rib in spring and the larva burrows between the surfaces, eventually pupating inside the mine. Adults fly in spring and summer in one brood. Widespread and common, even in cities.

Black scavenger fly or **ensign fly**
Sepsis punctum
Males of this distinctive little fly often congregate on vegetation in large mating swarms, using their spotted wings in wing-waving displays. The larvae feed on dung and decaying vegetation such as compost heaps. Found throughout most of the year; widespread and common on flowers.

Bluebottle *Calliphora vomitoria*
Bluebottles are mainly associated with putrification and can transmit a number of diseases, but are essential in breaking down carrion and decaying matter. Females lay several batches of up to 200 eggs each, which take two to three weeks to complete their life cycle. They are found almost everywhere, at all times of the year, often being the first insect seen sunning itself in early spring.

Cluster Fly *Pollenia rudis*
Identified by the dense golden hairs on the thorax and the wings held flat on the back, thousands of these flies cluster together in attics and outhouses in the winter, emerging in the spring to breed. Eggs are laid in the soil and the larvae are parasitoids of earthworms. Widespread, found in every month.

Tachinid fly *Tachina fera*
A large, bristly fly, found in damp places, near ponds, and often seen visiting water mint. The larvae are parasitoids inside larvae of Large White butterflies and various species of moth (mainly noctuids). Common and widespread. Adults are seen in May and June, and again more abundantly in late summer and early autumn.

Flesh fly *Sarcophaga carnaria*
A conspicuous fly with red eyes and large feet, whose chequered pattern changes according to the light. The female releases larvae, rather than eggs, onto carrion and the small maggots produce a liquid in which they live. Pupation occurs in the soil. Widespread, and found throughout the year. The commonest of several similar species.

Greenbottle *Lucilia caesar*
One of several metallic green flies, seen buzzing everywhere on flowers, dung, carrion and on human food, which they contaminate by vomiting and defecating. Their colour varies from brilliant green to bluish green, often with a violet or coppery sheen. The larvae emit a liquid in which they live, pupating in the ground after several days of feeding. Adults may occur throughout the year, in most parts of the country.

Fruit fly or **vinegar fly** *Drosophila* sp.
These tiny flies, with red eyes, are usually seen flying ponderously around fermenting fruit, wine bottles and compost heaps containing rotting fruit, where the larvae feed on decaying vegetation. Found throughout. Most common in the summer months, but found indoors all year.

Common House Fly *Musca domestica*
The commonest member of a large family, and abundant indoors and out, especially around rubbish dumps and farms, where horse dung is the preferred egg-laying site. Up to six batches, each containing 150 eggs, are laid in organic matter, the life cycle being completed in two to three weeks in warm weather. Found at all times, wherever humans live.

Yellow Dung Fly *Scathophaga stercoraria*
Females are greyer and less common than the furry ginger males, who spend much of their lives on and around dung, mating and preying on other insects, while the larvae live in and feed on dung. They also occur in other places, visiting flowers and often entering lighted windows at night. Common throughout the country, from spring until September.

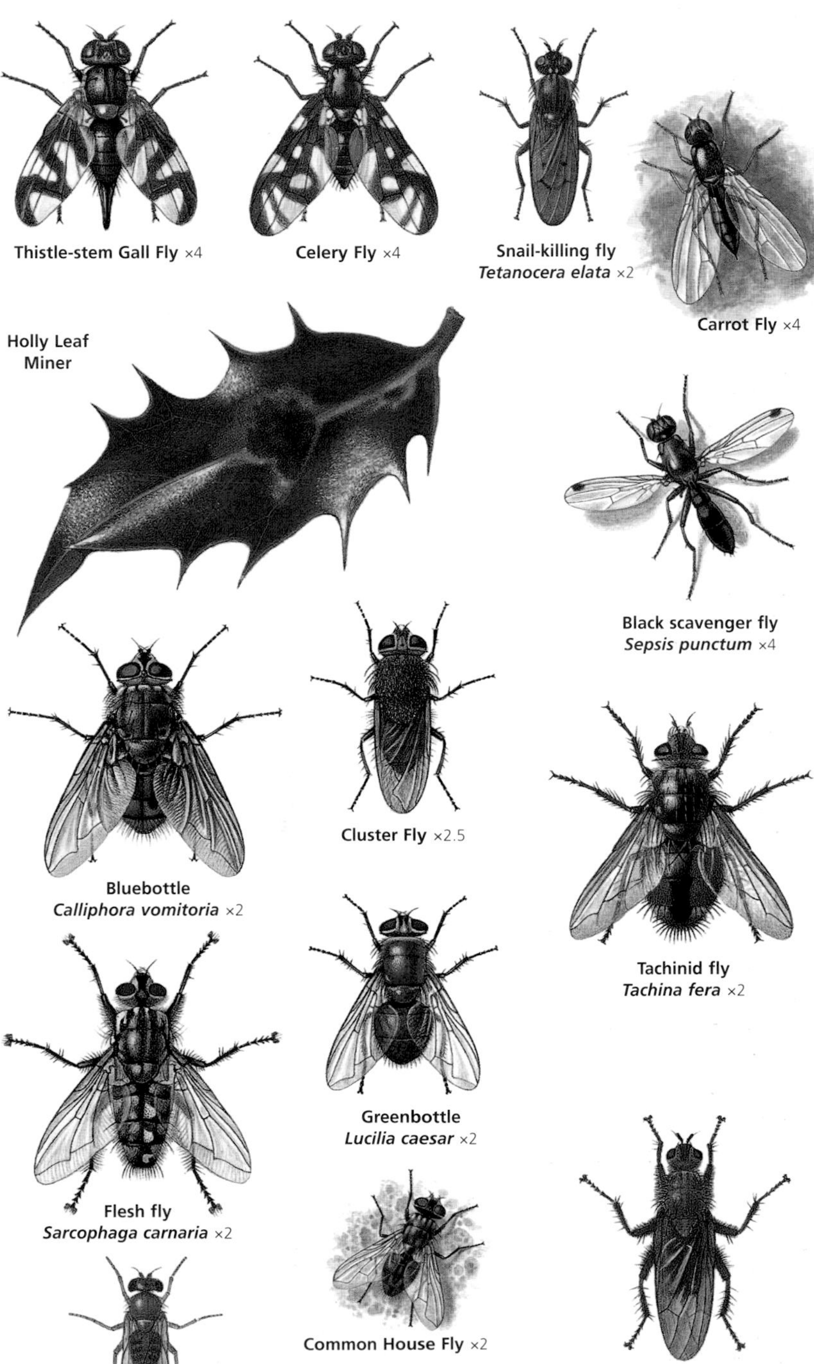
Thistle-stem Gall Fly ×4
Celery Fly ×4
Snail-killing fly
Tetanocera elata ×2
Carrot Fly ×4
Holly Leaf
Miner
Black scavenger fly
Sepsis punctum ×4
Cluster Fly ×2.5
Bluebottle
Calliphora vomitoria ×2
Tachinid fly
Tachina fera ×2
Greenbottle
Lucilia caesar ×2
Flesh fly
Sarcophaga carnaria ×2
Common House Fly ×2
Fruit fly
Drosophila sp. ×4
Yellow Dung Fly ×2

Bees, wasps, ants and allies
Hymenoptera

▲ The larva of the Rose Sawfly feeding on a leaf.

The Hymenoptera is a large and diverse group that contains more than 6,700 British species of bees, wasps and ants, and their relatives, and, apart from a few species, is one of the least well-known groups. The name Hymenoptera means 'membrane wing', a reference to the two pairs of membranous, veined wings of many, but not all, species. The group is split into two sub-orders: the Symphyta, the sawflies, and the Apocrita, which includes the Parasitica (ichneumon wasps and other parasites) and the Aculeata (social and solitary bees and wasps, and ants). The Aculeata contains some of the most highly advanced social insects, many of which play an important and indispensable role as pollinators of crops and garden plants. The parasitoids are equally important, as many species, including the myriads of tiny chalcid wasps, which make up more than a quarter of all Hymenoptera, play a vital part in controlling the populations of other invertebrates.

Sawflies are best separated from other Hymenoptera by the absence of a constricted waist and by the females' saw-like ovipositor, which is used to cut slits in plants for egg-laying. Adults are not well known but the larvae, some of which cause damage to garden plants and arable crops, are more likely to be encountered. Many of these resemble the larvae of moths and butterflies, but differ in having at least six pairs of false legs. The larvae of some are gregarious and live in conspicuous groups, clinging to the edges of leaves and frightening predators by suddenly flicking their bodies into a question-mark shape when threatened. Others, such as those of the various slug sawflies that feed in gardens on roses and some fruit trees, rely on a slimy secretion for protection when young, while the larva of the Woodwasp lives concealed in the heartwood of mainly coniferous trees, taking up to three years to develop on an innutritious diet of wood. Although concealed, they sometimes fall victim to another hymenopteran, the large ichneumon wasp *Rhyssa persuasoria,* which drills into the wood with its long, needle-like ovipositor to lay its egg in the host.

Of all the bees, the bumblebees and Western Honey Bee are the most familiar and popular, and play a major role in gardens. Queen bumblebees, with their sleepy, drunken flight, are one of the earliest signs that spring has arrived. After restoring her energy reserves with nectar, the queen establishes a nest and lays a batch of eggs that hatch into worker bees. These are also female, and possess pollen baskets on the hindlegs and a rarely used sting. The workers bring nectar and pollen back to the nest and raise further workers. Later in the season, males are produced that are stingless. These mate with new queens, after which the males die. The fertile queens hibernate until the following spring. Gardens provide important sources of food for bumblebees and Honey Bees. They return the favour by pollinating garden plants. Cuckoo bumblebees take over the nests of social bumblebees, employing the workers to rear their own offspring. They visit flowers to collect nectar and pollen, but only for their own consumption. Several of the 24 species of bumblebee that occur in the UK are threatened with extinction.

In addition to the bumblebees, there are many other unsung heroes among the Hymenoptera, particularly the many solitary bees that help pollinate a huge variety of plants, trees and shrubs. In many of these the tongue length varies, depending on the types of flowers they visit, but all are beneficial in transferring pollen as they move from flower to flower, collecting food for their young. As well as pollen baskets on the hindlegs, some species, such as the leaf-cutter bees, collect pollen on the underside of the abdomen. Most solitary bees, such as the mining bees and mason bees, nest in holes either in the ground or in old walls or rotten wood and, unlike the social bees, they provision the nest with food and leave the larvae to develop on their own.

▲ Western Honey Bees at the entrance to a hive.

Most people dislike social wasps, which can become a nuisance in late summer when their persistence around barbeques or in pub gardens can cause conflict, but they are not aggressive unless threatened or accidentally harmed, when they may sting. Unbeknown to most people, their benefits easily outweigh these inconveniences, as wasps collect huge numbers of insects, many of them garden pests, to feed their carnivorous young. The yellow-and-black-banded coloration of social wasps, warning of their stinging capabilities, is acknowledged by many other harmless insects which mimic the markings for their own protection against predators. These include many solitary wasps, hoverflies, the Hornet Moth and the Wasp Beetle, but whereas this may prove an effective means of protection against natural predators, the reaction of humans is often to strike out and kill, regardless.

Many of the less well-known wasps, such as the digger wasps, nest in the ground and lay their eggs on paralysed prey, whereas others, such as the ichneumon wasps, make no nest and lay their eggs directly into or on their victims. So effective are some species of parasitiod Hymenoptera in controlling other insects, that industry is turning to the commercial breeding of certain species as pest controllers, since some chemicals have proved less effective in putting right the imbalance in the natural world that we have caused. Some tiny species of wasp lay their eggs on plants, and their larvae feed inside galls, for example the Marble Gall found on oaks, the galls being the plant's reaction to the violation.

Like wasps, ants are generally unpopular, but on the whole they cause little harm and have fascinating social structures. They live in colonies, usually hidden underground or beneath stones, and, unlike wasp colonies, which die out in the autumn, may survive for many years.

Sawflies Symphyta

Woodwasp or **Horntail** *Urocerus gigas*
This large, harmless sawfly often causes alarm, as it is similar in size and colour to the Hornet and females have a long, sting-like ovipositor. Eggs are laid singly, drilled through the bark of pine trees into the heartwood, where the larvae live for up to three years. Adults fly in the sunshine from May until October, mainly in coniferous woodland, but they also occur where pine timber has been used for house building and in furniture making, or is stacked in woodpiles. Found throughout Britain and recently recorded from west Ireland, probably not endemic.

Birch sawfly *Cimbex femoratus*
The clubbed antennae, pale membrane at the base of the abdomen and dusky wing edges are characteristic of this large sawfly, which has a heavy, buzzing flight. The plump 'C'-shaped larva is powdery green with a dark dorsal line. It lives solitarily on the leaves of birch, and pupates on twigs, inside a tough brown cocoon. The adult emerges in spring. Common throughout Britain and Ireland. **Similar species** The **Hawthorn Sawfly** *Trichiosoma lucorum* is slightly smaller but is hairier and lacks the conspicuous pale membrane.

Turnip Sawfly *Athalia rosae*
A sluggish species that feeds on the nectar of various umbellifer and composite flowers, with several generations between May and October. It resembles the Gooseberry Sawfly, but can be distinguished by its shorter antennae. The larvae, which feed on the foliage of crucifers, sometimes cause damage to cultivated varieties in the vegetable garden, including cabbage, turnip and oil-seed rape. They pupate in silken cocoons in the soil. A pest in southern England and the Midlands.

Gooseberry Sawfly *Nematus ribesii*
The female Gooseberry Sawfly has a stout, orange abdomen, in contrast to the male which is smaller, with dark abdominal bands. The gregarious larvae of this well-known pest species can completely strip gooseberry and currant bushes of their foliage, reducing them to skeletons. Up to three generations are produced, the first adults appearing in April, with later broods lasting into September. Widely distributed, and the commonest of several similar species that attack gooseberries in gardens and allotments.

Solomon's-seal Sawfly *Phymatocera aterrima*
A shiny black sawfly, with a metallic sheen to the wings and long antennae. Adults fly sluggishly in gardens and are inconspicuous compared to their voracious larvae. These are pale blue-grey, speckled with black, and live gregariously on the leaves of Solomon's-seal, lily-of-the-valley and related plants in May and June, reducing the leaves to elongated veins. Common from the Midlands southwards.

Stem Sawfly *Cephus pygmeus*
The adults have cylindrical bodies and long antennae, and are a serious pest of cereal crops. They can often be seen in large numbers, flying slowly around yellow composite and umbellifer flowers in grasslands, between May and August. The larvae have vestigial legs and burrow into the stems of grasses and cereals. Found throughout England and Wales.

Bean Gall Sawfly *Pontania proxima*
The larvae of this and other closely related sawflies live within the conspicuous bean galls on the leaves of various species of willow. Adults are small, nondescript insects that appear in two broods, the first emerging in May from pupae formed in the soil. The galls are formed not by the larvae but from a secretion injected by the female whilst egg-laying. Occurs throughout Britain and in parts of Ireland.

Sawfly *Tenthredo arcuata*
One of a large and varied family of sawflies, some of which mimic wasps. Adults of this species, which appear in the spring and summer, have slightly clubbed antennae. The larvae feed on red and white clovers. Widespread throughout.

Pear-cherry Slug Sawfly *Caliroa cerasi*
The larvae of this small, black sawfly feed on the leaves of various members of the rose family, causing some damage in gardens to the foliage of apples, pears, cherries and almonds. It is black and covered in a slimy secretion, and when young, rasps on the upper leaf cuticle, creating opaque windows known as 'skeletonisation'. If larvae are present in large numbers, the leaves turn yellow and fall to the ground. Adults appear in two broods, from May until September. Found throughout Britain, locally common in Ireland.

Rose Slug Sawfly *Endelomyia aethiops*
The adult and its life cycle is similar to that of the Pear-cherry Slug Sawfly but the larvae feed gregariously on the leaves of cultivated roses, causing unsightly 'skeletonising' of the leaves but no serious damage. Two generations are produced, from May until September, and the larvae from the second brood overwinter in cocoons in the soil. Common and widespread.

Birch sawfly *Craesus septentrionalis*
Found on a variety of garden trees, but mainly on birch, the gregarious larvae cling to the leaf margins and flick their bodies into a question-mark shape when alarmed, at the same time releasing an unpleasant smell. Pupation takes place in the soil. The adult is black and orange and may be seen feeding from flowers throughout the summer months. Common and widespread.

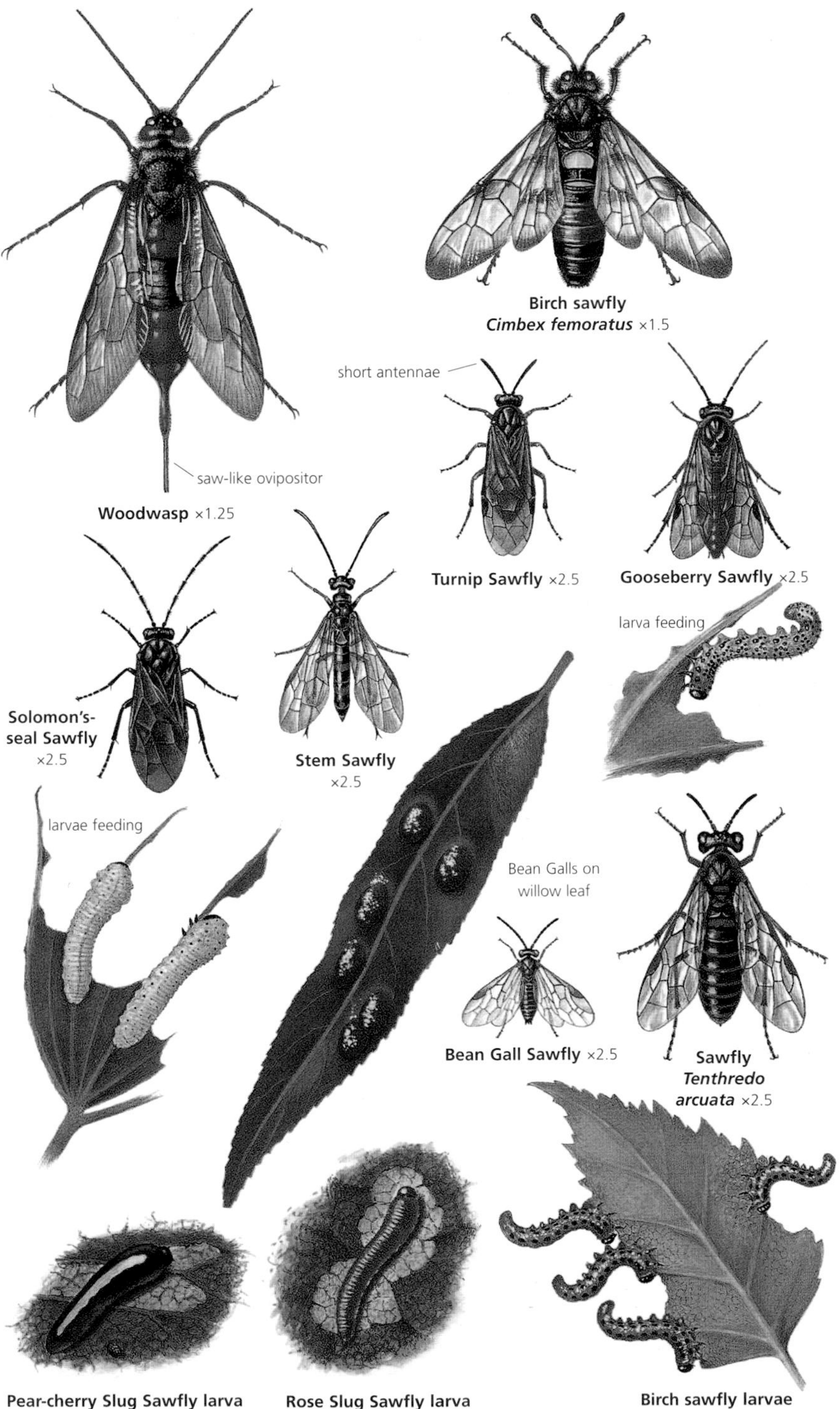

Woodwasp ×1.25

Birch sawfly
Cimbex femoratus ×1.5

Turnip Sawfly ×2.5

Gooseberry Sawfly ×2.5

Solomon's-seal Sawfly ×2.5

Stem Sawfly ×2.5

Bean Gall Sawfly ×2.5

Sawfly
Tenthredo arcuata ×2.5

Pear-cherry Slug Sawfly larva

Rose Slug Sawfly larva

Birch sawfly larvae
Craesus septentrionalis

Gall wasps, ichneumons and allies Parasitica

Oak Marble Gall Wasp *Andricus kollari*
Probably the most familiar of more than 40 galls found on oaks, caused by the tree's reaction to secretions from the newly hatched larva, which affects growth of the surrounding cells. Young galls are greenish, eventually reaching about 25mm in diameter and becoming brown with age, when they are most conspicuous in winter after the leaves have dropped. Pupation takes place inside the gall, and in autumn a parthenogenetic female emerges through an exit hole. This female lays eggs on the buds of Turkey oak, which causes a different 'ant pupa' gall to be formed; the resulting sexual generation emerges the following spring to start the cycle again. Several other species of wasp, known as 'inquilines', often develop along with the original gall-maker. Introduced into Britain in the 19th century, Marble Galls contain tannic acid used in the dyeing and ink-making industry. Widespread, found mainly on scrub oak and young oaks growing in hedgerows.

Robin's Pincushion or **Bedeguar Gall Wasp** *Diplolepis rosae*
The conspicuous mossy, red and green galls of this wasp are mainly seen on wild roses but may occasionally appear in gardens on cultivated roses. Up to 60 larvae, each in its own chamber, live and feed at the woody central core of the gall. In autumn and winter the gall becomes a brown, irregular lump in which the larvae overwinter until the following spring. In May, the adult wasps emerge; nearly all are females, males being very rare. As well as the gall-makers, several other species, 'inquilines', also emerge. Widespread throughout Britain and Ireland and very common on wild roses.

Chalcid wasp *Pteromalus puparum*
This is one of more than 500 species of chalcid wasp found in Britain, which are parasitoids on a wide range of insect hosts. Some species are available commercially as biological control agents against pest species such as aphids, whitefly and various weevils, but most act, along with other predators, as natural controllers of insect populations. The main chance of seeing these tiny metallic wasps is when large numbers emerge from a dead butterfly pupa in spring. Eggs are laid when the newly formed pupa is still soft. The grubs feed and then pupate inside the body, finally emerging through holes in the body wall. Several generations are produced in a year. Common and widespread.

Braconid wasp *Cotesia glomerata*
The most familiar part of the life cycle of this small black wasp are the yellow cocoons, often seen on walls, clustered around the shrivelled corpse of a Large White butterfly caterpillar. The female wasp injects about 80 eggs into a caterpillar and the tiny grubs feed, avoiding the vital organs, and emerge just as the host prepares to pupate. It is an important controller of Large White numbers and, as such, is a friend of the vegetable gardener throughout the country.

Ruby-tailed wasp *Chrysis ignita*
One of a family of brightly coloured, metallic wasps, known as cuckoo-wasps, which are parasitoids (they eventually kill the host) in the nests of other solitary wasps or bees. They have a hard, well-armoured body and are able to roll into a ball, gaining protection from bee stings when they enter nests to lay their eggs. Most active in the sunshine and often seen visiting flowers or running jerkily on walls and fences in search of entrance holes to bee nests. The plump grub feeds on the host larva and pupates in spring. Adults are widespread throughout the summer months.

Ichneumon wasp *Amblyteles armatorius*
A common ichneumon wasp that is a parasitoid of the larvae of several species of moth, especially noctuids. Both sexes gain protection from their wasp-like coloration but the female has rusty-brown legs and more yellow on the abdomen than the male. Adults hibernate in winter. Widely distributed and frequent on flowers in the summer months.

Ophion Wasp *Ophion obscuratus*
Resting in vegetation by day, this wasp is most frequently seen at dusk and at night, when it is attracted to outside lights, lighted windows and moth traps. It is one of many similar species in the huge family of ichneumon wasps and is an endoparasitoid (living inside and eventually killing its host) of the larvae of mainly noctuid and prominent moths. A variable species, several forms occur throughout the year, the most common garden form being the striped 'autumn giant', which flies from August to February. This wasp's appearance, with its arched abdomen, may cause alarm but it cannot sting, although the short ovipositor of the female can give a slight pinprick. Widespread and very common in gardens throughout the year. **Similar species** The **Yellow Ophion** *O. luteus* is another very common and equally variable species, which can only be separated by microscopic examination.

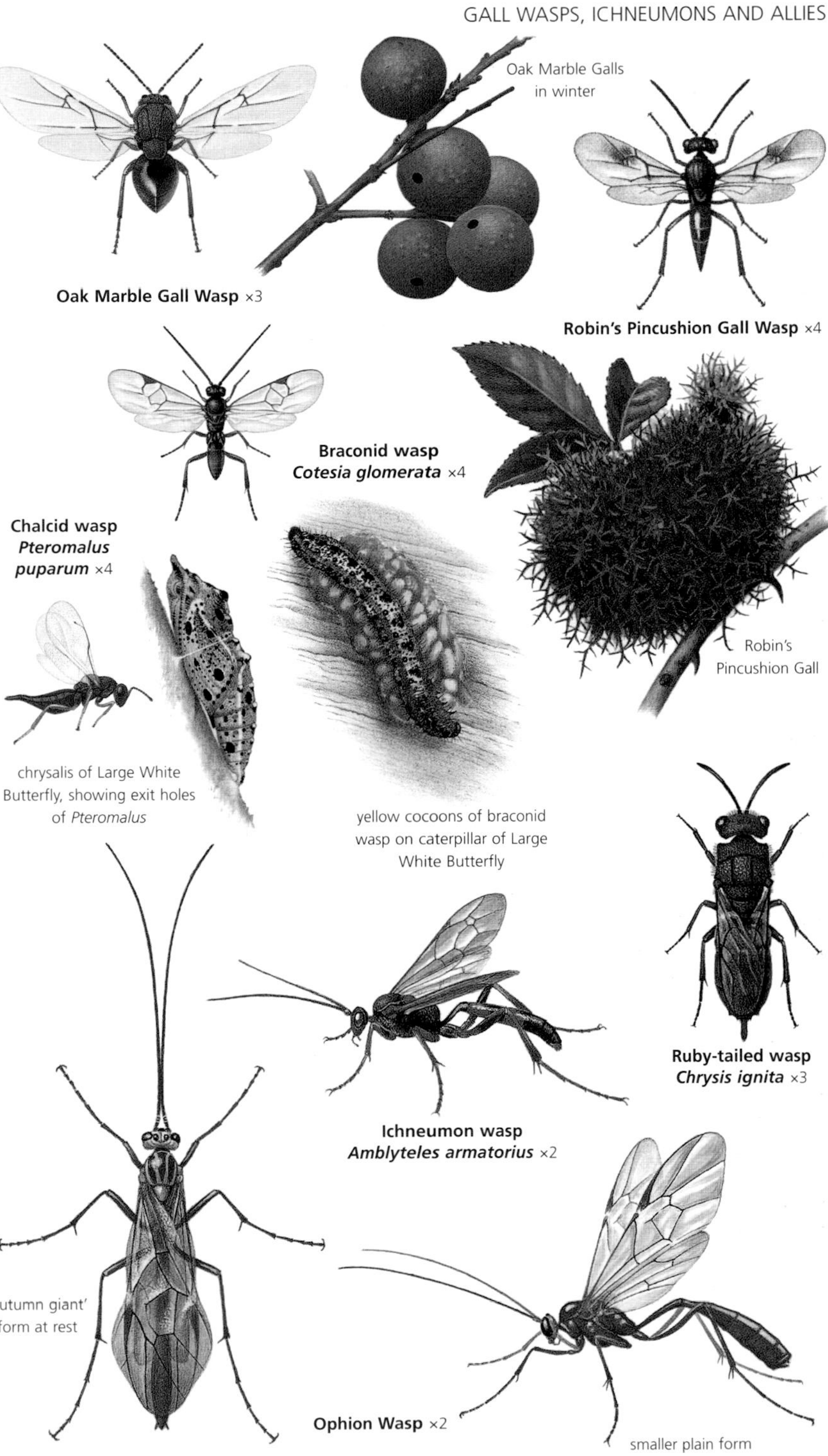

Oak Marble Gall Wasp ×3

Robin's Pincushion Gall Wasp ×4

Braconid wasp ***Cotesia glomerata*** ×4

Chalcid wasp ***Pteromalus puparum*** ×4

Ruby-tailed wasp ***Chrysis ignita*** ×3

Ichneumon wasp ***Amblyteles armatorius*** ×2

Ophion Wasp ×2

Ants, wasps and bees

Aculeata

Red ant *Myrmica ruginodis*
More formidable than the much smaller and paler Yellow Meadow Ant, this species is capable of giving a painful sting. It nests beneath stones and logs or in rotting wood or sheltered grass tussocks, in colonies of often more than 1,000 workers. Mainly vegetarian, it prefers nectar and honeydew but will also feed on plant seeds and small invertebrates. The most widespread ant, found commonly throughout Britain and Ireland.

Yellow Meadow Ant *Lasius flavus*
This small ant makes the large mounds often seen in meadows, which may be many years old, but in gardens, mowing and rolling prevent these from forming, although the nests remain intact below ground. The life cycle is similar to that of the Black Garden Ant, but this species lives almost entirely below ground, where it feeds on sweet secretions of root-feeding aphids. Widespread in many habitats except shaded woodlands.

Black Garden Ant *Lasius niger*
This abundant, dark brown rather than black ant is found everywhere in gardens, and sometimes indoors, searching for sweet food (often honeydew from aphids), insects and plant seeds. Its nest is made beneath paving slabs, in rotting tree stumps or underground, often also building above ground with particles of soil. The queen begins egg-laying in spring, producing workers which help enlarge the colony. On warm, humid afternoons in mid-summer, winged males and new queens take to the air to form new colonies, often swarming in huge numbers. These swarms may attract the attention of birds such as Starlings and House Sparrows, that readily take advantage of the short-lived bonanza. Very common almost everywhere, except the extreme north.

Wall Mason Wasp *Ancistrocerus parietum*
This solitary wasp, similar and closely related to the social wasps, folds its wings longitudinally in the same way and is often seen visiting flowers, especially umbellifers. The female nests in crumbling holes in mortar or around window frames, where ten or more cells are constructed, separated from each other with a mud partition. An egg is laid in each cell, which is provisioned with a number of small, paralysed lepidoptera larvae. Loose mortar or holes are then re-pointed, usually leaving a tell-tale ridge. Common in spring and summer in many parts of England, Wales and Ireland. **Similar species** *A. nigricornis* has a conspicuous black spot at the front of the abdomen; it is also common in gardens, mainly in the south.

Two-girdled Digger Wasp
Argogorytes mystaceus
The female of this digger wasp usually excavates a burrow in sandy soil, leaving tell-tale spoil heaps near the entrance hole. A series of six or more cells are formed along the chamber, which are provisioned with froghopper nymphs (the nymphs responsible for cuckoo spit, which is supposed to provide protection from predators, see page 94). An egg is laid in each cell and the larva feeds on a fresh diet of paralysed nymphs. Sometimes, before completion, the nest is raided by one of the related species of digger wasp, which lays its own eggs in the cells, like a cuckoo. Its larvae destroy the true occupant and proceed to feed on the store of froghopper nymphs. Widespread in Britain and Ireland.

Hornet *Vespa crabro*
Although the Hornet is the largest of the social wasps, it is less aggressive than smaller species and will sting only if provoked. The life cycle is similar to related species; the queen emerges from hibernation in April and searches for a nest site, usually in a hollow tree, where she builds a paper nest from wood scraped from trees and mixed with saliva. The grubs are carnivorous and are fed on insects, mainly flies; on average, each nest produces more than 900 workers and later in the season several hundred males and new queens emerge. Distribution has increased in the last 30 years, and the Hornet is now found throughout Britain as far north as Yorkshire.

Common Wasp *Vespula vulgaris*
Similar in appearance and habits to the German Wasp, the fertilised queen appears in spring, after hibernation, and having fed, sets about building her yellowish-brown paper nest either underground or in a loft. Thousands of carnivorous larvae are reared throughout the year, first by the queen and then by workers. It is not often appreciated just how useful wasps are in controlling many invertebrate pests in gardens. Common and widely distributed throughout.

German Wasp *Vespula germanica*
The other very common garden wasp, distinguished by the three black dots on the front of the head and the diamond at the front of the abdomen. It nests in similar places to the Common Wasp, but the nest is a uniform grey. Widely distributed, except for north-west Scotland and north-west Ireland.

Median Wasp *Dolichovespula media*
The large queen could be mistaken for a worker Hornet, but males and workers are smaller and distinguished by their heavily marked, sometimes almost all-black abdomens. The nest, usually suspended in a tree or shrub, is mainly grey but often has coloured bands that reflect the different types of wood used in its construction. The Median Wasp is usually less aggressive than the two common wasps, despite being dubbed the 'French killer wasp' by the press. First recorded in Britain in 1980, it has now spread throughout England and Wales. **Similar species** There are three other slightly smaller social wasps that make nests in trees and shrubs.

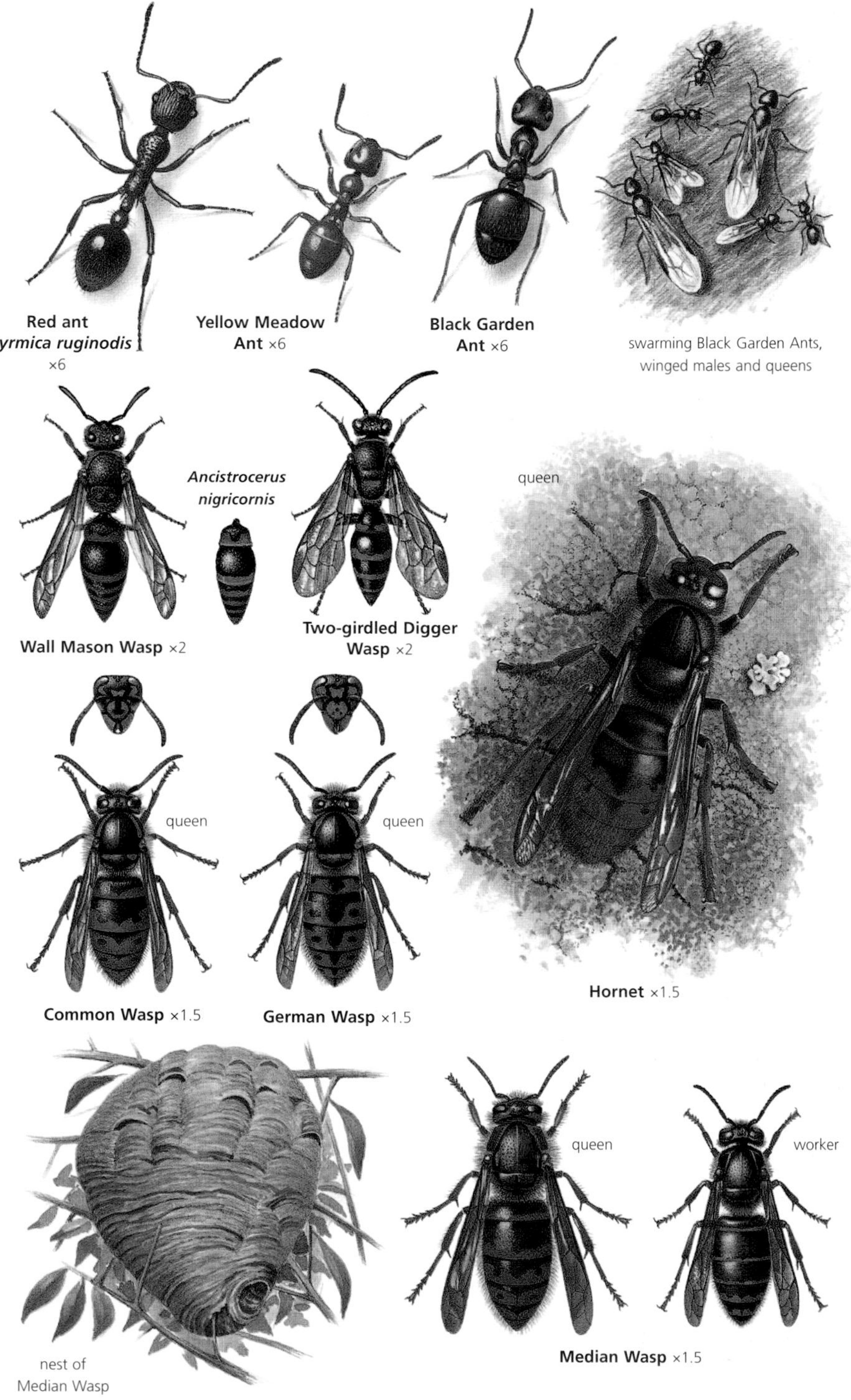

Red ant ***Myrmica ruginodis*** ×6

Yellow Meadow Ant ×6

Black Garden Ant ×6

swarming Black Garden Ants, winged males and queens

Wall Mason Wasp ×2

Ancistrocerus nigricornis

Two-girdled Digger Wasp ×2

Hornet ×1.5

Common Wasp ×1.5

German Wasp ×1.5

nest of Median Wasp

Median Wasp ×1.5

Solitary bees

Ivy Bee *Colletes hederae*
This autumnal bee, which only colonised Britain in 2001, has an unmistakeable broadly-banded buff-and-black abdomen. It nests in large aggregations, preferring warm, south-facing slopes in light, sparsely vegetated soil. Newly emerged females are often pounced upon by numerous males, forming a 'mating ball'. It favours pollen and nectar from ivy flowers but other plants may be visited before ivy comes into flower. Appears from early September, lasting into November. Widespread in southern England, south Wales and the Midlands, gradually spreading northwards.

Ashy Mining Bee *Andrena cineraria*
This distinctive mining bee with a grey-and-black-banded appearance is found in a wide range of habitats, including gardens. The sexes are similar, though the male is smaller with more white hairs than the female. It visits a variety of blossoms and flowers, usually from March to June, and nests in aggregations on sunny banks or lawns where the vegetation is sparse. Found throughout England, Wales and Ireland, with a few records from Scotland; in recent years it has become more common in southern and central England.

Tawny Mining Bee *Andrena fulva*
Conical mounds of soil on lawns are usually mines made by the bright, foxy-red female, who is also frequently seen pollinating the blossom of fruit trees and shrubs in gardens. The male is smaller and darker and is less often noticed. A 15–30cm shaft is dug, and larval cells, provisioned with a paste-like mix of pollen and honey, are made along its length. One generation a year is produced, appearing from April to June. Widely distributed throughout Britain; rare in Ireland.

Orange-tailed Mining Bee
Andrena haemorrhoa
Closely related to the Tawny Mining Bee, the female has a red thorax, a gingery tip to the otherwise shiny black abdomen, and white hairs on the face. The male is smaller, with long antennae, is less brightly marked and has pale brown hairs on the face. Adults emerge in early spring, when flowers such as sallow and blackthorn are in bloom, the females living until June; nests are often made on garden paths and lawns. One of the commonest and most widespread species of *Andrena*.

Orange-legged Furrow Bee
Halictus rubicundus
The bare patch on the fifth abdominal segment identifies female *Halictus* bees, of which there are many species. Males and females emerge in autumn, and after mating the males die, leaving only fertilised females to survive the winter. These emerge in spring to excavate their burrows, often colonially, in sandy soil. About six cells branch off from the burrow, in each of which an egg is provisioned with a ball of honey and pollen. Common and widely distributed.

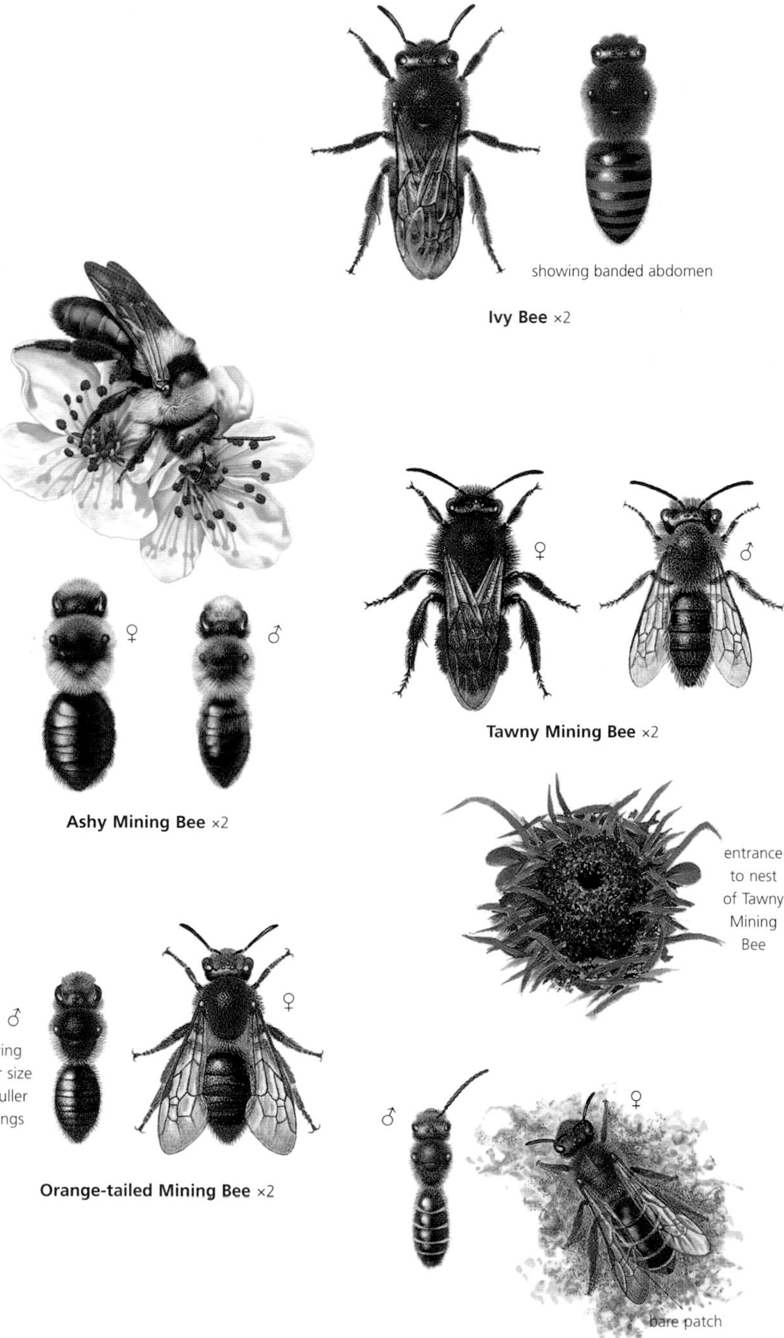

Ivy Bee ×2

Tawny Mining Bee ×2

Ashy Mining Bee ×2

Orange-tailed Mining Bee ×2

Orange-legged Furrow Bee ×2

Wool Carder Bee *Anthidium manicatum*
A big, robust bee. The male, unusually, is larger than the female, and is distinctively marked with yellow spots on the abdomen. The female strips the downy surface from leaves of plants such as lamb's ear and house leek and, using her toothed jaws to comb out the fibres, lines the inside of a nest tunnel, usually a hole in rotten wood. Each cell is lined with transparent saliva and an egg is floated on a liquid of honey and pollen. One generation a year occurs from May until September. Fairly common in England and Wales, being found as far north as southern Scotland; recently recorded from Ireland.

Red Mason Bee *Osmia bicornis*
The female has distinctive horns at the front of the head, used for tamping mud when nest-building. The head is black, becoming progressively gingery towards the end of the abdomen; the smaller male has longer antennae and a tuft of white hairs on the face. An important pollinator of many garden plants, like all mason bees, the female collects pollen in a basket beneath the abdomen. The nest is made in an existing hole in an old wall or dead tree stump, or in a special bee nestbox. Up to ten cells are formed along the tunnel and filled with a mixture of pollen and nectar. An egg is laid in each cell, which is then sealed with mud, and the process repeated until the tunnel is filled. The bees hatch in September but remain in the nest over winter, emerging in late March, continuing until early June. Common in England and Wales, but distributed as far north as southern Scotland; recently recorded from Ireland.

Patchwork Leafcutter Bee
Megachile centuncularis
Semi-circular holes in the leaves of garden roses are often the work of this bee which, although similar to the Honey Bee, is identified by the dense yellow hairs on the underside of the abdomen where pollen is collected. Oblong pieces of leaf are stuck together with saliva to line the nest tunnel, usually in a hole in wood. Cells are formed, each provisioned with a runny mix of nectar and pollen, and an egg is laid in each before being sealed with circular pieces of leaf. Emergence begins the following May, starting with the outer cells; these are always males, the females being towards the inner end of the tunnel. Flying continues until August. Common throughout most of England and Wales, rarer in Scotland and Ireland.

Gooden's Nomad Bee *Nomada goodeniana*
One of several related nomad bees, all of which are hairless and look more like wasps than bees. A cuckoo of other solitary bees, such as *Andrena* species, and is often seen around the entrance holes of their nests. The female lays her eggs in the cells of the host. These hatch and the larvae feed on the pollen and honey provided, and on the host's eggs or larvae. Mostly seen in spring and early summer. Widespread and one of the commoner species of nomad bee, but rare in Ireland.

Hairy-footed Flower Bee
Anthophora plumipes
One of the earliest springtime bees. The female is black with orange pollen baskets and resembles a small bumblebee, but with a fast humming flight, interspersed with hovering. Often flies with the long tongue extended. The male is paler, with a white face, and has conspicuous feathery extensions to the middle legs. In spring, the female makes a burrow in the ground or an old wall, and constructs several clay cells which are lined with a waterproof secretion; after filling them with pollen and honey, she lays a single egg in each. Adults appear from mid-March until June. Found throughout England and Wales, most commonly in the south; recently recorded from Scotland.

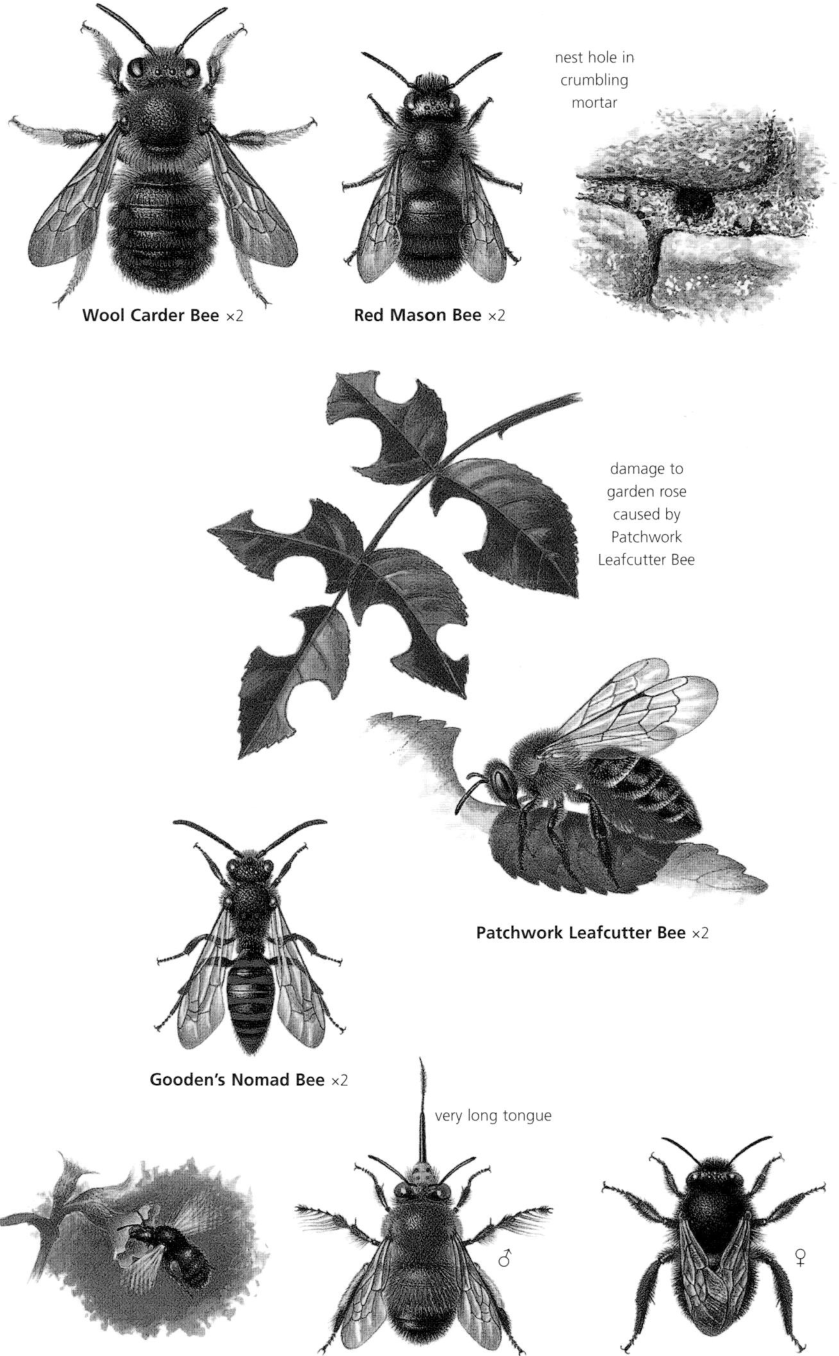

Wool Carder Bee ×2

Red Mason Bee ×2

Patchwork Leafcutter Bee ×2

Gooden's Nomad Bee ×2

Hairy-footed Flower Bee ×1.5

Bumblebees and Western Honey Bee

White-tailed Bumblebee *Bombus lucorum*
This bumblebee has black and 'clean' yellow banding, with a white tail, and has a face as long as wide, with a short tongue. It 'steals' nectar from long-necked flowers by making a hole in the base. Nests are built on or under the ground, always under cover, and are quite large, with around 200 workers. One of the earliest species to emerge from hibernation, the queens may be seen as early as February in the south. Widespread and very common, frequent in gardens. **Similar species** Workers of the **Buff-tailed Bumblebee** are very similar but their yellow coloration is 'dirty'.

Buff-tailed Bumblebee *Bombus terrestris*
This large bumblebee has black and 'dirty' yellow banding, with a white tail (occasionally buff-coloured in queens). The face is as long as wide, with a very short tongue (a 'nectar stealer', like the White-tailed Bumblebee). The nests are large, with up to 500 workers, invariably underground. It is one of the first species to emerge from hibernation, in early in February in the south. It is captive-bred in large numbers for glasshouse pollination. Very common and generally widespread, although scarce in Scotland. Frequent in gardens. **Similar species** Workers of the **White-tailed Bumblebee** are very similar but their yellow coloration is 'clean'.

Early Bumblebee *Bombus pratorum*
This is a relatively small species with black and 'clean' yellow banding and an orange tail, and the face as long as wide, with a short tongue. Males have distinctive yellow hairs on the face. Nests are small, with around 100 workers, and may be situated on or below ground, in crevices in trees, at the base of plants and other similar habitats. Queens emerge from hibernation very early, usually in February in the south. May manage two generations in a year. An important pollinator of soft fruits in gardens. Widespread and common.

Garden Bumblebee *Bombus hortorum*
The Garden Bumblebee has black and yellow banding and a white tail. The face is much longer than wide, with a very long tongue. Queens, males and workers are of similar coloration. Nests are on or under the ground, always under cover, with only around 100 workers. Queens emerge in March. Widespread and very common, especially in gardens on clover and dead-nettle. Often seen on foxgloves with the Common Carder Bee.

Red-tailed Bumblebee *Bombus lapidarius*
A large, distinctive species. Queens and workers are black with an orange-red tail; the male thorax has yellow bands. The face is as long as wide, with a medium-length tongue. Nests are formed underground and in cavities in walls and trees, usually in fairly open situations, and are quite large, often with more than 150 workers. Widespread and abundant. Shows a preference for yellow flowers, and is fond of bird's-foot-trefoil in wildlife gardens. Its nest is commonly taken over by the Red-tailed Cuckoo Bee *B. rupestris*, which appears to be increasing its range.

Tree Bumblebee *Bombus hypnorum*
First recorded in Britain in 2001, the Tree Bumblebee has distinctive ginger, black and white coloration. A bee of woodland margins, in Britain it is closely associated with human activity and has adapted well to urban regions; it is often the most common bee in parks and gardens. Queens appear in March and search for nesting sites, usually high up under eaves, in wall cavities and in bird nestboxes. Nests may have more than 150 workers, which gather pollen from a variety of cultivated and wild flowers. Two generations can be produced, with queens sometimes being seen as late as December. Found throughout England and much of Wales, spreading rapidly.

Common Carder Bee
Bombus pascuorum
Queens, males and workers are predominantly ginger-brown with black patches. The face is longer than wide, with a long tongue. These insects are called carder bees because of their habit of combing moss or dry grass to make their nest. The nests are built on or just below ground, covered with moss, and are quite small, rarely with more than 100 workers. Queens emerge from hibernation in March. It is common and widespread, and is a regular garden visitor. Frequent on flowers of dead-nettle and clover, and often seen on foxgloves, together with the Garden Bumblebee.

Vestal Cuckoo Bee *Bombus vestalis*
Similar in appearance to its host, the Buff-tailed Bumblebee, but without a yellow band at the front of the shiny abdomen and with much darker wings. The face is as long as wide, with a short tongue. Queens are seen in March or April, searching for nests of the Buff-tailed Bumblebee to parasitise. Only queens and males emerge from the nest of their host. Generally widespread and common. Has started moving north and is now found in Scotland and Ireland.

Western Honey Bee *Apis mellifera*
This familiar domesticated bee is orange-brown, with a long, narrow cell near the wing tip. Its nests are very large, with a queen and several tens of thousands of workers that visit a wide variety of garden flowers from early spring to autumn, often flying several kilometres in search of pollen and nectar. Male drones are produced from late spring onwards and form mating swarms with new queens. At other times, old queens leave the nest with about half the workers to make way for the new queen. These may form large swarms that hang from tree branches. Originally from south-east Asia, it is now widespread in artificial hives and in the wild, where it usually nests in hollow trees.

All bumblebees illustrated are queens

White-tailed Bumblebee ×1.5

Buff-tailed Bumblebee ×1.5

Early Bumblebee ×1.5

Garden Bumblebee ×1.5

Red-tailed Bumblebee ×1.5

Tree Bumblebee ×1.5

Common Carder Bee ×1.5

Vestal Cuckoo Bee ×1.5

Western Honey Bee ×1.5

Western Honey Bee swarm

Beetles Coleoptera

▲ A male Cockchafer in flight, showing the raised elytra and the extended hindwings.

Beetles are the most successful of all insects, and occur throughout the world in virtually every known habitat, terrestrial and aquatic; they make up 40% of all insects. More than 4,000 species of beetle occur in Britain. The name 'Coleoptera' means 'sheath wing' and, although beetles vary greatly in their shapes, colours and adaptations, the most obvious distinguishing features are the forewings, or elytra. These are modified into rigid curved plates that meet in a central line down the back, covering the membranous hindwings, which are folded away underneath. In some species, the hindwings are reduced or absent and the elytra are fused together, so that the insect is unable to fly. Beetles are not the most manoeuvrable of insects in flight, but many species take to the wing in sunshine or at night, first raising the elytra away from the body and then extending the hindwings before take-off. Several species, notably dung beetles and the Cockchafer, are often drawn to artificial light at night, and blunder indoors through open windows.

The tough, armour-plated structure, which extends to the rest of the body and legs, accounts for the success of beetles, protecting them from predators, allowing them to squeeze into tight crevices and preventing desiccation or water-logging in extreme weather. They have chewing and biting mouthparts and although the majority are herbivorous, some are predatory, whilst others scavenge or bore into wood or fungi. The tremendous range in size, even among garden beetles, begins with the tiny pollen beetles, flea beetles and weevils at no more than 1.5mm, up to the giant male Stag Beetle, which can reach 75mm.

Beetle larvae, like the adults, vary greatly and feed on a wide range of materials. They can usually be identified by the hardened, shiny head capsule and three pairs of thoracic legs, although these may be absent in wood borers. While many are grub-like and inactive, other larvae, such as those of the ladybirds, are colourful and agile hunters. Larvae of ground beetles and water beetles are active, fast-moving predators that seize their victims aggressively. The pupal stage is usually formed in a hidden chamber or cocoon, since this soft, immobile stage is when the beetle is most vulnerable. The pupa appears transitional between larva and adult, with

▲ A Rose Chafer on blossom.

the appendages clearly visible and separate from the body.

With a few exceptions, such as the Strawberry Seed Beetle, ground beetles are some of the most beneficial garden insects, many of which are predatory night hunters that feed on invertebrate pests, including slugs and various insect larvae. The Violet Ground Beetle is a good example, as both adult and larva are fierce hunters.

A large family containing more than a quarter of the British beetle species, the rove beetles are characterised by their short elytra, which expose the long, cylindrical abdomen. The largest member of the family, the Devil's Coach-horse, is a formidable hunter, and if threatened, postures by opening its jaws and curling its tail over its back. It is mainly nocturnal, but many of the smaller rove beetles are active in the daytime and often fly in sunshine, using their abdomen to tuck away the hindwings after flight. As a part of their defence mechanism, they can also emit a caustic irritant from their rear end.

Closely related are the burying beetles, which are night flyers and are usually either entirely black or boldly banded with orange and black. They seek out the corpses of small mammals, birds and reptiles, and set about excavating the ground beneath the carcass until it has disappeared, finally laying their eggs in a nearby shaft. Their smell reflects their occupation, but they play an important role in disposing of carcasses. Accompanying them in their night-time activities, and doing an equally unpleasant yet essential task, are the dung beetles. They are found mainly on farmland, where they help to dispose of the dung of cattle, sheep and horses, but they are also common visitors to rural gardens.

Many beetles from many different families visit flowers for nectar and pollen, making an important contribution to pollination. Several fly by day and are brightly coloured, warning predators they are unpalatable. Two of those commonly seen in gardens are the Black-and-yellow Longhorn Beetle and the Wasp Beetle. The cardinal beetle is another large, brightly coloured beetle often seen in the daytime on flowers. Its larva is associated with rotting wood, but it feeds not on the wood but on the invertebrates that share the habitat.

Perhaps the largest and most diverse group of beetles found in the garden, many of which cause problems to vegetable and flower growers, are the herbivores, which include the leaf beetles, flea beetles and weevils. These are many and varied and, as well as native species that take advantage of an abundance of healthy cultivated foliage laid out in easily accessible rows, there are also accidentally introduced aliens. Notable amongst these are the Rosemary Leaf Beetle and the notorious but infrequent Colorado Beetle, which have arrived courtesy of the horticultural industry and which may, with the aid of climate change, become more securely established. Several species of flea beetle, all of which are tiny but often beautifully coloured, cause some damage to vegetables. The brightly coloured Asparagus Beetle can strip the fronds of its host plant but, at the moment, the most notorious of the beetle villains, ranking even higher than the dreaded Vine Weevil, is the handsome Lily Beetle. It and its larvae, concealed in their own excrement for protection, munch their way through fritillaries, Solomon's-seal and lilies, and are a fine example of opportunism in the insect world.

Violet Ground Beetle *Carabus violaceus*
One of several large, fast-moving, black ground beetles, distinguished by the violet or blue margins to the thorax and wing cases. Active mostly at night, the flightless adults and the larvae feed on invertebrates, including many insect pests, worms and slugs. By day, it is often disturbed from beneath stones and logs. It occurs all year but is especially common from June to August, in gardens throughout the country.

Copper Greenclock *Poecilus cupreus*
This very variable beetle ranges from bronzy-green, coppery or purple, to almost black, with the two basal segments of the antennae orange. Common in gardens, it occurs in damp places, under stones and rotten wood, emerging at night to feed. Found mainly in southern Britain and parts of Ireland.

Strawberry Seed Beetle *Harpalus rufipes*
This is distinguished from other ground beetles by the dull, velvety appearance of the wing cases and the reddish-brown legs and antennae. Adults and larvae are almost exclusively vegetarian, preferring the seeds of fat hen, but also causing some damage to strawberries. Beetles emerge in the late summer and live for more than two years. They are mainly nocturnal and, although they can fly and are sometimes attracted to light, they are usually found on the ground. Very common in gardens, and sometimes enters houses.

Common Sun Beetle *Amara aenea*
A shiny, oval-shaped beetle, which ranges in colour from coppery-green to almost black, with three orange basal segments to the antennae. Often seen flying in the sunshine or scurrying for shelter on paths, when disturbed it emits an unpleasant-smelling fluid. It is omnivorous, feeding on vegetable and animal matter, including small invertebrates and their larvae. Common everywhere; found throughout the year but most often seen in spring.

Ground beetle *Notiophilus biguttatus*
A tiny, shiny bronze ground beetle, the commonest of eight closely related species, with very large eyes, often seen running jerkily in bright sunshine. Adults hibernate and emerge in spring to feed on tiny invertebrates such as springtails. Found in many habitats throughout the country; very common in gardens.

Great Diving Beetle *Dytiscus marginalis*
Best known of all the water beetles, and the commonest of six closely related species, often seen taking in air at the water's surface. The male is shiny olive-brown with a greenish sheen, and has disc-like suckers on the forelegs, used for gripping the female during mating. The female is duller and usually has longitudinal grooves on the wing cases. Eggs are laid in the stems of water plants in March and April, and both adults and larvae are voracious predators, attacking tadpoles and small fish as well as aquatic invertebrates. Diving beetles fly at night and are often attracted to light, sometimes mistaking glass roofs and wet roads for deeper water. Adults can live for up to three years. Found in weedy ponds throughout Britain and Ireland.

Water beetle *Agabus bipustulatus*
A very common, black water beetle, with a metallic sheen and two obscure reddish spots on the head. It flies readily at night and often visits garden ponds. It can tolerate quite stagnant water and is sometimes found in damp muddy crevices in periods of drought when ponds dry out. The predatory larva pupates inside a spherical cell made from mud at the water's edge. Widespread and very common, found throughout the year.

Diving beetle *Hygrotus inaequalis*
A common, often abundant beetle, which varies in colour, some specimens having entirely black wing cases. Found in well-vegetated ponds and small lakes throughout Britain and Ireland.

Scavenger water beetle *Enochrus testaceus*
This shiny brown beetle, with maxillary palps longer than the antennae, is found in vegetation around the shallow margins of ponds and sluggish water. The female lays about a dozen eggs, contained in a triangular silken bag attached to duckweed. The larvae crawl, caterpillar-like, through the vegetation. Widespread throughout Britain and Ireland, scarcer further north.

Scavenger water beetle
Helophorus brevipalpis
One of several similar species, with a characteristic metallic green thorax with five vertical furrows, and clubbed antennae. Neither adults nor larvae swim, but crawl amongst water plants and debris around the water's edge. They feed on plants or decomposing vegetation and are found commonly in ponds and stagnant pools throughout the country.

Common Whirligig Beetle
Gyrinus substriatus
Whirligig beetles, of which there are 12 species, are amongst the most conspicuous water beetles as they spend most of their time, particularly in warm, calm weather, gyrating in 'schools' on the surface of ponds. This species is typical of the family, having a glossy black oval appearance and modified paddle-shaped middle and hindlegs, enabling it to whirl wildly around on the surface. The eyes are separated horizontally, forming an upper eye and lower eye, allowing the beetle to see above and below the surface; when alarmed, it dives into submerged vegetation. In spring, small batches of eggs are laid on underwater vegetation. The larva, which resembles that of alderflies, with a row of gills along each side of the abdomen, feeds mainly on mosquito and other aquatic larvae. Pupation takes place in a mud cell at the water's edge. Found throughout Britain and Ireland, in many still-water habitats, including newly-created garden ponds.

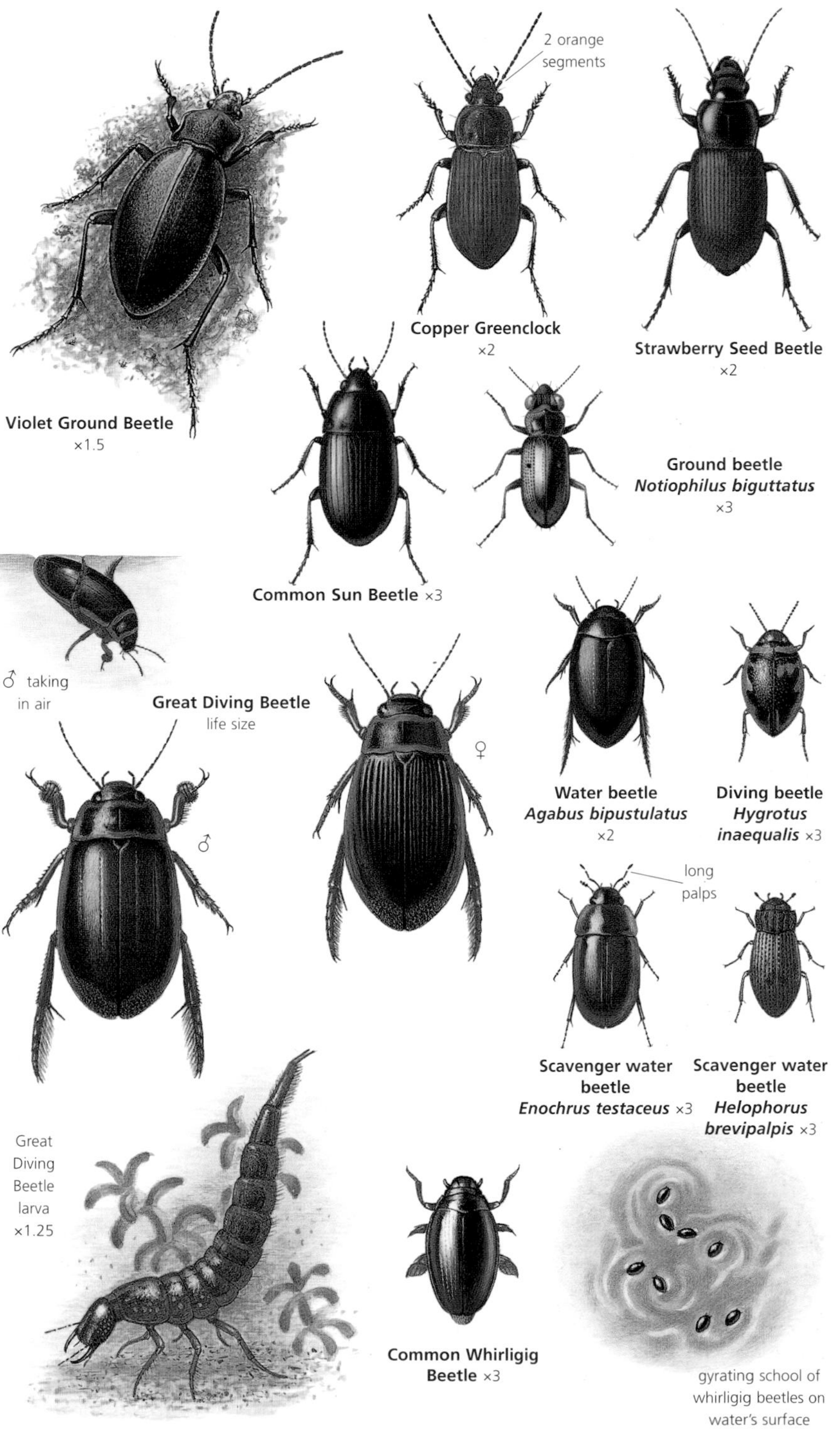

Violet Ground Beetle ×1.5

Copper Greenclock ×2

Strawberry Seed Beetle ×2

Common Sun Beetle ×3

Ground beetle *Notiophilus biguttatus* ×3

Great Diving Beetle life size

Water beetle *Agabus bipustulatus* ×2

Diving beetle *Hygrotus inaequalis* ×3

Scavenger water beetle *Enochrus testaceus* ×3

Scavenger water beetle *Helophorus brevipalpis* ×3

Great Diving Beetle larva ×1.25

Common Whirligig Beetle ×3

gyrating school of whirligig beetles on water's surface

Devil's Coach-horse *Ocypus olens*
The largest and best-known member of the huge rove beetle family, this sooty black species usually hides under stones and debris by day, emerging at night to hunt. Adults and the equally voracious larvae feed on a wide variety of invertebrates, including insects, spiders, woodlice, snails and worms. When alarmed, it opens its jaws and curls its tail over its back threateningly, giving rise to its other name of Cock Tail. It can also discharge a repellent odour to deter predators and is capable of giving a sharp nip with its powerful jaws. Widely distributed and frequent in gardens.

Rove beetle *Tachyporus hypnorum*
One of many species of small red and black rove beetles whose colours warn of its unpleasant taste. Found among garden debris, in compost heaps and under stones, where it hunts small invertebrates such as aphids. Widespread and especially common sunning itself on foliage in spring.

Rove beetle *Xantholinus linearis*
A narrow, parallel-sided rove beetle, one of six *Xantholinus* species that occur in Britain. Widespread and found commonly in moss, grass and leaf litter in various habitats, including gardens.

Click beetle *Athous haemorrhoidalis*
Click beetles, or 'skipjacks', are able to spring into the air, with an audible click, in order to avoid danger. This species is common on trees and shrubs, and in spring, batches of eggs are laid in the soil. The larvae, the well-known wireworms, take several years to mature and may cause damage to root vegetables, seedlings and ornamental plants. Widely distributed throughout Britain and parts of Ireland; a pest in gardens, allotments and farmland.

Lined Click Beetle *Agriotes lineatus*
Larvae of this and the closely related *A. obscurus* and *A. sputator* are the most damaging of all root-feeding pest species. Roots, tubers and bulbs of many plants are tunnelled into, allowing other pests such as slugs to continue the damage. They are mainly active from March to May, and again from September to October, and can live in the soil for up to five years, pupating in the autumn in an earthen chamber several centimetres below the surface. Adults hatch after a few weeks, but remain below ground until the following spring and are most common from May to August. Frequent everywhere.

Sexton beetle *Nicrophorus vespillo*
Six of the eight species of *Nicrophorus* (meaning 'grave digger') are orange and black; this species, with its curved hind legs, is one of the commonest. An important recycler of dead birds and animals, it flies at night in spring, searching by scent for decaying corpses, and is often attracted to light. It feeds on flesh and also on any fly maggots present on the corpse, and then begins to excavate beneath it. When burial is completed, about 15 eggs are laid in a nearby shaft and the young larvae are cared for and fed by the female until they can look after themselves. Common in spring and autumn in the south, but scarcer further north.

Black sexton beetle *Nicrophorus humator*
This is the commonest of two black burying beetles, with a similar life cycle to that of the sexton beetle. Seen crawling over decaying carcases or attracted to light at night, it is often covered in *Gamasus* mites, which feed from the beetle but do little harm. Widespread and found in many habitats, mainly from spring to autumn.

Common Malachite Beetle
Malachius bipustulatus
This beetle is often seen on sunny summer days, when it visits a variety of garden flowers and grasses to feed on pollen, nectar and other insects. The distinctive bright colours warn that it is poisonous, and when disturbed it can inflate protuberances from the sides of the thorax to deter predators. The larva is carnivorous, and lives under bark and leaf litter. Common in England and Wales, rarer in Scotland.

Common Red Soldier Beetle or
Bloodsucker *Rhagonycha fulva*
Despite the name 'Bloodsucker', this is a harmless beetle, commonly seen in summer on a variety of flowers, particularly umbellifers, mating or feeding on other smaller insects. They fly readily and have characteristic soft, orange wing cases with black tips. The larva is predatory, living on the ground in moss and leaf litter. This is the commonest soldier beetle. It is widely distributed, but less frequent in the far north.

Flower beetle *Oedemera lurida*
A dull metallic green beetle, often seen feeding in groups in sunshine on the pollen of umbellifers, hawkweeds and buttercups. The larvae feed on decaying wood and in stems of various herbaceous plants. Locally common and widespread.

Red-headed Cardinal Beetle
Pyrochroa serraticornis
The commonest of three cardinal beetles, distinguished by the lack of any black markings on the head or thorax. Often seen in the daytime on flowers, feeding on pollen and nectar, or crawling on the trunks of fallen trees. The flattened larva lives for up to two years under the damp bark of old tree stumps, where it feeds on invertebrates. Found in England, Wales and parts of Ireland.

Rustic Sailor Beetle *Cantharis rustica*
This is one of the largest and commonest of 15 species of *Cantharis*, often found in the company of the Common Red Soldier Beetle and with a similar life cycle. Adults and larvae are predators and are sometimes cannibalistic. Found throughout the country, in any suitable flowery habitat.

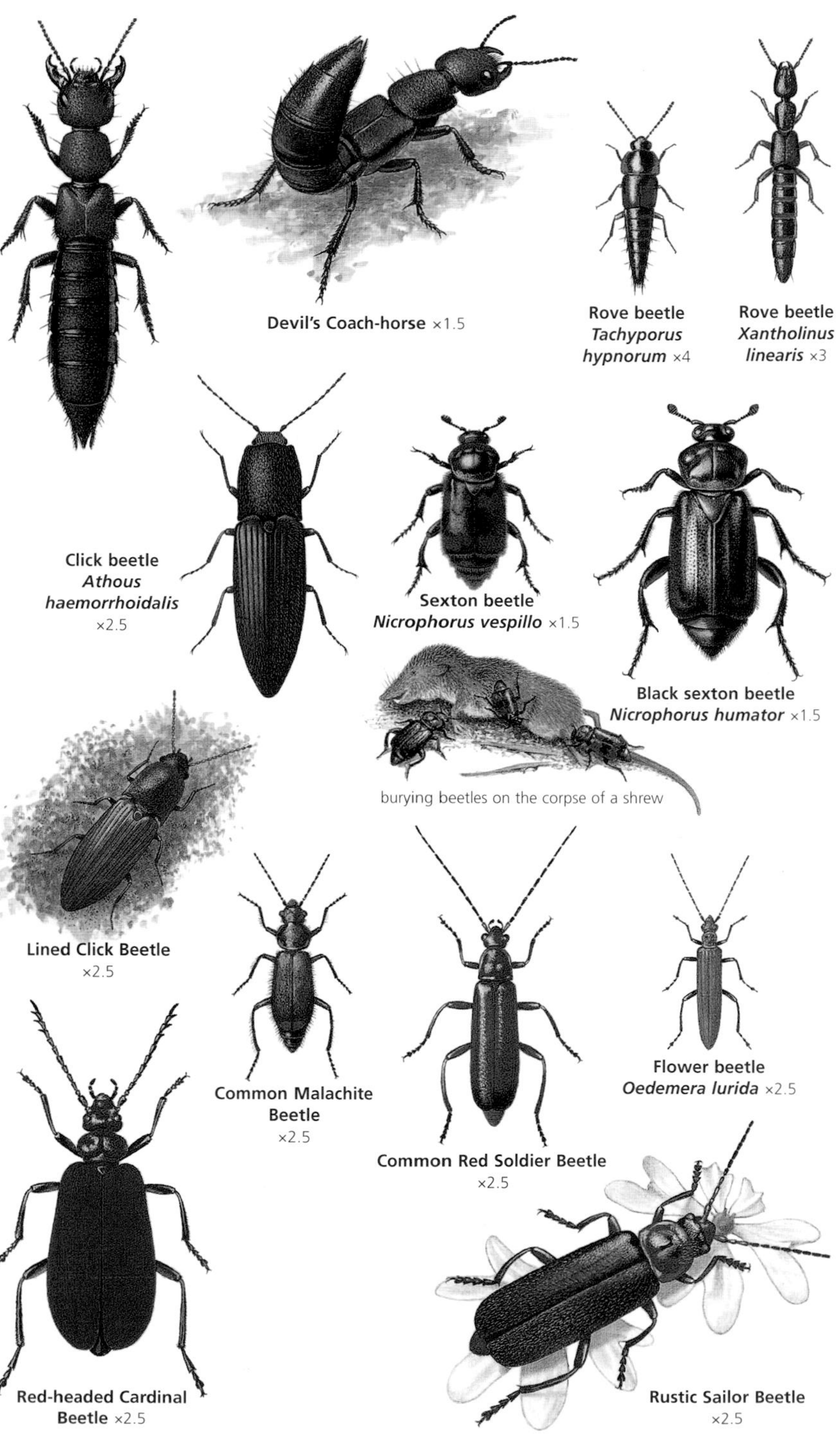
Devil's Coach-horse ×1.5
Rove beetle
Tachyporus hypnorum ×4
Rove beetle
Xantholinus linearis ×3
Click beetle
Athous haemorrhoidalis
×2.5
Sexton beetle
Nicrophorus vespillo ×1.5
Black sexton beetle
Nicrophorus humator ×1.5
burying beetles on the corpse of a shrew
Lined Click Beetle
×2.5
Common Malachite Beetle
×2.5
Common Red Soldier Beetle
×2.5
Flower beetle
Oedemera lurida ×2.5
Red-headed Cardinal Beetle ×2.5
Rustic Sailor Beetle
×2.5

Dung beetle *Aphodius rufipes*
This species is one of the largest and commonest of more than 40 species of *Aphodius* beetles. Mostly active at night, it is regularly attracted to lighted windows and, along with other dung beetles, plays an important part in the diet of bats. Eggs are laid in the dung of horses, sheep and cattle, with up to 100 larvae found in a single cow pat. When fully grown the larvae pupate in the soil, the adults being most common in late summer.

Dor Beetle *Geotrupes stercorarius*
An important recycler of animal droppings, the Dor Beetle is a large, shiny metallic beetle, often seen flying clumsily on summer evenings. It is also known as the 'Lousy Watchman' as it is frequently infested with tiny yellowish-brown *Gamasus* mites that feed from the soft parts of its body. Eggs are laid below ground in dung-filled chambers leading from a shaft, which may be up to 60cm deep. The larvae feed for several months before pupating in the soil, and adults appear the following spring, continuing until the autumn. Common in farmland and pastures and often visits rural gardens.

Garden Chafer *Phyllopertha horticola*
This small chafer, with a metallic green thorax, may often be seen flying in sunshine around fruit trees and ornamental shrubs in orchards and gardens, where it may cause some damage by nibbling leaves and buds. Eggs are laid up to 25cm below ground and, when present in large numbers, the 'C'-shaped white grubs, which feed on roots, may cause considerable damage to lawns. They live for about a year, moving deeper into the soil in the cold winter months, and pupate the following spring, being most common in May and June. Becoming less common but widespread throughout the country, especially on light chalky soil.

Summer Chafer *Amphimallon solstitialis*
Often seen flying around mature deciduous and conifer trees in gardens at dusk in June and July, the Summer Chafer has a similar life cycle to other chafers but completes its larval stage in two years. Like a smaller version of the more common Cockchafer, fresh specimens are covered in dense hair, although this rubs off with age. Eggs are laid into grass turf and the larvae feed exclusively on the roots, sometimes causing damage to lawns. They pupate in the spring after the second year. Locally common in England and Wales.

Cockchafer or **May Bug**
Melolontha melolontha
This big, clumsy chafer often swarms in large numbers around trees and shrubs, with an audible humming sound, on warm nights in May and June. It feeds on foliage, with a preference for oak and apple, and may cause considerable damage; it also causes alarm when entering lighted windows at night. Males have well-developed, fan-like antennae, and both sexes have prominent white triangles along the sides of the body. Batches of up to 20 eggs are laid about 20cm below ground, and the white larvae can cause damage by eating the roots of grasses, cereals and young shrubs. After the third summer, the larva pupates at a depth of up to 60cm; the adult emerges in October, but remains underground until the following spring. Widespread and very common, but scarcer in the north where a similar but much rarer species, *M. hippocastani*, also occurs.

Rose Chafer *Cetonia aurata*
To most people, the sight of this beautiful metallic green beetle, often with a coppery sheen, resting among rose petals in June, is worth the sacrifice of a few leaves and blooms. It flies readily in the sunshine and has a heavy, buzzing flight. The plump, 'C'-shaped larva lives in soft rotting wood, leaf litter and compost; it completes its growth in one to two years. Widely distributed and locally common in the south.

Lesser Stag Beetle *Dorcus parallelipipedus*
This resembles a small female Stag Beetle, but can be identified by its broader, squarer head, particularly in the male, a duller body, and by one spine, rather than three spines, on the tibia of the middle and hindlegs. Eggs are laid in decaying wood of various deciduous trees and the larvae take several years to mature. Adults hide by day in rotten wood, emerging sluggishly at night and sometimes flying to light. It occurs throughout the year but is most often seen in the spring and summer months. Locally common in England, Wales and Ireland.

Stag Beetle *Lucanus cervus*
The Stag Beetle is the largest and most impressive land beetle; males, with their enormous antlers, can reach a length of 75mm. The female lacks the intimidating jaws of the male but can inflict a more painful nip with her sharp, pincer-like mandibles. Each female produces a total of about 70 eggs, which are laid in small batches in damp, rotting stumps of oak, apple and other deciduous trees. The larva takes up to four years to mature and, after hatching in the autumn, the adult remains in its cell until the following spring. Found locally in the south and south-east of England, it has declined, mainly as a result of the tidying up of tree stumps and decaying wood in parks and gardens. A Biodiversity Action Plan was developed to encourage retention of dead wood, not removing tree stumps, and the creation of wood piles.

all shown life size
except where indicated

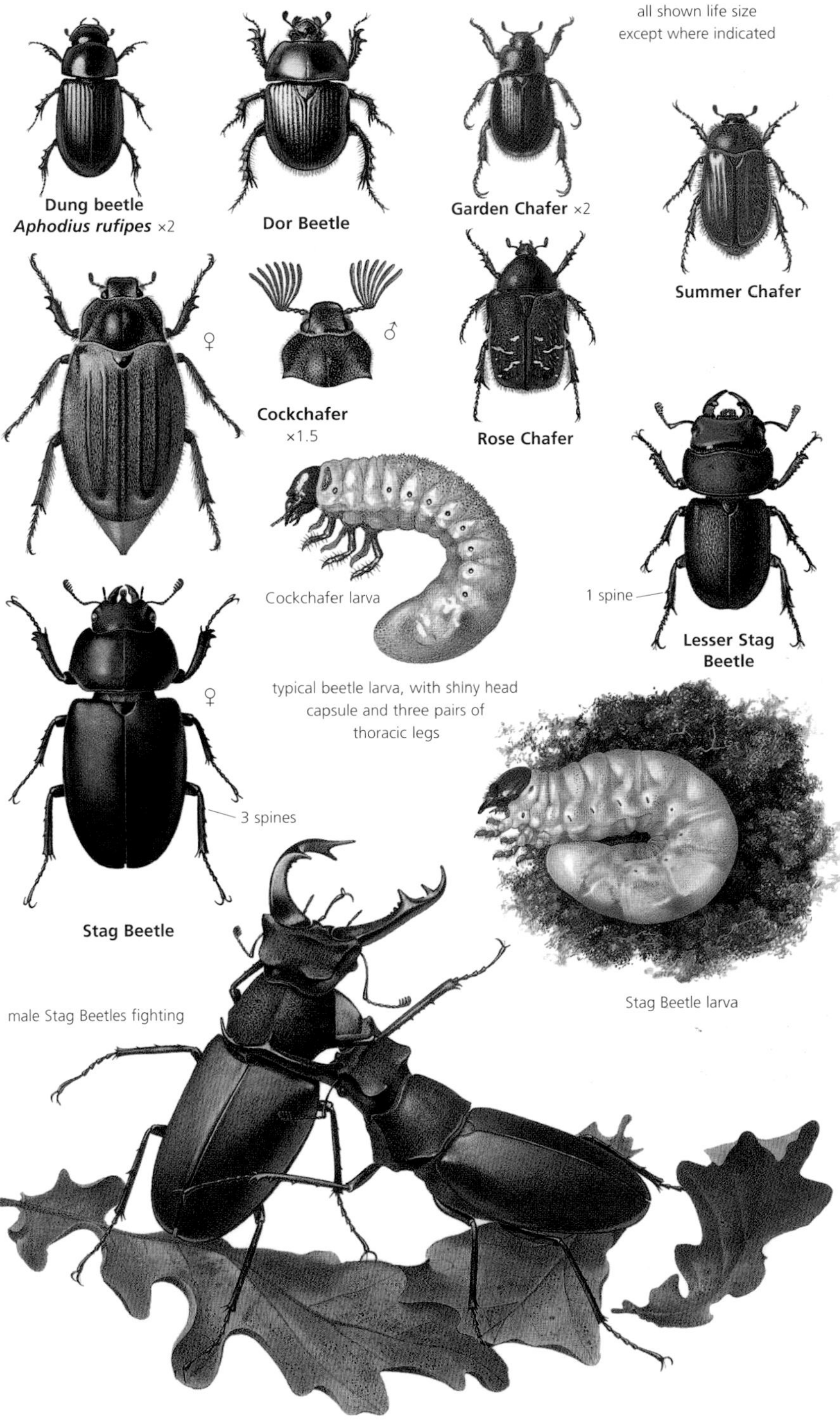

typical beetle larva, with shiny head capsule and three pairs of thoracic legs

Stag Beetle larva

male Stag Beetles fighting

7-spot Ladybird *Coccinella septempunctata*
The most familiar ladybird, known for its bright colours and popular with gardeners for its voracious appetite for aphids. Adults overwinter, often communally, in sheltered nooks, appearing in gardens in spring and summer. After mating, the female lays batches of yellow eggs on aphid-infested plants. The active larva lives for up to six weeks, eating several hundred aphids before pupating on vegetation, the full life cycle taking about two months to complete. A widespread and abundant beneficial insect found throughout Britain and Ireland.

Orange Ladybird *Halyzia sedecimguttata*
A distinctive ladybird with 12–16 white spots and a partially translucent thorax, found on many trees and bushes, especially birches, sycamore and ash, where it feeds on powdery mildew. It often flies at night and may be attracted to lighted windows and moth traps. Most common in August and September. Widespread throughout Britain and Ireland; in southern England, its range and frequency has increased in recent years.

Harlequin Ladybird *Harmonia axyridis*
This recent alien arrival into Britain has caused much alarm. It is a predatory species, which out-competes other ladybirds for food and then feeds on them and other insects when food becomes scarce, possibly affecting the future of some native species. Markings vary greatly, the most typical form resembling the size and colour of the 7-spot Ladybird but with up to 21 black spots. Found on various trees, especially lime and sycamore. First recorded from the south-east in 2003, it has spread rapidly north and west and now also occurs in Wales, Scotland and Ireland.

Cream-spot Ladybird
Calvia quattuordecimguttata
Another white-spotted ladybird with little variation. It has a rusty-red ground colour and occurs on small deciduous trees and shrubs, where it feeds on aphids and plant lice. It hibernates in crevices and emerges in spring. Frequent in gardens throughout Britain and Ireland.

10-spot Ladybird *Adalia decempunctata*
A very variable and abundant ladybird best told from related species by the pale-coloured legs. Widely distributed and found on many deciduous trees and shrubs, where it feeds on aphids.

2-spot Ladybird *Adalia bipunctata*
A very common species with a great range of markings, the most frequent being red with two conspicuous back spots on the wing cases; all forms have black legs. Both adults and larvae are beneficial in the garden, predating aphids on many trees, shrubs and plants. Large groups of hibernating adults may sometimes be found either in houses or outdoors, behind bark or in bird nestboxes. They emerge in the first warm days of spring and can be found throughout Britain and parts of Ireland. **Similar species** The **10-spot Ladybird** is a similar size and is equally variable, but has paler legs.

14-spot Ladybird
Propylea quattuordecimpunctata
The angular spots of this variable yellow and black ladybird are often confluent, but the central dorsal line is always present. It lives on a variety of mainly low-growing plants, where it and its larvae feed on aphids. Common in England, Wales and Ireland, with a few scattered records from Scotland. **Similar species** The **22-spot Ladybird** is smaller, with more regular, rounded spots.

22-spot Ladybird
Psyllobora vigintiduopunctata
A tiny, but easily recognised ladybird that varies little and is found in low vegetation, such as nettles, hogweed and amongst grasses, where it feeds on mildew. Quite common in England, Wales and eastern Ireland, but rare in Scotland.

24-spot Ladybird
Subcoccinella vigintiquattuorpunctata
The number of spots on this small, russet-coloured ladybird, which is covered in fine grey hairs, varies from none to 24. It is a non-carnivorous species, feeding mainly on campions and false oat-grass. Widely distributed, it is locally common in England, Wales and parts of Scotland.

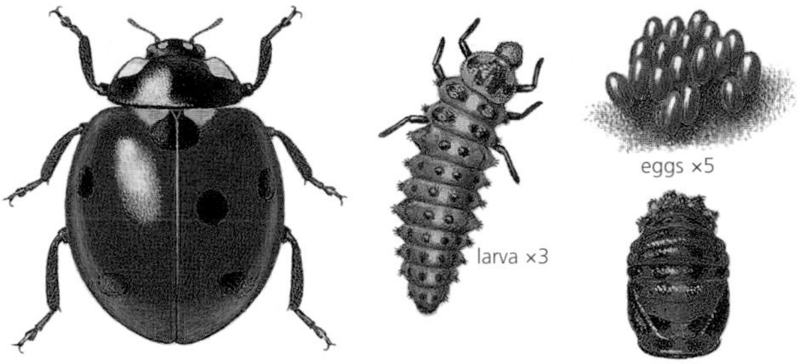

×4
larva ×3
eggs ×5
pupa ×3

7-spot Ladybird

Orange Ladybird ×4

×4
dimple at the rear of each elytron
pupa ×3
Harlequin Ladybird larva ×3

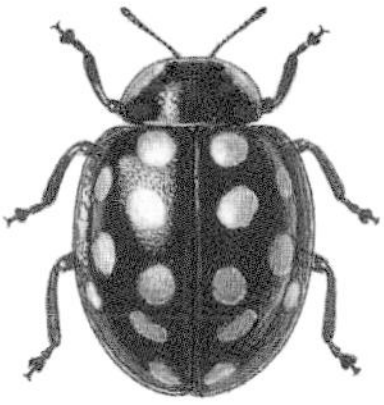

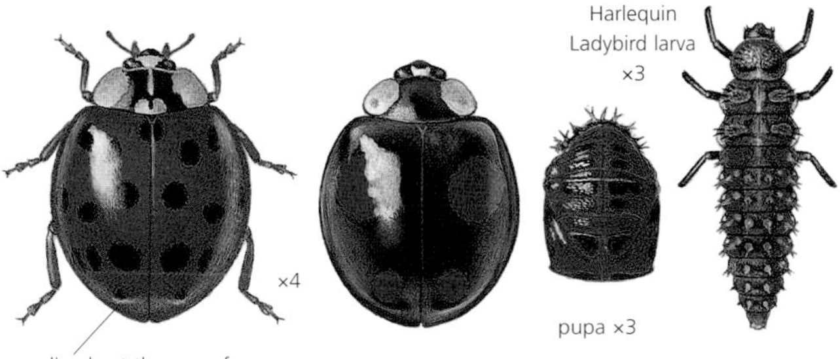

Harlequin Ladybird

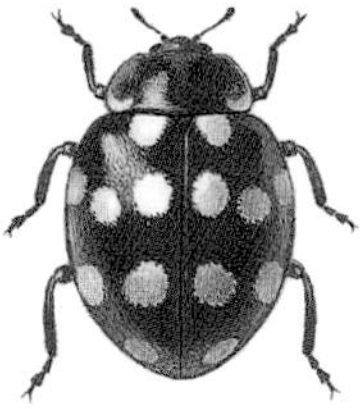

Cream-spot Ladybird ×4

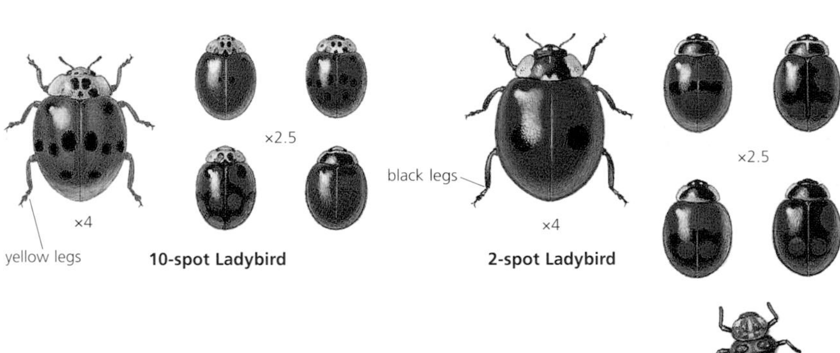

×4
×2.5
yellow legs

10-spot Ladybird

black legs
×4
×2.5
2-spot Ladybird larva ×3

2-spot Ladybird

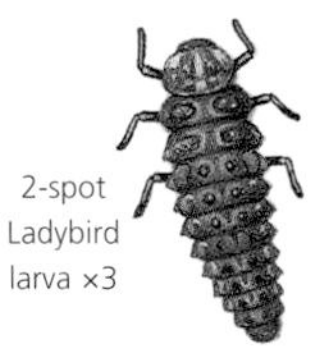

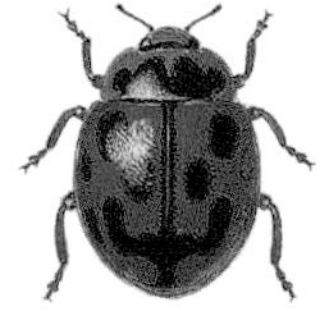

14-spot Ladybird ×4

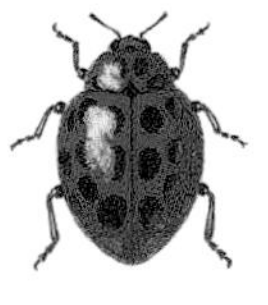

22-spot Ladybird ×4

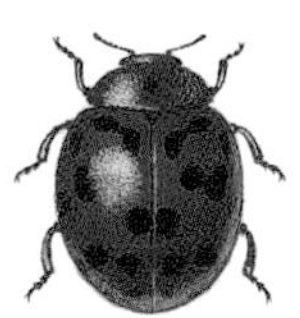

24-spot Ladybird ×4

Larder Beetle or **Bacon Beetle**
Dermestes lardarius
Often found indoors, where the larva is sometimes a pest of dry foodstuff, outdoors it breeds in the nests of birds and rodents. The female lays up to 150 eggs throughout her life in a single generation, with the complete life cycle taking 2–3 months. Outside, the winter is passed as an adult. Cosmopolitan, being found in most parts of Britain.

Fur Beetle or **Two-spotted Carpet Beetle**
Attagenus pellio
The larva has an even wider dietary range than that of the Larder Beetle, including carpets, furniture upholstery and museum specimens. Outdoors, it lives in birds' nests and dried animal corpses, taking 1–3 years to mature; the harmless adult feeds on pollen from many plants and shrubs. Overwinters as an adult; widespread throughout Britain.

Furniture Beetle or **Woodworm**
Anobium punctatum
Considered mainly an indoor pest, the Woodworm is common in gardens, where the larva tunnels for up to five years in fence posts and dead branches. Adults, which from the side appear to have a hood over the head, mate soon after emergence between May and August, and females lay about 40 eggs in crevices, including old emergence holes in both softwoods and hardwoods. Common and widespread throughout Britain and Ireland.

Carpet Beetle *Anthrenus verbasci*
Another species whose larva, the notorious 'Woolly Bear', causes damage indoors, but outdoors lives mainly in birds' nests. Adults become active in spring and early summer and are often seen flying in the sunshine or feeding from the flowers of *Spiraea* or umbellifers. Widespread in England, Wales and Ireland.

Churchyard Beetle or **Cellar Beetle**
Blaps mucronata
This large, flightless, black beetle is mainly active at night in damp barns and outhouses, where it scavenges omnivorously on organic matter; its larva also scavenges, but only on vegetable matter. Adults, which may live for several years, move slowly and often climb walls, and when alarmed discharge a foul-smelling liquid. The commonest of three closely-related species, it is locally common throughout Britain and also present in Ireland.

Yellow Mealworm Beetle *Tenebrio molitor*
A common pest of stored foods, the Yellow Mealworm is bred in large numbers for wild and caged birds and for pet food. It also occurs outdoors in birds' nests and chicken coups, the adults and larvae scavenging on all kinds of organic matter but preferring grain products. Outdoors, larvae hibernate and adults emerge in April and May, but indoors adults occur throughout the year. Probably not native to Britain but it is now cosmopolitan in distribution.

Black-and-yellow Longhorn Beetle
Rutpela maculata
This brightly coloured beetle, whose yellow and black markings vary greatly, is commonly seen flying in the sunshine and visiting flowers such as umbellifers. The larva lives for up to three years, feeding on the sapwood in damp, decaying stumps of various deciduous trees, particularly birch, or in pine. In spring, it pupates near the surface and adults are seen from May to September. Common and widely distributed in England and Wales but scarcer in Scotland and Ireland.

Thick-legged Flower Beetle
Oedemera nobilis
Most often seen feeding on pollen from the flowers of oxeye daisies, bramble and various umbels, only the male of this bright, metallic-green beetle has the conspicuous swollen thighs that are characteristic of the species. The larva lives concealed in hollow plant stems. Common from April to September, and widespread throughout England and Wales. The first record in Ireland was recently confirmed in Waterford.

Lily Beetle *Lilioceris lilii*
Well known to gardeners as a pest of various lilies, fritillaries and Solomon's-seal, this conspicuous beetle emerges from hibernation in early April and continues into the autumn. The female lays several hundred eggs in small batches on foliage and stems, and the larva gains protection by covering itself in slimy black excrement. Damage by adults and larvae can cause serious defoliation, and when removed by hand adult beetles make an audible squeaking sound. Found throughout England and Wales; it has spread northwards in recent years, with scattered records from Scotland and Ireland.

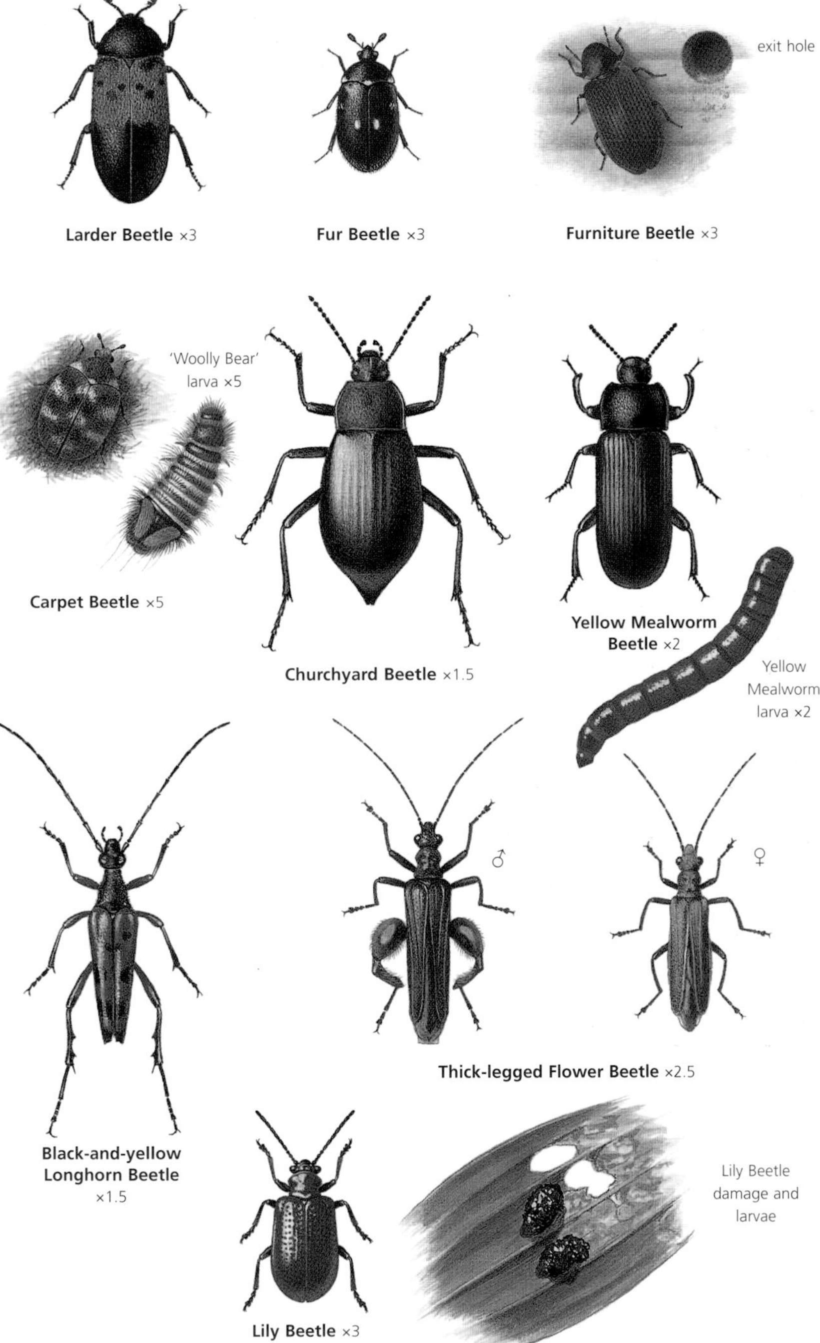

Larder Beetle ×3

Fur Beetle ×3

Furniture Beetle ×3

Carpet Beetle ×5

Churchyard Beetle ×1.5

Yellow Mealworm Beetle ×2

Thick-legged Flower Beetle ×2.5

Black-and-yellow Longhorn Beetle ×1.5

Lily Beetle ×3

Wasp Beetle *Clytus arietis*
This beetle gains protection from its wasp-like markings. It also flies in the sunshine and moves jerkily, like a wasp. It is most often seen visiting flowers or on woodpiles, from May to July. The larva feeds in old fence posts and fallen branches of various deciduous trees, particularly willows and birches. Found in all parts of Britain, most common in the south, scarce in Scotland and Ireland.

Common Grammoptera
Grammoptera ruficornis
This is one of the smaller and less spectacular longhorn beetles, often seen in April and July visiting flowers of hawthorn, and umbellifers. The larva feeds in dead twigs of various deciduous trees. The commonest of three closely related species, it is found throughout Britain except in the far north and also occurs in Ireland.

Asparagus Beetle *Crioceris asparagi*
Another distinctively marked pest found, along with its larvae, on the leaves of asparagus where it can cause serious defoliation. Eggs are laid in batches on the feathery fronds and the greenish-grey larvae feed for about two weeks, stripping the foliage and leaving only dry, yellowish-brown stems. Adults hibernate amongst garden debris and become active in May; they produce several generations throughout the year, lasting into October. Occurs mainly in southern Britain.

Rosemary Leaf Beetle *Chrysolina americana*
Originating from southern Europe and North Africa and first recorded in Britain over 50 years ago, it is only in the last five years that this beetle has been regarded as an established pest species, feeding mainly on rosemary, but also on lavender, thyme and sage. The flightless adults emerge in spring but are mostly active from early summer, when they mate and lay their eggs. Its range is expanding, being found mainly around London and the south-east, but with widely scattered records in Wales, Scotland and Ireland.

Knotgrass Leaf Beetle *Chrysolina polita*
The commonest of the leaf beetles, found on a wide range of low-growing plants and occurring in gardens on various mints, marjoram and ground ivy. Adult beetles appear after hibernation in spring and continue into the autumn. Found throughout most of Britain and Ireland.

Mint Leaf Beetle *Chrysolina herbacea*
A sluggish, metallic green beetle, usually found in damp places on various mints and related species. Appearing from May until September, widespread, sometimes occurring on cultivated mint in herb gardens and around garden ponds on water mint.

Colorado Beetle *Leptinotarsa decemlineata*
This infamous and notifiable pest of potatoes is a native of North America and, although not established in Britain, it has become widespread in mainland Europe following its introduction in 1922. Adults emerge from their hibernation in the soil in spring, and the female lays more than 400 orange eggs in batches of about 30 on the undersides of potato and, less often, tomato leaves. Depending on temperature, these usually hatch in 1–2 weeks and the larvae live for a further 2–4 weeks before entering the soil to pupate. Several generations may be produced in favourable conditions. Most reported specimens are imported into Britain with consignments of parsley or potatoes from southern Europe. Any specimens discovered should be reported immediately to Defra.

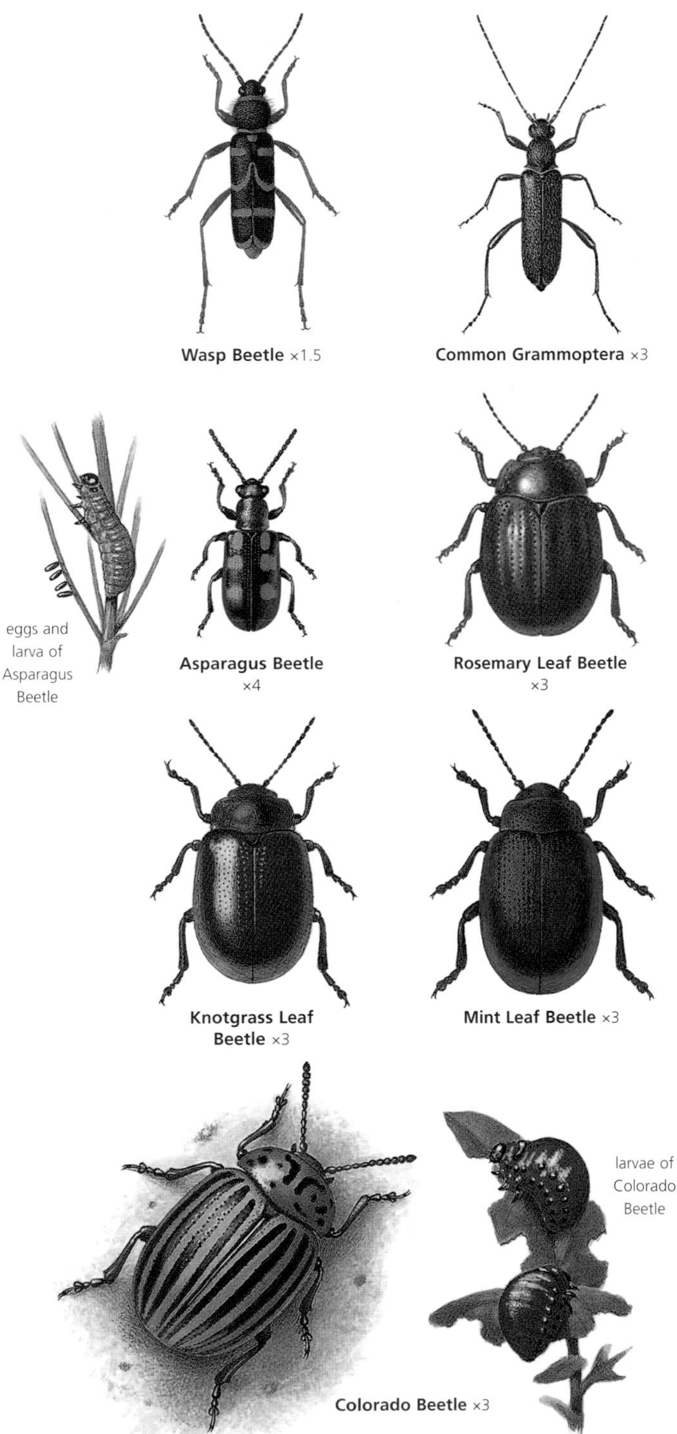

Wasp Beetle ×1.5

Common Grammoptera ×3

Asparagus Beetle ×4

Rosemary Leaf Beetle ×3

Knotgrass Leaf Beetle ×3

Mint Leaf Beetle ×3

Colorado Beetle ×3

Willow Flea Beetle *Crepidodera aurea*
A beautiful little metallic beetle, found on the leaves of willows and poplars. Adults emerge from hibernation in spring and the female lays batches of eggs on the undersides of leaves. The larva feeds on the surface tissue, leaving the veins exposed; it pupates in the soil, producing a second generation in August. Widespread and common, mainly in the south.

Turnip Flea Beetle *Phyllotreta nemorum*
This is one of many beetles that leap, flea-like, to avoid predation, aided by enlarged hind femora. Adults hibernate, emerging in spring to mate and lay eggs in the soil, close to various brassicas, including turnips. Adults make small holes and pits in seedlings, and the larvae tunnel in the leaves. Common and widespread in gardens and allotments.

Flea beetle *Phyllotreta nigripes*
This has a similar life cycle to related species and is found on brassicas and other low-growing plants, but the larvae feed on roots rather than foliage. Common and widespread in gardens and allotments.

Potato Flea Beetle *Psylliodes affinis*
Found on potatoes, tomatoes and related species such as woody nightshade. The adults riddle the leaves with small shot-holes, while the larvae feed on roots. Locally widespread but not usually causing much damage.

Pea Beetle *Bruchus pisorum*
Originating from Asia, this pest species is now cosmopolitan and causes damage to both growing and stored legumes. Adults hibernate in crevices and emerge in spring. After feeding from pollen, each female lays several hundred eggs on soft, developing pods. The newly hatched larva bores inside the pod and the plump white grub develops inside the seed.

Pea Leaf Weevil *Sitona lineatus*
This weevil causes characteristic semi-circular holes to the leaf edges of tender pea and bean plants, as well as to other legumes in gardens. Adults can be seen anywhere in the garden, on paths, soil or plants, and if disturbed drop to the ground and play dead. Eggs are laid in the soil and the larvae feed on roots for about a month before pupating, the adults emerging in June and July. A very common pest that has spread to many parts of the world and that carries some viral diseases.

Small Nettle Weevil
Nedyus quadrimaculatus
This dumpy little weevil is common on nettles, its larvae feeding low down in the stems and roots. Abundant throughout Britain and parts of Ireland wherever nettles grow.

Common Leaf Weevil *Phyllobius pyri*
One of several similar weevils covered in green scales, often tinted with copper or gold, which rub off with age, exposing black below. The adults are most often seen in May and June sunning themselves, mating and feeding on many young trees, shrubs, and frequently on nettles, although the larvae are root feeders. Widespread, but causes little damage in gardens.

Apple Blossom Weevil
Anthonomus pomorum
This weevil emerges from hibernation in spring, when the female seeks out the developing buds of apple and pear trees. Eggs are laid in the unopened buds and the larva feeds inside, preventing the flowers from opening properly. It pupates in the brown withered petals and the adult emerges in June and July, hibernating behind bark in early autumn. Widespread and common in England and Wales, scarce in Scotland and Ireland.

Figwort Weevil *Cionus scrophulariae*
Found in gardens on mulleins, figworts and orange ball buddleia, this distinctive weevil is one of the largest species of *Cionus*. The larva looks like a tiny orange slug, and gains protection from a thick covering of slime. It pupates in a cocoon attached to the foodplant, and after emergence the adult hibernates in leaf litter and garden debris. Common throughout Britain.

Thistle Tortoise Beetle *Cassida rubiginosa*
Named after its flattened, tortoise-like appearance, this species is common on thistles but is well camouflaged and is not often seen, although it flies readily in the sunshine. The strange spiny larva gains protection by attaching old skins and excrement to itself. Occurs in spring and summer throughout Britain and Ireland.

Vine Weevil *Otiorhynchus sulcatus*
One of several similar species and a troublesome pest of plants growing in containers indoors, but also causes damage out of doors, especially to strawberries and primulas. The adults, which are unable to fly and are mainly active at night, are unusual in that males are very rare and are not necessary for fertilisation. Each female can produce many hundreds of eggs, which are laid in the soil; the white, grub-like larva lives for several months, feeding on roots and tubers, causing the plants to wilt and die. Widespread and common throughout.

Large Elm Bark Beetle *Scolytus scolytus*
This beetle is the carrier of the deadly fungal spores that infect the sap of elm trees, causing Dutch Elm Disease. Adult beetles emerge from exit holes from May to October and seek new elm trees on which to feed and breed. The female bores a gallery between the bark and sapwood, and lays about 70 eggs along its length. The larvae feed, radiating out from the gallery, causing a distinctive fan-shaped pattern. Widespread and common.

European Oak Bark Beetle
Scolytus intricatus
The life cycle is similar to the Large Elm Bark Beetle, but the female makes a horizontal gallery under the bark of oak and some other trees. Occurs mainly in southern England.

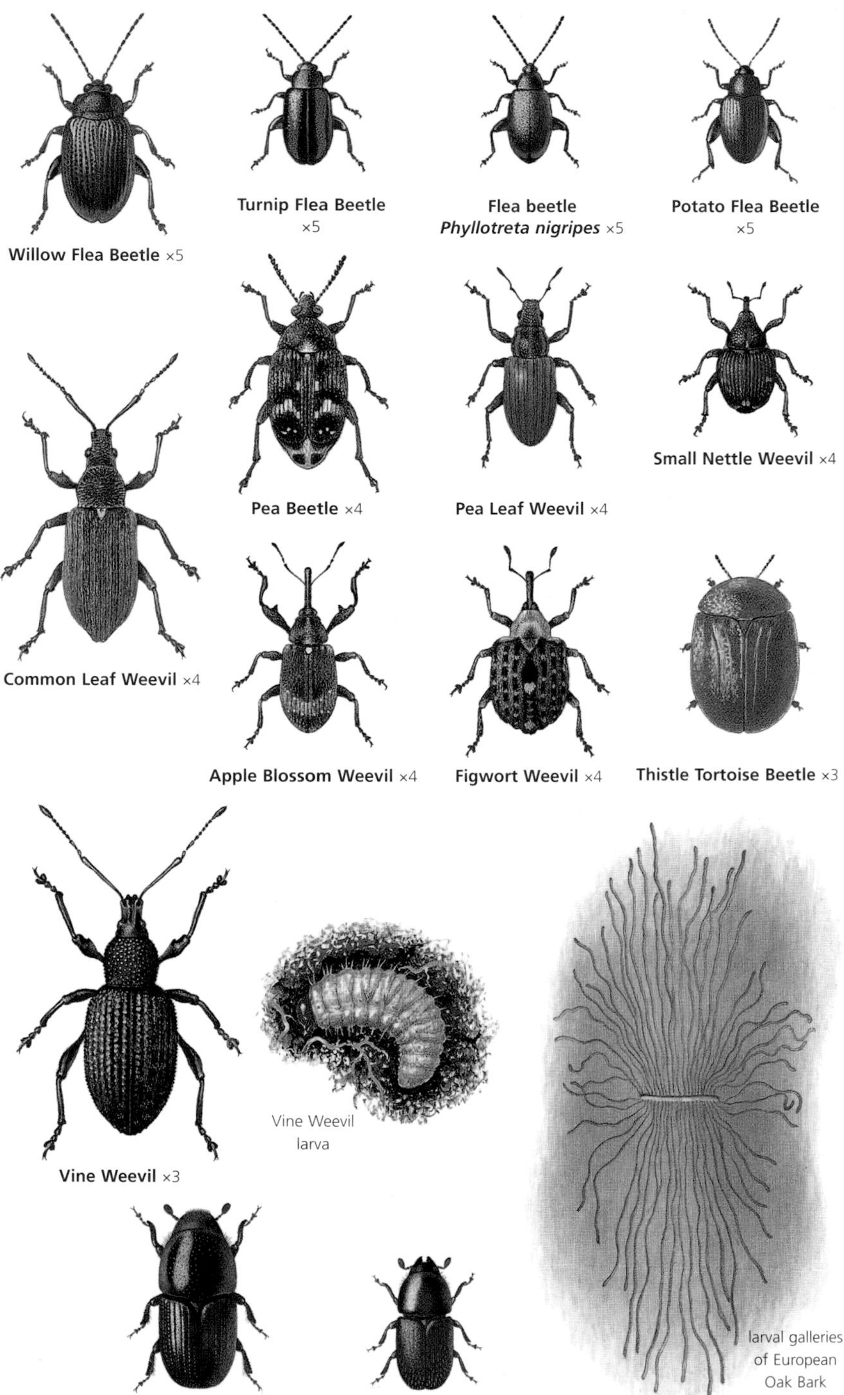

Willow Flea Beetle ×5

Turnip Flea Beetle ×5

Flea beetle ***Phyllotreta nigripes*** ×5

Potato Flea Beetle ×5

Common Leaf Weevil ×4

Pea Beetle ×4

Pea Leaf Weevil ×4

Small Nettle Weevil ×4

Apple Blossom Weevil ×4

Figwort Weevil ×4

Thistle Tortoise Beetle ×3

Vine Weevil ×3

Large Elm Bark Beetle ×4

European Oak Bark Beetle ×4

Woodlice
Terrestrial Isopoda

Woodlice are among the most familiar of garden animals. They may be abundant under stones, in leaf litter and on compost heaps. Of the 37 species that occur out of doors in Britain, seven are likely to be found in gardens. All species have seven pairs of legs and the females carry their young in a brood pouch for several weeks before releasing them. The tip of the antenna (flagellum) may be of two or three subsegments, or tapers to a sharp point. Some species have prominent white patches (lungs) on their underside.

Rosy Woodlouse *Androniscus dentiger*
A pretty little pink or rose-red species, with a double yellow stripe. Pale cream or white forms are occasionally found. The body surface is covered in small bumps and spines. Each eye has only one large black eye lens. **Habitat and distribution** Found in damp soil under bricks and stones. Widespread and fairly common.

Common Pygmy Woodlouse
Trichoniscus pusillus
This woodlouse is a uniform reddish brown, with a smooth body surface. Flagellum of antenna tapers to a fine point. Each eye has three lenses in a tight group. **Habitat and distribution** Found in damp soil and wet leaf litter. Widespread and very common, and is probably the most abundant woodlouse in Britain and Ireland.

Rough Woodlouse *Porcellio scaber*
The 'typical' woodlouse, a dark slate grey in colour, with a 'warty' appearance, and feels rough to the touch. Mottled brown or reddish specimens are sometimes found, especially in gardens near the sea. Flagellum of antenna has two subsegments. Two pairs of lungs. It is more likely to run away when disturbed than the Common Shiny Woodlouse. **Habitat and distribution** Extremely common under bricks and stones, dead wood, planks and other surface debris. Forms large aggregations under loose bark on trees. The most common woodlouse in gardens, found in drier situations than the Common Shiny Woodlouse. Often enters houses, where it forms the main diet of the spider *Pholcus phalangioides*.

Ant Woodlouse *Platyarthrus hoffmannseggi*
This woodlouse is white (although the dark gut contents may show through the cuticle). It is only found in the nests of ants, where it scavenges on their regurgitated food remains. It runs rapidly when disturbed and vibrates its antennae from side to side. It is blind. **Habitat and distribution** Occurs in the nests of most species of ants. Lifting paving stones to reveal ant nests is the best way to find this species. Common in Wales and southern England but becomes more scattered north of a line from Liverpool to Hull. Occurs in southern Ireland.

Common Shiny Woodlouse *Oniscus asellus*
Greyish, with light markings and rows of yellow patches. The body surface is usually smooth and shiny. Flagellum of antenna has three subsections. Lungs absent. It tends to clamp down when disturbed, rather than run away. **Habitat and distribution** Found under stones and dead wood, and is common in leaf litter. It is found in damper habitats than Rough Woodlouse. Widespread and very common. **Similar species** *Porcellio spinicornis* (found on limestone walls and buildings) is superficially similar but has a jet-black head, antennal flagellum with only two subsegments, and two pairs of lungs.

Common Pill Woodlouse
Armadillidium vulgare
This species is usually a uniform slate grey in colour, but pink, reddish or brown forms with yellow mottling are common. The only pill woodlouse that can roll into a perfect sphere and not leave a gap. **Habitat and distribution** Common in a wide range of habitats. It is quite resistant to desiccation and can be found under quite dry stones and vegetation. Widespread in south and east England, but much more coastal and associated with buildings north of these areas. **Similar species** *A. depressum* (common in gardens in Bristol, Bath and south Wales) leaves a gap when it rolls up. *A. nasatum* (sometimes abundant in glasshouses) also leaves a gap and has longitudinal stripes on the body and a prominent 'snout' on top of the head.

Striped Woodlouse *Philoscia muscorum*
Mottled brown, sometimes yellow, red or greenish, with a central dark stripe. The body surface is smooth and very shiny. Flagellum of antenna has three subsections. Lungs absent. Outline of body stepped between the front leg-bearing section and the rear part. Runs rapidly when disturbed and feels soft to the touch. **Habitat and distribution** A characteristic species of grassland, particularly common at the base of tussocks. Widespread and common.

Hoppers Amphipoda

Hoppers (amphipods) are flattened from side to side. This makes it difficult for them to walk without falling over, so they jump, hence their common name of 'hoppers'. One truly terrestrial species is a relatively recent addition to the British garden fauna. There are several other freshwater and seashore amphipods, but these must all return to water to breed.

Landhopper *Arcitalitrus dorrieni*
First found on the Scilly Isles in 1925, and subsequently discovered to be native to Australia. Does not need to return to water to reproduce. **Habitat and distribution** Found in leaf litter and under stones in sites rich in organic matter. Widespread and locally abundant in gardens near the coast in south-west England and south Wales. Isolated populations elsewhere (e.g. Kew Gardens and in Northern Ireland).

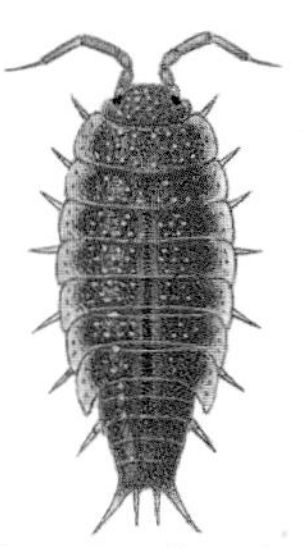

Rosy Woodlouse ×4

Common Pygmy Woodlouse ×4

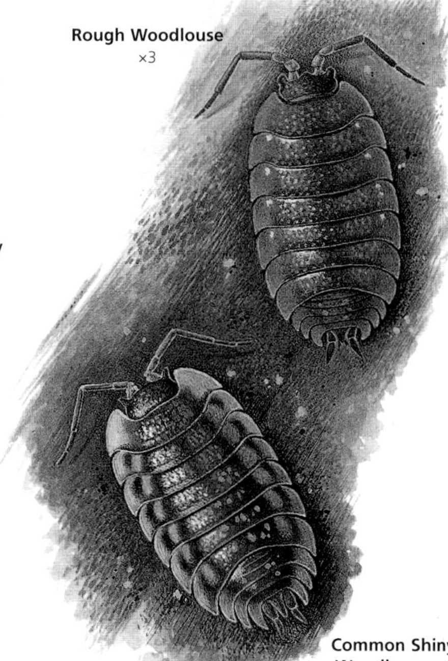

Rough Woodlouse ×3

Common Shiny Woodlouse ×3

found only in ants' nests

Ant Woodlouse ×8

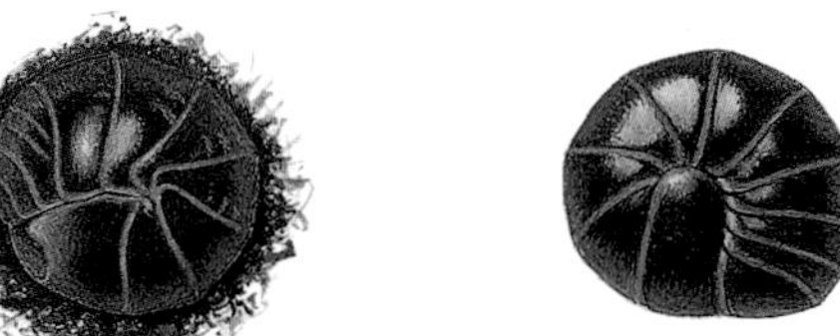

a more irregular, less spherical ball than Common Pill Woodlouse

Common Pill Woodlouse ×3

Pill Millipede ×3

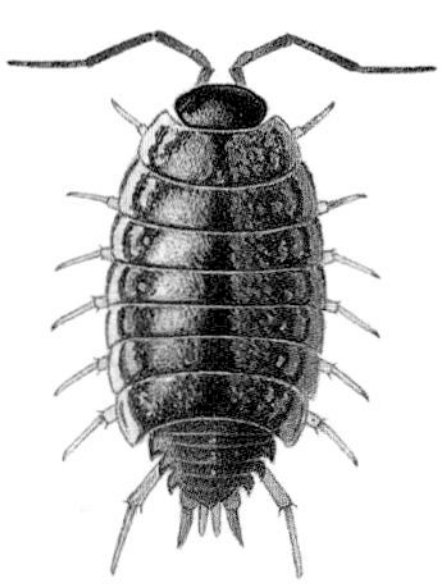

Striped Woodlouse ×4

Landhopper ×3

Millipedes Diplopoda

Milipedes are usually elongated and slow-moving, with two pairs of limbs to most body segments. They are almost entirely vegetarian, with a very few species occasionally causing damage to roots and soft fruit, but some species will scavenge on dead invertebrates. Nocturnal. Many species are found in compost heaps or under paving slabs, and require a moist environment. Eighty species have been recorded in Britain and Ireland.

Pill Millipede *Glomeris marginata*
The Pill Millipede is usually shiny black with pale edges to the segments, but also occurs in yellow, brown and red forms. When threatened, the Pill Millipede rolls into a tight ball, resembling a Common Pill Woodlouse (see page 176). It lives among fallen leaves and beneath hedges, particularly on calcareous soil, and is more tolerant of drier conditions than other millipedes. Widespread.

Common Flat-back *Polydesmus angustus*
This is the largest and commonest member of its family, with 20 body segments and finely sculptured 'winged' plates along its back. It can vary in colour from pale to dark brown. It is blind and is more vulnerable than most to desiccation, so remains in moist places. The female constructs a tiny earthen nest and remains with the eggs during incubation. When disturbed, it gives off a toxic, almond-smelling secretion.

Bristly Millipede *Polyxenus lagurus*
This strange, rarely encountered millipede is more reminiscent of a 'Woolly Bear', the larva of the Carpet Beetle, than of a millipede. Often common under lichen on crumbling walls, and beneath bark and organic matter. It has also been recorded in direct sunlight and living in the nests of Wood Ants. Widely distributed but most frequent in southern England.

White-legged Snake Millipede
Tachypodoiulus niger
This 'typical' black millipede coils into a 'watch spring' when disturbed. By day, it hides in the soil or behind bark, and emerges at night, often climbing trees and bushes to feed on living and decaying vegetable matter, including soft fruit. A common and widely distributed species, found throughout Britain and Ireland, particularly on chalk and limestone.

Red-spotted Millipede *Blaniulus guttulatus*
This pest species has a distinctive row of stink glands, which show through as red spots along each side of the body and produce an unpleasant fluid to repel predators. Common under paving slabs but is most often encountered in potatoes, bulbs, strawberries and other crops, where it probably enters through existing wounds as its jaws are too weak to penetrate the outer skin. Up to 100 individuals may occur in a single potato, taking advantage of the moisture in dry weather.

Symphylid *Scutigerella immaculata*
These small, colourless invertebrates belong to the Order Symphyla and resemble tiny centipedes, growing to no more than 1cm in length. They sometimes occur in such abundance that they can become pests in gardens, allotments and greenhouses. They feed on the tiny rootlets of many flowers and vegetables, particularly where the soil is moist, and in dry weather descend up to 2m below the surface.

Centipedes Chilopoda

Centipedes are elusive, mostly fast-moving predators that have only one pair of limbs to each body segment and possess sharp poison fangs, which are harmless to humans. Mostly beneficial in gardens, eating large numbers of soil pests, but one species can occasionally damage root crops. Most live in dark, damp places and emerge at night to hunt invertebrates; others live within the soil. Around 60 species have been recorded in Britain and Ireland.

Western Yellow Centipede
Haplophilus subterraneus
A long, cream-coloured, soil-dwelling centipede that twists and rolls when it is unearthed, and the one species that may cause some root damage to plants. The female uses her long, flexible body to encircle and protect her eggs and young. Ubiquitous in gardens, allotments and agricultural land.

Luminous Centipede *Geophilus carpophagus*
Dark and sombrely marked, this centipede is sometimes known as the 'glow worm' as it gives off phosphorescent light at night. Found under loose bark and fallen logs, and in damp sheds and buildings. Widespread, it appears to be essentially coastal in northern England and Scotland.

Long-horned Geophilus *Geophilus flavus*
A very common blind centipede, with long antennae and a dark red head. Its slender, worm-like body is typical of the geophilids, allowing it to negotiate tiny cracks and crevices in its subterranean lifestyle.

Common Cryptops *Cryptops hortensis*
This fast-moving member of the scolopendrids is a 'runner' centipede, found regularly in gardens, under logs and stones. Distinguished in having 21 pairs of legs, the rear pair appearing stoutly robust. Widely distributed and also found in woods and meadows. **Similar species** The **Greater Cryptops** *C. anomalans* is much larger and occurs in town gardens in the south-east.

Brown Centipede *Lithobius forficatus*
This familiar, fast-moving centipede with eyes can be found hiding under logs and beneath bark in the daytime, emerging at night to hunt invertebrates. At birth, the young have only seven pairs of legs, but after moulting end up with 15 pairs, the two rear pairs being particularly long. Ubiquitous. Found in many habitats and sometimes enters damp houses at night.

Pill Millipede ×2.5

Common Flat-back ×2.5

White-legged Snake Millipede ×2.5

Bristly Millipede ×10

millipedes have two pairs of legs on most segments

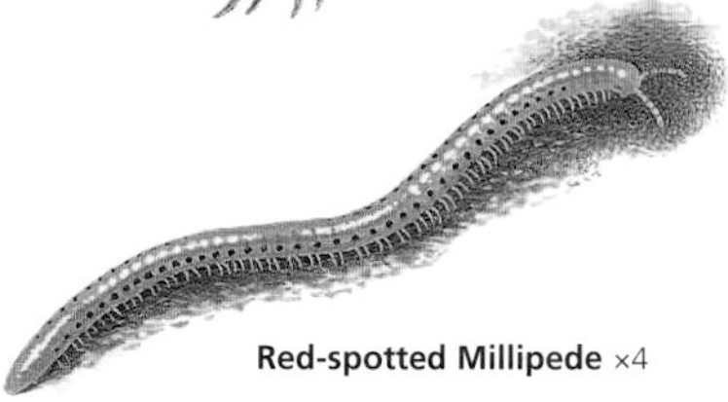

Red-spotted Millipede ×4

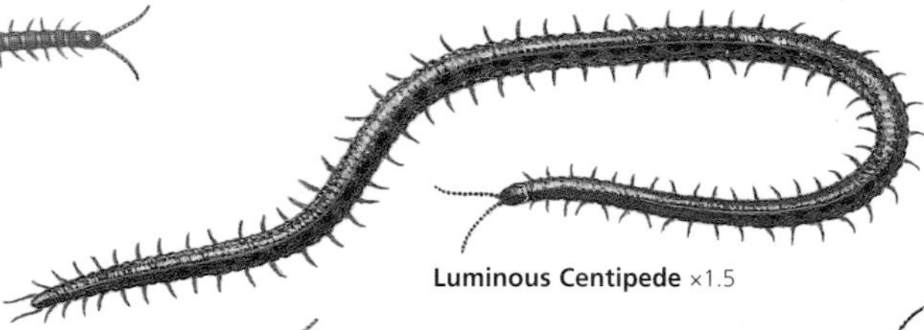

Symphylid
Scutigerella immaculata ×4

Luminous Centipede ×1.5

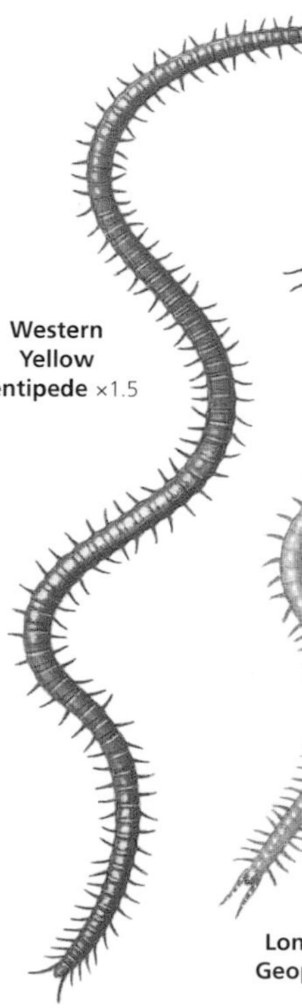

Western Yellow Centipede ×1.5

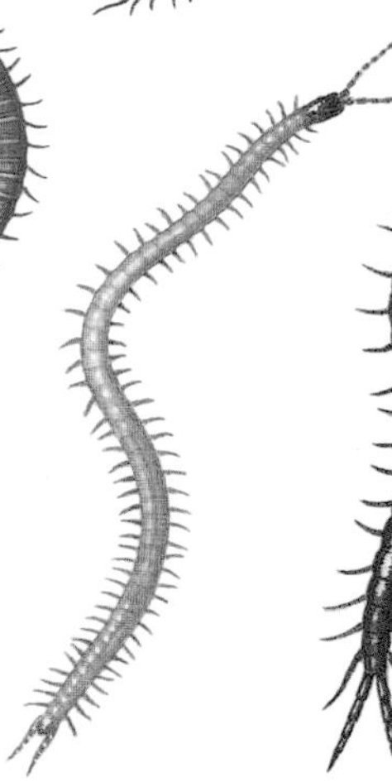

centipedes have one pair of legs on each segment

Long-horned Geophilus ×1.5

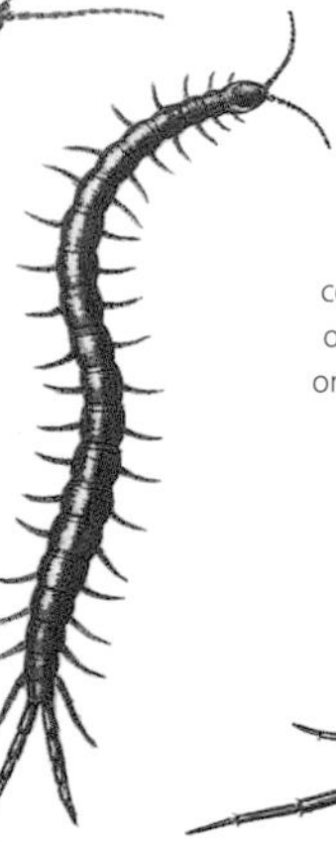

Common Cryptops ×1.5

Brown Centipede ×1.5

Spiders, harvestmen and allies
Arachnida

▲ A garden hedge covered in the webs of money spiders.

Like insects and crustaceans, arachnids are Arthropods, meaning 'jointed foot' (although this more accurately refers to their legs), but they differ from insects, in particular, in a number of ways. Most notably, they have four pairs of legs, simple rather than compound eyes, and their bodies are divided into two, rather than three distinct segments, the cephalothorax and the abdomen. In mites and harvestmen, these may appear fused as one. They also lack wings or antennae.

Spiders are by far the most familiar and often feared of the arachnids, distinguished from other members of the group in having spinners at the tip of the abdomen which are capable of producing silk, although not all species build webs. They also usually have eight or, less often, six eyes. Apart from web making, silk is also used to make protective egg sacs or to construct silken retreats for shelter. Many egg sacs are distinctively shaped and coloured and, depending on the species, each female lays between a few dozen to several thousand eggs. After hatching, some spiderlings are protected by their mother until ready to disperse, in the case of some wolf spiders riding on her back. Others disperse immediately by releasing a silken thread into the air and 'ballooning' away. Like all arthropods with exoskeletons, the newly hatched spiders shed their skins as they grow, some species having up to ten moults before reaching maturity.

Although many of Britain's 670 or so species are found in and around gardens and houses, most belong to the family of tiny 'money spiders', the Linyphiidae, so are seldom noticed. A few of the larger members of this family, which reach no more than 6mm, hang below small sheet webs in low vegetation, while many of the tinier species, which may reach no more than 1.5mm, make their webs beneath logs and stones, where they feed on tiny invertebrates such as springtails and mites.

In gardens, orb weavers painstakingly construct their webs of ever increasing spirals among vegetation, the most familiar being that of the plump female Garden Spider.

Other webs, made by species such as lace-webbed spiders and the house spiders, have a tubular silken retreat where the spider lurks; these webs are usually constructed around walls, sheds and log piles. Another conspicuous web, made in long grass and scrub, is that of the Nurseryweb Spider. This tent-like web is guarded by the female to protect the eggs and young spiders after they have hatched. Of the non-web builders, wolf spiders and jumping spiders rely on agility and surprise to catch their prey, whereas crab spiders wait for unsuspecting prey, camouflaged amongst their surroundings.

Mature males can be distinguished from females by the boxing-glove-like palps at the front of the head. During mating, these structures are used for transferring sperm to the epigyne, a structure on the underside of the female's abdomen. These organs of both sexes are complex and varied in design, and are the main critera for positive identification. Courtship in some species is often an elaborate affair, involving the male signalling with his prominent palps and offering prey wrapped in silk as a distraction to the female. This can be a risky time for the male as he is usually much smaller than the female. There is one species of linyphiid whose female feeds from the blood of her mate as they copulate.

▲ A Woodlouse Spider.

Spiders are most abundant from late spring until autumn, and although some species may be found as adults at any time of the year, most spend the winter months as eggs, usually wrapped in a protective silken sac, or as immature spiderlings.

Spiders are carnivorous predators with sharp fangs (chelicerae) which produce poison. However, the fear spiders engender, fuelled by the annual media hysteria over 'killer' Noble False Widows, is irrational, and no-one in Britain should worry about spider bites. Indeed, most species are beneficial and capture many harmful insects. As well as being predators, they are prey themselves for many insectivorous birds, reptiles, small mammals and countless invertebrates. They also assist birds who use silk from the spiders' webs to weave into their nests.

Harvestmen, or Harvest Spiders, differ from true spiders in having the cephalothorax, the front part, and the weakly segmented abdomen fused together without a waist, and in having only two eyes set on a raised tubercle, the ocularium. The legs of many species are extremely long and are often shed to escape capture. However, if the second pair, which are always the longest and are used as sensors, are lost, the harvestman will perish. The palps at the front of the head often resemble an extra pair of legs and are also used as sensors, to detect food. Harvestmen are mainly carnivorous, but produce no venom or silk and, although their diet includes scavenged dead corpses, bird droppings and over-ripe fruit, they also hunt soft-bodied invertebrates. The peak of abundance is reached at harvest time, hence the name.

False-scorpions resemble miniature true scorpions but without the sting. They live mainly in leaf litter but, because of their size (the largest British false-scorpion being barely 4mm long), they are rarely encountered. Entirely carnivorous, they kill their prey by injecting venom from the palps and then suck up the fluid produced by enzymes, with their jaws. They are also able to produce silk from the palps, which is used to construct a cocoon that acts as a shelter and a nest.

Mites are undoubtedly the most numerous arachnids in gardens, but most are under 2mm long. However, vast numbers occur in soil and leaf litter, scavenging or feeding on decaying organic matter, and some vegetarian species are so prolific that they can cause serious damage to cultivated plants. They are unusual among arachnids in that the young of some species have only six legs.

Common Candy-striped Spider
Enoplognatha ovata
This spider occurs in several colour forms, ranging from plain cream with dark spots to yellow with rose-coloured stripes. The female constructs a small, sticky web and is capable of ensnaring quite large insects. Most of her later life is spent concealed in a curled leaf, often among common nettles, making a tent-like structure that resembles that of a Red Admiral caterpillar; here, she may be found guarding her blue-grey egg sac. **Habitat and distribution** Found in abundance in gardens, throughout the summer months, in low vegetation, amongst brambles, nettles and the foliage of many trees and shrubs. Very common and widespread throughout Britain and Ireland.

Comb-footed spider *Phylloneta sisyphia*
The abdominal markings of this spider vary, but the general pattern is usually clearly defined. Although the sexes are similar, the male is slightly smaller. The female makes an untidy, tangled web in low vegetation and shrubs, and hides in a retreat constructed at the top of the web. Here, she produces a greenish-blue egg sac and, after they hatch, protects the young and cares for them in a unique way, feeding them with liquid from her mouth. **Distribution** Widespread throughout Britain, with scattered records in Ireland.

Comb-footed spider *Steatoda bipunctata*
Easily identified by the glossy dimpled abdomen, this species varies from coffee-brown to almost black. The male is especially dark, but all specimens have a pale edge at the front of the abdomen. Males are active from early spring, with females sometimes living for several years. **Habitat and distribution** Common throughout Britain and Ireland, being found mainly in and around human habitation, often in sheds and dry, neglected places, but also behind loose bark or in bird nestboxes. **Similar species** The female *S. grossa* is larger, up to 10mm, and is generally darker, and the male has white abdominal markings. Found in similar habitats and, although much scarcer, is expanding its range.

Noble False Widow Spider *Steatoda nobilis*
The female Noble False Widow Spider, the largest of the six species of British *Steatoda,* has a shiny, globular abdomen, which is variably marked cream and dark brown, though some specimens may be very dark. Its web is a strong structure with a retreat where the spider lays in wait, moving swiftly if an insect becomes ensnared. If threatened, females have occasionally been known to pierce human skin. **Habitat and distribution** Closely associated with human habitation, it is a non-native species, common in central and southern England, expanding its range northwards. Recently recorded in Ireland. **Similar species** *S. grossa* is slightly smaller; microscopic examination is often required to separate the two species.

Money spider *Lepthyphantes leprosus*
This is one of a huge family of small spiders, the Linyphiidae, which includes more than 280 British species. The female *Lepthyphantes leprosus* makes a sheet web typical of the family, and can be found throughout the year. **Habitat and distribution** Occurs in buildings and outhouses, on walls and behind loose bark on trees. Common and widespread. **Similar species** *Megalepthyphantes nebulosus* is found in similar places but is larger, with a dark 'Y'-shaped mark on the carapace.

Long-jawed Orbweb Spider
Tetragnatha montana
Spiders of this family all have elongated legs and bodies, accentuated by their resting posture. Females build a flimsy web and rest stretched on silken strands or on nearby stems. The huge fangs are used whilst mating, the male locking the female's fangs open to avoid being bitten. **Habitat and distribution** Found throughout Britain and Ireland, often near sheltered garden ponds but also away from water in shrubs and low vegetation. **Similar species** *T. extensa* is also common in gardens, but is less often found away from water. Usually slightly paler; close examination is necessary to separate the two species.

Common Sheetweb Spider
Linyphia triangularis
The best-known and largest member of the family, with a characteristic leaf-like pattern on the abdomen and tuning-fork mark on the carapace. The female builds a slightly domed sheet web, which is very common in vegetation from ground level up to several metres above the ground. Here, the spider patiently hangs upside-down, waiting for insects to blunder into the tangle of silk above; she then grabs the prey from below. **Habitat and distribution** Abundant throughout, in gardens and many other habitats. Most frequently seen in mid summer and in autumn, when the webs become conspicuous in the morning dew. **Similar species** Some similar species occur, but all are smaller and less common in gardens.

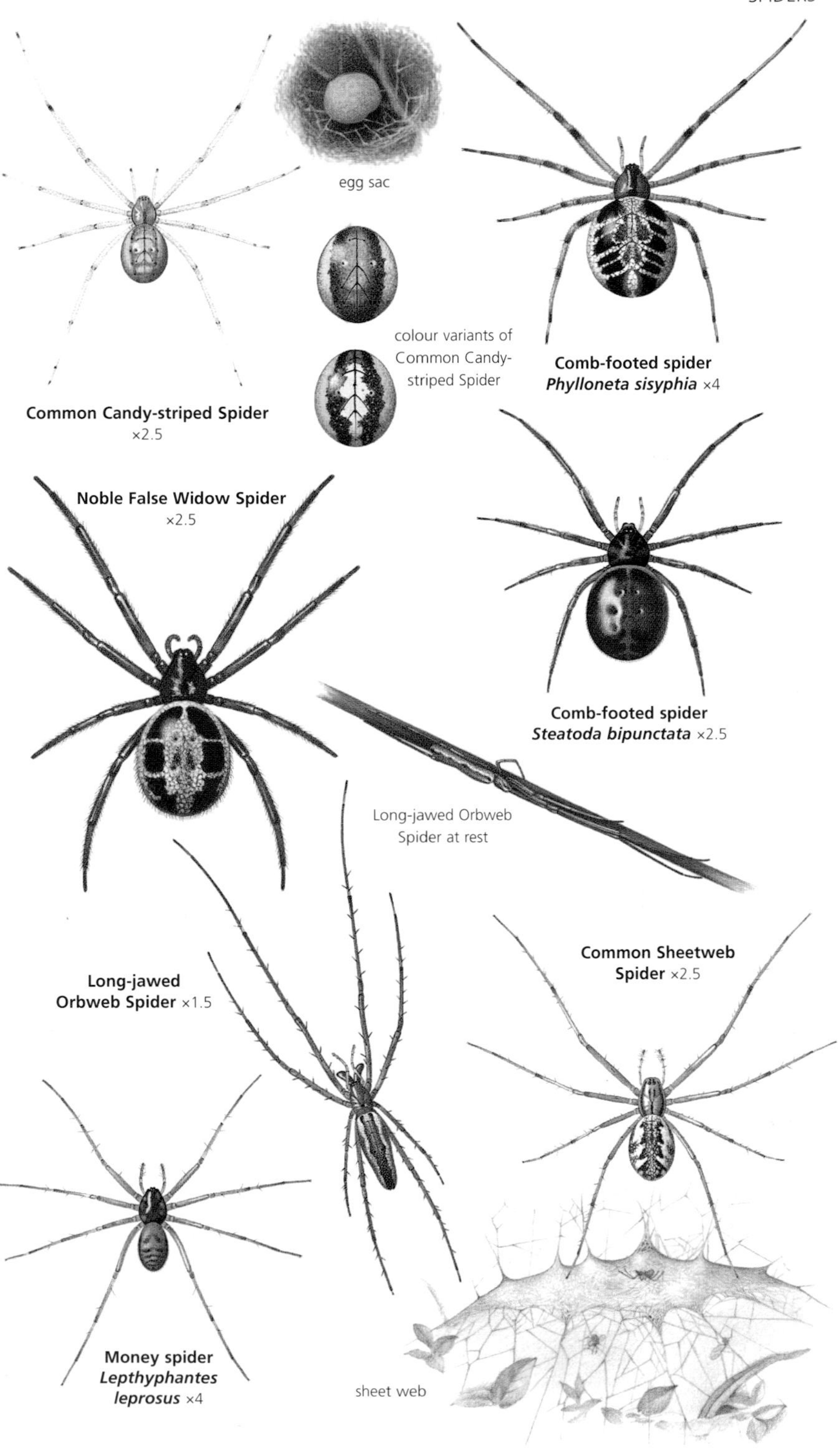

Common Candy-striped Spider ×2.5

Comb-footed spider *Phylloneta sisyphia* ×4

Noble False Widow Spider ×2.5

Comb-footed spider *Steatoda bipunctata* ×2.5

Long-jawed Orbweb Spider ×1.5

Common Sheetweb Spider ×2.5

Money spider *Lepthyphantes leprosus* ×4

Four-spotted Orbweb Spider
Araneus quadratus
The bulkiest of all our spiders, this variable species always has four pale spots on its globular abdomen, which ranges from pale yellow, green or orange to reddish brown. The female makes a large orb web, with a tough silken retreat nearby where she waits, ready to capture prey that becomes entangled. **Habitat and distribution** Found low down in scrubby vegetation, including in wilder gardens. Common throughout, but less so than the Garden Spider. **Similar species** The **Garden Spider** has a more angular abdomen, which usually has a clearly defined white cross.

Garden Spider *Araneus diadematus*
Also known as the Diadem Spider, this is our most familiar orb-web spider, its colour varying from orange to dark brown, with a central cross formed by white spots. The markings of the male are similar to those of the female but he is much smaller, with longer legs. The female builds a web in low vegetation, bushes and trees, which is most conspicuous when covered in dew on autumn mornings. In late autumn, she leaves her web to lay an egg batch; this is covered in dense silk to protect it through the winter. On hatching, in spring, the young spiderlings live gregariously, huddled together in a tight, golden ball for protection, but they quickly disperse when disturbed. **Habitat and distribution** Found everywhere, from gardens and hedgerows to more open countryside.

Common Cucumber Spider
Araniella cucurbitina
The attractive yellow and green coloration of this little spider provides excellent camouflage when resting, often well above the ground, in the foliage of trees and shrubs, where the female constructs her small orb web. This is often spun horizontally, and may only span a single leaf. The male is smaller, with more boldly marked legs, but both sexes have bright red markings near the spinners at the tip of the abdomen. Maturity is from May onwards, when the young spiderlings develop their full green colour. **Habitat and distribution** Found commonly in trees, shrubs and bushes throughout Britain and Ireland. **Similar species** The common and almost identical *A. opisthographa* can only be separated by microscopic examination.

Walnut Orbweb Spider *Nuctenea umbratica*
This dark, rather sinister spider is most likely to be seen suspended in the centre of its orb web at night, as during the daytime it hides, concealed in a nearby retreat. It has a shiny, flattened abdomen, well adapted to squeezing into narrow crevices in fences or behind bark. If disturbed in the daytime it will feign death and drop to the ground on a silken thread, its legs held tightly to its body. The female usually makes a new web each night, constructed from strong, flexible silk and capable of ensnaring quite large nocturnal insects. She may be found throughout the year, but the male is active only in the summer months. **Habitat and distribution** Found around human habitation, on fences, posts, sheds and tree trunks. Common throughout.

Missing-sector Orbweb Spider
Zygiella x-notata
Webs of this common spider and its two close relatives are distinctive, having a wedge-shaped segment missing and a strong thread running from the centre to a hidden retreat. Here, the occupant waits, feeling the thread, like an angler waiting for a bite. The spider has a greyish-brown, leaf-like pattern on its abdomen, with a silvery-white flash towards the front. Females lay their egg batches around window frames, protecting them with a conspicuous yellow, silken cocoon. **Habitat and distribution** Nearly always found near habitation, especially on sheds, fences and greenhouses, and around window frames. Widely distributed and found commonly throughout the year. **Similar species** *Z. atrica* usually has a reddish tint to the abdomen and is less often found near to human habitation.

Orbweb spider *Metellina segmentata*
The abdominal markings of this spider vary in colour, but the characteristic dark marking on the carapace is constant. The underside of the abdomen, which is most often seen as the spider hangs in the centre of the web, has a dark, longitudinal stripe. The orb web is distinctive, with the central area missing, and in the autumn most webs have a male lurking at the edge in addition to the female in the centre. Unusually for spiders, the male is often larger, with much longer legs than the female, but it is only after she has caught prey that mating takes place. **Habitat and distribution** Found throughout, this is one of the commonest spiders, occurring in low vegetation, herbs and bushes. **Similar species** The equally common *M. mengei* was once thought to be a subspecies of *M. segmentata*. It occurs earlier in the year, is smaller, and the markings at the front of the abdomen are more rounded.

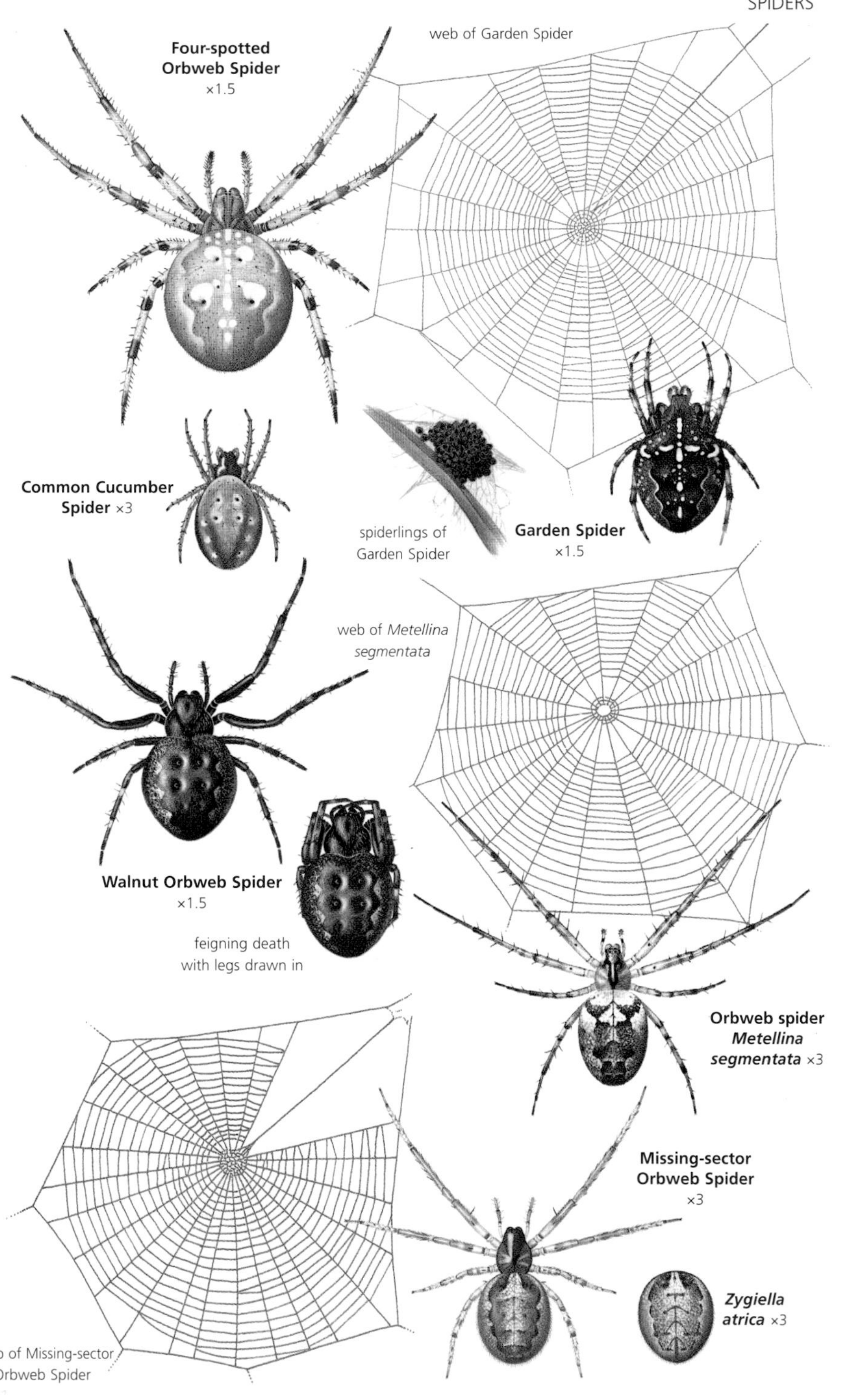

Four-spotted Orbweb Spider ×1.5
web of Garden Spider
Common Cucumber Spider ×3
spiderlings of Garden Spider
Garden Spider ×1.5
web of *Metellina segmentata*
Walnut Orbweb Spider ×1.5
feigning death with legs drawn in
Orbweb spider *Metellina segmentata* ×3
Missing-sector Orbweb Spider ×3
Zygiella atrica ×3
web of Missing-sector Orbweb Spider

Woodlouse Spider *Dysdera crocata*
The huge dark-red fangs, pale, shiny abdomen, and only six eyes make this spider easily recognisable. It builds no web to capture its prey but hunts at night, specialising in feeding on woodlice, aided by its powerful jaws which are able to pierce the tough outer armour. One of the very few spiders able to pierce human skin. **Habitat and distribution** Sometimes found in damp outhouses, but mainly in warm places under stones and logs, hidden by day in a silken cell. Maturity is reached in early summer but adults may occur throughout the year. More common in the south, but extends into southern Scotland and Ireland. **Similar species** *D. erythrina* is usually slightly smaller but is only separable by microscopic examination.

Wolf spider *Pardosa amentata*
This is one of the commonest of a large family of spiders, found in abundance amongst rough ground vegetation in the summer months. The male is smaller and much darker than the female, and has dark, swollen palps which he vibrates and displays in an elaborate courtship. The female may be seen carrying her pale egg sac around beneath her abdomen prior to the eggs hatching. After emerging, the young spiderlings crawl onto the mother's back, where they gain protection until they can fend for themselves. Wolf spiders do not make webs and, as their name suggests, rely on speed for chasing and catching their prey. **Habitat and distribution** Common throughout, in sheltered, grassy places exposed to the sun. **Similar species** There are many similar species of wolf spider, which need close examination to separate.

Large House Spider *Tegenaria gigantea*
This harmless species is perhaps the spider most feared by arachnophobes, as it is the one most often seen dashing across carpets on autumn evenings, or found trapped in the bath. The familiar sheet web, which may be several feet across, is often constructed in sheds and outbuildings, but may also be outside in woodpiles and on banks, the female waiting at the entrance of the tubular retreat. She may live for several years, and is able to withstand long periods in desiccated habitats, without the need for moisture. Although smaller in body size, the male has much longer legs than the female and it is he that is most often seen. After mating, he often shares the female's web and may be eaten by her when he dies. **Habitat and distribution** Common around human habitation, both indoors and out. Found in eastern and northern England, and in Scotland, Wales and Ireland. Females can be found at any time of year, but males are most frequent in the autumn, when they seek out females. **Similar species** There are several very similar species of *Tegenaria*, including *T. saeva*, which is almost indistiguishable and is found in the West Country, Wales, northern England and Scotland, and *T. parietina*, the large **Cardinal Spider**, so-called because it was said to have terrified Cardinal Wolsey in Hampton Court. The males of this latter species may have a legspan of 10cm.

Nurseryweb Spider *Pisaura mirabilis*
The variable markings of this spider can range from plain buff to pale orange with black patches, but all forms have a pale, black-edged streak on the carapace. A fairly large and conspicuous spider, it is often seen basking in the sun or hurrying through rough grassy vegetation. Courtship in this species is unique, and involves the male catching, posturing with, and then offering prey wrapped in silk to the female to distract her while he mates. The female carries her white egg sac in her jaws beneath the body; just before they hatch, the eggs are attached to grasses, and a silken dome, the nursery-web, is constructed over them. Here, the female rests, guarding the eggs and then the young, until they are old enough to disperse. **Habitat and distribution** Common in long grass and herbage, maturing in June. Widely distributed throughout Britain and Ireland.

Lace-webbed spider *Amaurobius similis*
The sharply-defined, dark mark on the abdomen, separated by a pale central band, and the shiny black raised head distinguish this spider from close relatives. Females make an often untidy, tubular retreat by brushing bluish silk with a comb-like structure on the hind legs called a calamistrum. This activity and the male's courtship take place at night. **Habitat and distribution** Webs are most often seen on sheds, around window frames and in cracks in dry walls. Common and widespread throughout, females may appear at any time of the year. **Similar species** *A. fenestralis* has the dark mark on the abdomen only faintly separated with a pale band; found in slightly damper places. *A. ferox* is larger and more sombrely-marked greyish black; often found in damp outhouses.

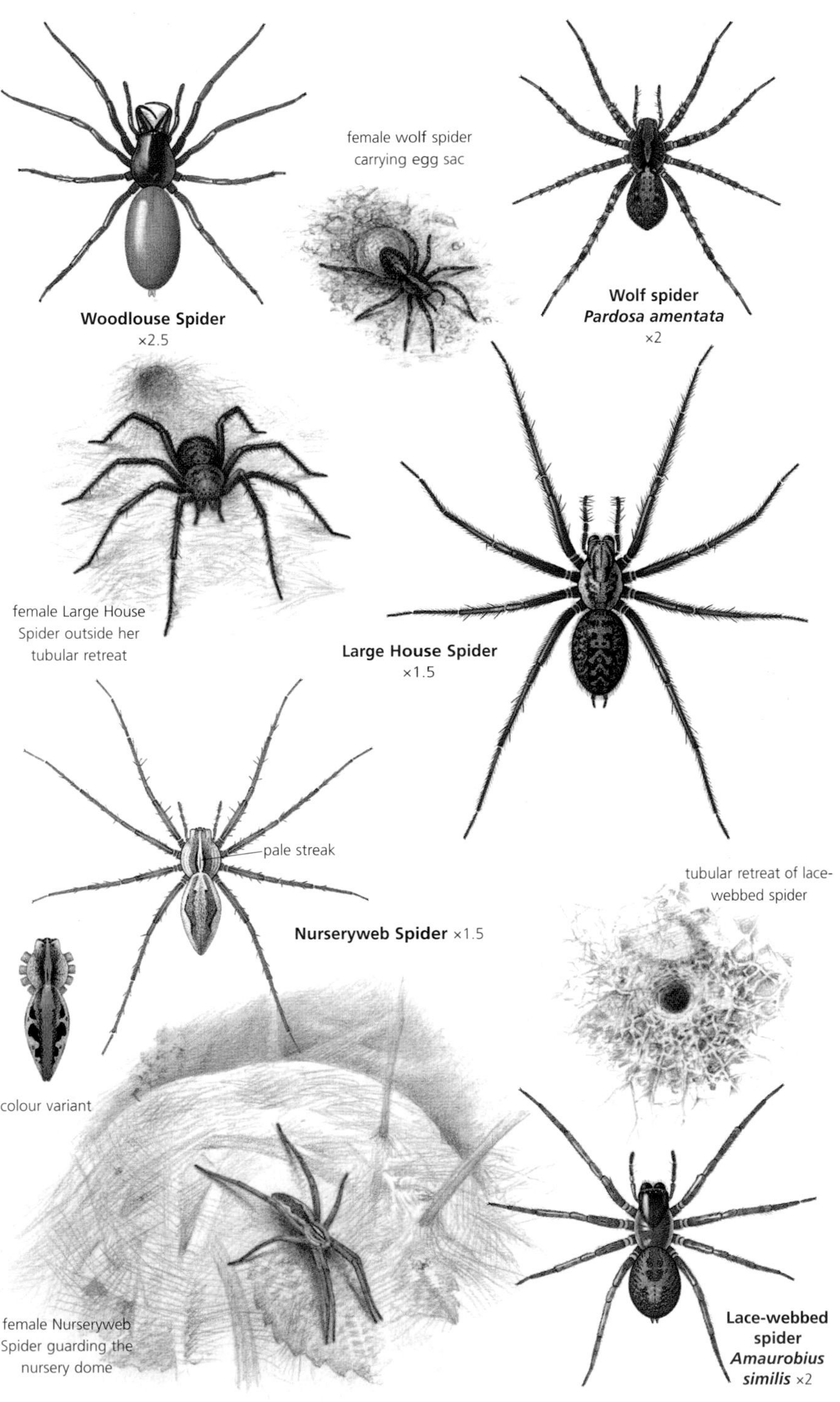

Woodlouse Spider
×2.5

Wolf spider
Pardosa amentata
×2

Large House Spider
×1.5

Nurseryweb Spider ×1.5

Lace-webbed spider *Amaurobius similis* ×2

Meshweb spider *Dictyna arundinacea*
The conspicuous tangled web of this tiny spider can be seen on dry flower- and grass-heads, where the female spider rests, hidden inside the structure. The male is slightly smaller and darker than the female. This is by far the commonest of five British *Dictyna* species, none of which exceed 4mm in length. **Habitat and distribution** Common in grassy, scrubby places throughout Britain and Ireland.

Running crab spider *Philodromus dispar*
This group of crab spiders are active hunters that run down their prey, as well as laying in wait. They are less crab-like than others in the group, with longer, more even-length legs. The male *P. dispar* is quite unlike the female, hence the name *dispar*; she is plumper, especially before egg-laying, with a much paler, buff abdomen. This gives better protection when guarding her egg sac, which is attached to vegetation. **Habitat and distribution** Found on trees, shrubs, rough herbage and ground vegetation. Common in spring and summer. **Similar species** *P. aureolus* is the other very common *Philodromus* species found in gardens. The female has a more reddish abdomen, and the male an all-over dark, metallic iridescence.

Crab spider *Xysticus cristatus*
Crab spiders rely on camouflage rather than webs to capture their prey, ambushing or scurrying crab-like after insects that get too close. *X. cristatus* is the commonest of about 12 closely related species, and can be recognised by the wedge-shaped 'V' on the carapace which ends in a sharp, black point. All species have the first and second pair of legs much longer than the others, and males are usually much smaller and darker than females. Mature by early summer. **Habitat and distribution** Lives in low vegetation and shrubs. Widely distributed.

Green Crab Spider *Diaea dorsata*
The sexes of this distinctive crab spider are similar, although the male is slightly smaller and darker than the female. Maturity is reached in May and adults can be seen throughout the summer. **Habitat and distribution** Mainly found on evergreens, and especially on box, but also on pine, yew and oak. Locally common, found mainly in southern England.

Flower Crab Spider *Misumena vatia*
The female of this crab spider is a master of camouflage, able to adjust her colour according to the flowers on which she rests, ranging from white, through pale green, to yellow, with or without darker stripes. She waits motionless, the two long pairs of front legs raised and spread, ready to grab any unsuspecting insects that venture too close. Her venom is powerful, capable of killing quite large insects such as hoverflies and bees. By comparison, the male is tiny, barely 4mm long, darker and is rarely noticed. Found throughout the summer. **Habitat and distribution** Occurs mainly on white or yellow flowers. More frequent in the south.

Common Zebra Spider *Salticus scenicus*
The best known of the jumping spiders, this sun-loving species relies on four large, forward-facing eyes to detect its prey. It does not build a web, but instead moves with a jerky gait, stalking and then leaping on unsuspecting insects. The variable markings are made up from coarse flattened hairs, giving a granular appearance. The sexes are similar, but the male has large, forward-projecting jaws, used in confrontations with rival males. Adults are found in the spring and summer. **Habitat and distribution** Most common on sunny walls, sheds and fences, but also found on rocks and tree trunks. Widely distributed throughout Britain and Ireland.

Sun jumping spider *Heliophanus flavipes*
A distinctive jumping spider, separated from similar species by the plain, greenish-yellow legs, although the two rear pairs sometimes have a black basal streak. Males are similar to, but smaller than, the females. **Habitat and distribution** Widely distributed and common amongst low vegetation. **Similar species** *H. cupreus* is found in similar places and is equally common. It has more heavily-streaked legs and the abdomen and thorax often have white patches.

Jumping spider *Pseudeuophrys lanigera*
The male of this small jumping spider has similar, but more clearly contrasting, markings than the female. **Habitat and distribution** Locally common, mainly in the south. Found mostly around human habitation on walls, roofs and sometimes indoors. Females can be found at all times of the year.

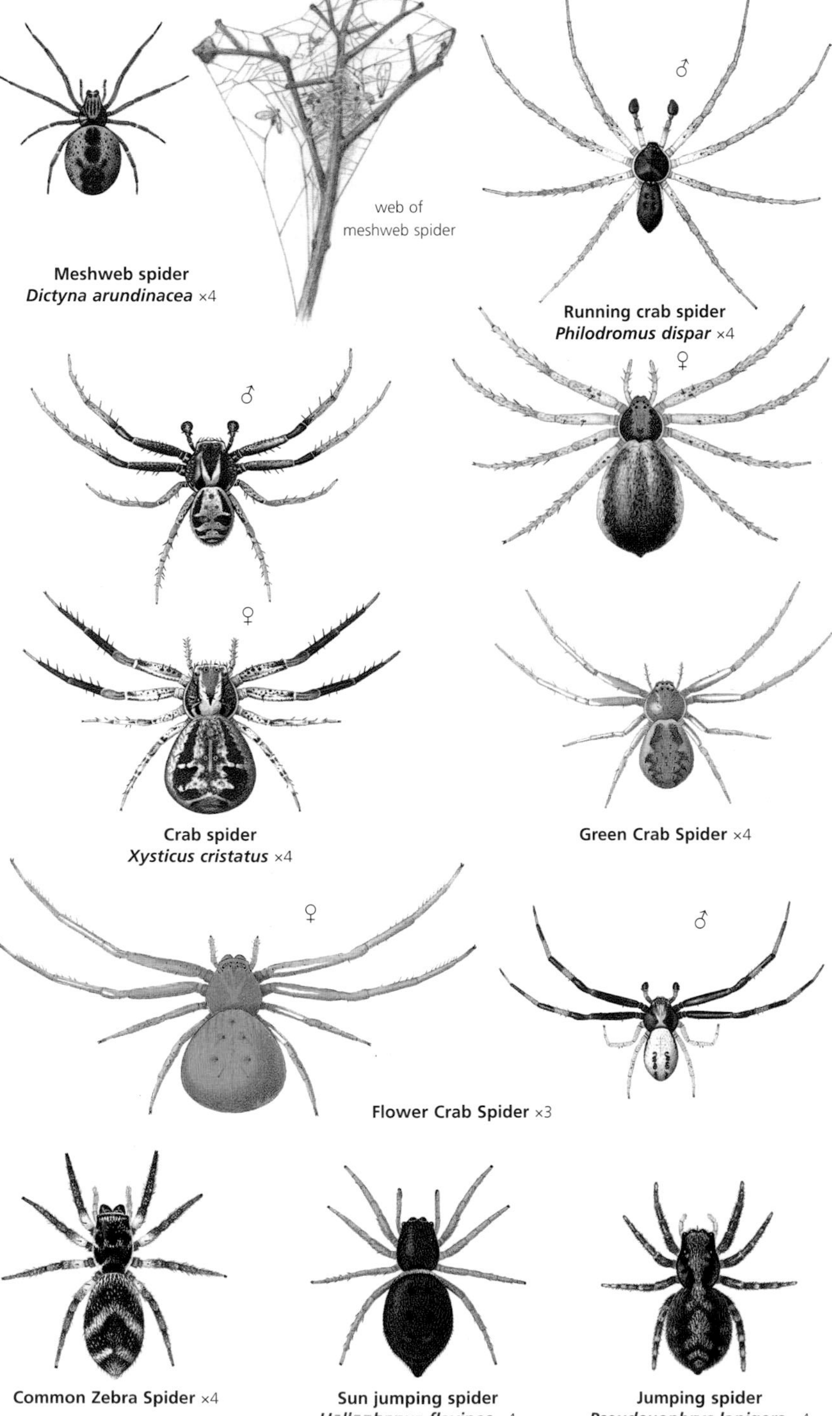

Meshweb spider
Dictyna arundinacea ×4

Running crab spider
Philodromus dispar ×4

Crab spider
Xysticus cristatus ×4

Green Crab Spider ×4

Flower Crab Spider ×3

Common Zebra Spider ×4

Sun jumping spider
Hellophanus flavipes ×4

Jumping spider
Pseudeuophrys lanigera ×4

False-scorpion, mites

False-scorpion *Neobisium carcinoides*
Resembling tiny true scorpions but without the sting, or miniature lobsters, the largest British false-scorpion is barely 4mm long, so they are rarely encountered. However, they have a fascinating and complex life history worthy of detailed study. This species lives in damp leaf litter, moss, rotting wood, under stones and sometimes in garden compost heaps. It is active at night, feeding on small invertebrates, such as mites, psocids and springtails, catching and killing them by injecting venom from the palps. Females are sometimes phoretic, that is, they attach themselves to the legs of other, more mobile, insects; this is thought possibly to be a means of dispersal to better hunting grounds. **Habitat and distribution** Widely distributed and found in many habitats.

Velvet Mite *Eutrombidium rostratus*
Sometimes mistaken by gardeners for the much smaller and destructive Fruit Tree Red Spider Mite, this attractive species is harmless and is commonly seen walking over soil and paths, hunting for small invertebrates and their eggs. Velvet Mite eggs are laid in the soil, and after hatching the larvae seek out an insect host, such as a grasshopper, on which to live. After a few days they drop to the ground to mature and live freely. **Habitat and distribution** Common and widespread in gardens, especially in the spring, after hibernation.

Glasshouse Red Spider Mite *Tetranychus urticae*
Found outdoors, as well as in glasshouses, on many plants such as strawberries, tomatoes, cucumbers, beans and other cultivated fruit and vegetables. As well as damaging leaves, flowers and fruit, when infestations are heavy a mass of fine silken webs clothe the plants. In summer it has two conspicuous spots on each side, but in winter the adults hibernate and turn orange-red. **Distribution** A common worldwide pest; breeding is accelerated in hotter weather.

Fruit Tree Red Spider Mite *Panonychus ulmi*
An infamous pest species, infestations of which have become more serious since its resistance to chemical insecticides in the 1960s. These were non-selective and killed the natural predators as well as the pests, leaving the mites to multiply unchecked. Colonies become established from April, breeding quickly and causing extensive damage to the fruit and foliage of apple, pear, plum and many other fruit and ornamental trees and shrubs. Eggs are laid on leaves in up to five summer generations, but winter eggs are laid on bark, giving twigs a red appearance if infestations are heavy. **Distribution** A worldwide pest species.

Harvestmen Opiliones

Harvestmen reach the peak of abundance at harvest time, hence the name. They differ from true spiders in having the cephalothorax and abdomen fused together without a waist. The legs of many species are extremely long, the second pair always being longer than the rest, and although they are carnivorous, they produce no venom or silk. They have two eyes, set on a raised ocularium, and often hunt soft-bodied invertebrates, although their diet also includes scavenged corpses, bird droppings and over-ripe fruit.

Harvestman *Leiobunum rotundum*
This distinctive species has exceptionally long, dark legs and a small, rotund body, plain orange in the male and with a distinct dark saddle in the female. Maturity is reached in July, with some specimens living on into December. **Habitat and distribution** It is found in a variety of habitats, including rank vegetation, trees, bushes and walls, and often congregates on shaded tree trunks. Widespread throughout Britain and Ireland; most abundant in the south.

Harvestman *Nemastoma bimaculatum*
This tiny, relatively short-legged harvestman is entirely ground-living, and is found under logs, stones and moss in a variety of habitats, including gardens. Adults can be found at any time of the year, and live for up to 18 months. **Distribution** Common and widely distributed throughout Britain and Ireland, especially on limestone soil.

Harvestman *Dicranopalpus ramosus*
First recorded in England 60 years ago, this variably coloured species is easily recognised by the long forked pedipalps and by its characteristic splayed resting posture. It was probably accidentally introduced, and is mostly associated with human habitation. **Habitat and distribution** Adults are found from late July until November, occurring on walls and in trees, bushes, and hedgerows in parks and gardens. It was first found on the south coast but has spread rapidly northwards to Scotland and Ireland.

Harvestman *Paroligolophus agrestis*
This variable species, usually with a pale central band down the abdomen, is probably the commonest harvestman in Britain. Maturity is reached from July, and adults may survive until February in mild winters. **Habitat and distribution** Found in many habitats and can be abundant in parks and gardens. Widely distributed.

Harvestman *Phalangium opilio*
A very common species, usually with a distinct saddle and a white underside. The male is immediately identified by the horn-like projection on the jaws, and the long pedipalps. The immature stages are usually found on the ground; maturity is reached in June, with adults lasting into December. **Habitat and distribution** Found in rough vegetation, trees and shrubs in many habitats, including gardens. Common and widely distributed almost everywhere, including the far north.

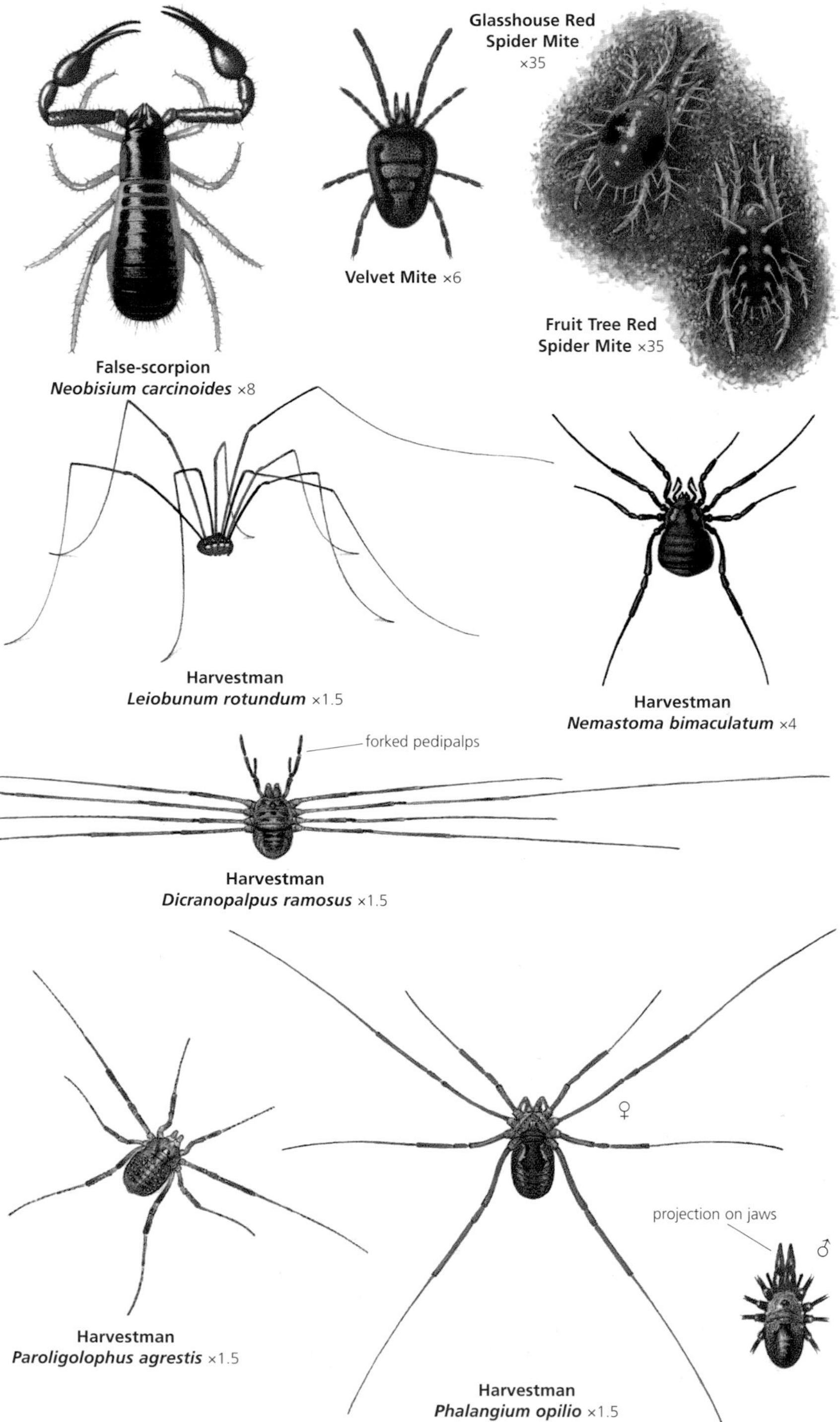

Glasshouse Red Spider Mite ×35

Velvet Mite ×6

Fruit Tree Red Spider Mite ×35

False-scorpion
Neobisium carcinoides ×8

Harvestman
Leiobunum rotundum ×1.5

Harvestman
Nemastoma bimaculatum ×4

Harvestman
Dicranopalpus ramosus ×1.5

Harvestman
Paroligolophus agrestis ×1.5

Harvestman
Phalangium opilio ×1.5

Slugs and snails Terrestrial Gastropoda

▲ A cluster of Garden Snails on a fence post.

Slugs and snails are gastropods and are part of the huge and ancient group of Mollusca, which includes bivalves such as cockles and mussels, and cephalopods such as octopuses and squid. They are the only molluscs that inhabit dry land. The name gastropod means 'belly foot', a reference to the large muscular foot used for locomotion. The whole of the body and the underside of the foot, the sole, are coated in a layer of either clear or coloured mucus, secreted from various glands, which acts as a lubricant when moving and often leaves a characteristic silvery trail when it dries. The majority of species have four retractable tentacles, the longest pair having tiny black eyes at the tips, the shorter pair being equipped with sensory scent organs.

The division between gastropods with shells (snails), and those that have lost or only have tiny, vestigial shells (slugs), is not always clearly defined. Some species have intermediate characteristics, and most slugs have a small internal shell, which in some may be reduced to a few chalky granules. Most species are vegetarian and feed on living and decaying plant material, fungi and algae, although some scavenge on excrement and carrion, and a few are carnivorous. They feed by rasping away with a horny, file-like structure covered in tiny teeth, called a radula, which grows continually from the base as it wears away at the front end.

Gastropods prefer moist, humid weather and are active mainly at night. By day, they shelter under logs and stones, in leaf litter or in drains, where they can keep damp and concealed from predators. In unsuitable weather, when the temperature is below freezing, or in the heat of summer, snails often enter a state of torpor and can survive long periods of dry conditions. Slugs rely on their thicker coating of mucus and also burrow deep into the soil to avoid drying out. Because shells need calcium to grow, more species of both snails and slugs are found on chalk and limestone soil than on sandy or acidic soil.

Nearly all gastropods are hermaphrodite and contain both male and female sex organs. However, most species require a mate to reproduce. Courtship in some species is an elaborate affair, involving the insertion of a 'love dart' through the body wall; this is thought to stimulate mating and an exchange of sperm. The eggs are laid mainly in the summer or autumn months. They are either transparent spheres or chalky and opaque, and are usually laid either singly or in batches of up to about 100, in damp places such as under logs or in crevices in the soil. The young, which resemble miniature adults, usually hatch after a few weeks and may take up to four years to mature, with adulthood lasting from a year to up ten years in some larger species.

Slugs and land snails are well known, but usually unwelcome, garden inhabitants, associated with causing damage to fruit, vegetables and ornamental plants. However, only a very few of the 140 or so British species actually cause problems in gardens, the majority being important recyclers, efficiently breaking down decaying plant and organic matter.

Snails have a coiled shell made of whorls that are added to and widened as the snail grows, gradually opening into a broad aperture or mouth. When danger threatens, the soft body of the snail can retreat entirely into the shell, and in dry weather the opening can be sealed with calcified mucus to prevent desiccation. Most are vegetarian and feed mainly on decomposing plant material but, as gardeners know, the two main pest species – the Garden Snail and the Strawberry Snail – will eat seedlings and tender plants, as will some other species if all the leaf litter and organic matter has been tidied away.

Slugs can be divided into three groups: the round-backed slugs, keeled slugs and shelled slugs. Lacking a visible shell, the two former groups are best identified using a combination of features, including the body and sole colour, the position of the breathing hole on the mantle and the presence or absence of a keel along the back. The three species of shelled slug found in Britain are mainly associated with human habitation, but are rarely encountered as they live a partly subterranean life, feeding on earthworms.

Being slow-moving, slugs and snails are vulnerable to predation, and mortality is highest in the early stages. Several vertebrates prey on them, including Hedgehogs, rats, shrews, mice, Slow Worms and frogs. The Song Thrush is well known for hammering snails from their shells on a 'thrush's anvil'. Some species of ground and rove beetles and their larvae also help to control numbers.

Mainly as a result of man's activities, for example in the horticultural and agricultural industries, some non-native species, such as the Budapest Slug, have been accidentally introduced into Britain and have become pests. Others, such as the Field Slug, now cause problems in many parts of the world where they have been accidentally introduced. As a result of the way we have altered habitats for food production and recreation, many species have become scarce, while others have benefited and have perhaps become too successful. The chemical method of control used to treat the handful of species that sometimes cause problems is controversial, and the generally accepted opinion is that, for the well-being of other garden inhabitants, chemical molluscicides should be avoided at all costs.

▲ The red form of the Large Black Slug feeding on celery.

Round-backed slugs

This group of slugs, containing all the *Arion* species, differ from the keeled slugs in having the breathing pore towards the front of the mantle, which is roughened, rather than having a concentrically grooved pattern. They also lack a dorsal keel, but the body is often deeply furrowed along its length. The tail is rather rounded and bears a mucus gland just above the tip.

Dusky Slug *Arion subfuscus*
Northern Dusky Slug *Arion fuscus*

Recent genetic examination of the Dusky Slug has found that in fact it comprises two separate species, which range in colour from bright orange, to greyish brown, with a darker longitudinal line along the sides. When touched, the sticky body mucus stains bright yellow and is hard to remove, although the mucus on the foot is colourless. Fully grown adults reach 7cm, and, unlike related species, are unable to contract into a tight hemispherical dome. Feeding mainly on decaying vegetation, little damage is caused to growing plants in the garden. **Habitat and distribution** Found resting under stones and logs by day and in dry weather, in a wide range of habitats throughout Britain and Ireland.

Garden Slug *Arion hortensis*

A common and serious pest species that feeds on root crops, lettuce, strawberries and many other cultivated plants. It grows up to 3–4cm long, and is dark bluish-black with a black lateral band and a reddish tinge to the tentacles. The underside sole and the body mucus are yellow-orange, and when contracted and viewed end on, it appears circular without a splayed foot fringe. **Habitat and distribution** Found beneath stones amongst rubbish and disturbed ground in gardens, allotments and agricultural land throughout Britain and Ireland.

Large Black Slug *Arion ater*

This is our largest *Arion* slug, which may reach 13cm in length and ranges in colour from orange or reddish brown, to pale grey or jet black, the latter being the form that is most common in the north. The body, which is covered in deep, elongated furrows, can be contracted into a domed hemisphere that can be rocked when disturbed or prodded. It has a thick coating of usually colourless mucus, which may form a globule near the mucus gland by the tail; this slime is sticky and hard to remove from the fingers, and leaves a trail on vegetation. Although it may occur in large numbers, this species causes less damage in gardens than some of the smaller species, as it prefers decaying vegetation, dung and carrion to living plant material. **Habitat and distribution** Mainly active after rain, in the evening and at night. Very common, found throughout Britain and Ireland in almost any habitat, including urban areas and gardens.

Dotted Slug *Arion circumscriptus*

A fairly small slug reaching up to 4cm, this species is variable greyish yellow, with an indistinct dark lateral band, bordered with grey, and a characteristic dark-speckled mantle. When contracted and viewed end on, it appears bell-shaped with a splayed-out foot fringe. It feeds on decaying matter and fungi and is not as destructive as its close relatives. **Habitat and distribution** Common in all habitats and generally distributed throughout. **Similar species** *A. silvaticus* lacks the dark speckling on the mantle and has greater contrast below the lateral bands.

Hedgehog Slug *Arion intermedius*

This small slug gets its name from its spiky, domed appearance when the body contracts. It reaches 1.5–2cm in length and is usually greyish yellow, with a darker head and tentacles and yellow mucus on the pale sole. A self-fertilising pest that has been accidentally introduced into many parts of the world, it breeds in autumn, laying batches of up to 24 eggs under stones and in crevices in the soil. **Habitat and distribution** Found in many habitats, including cultivated land, waste ground, roadside verges and less often in gardens. Common and widespread in all parts of Britain and Ireland.

Keeled slugs

These slugs, which include those on page 196, differ from the round-backed slugs in having a ridge or keel, either near the tail or running the full length of their backs. Some species have a fingerprint-like, ridged impression on the mantle and all have a breathing pore on the rear part of the mantle, to the right-hand side.

Field or Netted Slug *Deroceras reticulatum*

This is undoubtedly the most destructive pest species, detested by all gardeners. It grows to 5cm and ranges in colour from pale buff to greyish brown, often with a reticulated, netted pattern on the body. Regularly found hiding beneath leaves or under stones, where it contracts its body into a dome. It has a shiny, slimy appearance, and if disturbed exudes milky-white mucus. Breeding occurs throughout the year but peaks in spring and autumn. Because of its close association with cultivated places it has been accidentally introduced to many parts of the world. **Habitat and distribution** Abundant in gardens, allotments and agricultural land, as well as scrubby grassland and hedgerows throughout the country. **Similar species** There are several other very similar species of *Deroceras*, of which only *D. panormitanum* occurs regularly in gardens, especially in the south.

Worm Slug *Boettgerilla pallens*

This slender little slug was probably accidentally introduced into Britain from south-eastern Europe about 50 years ago, and has spread quite rapidly in recent years. It reaches 4cm when fully extended, and has a translucent greyish-yellow, worm-like appearance, with a dark tail, head and tentacles. **Habitat and distribution** Found mainly in cultivated places, including gardens, with widely scattered records throughout Britain and Ireland.

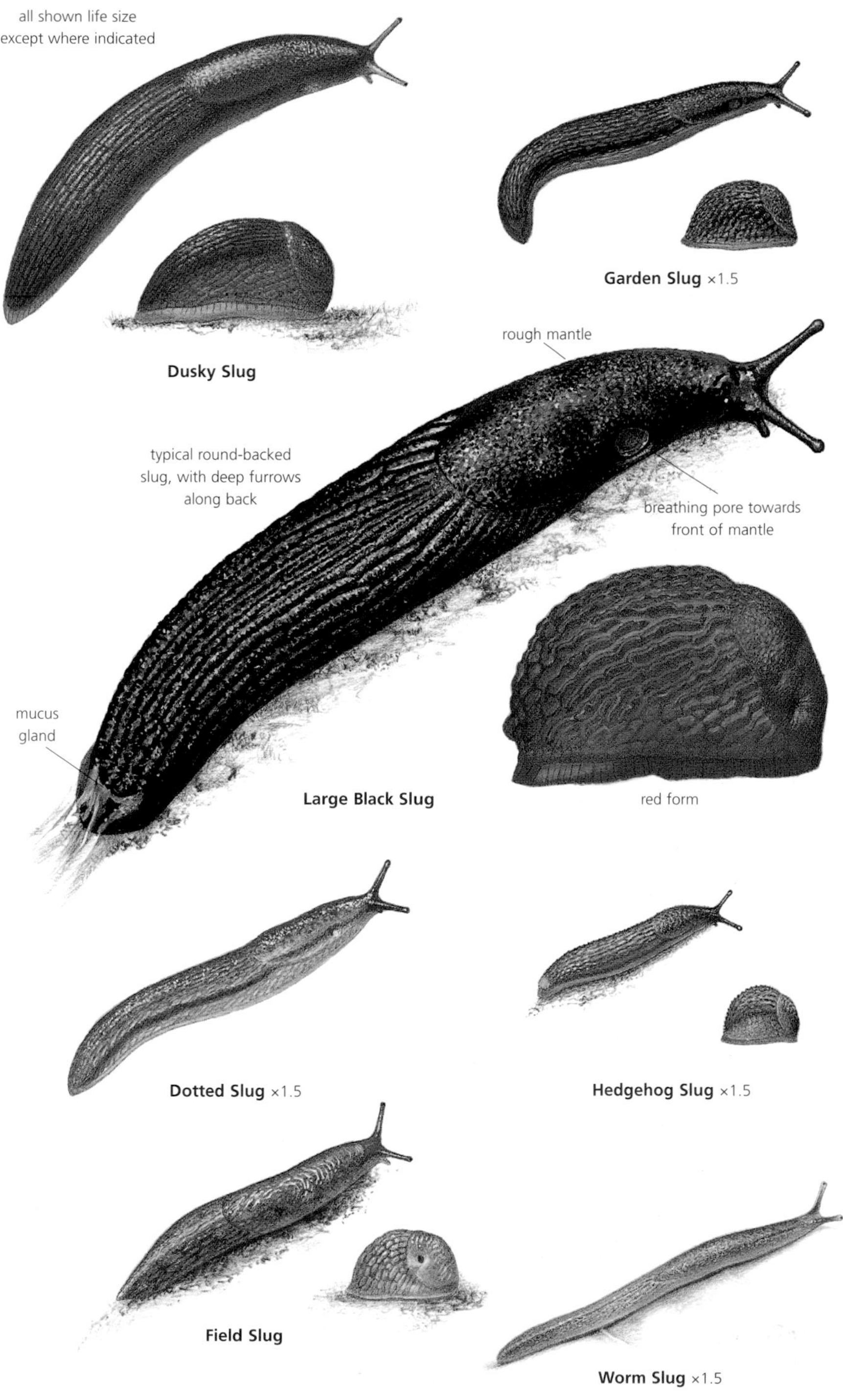

Garden Slug ×1.5

Dusky Slug

Large Black Slug

Dotted Slug ×1.5

Hedgehog Slug ×1.5

Field Slug

Worm Slug ×1.5

Sowerby's Slug *Tandonia sowerbyi*
A greyish-brown slug, speckled with black and with a pale keel running the length of the body. The grooves running along the slightly compressed body are dark pigmented, and although the body is rather dry, the sole has thick yellow mucus. It reaches a length of 7.5cm. **Habitat and distribution** A common pest species that spends most of its time below ground feeding on the roots and tubers of cultivated plants. Widely distributed throughout Britain and Ireland but absent from parts of the north.

Smooth Jet Slug *Milax gagates*
A dark grey-brown to black slug, slightly paler below and with an off-white sole that has colourless mucus. It reaches 6cm, and has a smooth appearance, with a prominent keel running down the full length of the back, truncated near the tail. **Habitat and distribution** Fairly common in gardens and occasionally damages crops. It is more frequent in the south, particularly in coastal areas.

Budapest Slug *Tandonia budapestensis*
This slug occurs in various shades, from yellowish grey to dark greyish brown speckled with black. The keel is orange and the sole, which has thick clear mucus, has a dark central band running down the middle. It is narrow and elongate when fully extended, reaching 6cm but, unlike closely-related species, forms a 'C' shape when at rest. **Habitat and distribution** A serious pest mainly associated with cultivated places, including gardens, this is the commonest keeled slug to be found in arable land. Abundant and generally distributed throughout Britain; more local in Ireland.

Great Grey or **Leopard Slug** *Limax maximus*
One of the largest slugs, this species has a variety of colour forms, the most striking being a grey and buff coloured body and mantle, banded and marbled with black. The tentacles are tinted with red, and the whitish sole has clear sticky mucus. As well as its impressive size, which can reach 20cm, this slug is well known for its elaborate courtship behaviour. When they meet, the pair perform a strange circular dance, leading to them climbing a tree or wall. They then descend, entwining themselves on a twisting rope of thick mucus, and mating then takes place suspended in mid-air. The Great Grey Slug hides beneath damp logs and rocks by day and is active mainly at night, laying batches of up to 100 eggs. It feeds mainly on decaying vegetable matter and fungi rather than growing plants, and does little damage in the garden. **Habitat and distribution** Usually associated with human habitation such as parks and gardens, and is found throughout Britain and Ireland.

Yellow Slug *Limacus flavus*
This distinctive slug, with its pale blue tentacles and smooth, greenish-yellow, mottled body, is a streamlined species that sometimes appears indoors in old, damp houses, leaving a slime trail across carpets and walls. A large, handsome slug growing to more than 10cm, it has a short keel running up from the tail. It is nearly always found near human habitation, and for this reason it has been accidentally introduced to other parts of the world, where it is regarded as a pest species. Most of its diet consists of decaying vegetable matter, but it may do some damage to growing plants. **Habitat and distribution** Prefers damp, humid places, where it may congregate in groups beneath rocks, in drains and cellars around human habitation. Widespread and common, especially in the south.

Golden Shelled Slug *Testacella scutulum*
Although this slug is mainly associated with gardens and cultivated places, it is rarely seen as it is nocturnal and spends most of its life underground. It is a large, creamy-yellow slug, speckled with brown and with a rather dry, waxy texture. It reaches 10cm when extended, and has a small, flat, ear-shaped shell at the rear of the body, and a branched groove running along the sides. When it is inactive the body is rounded or pear-shaped but it becomes very narrow when fully extended, an adaptation to its carnivorous, subterranean life, spent hunting earthworms and, less often, other species of slug. The recent invasion of the New Zealand Flatworm (see page 202), which also preys on earthworms, could affect the survival of shelled slugs. **Habitat and distribution** Mainly found in cultivated places, around compost heaps and where the soil is rich, containing good numbers of earthworms. Widely distributed throughout Britain and Ireland, apart from the extreme north; most frequent in the south, particularly in Devon. **Similar species** Two other species of shelled slug occur in Britain: *T. haliotidea,* which is cream-coloured with a larger, more rounded shell, and *T. maugei,* which has a darker body and a larger, more oblong shell.

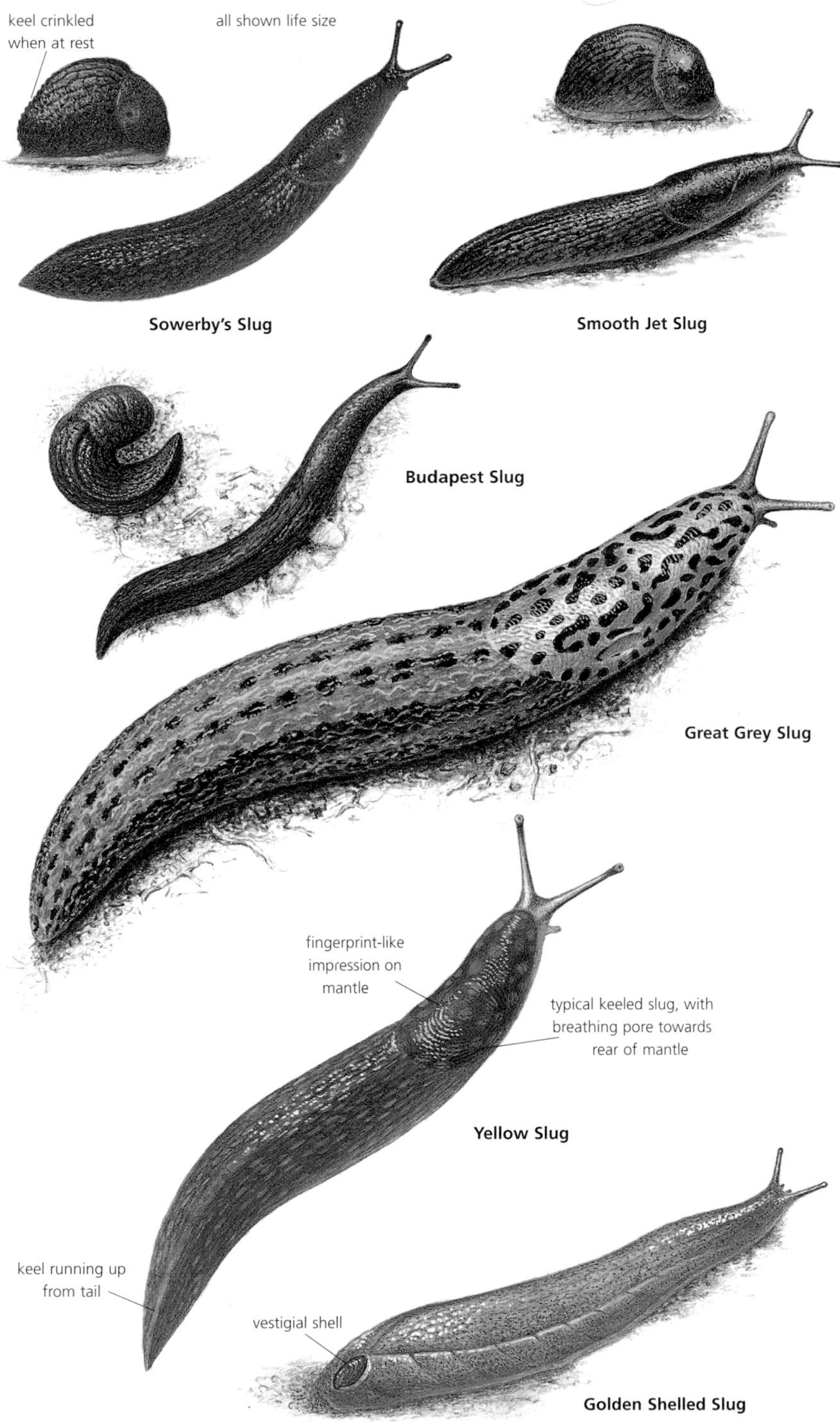
keel crinkled
when at rest
all shown life size
Sowerby's Slug
Smooth Jet Slug
Budapest Slug
Great Grey Slug
fingerprint-like
impression on
mantle
typical keeled slug, with
breathing pore towards
rear of mantle
Yellow Slug
keel running up
from tail
vestigial shell
Golden Shelled Slug

Two-toothed Door Snail *Clausilia bidentata*
This is one of many small, spindle-shaped snails that have a flexible plate, enabling them to seal the entrance of the shell, preventing the entry of small insects and predators. Fresh specimens range from reddish brown to black, with older individuals becoming partly or wholly bleached grey. **Habitat and distribution** Lives in leaf litter, rockeries and old walls, and emerges at night to climb banks and tree trunks to feed on lichens and algae. The commonest member of the family, distributed throughout Britain and Ireland.

Garden Snail *Cornu aspersum*
This is the most common pest species of snail in gardens and allotments, and is responsible for damage to fruit, vegetables and many tender bedding plants. A variably marked species, with an irregularly ridged shell, often attractively marbled and flecked with brown, yellow and black. On mild, wet nights it often forages across paths and lawns, but in dry weather and in winter large numbers may congregate beneath flowerpots or in drains, their shells sealed with dried mucus. **Habitat and distribution** Occurs in many habitats in Britain and Ireland, except in central northern parts.

Rounded Snail *Discus rotundatus*
This small, yellowish-brown snail has distinctive dark-reddish bands curving across the ribbed whorls, and a bluish-grey body, paler near the foot. The hollow on the underside of the flat shell, the umbilicus, is large and covers a third of the shell's diameter. **Habitat and distribution** Found in shady places in gardens, under stones and logs, in moss and leaf debris. It feeds on fungi and decaying vegetation and is widely distributed in all but the driest places.

Brown-lipped Banded Snail
Cepaea nemoralis
One of the most familiar snails, occurring in many colour forms. The yellow-and-black-banded form is the most typical, but plain yellow, dark brown or even pink forms may occur, depending on habitat. Occasionally the lip may be white. **Habitat and distribution** Very common in many habitats, including well-vegetated gardens. It rarely causes much damage but may sometimes nibble tender plants such as lettuce. Occurs in all parts of Britain and Ireland except the far north of Scotland. **Similar species** The **White-lipped Banded Snail** (see below).

White-lipped Banded Snail
Cepaea hortensis
This snail, which may be confused with its close relative above, also occurs in many colour forms but is generally smaller. Occasionally the lip may be brown. **Habitat and distribution** Occurs in a variety of habitats and is often found with the Brown-lipped Banded Snail, but is less often seen in gardens and prefers rather moister places. Widely distributed but fewer records from the far north and west.

Kentish Snail *Monacha cantiana*
A pale, globular snail often tinged with pink, the Kentish Snail was first described in Britain in 1803. **Habitat and distribution** Mainly found in more unkempt parts of gardens, where longer grasses and scrub grow. Widespread and most common in southern and eastern England. Absent from Ireland. **Similar species** The **Carthusian Snail** *M. cartusiana* is slightly smaller and restricted mainly to south-east England.

Two-toothed Door Snail ×2

Garden Snail ×1.25

Rounded Snail ×2

White-lipped Banded Snail ×1.25

Brown-lipped Banded Snail ×1.25

Song Thrush's 'anvil'

plain and banded forms of Brown-lipped Banded Snail

Kentish Snail ×1.25

Girdled Snail *Hygromia cinctella*
An alien species that has only been recorded in Britain since the 1950s, the Girdled Snail originates from the Mediterranean and was probably accidentally imported with garden plants. It ranges from light to dark brown and has a distinctive white 'girdle' or ridge running around the shell. **Habitat and distribution** Found in gardens, waste ground and roadside verges, among low vegetation and grasses. Common in gardens in Devon and Cornwall, but has spread east, and as far north as Yorkshire and Northern Ireland.

Strawberry Snail *Trochulus striolatus*
Some examples of this variable pest species may be cream coloured, but most are dark reddish brown with a pale lip. There are coarse ridges across the whorls, and when young the surface is clothed in short hairs which wear off by adulthood. **Habitat and distribution** Found beneath logs, stones and low-growing plants in gardens and allotments, where it damages plants such as strawberries, lettuces and other cultivated crops. **Similar species** The **Hairy Snail** *T. hispidus* occurs less frequently in gardens. It is smaller and retains a covering of short, curved hairs into adulthood, although patches may get rubbed off.

Smooth Snail *Aegopinella nitidula*
Similar to the *Oxychilus* snails but with a waxy, amber-coloured shell which, although slightly translucent, lacks a glossy sheen. **Habitat and distribution** Occurs in a variety of damp places among plants and shrubs, often around human habitation. Widely distributed throughout Britain and Ireland.

Cellar Snail *Oxychilus cellarius*
Both the shell and the body are paler than closely related species, but the amber shell has the characteristic highly polished surface typical of the genus. It feeds on decaying vegetable matter and fungi, but also eats small snails and invertebrates. If disturbed, may give off a pungent smell. **Habitat and distribution** Lives in damp places in gardens, under hedges and in leaf litter, but may enter outbuildings and moist cellars. **Similar species** The **Garlic Snail** *O. alliarius* is also found in gardens and is more tolerant of acidic soil. It is smaller, 6mm, darker and gives off a strong smell of garlic when handled.

Draparnaud's Glass Snail
Oxychilus draparnaudi
The largest and least shiny of the *Oxychilus* species, whose shell may reach 15mm across. The waxy, yellowish-brown shell is slightly darker near the opening, and the body is blue-grey. A carnivorous snail, it feeds mostly on earthworms and other small invertebrates. **Habitat and distribution** Found in damp shady places, among garden rubbish and leaf litter. Widely distributed and expanding its range.

Glossy Glass Snail
Oxychilus navarricus helveticus
A very glossy species, whose jet-black mantle, the part of the body near the shell, forms a black band near the mouth. When disturbed, it has a faint smell of garlic, although less pungent than that of the Garlic Snail. **Habitat and distribution** Common under logs and stones and among damp leaf litter. Found throughout England and Wales but most common in the south, with few records from Scotland. **Similar species** The **Garlic Snail** (see Cellar Snail, above).

Girdled Snail ×.2.5

Strawberry Snail ×2.5

Smooth Snail ×.2.5

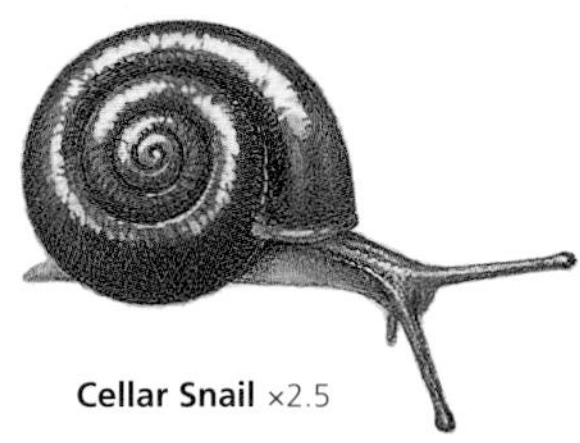

Cellar Snail ×2.5

Draparnaud's Glass Snail ×2.5

Glossy Glass Snail ×2.5

Earthworms and flatworms
Oligochaeta and Turbellaria

Earthworms play a vital role in maintaining the structure of soil by breaking down organic matter and aerating through burrowing, thus creating good moisture balance and an improvement in microbial activity. Valued by all who work on the land, the presence of earthworm populations is often used to calculate the quality of soil, both from a horticultural and an ecological viewpoint.

Flatworms are primitive, elongated invertebrates related to tapeworms, most frequently encountered beneath damp logs and stones. They glide slowly, leaving a trail of mucus, and feed either on live or dead earthworms or slugs, sucking in a liquid formed by enzymes exuded onto the victim and then ejecting waste through the mouth. Although hermaphrodites, not all species mate as some are able to reproduce by breaking in half.

Long-worm or **Blackhead** *Aporrectodea longa*
This is the worm mainly responsible for the surface casts on lawns and bowling greens, especially in spring and autumn when the ground is moist. A deep vertical-burrowing species, in the summer when the ground is dry it enters a resting stage and is often dug up in a tight knot, which helps it to prevent desiccation. The cylindrical body is dark muddy brown, becoming paler towards the tail, and reaches a length of around 17cm. Mating takes place in the soil rather than on the surface. Burrows may be up to 60cm deep, and if the soil is vibrated with a fork, worms emerge rapidly to the surface. Widespread throughout Britain and Ireland, and common in gardens, parks and allotments.

Red Worm *Lumbricus rubellus*
This medium-sized worm, reaching a length of 14cm, is deep purplish red above, towards the front end, and pale yellow below. Usually occurs near the surface, beneath leaf litter and under stones, where the soil is moist and rich in organic matter. Popular with anglers as bait. Common and widely distributed.

Lob Worm *Lumbricus terrestris*
The largest and best known earthworm, reaching up to 35cm and easily recognised by the plump, cylindrical body with a distinctly flattened tail, and by its purplish-brown colour, paler yellow on the underside. It is the only species that mates on the surface, usually on damp nights, when pairs can be seen by torchlight, lying head to tail. Mating may last for four hours, making them vulnerable to predation by Foxes, Hedgehogs and owls. However, they are able to withdraw rapidly into their burrows if disturbed, aided by short bristles, or setae, which grip the inside of the burrow. A deep-burrowing species that makes permanent tunnels reaching 3m deep, the Lob Worm comes to the surface to feed, drawing leaves and other organic matter into its hole, often leaving a little cluster of twigs and leaves poking out of the entrance. Maturity is reached in about three years, and individuals can live for several decades. Widespread in Britain and Ireland; found in many habitats, including garden lawns, and especially common in clay soil. A favourite bait of anglers.

Grey Worm or **Turgid Worm**
Aporrectodea caliginosa
Four distinct forms of this worm occur, the most familiar, which occurs abundantly in cultivated soil, being mainly pale blue-grey, with a pale orange clitellum (a protective mucus collar for the eggs) and a pinkish front end. It grows to a length of 8cm and makes a horizontal burrow in the top 8cm of soil, coming to the surface when disturbed by vibration. Widespread, it is found in many habitats, and is often the commonest worm in gardens.

Brandling *Eisenia fetida*
This distinctively banded worm, which gives off an unpleasant-smelling (fetid) yellow fluid when handled, may reach 13cm, but is usually much smaller. Bred commercially for high-protein feed for livestock and fish, they are also supplied to gardeners in wormeries to help improve compost heaps. Widely distributed; usually found in rich organic matter such as in compost heaps and beneath manure.

Flatworm *Microplana terrestris*
The commonest native flatworm, usually black or dark grey, which grows to about 2cm. It lives in damp places under logs and stones, and scavenges on dead slugs and earthworms. Widespread throughout Britain.

New Zealand Flatworm
Arthurdendyus triangulatus
Smooth, shiny and covered in mucus, which can cause skin irritation, this alien flatworm reaches 20cm when extended but when resting it curls into a flat coil about 2cm across. It is most often encountered beneath plant pots, logs and stones in moist, shaded places, along with its egg capsules, which resemble slightly flattened blackcurrants. These each contain up to eight eggs, which hatch into pale juveniles about 2.5cm long. First recorded in the early 1960s, the species was probably accidentally introduced from New Zealand by the horticultural industry. It has since gained notoriety as it preys entirely on earthworms, particularly the deep-burrowing species that come to the surface, sometimes virtually eradicating them, resulting in deterioration in soil structure. This has had a knock-on effect on populations of small mammals such as Moles and Hedgehogs, and some birds that feed mainly on earthworms. At present, there are no control methods available. Locally very common in gardens and allotments in central and southern Scotland, northern England and Ireland, with scattered records from other parts of Britain.

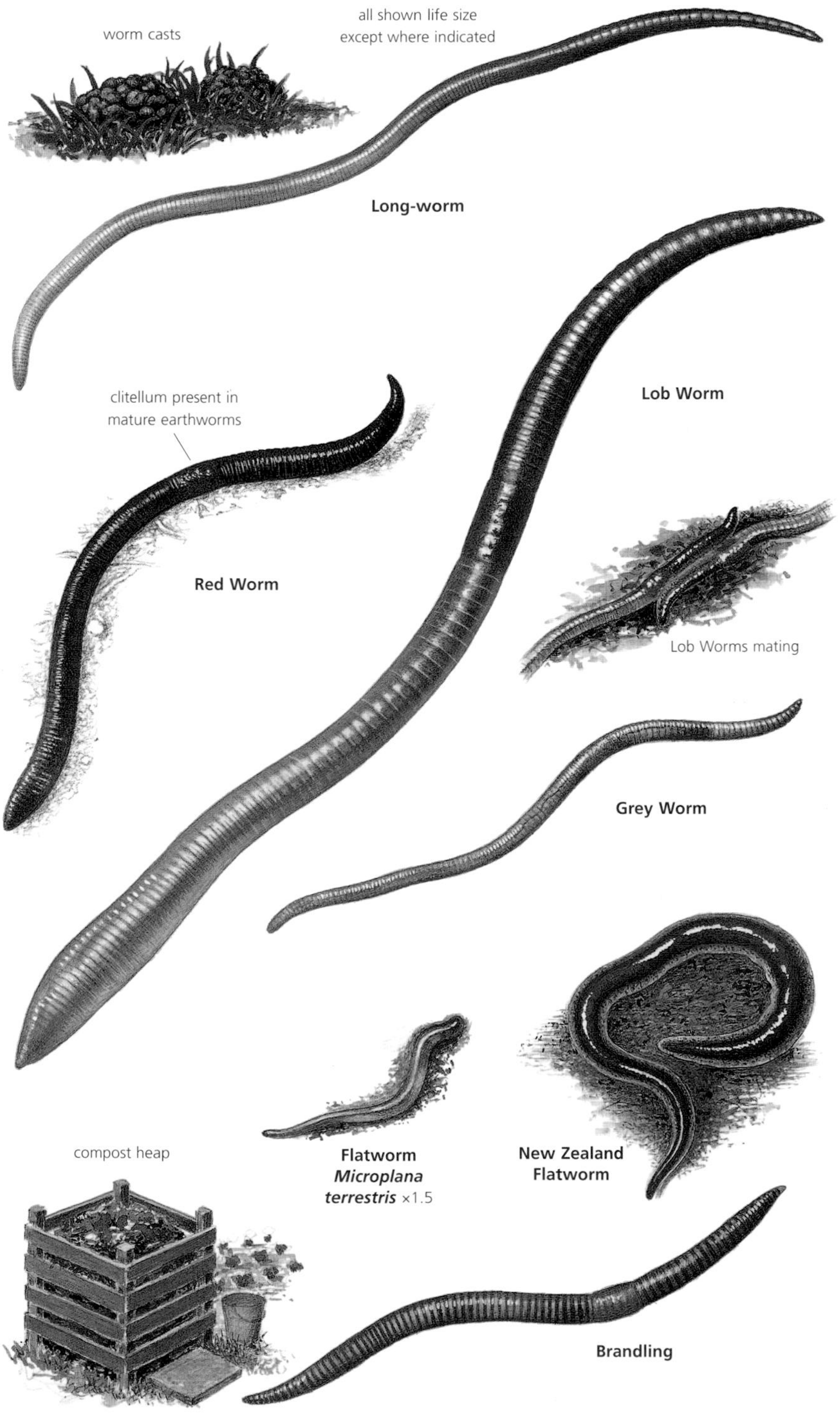
worm casts
all shown life size
except where indicated
Long-worm
clitellum present in
mature earthworms
Lob Worm
Red Worm
Lob Worms mating
Grey Worm
compost heap
Flatworm
Microplana terrestris ×1.5
New Zealand
Flatworm
Brandling

Pondlife

▲ Frogs will breed in even the smallest of garden ponds.

In the past 100 years, 70% of our ponds have been lost from the wider countryside, mainly as a result of drainage, infilling and pollution. It follows that garden ponds have become a key resource for some wildlife, such as frogs, and there is no better way of increasing the diversity of wildlife in your garden than by having a pond.

Anything from the size of a small tub upwards will provide a habitat for wildlife. The ideal would be about 3m × 4m, with the deepest point about 60cm, positioned predominantly in sunlight. Have a sloping, shallow end with planted shelves, since shallow, well-vegetated areas are best for small animals. Dragonflies and damselflies are the jewel in the pond's crown and to attract these spectacular insects size matters. A minimum of about 3.5m^2 will encourage some of the commoner damselflies such as the Azure and Common Blue Damselflies to breed, while a pond of 12m^2 is large enough to attract any of the still-water species, including our largest dragonfly, the impressive Emperor.

In ponds, water quality is all. The best water supply is rainwater collected naturally or from a nearby roof. Avoid tap water if possible because it usually contains chlorine, together with dissolved phosphates, added to reduce lead in drinking water. These phosphates, along with any fertiliser leaking in from the garden, will cause problems with weed and algae.

A good mix of native and some non-native submerged and floating plants will keep the water clear and give shelter to the inhabitants, and marginal and bog garden plants will help to create a more natural look. Care though, should be taken to avoid the introduction of invasive aliens such as the water fern *Azolla filiculoides.* Regardless of whether animal life is introduced or is allowed to colonise naturally, life will begin to appear, often within days, depending on the time of year. Fish and wildlife do not mix and the temptation to introduce ornamental fish, or even Stickle-backs, should be resisted, as they will drastically reduce the animal life, making the pond a much less interesting place to observe the behaviour of the smaller inhabitants, and eventually polluting the water with their waste, if you feed them.

In the first season, larger predatory insects such as dragonflies and diving

▲ The Great Diving Beetle often visits weedy garden ponds.

beetles will arrive to lay eggs, and their larvae will feed on the young of other insects such as mayflies, flies and bugs. Many other insects, particularly bugs like the Backswimmer and Pondskater, which are only ever seen beneath or on the surface of the pond in the daytime, fly at night and will soon colonise new ponds. Several species of fly, such as the long-legged fly and the familiar yellow-and-black hoverfly *Helophilus pendulus,* will colonise the pond margins, resting on floating lily pads and other surface vegetation. Less welcome insects such as mosquitoes will visit and, although potentially a nuisance in gardens, especially on warm summer evenings, they are an important food source for many creatures and most will be eaten in a healthy wildlife garden by countless other invertebrates.

The three common amphibians, Common Frog, Common Toad and Smooth Newt, nearly always appear naturally, especially if there are ponds or other waterbodies nearby. However, ponds in gardens completely enclosed with fence panels or walls (both of which are to be discouraged) may need a helping hand, although the transference of frogs and frogspawn is not recommended as this may contribute to the spread of Ranavirus Disease. In early spring, the entertaining antics of mating frogs and toads soon die down after the eggs have been laid, but the fascinating tail-wagging courtship of newts continues into the summer months. The arrival of these amphibians may in turn attract the Grass Snake, if the surrounding habitats are suitable, as the Common Frog forms a major part of its diet. If a suitable compost heap is nearby, its warmth may provide the right conditions for the Grass Snake to lay eggs.

A log pile positioned in a cool, shady spot close to the pond will benefit many creatures, giving shelter to small mammals such as voles, mice and Hedgehogs that will drink from the pond, as well as giving refuge to newts after they have left the water in late summer following breeding. Although most garden ponds are too small to attract water birds such as Mallard and Moorhens, which prefer larger, more open water, many garden birds such as Blackbirds, Greenfinches and Starlings will take advantage by drinking and bathing in the shallows, and others like the Song Thrush and even House Martins will collect mud from the margins to help make their nests.

Herons often become regular but unwelcome visitors, especially to garden ponds stocked with fish. They are less troublesome in wildlife ponds, but may interrupt the breeding activities of frogs in the early spring, when their voracious, demanding young are in the nest. Gardens with a river or larger lake nearby could be visited by the most exotic of all our water birds, the Kingfisher, and a branch leaning out over the water will provide a convenient perch for this and other hunters such as dragonflies to launch their attacks.

Undoubtedly, the garden pond forms an important mini-ecosystem upon which many animals depend, and is a source of constant interest and activity; as a result, the would-be pond installer should be aware that this interest can become addictive, and there is no known cure!

Creating a garden pond

▲ Birds will visit garden ponds to drink and bathe.

Why have a pond?

The introduction stressed that having a pond undoubtedly contributes more to a wildlife-friendly garden than any other feature, attracting a wide range of permanent and visiting animal life, as well as giving great pleasure to young and old, and to both serious and casual wildlife observers. Before the often demanding but unavoidable task of digging the hole begins, various considerations regarding location and construction should be decided.

Size and location

All sizes of garden will benefit from having a pond, and anything from the size of a baby's bath or a sink upwards will support wildlife of some sort, but in general, so far as attracting a greater variety of animal and bird life is concerned, the larger the pond, the better. A good, average size would be 3m × 4m, with a minimum depth at the deepest point of 60cm to prevent it from freezing solid in winter or heating up during the summer. An irregular but not too complicated shape looks more natural, and shallow and medium-depth areas are also essential. These provide a range of temperatures to suit a variety of plant and animal life; they also provide a means of escape for animals that may accidentally fall in. A location in the garden that gives shelter, plenty of sunlight, but also a little shade is best, and to avoid too many leaves falling into the pond in the autumn, it is best not to site it too close to large trees.

Choosing and measuring a lining

In recent years, ponds lined with butyl rubber have proved the most suitable, as they are adaptable and can be made to measure. However, moulded plastic or fibreglass liners can also be satisfactory, especially for small ponds, although they often lack shallow or gently sloping edges. Once the size and depth of the pond has been established, the size of the liner can be calculated. This is done by taking the length + twice the maximum depth + 50cm, and the width + twice the maximum depth + 50cm. So, for example, a 3m × 4m pond, with a maximum depth of 60cm, would require a liner of 5.70m × 4.70m.

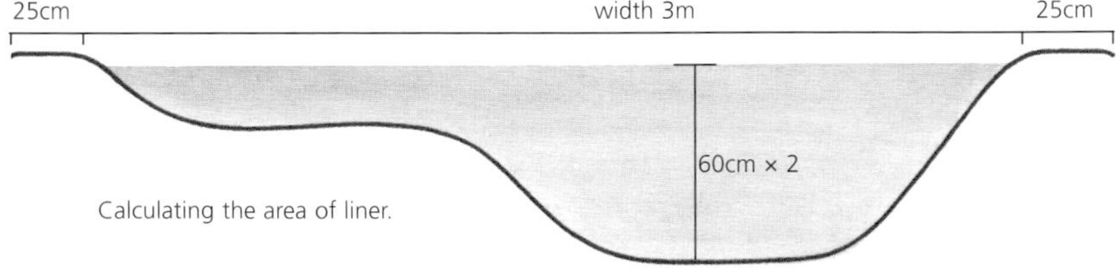

Calculating the area of liner.

Construction

Make sure the site for the pond is level, and consider using the soil from the excavation to create a bank or rockery nearby to provide shelter. Once dug, any stones and other sharp objects should be removed from the hole, and the bed covered with a layer of soft, damp sand or soil, followed by a layer of old carpet or underlay. The liner can then be placed over the hole and gently pressed into shape. Before filling, the edges can be anchored with flat rocks or turfs, which can be properly positioned when the water has moulded the liner into place. Rainwater is preferable, but tapwater can be used to gradually fill the pond. When full, it must be left for several days to allow the release of chlorine from the water.

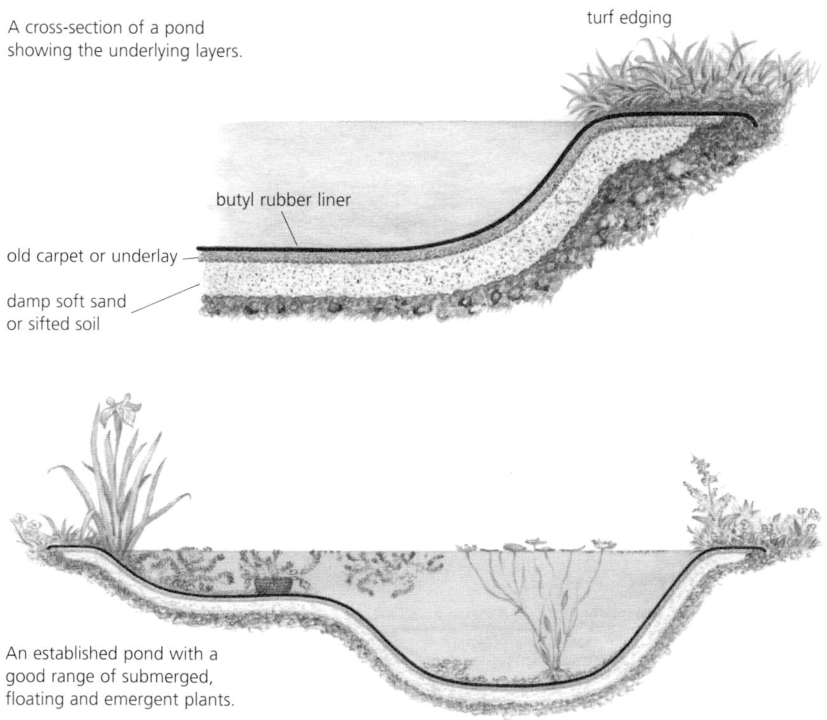

A cross-section of a pond showing the underlying layers.

An established pond with a good range of submerged, floating and emergent plants.

Stocking

A newly-created pond will soon start to become colonised naturally, with animal and plant life coming and going as the pond develops. In fact, after just a few years of existence, without assistance, the variety of wildlife may well equal that of a pond many decades old. But, for the less patient, who want to give their pond an established appearance, the planting of submerged, floating and marginal plants will speed up the process, although rampant species, and especially alien invasive species, must be avoided. The introduction of a bucket-full of water from an established pond will introduce smaller organisms, which will become the basis of a wide community of diverse food chains, but again, care must be taken to avoid fish fry, which could go on to reduce that diversity. Fluctuation in the water level is natural, and topping up the pond need only be done if there is danger of the pond drying out completely. Maintenance, such as the thinning out of vegetation, is best done in late autumn, so that life in the bottom can re-adjust before the onset of winter.

Cinnamon Sedge
Limnephilus rhombicus larva and case
Caddisfly larvae found in garden ponds are members of the 'case-maker' group, which construct their mobile homes from plant materials, small stones, sand grains or snails' shells. Many cases are similar, but some can be identified by their structure. The larvae feed mainly on vegetable matter and, when fully grown, seal the case, securing it to a stone or plant prior to pupation. For adult, see page 98.

Mottled Sedge *Glyphotaelius pellucidus* case
The distinctive, flattened case of this caddisfly is constructed from pieces of overlapping leaf, spun together with silk. The larva pupates inside the case and, after about two weeks, cuts itself out of the case and scrambles to the surface. The adult emerges and inflates its wings like a butterfly. Common in weedy ponds and ditches. For adult, see page 98.

Southern Hawker
Aeshna cyanea larva
A large, cryptically camouflaged larva, which ambushes prey up to the size of tadpoles and small fish. Victims are grabbed with the hinged lower lip, which shoots out at amazing speed. Fully grown after three years, the larva crawls up waterside vegetation and the adult dragonfly emerges, leaving only the dried empty larval skin, or exuvia, still clinging to the vegetation. For adult, see page 80.

Great Diving Beetle
Dytiscus marginalis larva
Even fiercer than the adult, this larva waits amongst weed, with jaws wide open, seizing prey often larger than itself, such as small fish and tadpoles. Fully grown after a year, it leaves the water and burrows into soft mud to form a cell, where it pupates. The adult emerges after three weeks and, when hardened off, leaves the cell and heads for water, where it descends into the muddy bottom to spend the winter. For adult, see page 162.

Alderfly *Sialis lutaria* larva
A distinctive larva, with seven pairs of segmented abdominal gills. It lives for up to two years in the muddy bottom of ponds, where it preys on insect larvae and other invertebrates. When fully grown it leaves the water and pupates in a cell constructed in damp soil. The pupa digs its way out of the cell in spring and the adult finally emerges. For adult, see page 98.

Azure Damselfly *Coenagrion puella* larva
This damselfly has a similar life cycle to the larger hawker dragonfly, but is more delicate, feeding on water fleas, small crustaceans and insect larvae. It takes one, occasionally two, years to become fully grown and is one of the commonest and most frequently encountered damselfly larvae found in weedy garden ponds. For adult, see page 78.

Pond Olive *Cloeon dipterum* nymph
The most abundant mayfly to occur in nutrient-rich garden ponds, water butts and cisterns. It has seven pairs of gills along the abdomen and three tails, and when disturbed, dashes with amazing bursts of speed. Feeds on organic detritus and has a one-year life cycle. The fully-grown nymph rises to the surface of the pond and without delay, to avoid predation, the sub-adult insect emerges. It then flies to nearby vegetation and, unlike other insects, undergoes a further moult into the mature mayfly, known to anglers as a 'spinner'. For adult, see page 78.

Phantom midge *Chaoborus* sp. larva
A strange, transparent larva, which hangs motionless in a horizontal plane, almost invisible apart from two dark bladders at either end. It moves with a sudden flick when disturbed, reappearing some distance away. It feeds on tiny crustaceans and insect larvae, which it catches with its modified antennae, and is able to withstand the coldest winter temperatures. The pupa is similar to the mosquito pupa but with longer, ear-like breathing tubes. The non-biting adults emerge from spring onwards, and resemble some chironomid midges.

Non-biting chironomid midge
Chironomus sp. larva
Known as 'bloodworms', their red bodies indicate the presence of haemoglobin, which enables them to survive in stagnant, muddy water with a low oxygen content. They feed on organic matter and live in tubular retreats, constructed from sand and organic particles, mixed with silk, in mud and debris at the bottom of ponds and water butts. When oxygen levels are especially low they swim to the surface with a jerky looping action. The pupa is formed in mud and has tufts of filaments on the head to help absorb oxygen. Bloodworms form a major part of the diet of many invertebrates and vertebrates. For adult, see page 138.

Drone fly
Eristalis sp. larva (rat-tailed maggot)
Adapted to living in stagnant, foul-smelling water, and feeding on organic particles in the mud, this strange, semi-transparent larva breathes by means of an extensible telescopic tube, which reaches the surface of the water. The pupa is formed in marginal mud and resembles a dark, shrivelled larva with a pair of long breathing tubes at the front. For adult, see page 142.

Common Mosquito *Culex pipiens* egg, larva and pupa
Larvae hatch from a buoyant, floating 'raft' of eggs, and hang, along with pupae, below the surface-film of water butts and ponds, diving in an energetic wriggling motion when disturbed. All stages of the life cycle are fed on by a wide range of creatures. For adult, see page 138.

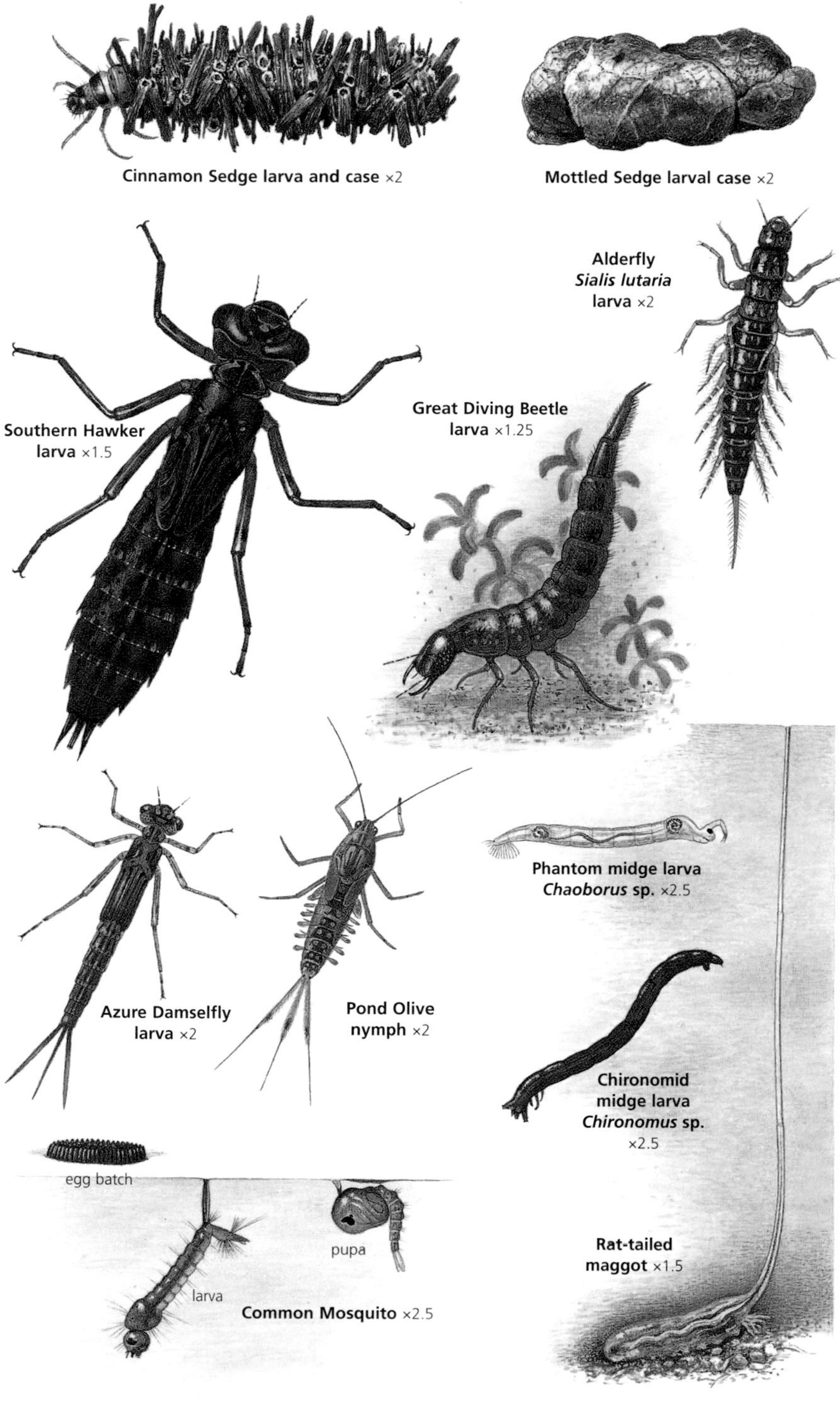

Cinnamon Sedge larva and case ×2

Mottled Sedge larval case ×2

Alderfly *Sialis lutaria* larva ×2

Southern Hawker larva ×1.5

Great Diving Beetle larva ×1.25

Phantom midge larva *Chaoborus* sp. ×2.5

Azure Damselfly larva ×2

Pond Olive nymph ×2

Chironomid midge larva *Chironomus* sp. ×2.5

Rat-tailed maggot ×1.5

Common Mosquito ×2.5

Water mite *Eylais* sp.
Water mite *Limnesia fulgida*
Related to spiders, free-living adult mites are often seen swimming or crawling amongst vegetation in ponds, where they feed on planktonic invertebrates. Eggs are laid in a gelatinous mass attached to stones or vegetation, and the juveniles, which have only six legs, develop as parasites on various aquatic bugs and beetles. Britain has about 300 species.

Great Ramshorn Snail *Planorbarius corneus*
The largest of many hard-to-identify ramshorn snails, reaching in excess of 30mm across. Sixty or so eggs are laid in a flat, gelatinous egg-mass, attached to a plant or other firm surface. Strictly herbivorous, they are kept in aquariums and often released into garden ponds. Their blood contains haemoglobin, allowing them to survive in stagnant water. Widespread, but scarcer further north and west.

Common Bithynia *Bithynia tentaculata*
One of the operculate snails, which have a circular, chalky lid that seals off the entrance of the shell. Usually found in larger weedy ponds and slow-moving rivers. Gelatinous egg capsules are laid in double rows on stones or vegetation. Common in most parts of Britain and Ireland, except the far north.

Wandering Snail *Radix peregra*
The commonest and most widespread water snail, found in virtually every freshwater habitat, still and moving, throughout Britain and Ireland. It varies considerably in size and shape, according to water type.

Great Pond Snail *Lymnaea stagnalis*
This large and familiar pond snail, reaching 50mm in length, is often seen at the water's surface, taking in air. Capable of surviving in quite stagnant water, its diet includes dead animals as well as vegetable matter. The sausage-shaped, gelatinous egg batches, often containing several hundred eggs, are laid on dead leaves or near the surface, on the underside of water-lily leaves. Common throughout Britain and Ireland.

Flatworm *Polycelis nigra*
A small, dark flatworm, which has many minute eyes arranged around the margins of the front end. Mature specimens reach about 12mm. They feed on decaying organic matter and lay yellow egg cocoons on plants and stones. Often abundant under leaves and detritus, in ponds and slow-moving water.

Flatworm *Dendrocoelum lacteum*
A sticky, milky-white flatworm, which glides smoothly across leaves and stones, hunting for invertebrates such as the Two-spotted Water Louse. Flatworms are hermaphrodites but still require mates to reproduce, although if accidentally cut in half, will grow into two separate individuals. Widespread and common in ponds and lakes.

Horse Leech *Haemopis sanguisuga*
An impressive animal, about 4cm at rest but reaching 15cm when extended. Usually found in ponds in mud, beneath submerged logs and under stones, but also on land, where it lays its egg cocoon in mud. Its jaws are incapable of piercing the skin of horses or man; instead, it feeds on worms, molluscs, tadpoles, small frogs and fish, which it swallows rather than sucks. Widespread and locally common.

Copepod *Cyclops* sp.
Abundant in many types of permanent or semi-permanent water, where they swim jerkily in the company of other plankton, or in debris at the bottom, feeding on tiny organic particles and microscopic animal and vegetable life. Females are most obvious, with their double sacs of dark eggs slung either side of the tapering body. During mating, the male holds the female firmly with his bristly antennae. About 40 species occur in Britain.

Water flea *Daphnia* sp.
Water flea is a general term for many microscopic crustaceans. They form an important food resource for many pond inhabitants, as well as being popular with aquarists as fish food. *Daphnia* are perhaps the best known; they swim jerkily, with the aid of their antennae, and in the summer months reproduce rapidly, without mating. When present in large numbers, the haemoglobin in their blood can give a discoloured, pinkish-brown hue to pond water.

Two-spotted Water Louse *Asellus aquaticus*
A flattened, aquatic relative of the woodlouse which, like them, has seven, though much longer, pairs of legs. The larger male carries the female beneath him prior to mating, and the eggs are laid and protected in a brood pouch beneath her body. Two-spotted Water Lice do not swim well, but bumble around in waterweed, and in mud and detritus at the bottom of ponds and lakes, scavenging on organic debris and algae, often tolerating stagnant water, low in oxygen. **Similar species** *A. meridianus* is smaller, with shorter antennae, and the two pale spots on the head are joined to make an elongated band. Both species are common and widespread in Britain and Ireland.

Freshwater shrimp
Crangonyx pseudogracilis
An introduced species from North America, more likely to be found in still-water ponds than *Gammarus* species of shrimp, which need a higher oxygen content. It walks upright amongst aquatic vegetation rather than scrambling sideways under stones, and reaches no more than 10mm. It feeds on decaying organic matter. Females can be found carrying their eggs in a brood pouch beneath the thorax. Common in the south and Midlands, and has spread to Scotland and Ireland.

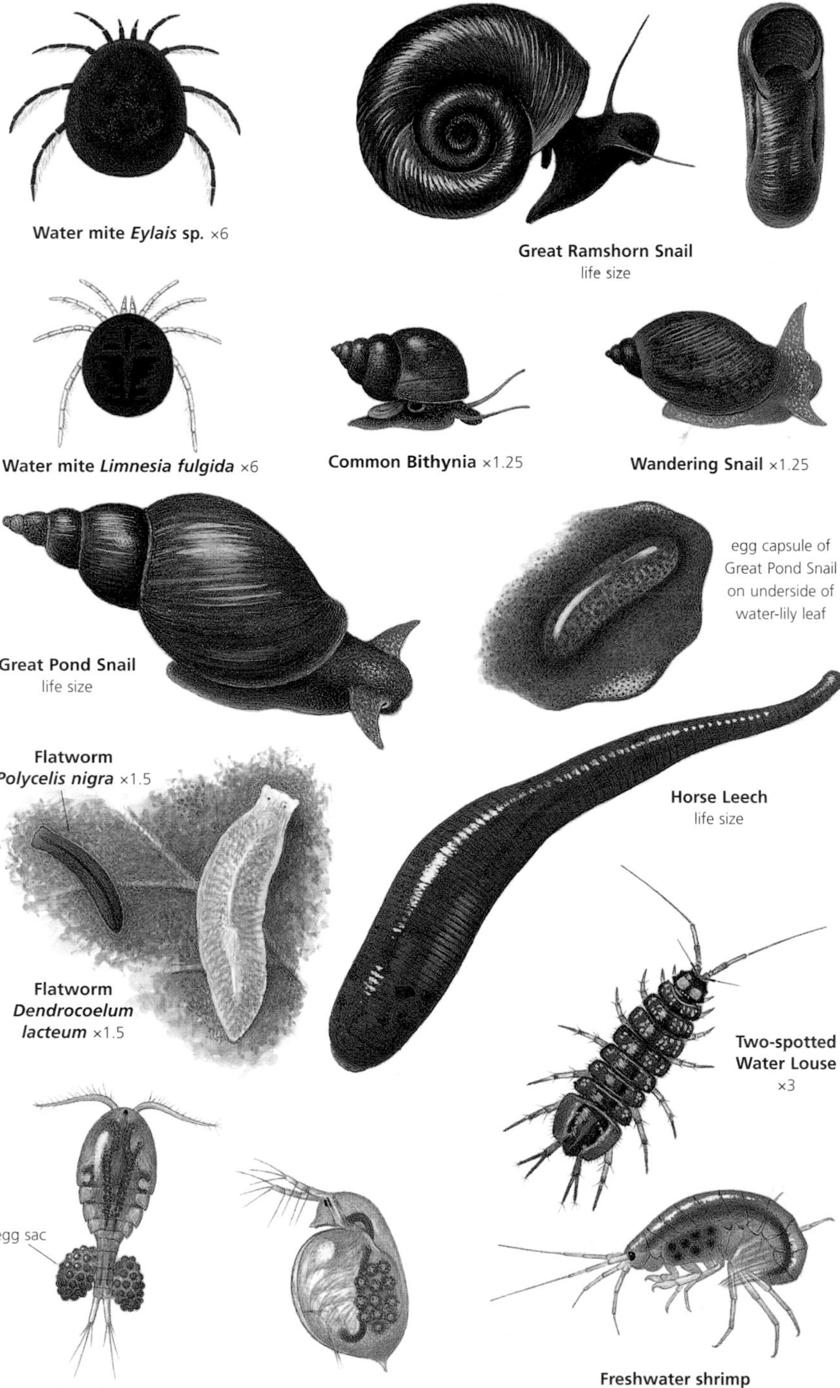

Water mite *Eylais* sp. ×6

Great Ramshorn Snail
life size

Water mite *Limnesia fulgida* ×6

Common Bithynia ×1.25

Wandering Snail ×1.25

Great Pond Snail
life size

Flatworm
Polycelis nigra ×1.5

Horse Leech
life size

Flatworm
Dendrocoelum lacteum ×1.5

Two-spotted Water Louse
×3

Copepod *Cyclops* sp. ×12

Water flea *Daphnia* sp. ×12

Freshwater shrimp
Crangonyx pseudogracilis ×3

Glossary

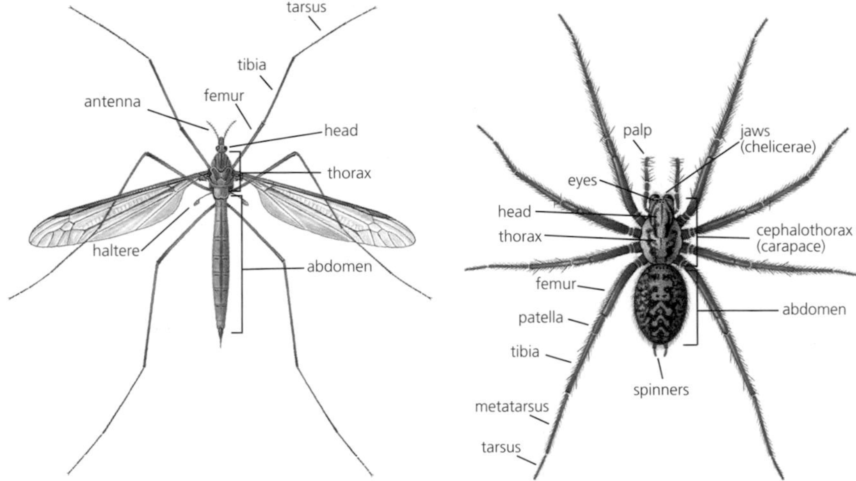

Cranefly and a Large House Spider, showing the basic features of an insect and a spider body.

Calamistrum A comb-like structure on the rear metatarsi of lace-webbed spiders, used in web-making.

Carapace The hard external covering of the cephalothorax of a spider or harvestman.

Cephalothorax The front section of the two divisions of a spider's body.

Cerci A pair of appendages, often very long, at the tip of the abdomen of many arthropods, such as mayflies.

Chelicerae Jaws of a spider, each made up of a base and a fang.

Clitellum A collar, towards the front end of a mature earthworm, often pink or orange, which protects the eggs.

Cocoon A structure, made mainly from silk, by a larva, to protect it after pupation, or by spiders to protect their eggs.

Dorsal The back or upper surface (opposite of ventral).

Elytra The hardened, curved forewings of beetles and earwigs, not used for flying.

Endoparasitoid Insect whose larva lives inside the body of a host, eventually killing it.

Epigyne The genital opening of mature female spiders, situated towards the front, on the underside of the abdomen, often used to identify species.

Exoskeleton The external skeleton of arthropods, necessitating the moulting of the outer cuticle as they grow.

Exuvia The cast-off skin of arthropods, most notably dragonflies and damselflies.

Femur/femora (plural) The third leg segment from the body, and often the largest.

Flagellum The tip of the antenna.

Furcula The forked springing organ held beneath the abdomen, found on springtails.

Halteres Club-shaped, modified hindwings of true flies (Diptera), which act as stabilisers and are essential for balancing whilst in flight.

Hemimetabolism An incomplete metamorphosis with no pupal stage, as in true bugs, dragonflies and earwigs.

Hibernaculum A winter retreat for hibernating animals.

Inquiline An animal that shares the home and food of another, for example, various wasps that live in the galls of other wasps.

Kleptoparasite A parasite that obtains its food by theft, sometimes eating the host and often stealing its food supply; e.g. ruby-tailed wasps, whose larvae live in the nests of solitary wasps.

Larva/larvae (plural) The immature stage of an insect (also known as a caterpillar in butterflies), following emergence from the egg, when most eating and growing is done; quite unlike the adult.

Metamorphosis The changes throughout the life cycle, from egg to adult.

Metatarsus Section of a spider's leg between the tibia and the tarsus.

Nymph The immature stage of some insects, which have an incomplete metamorphosis, such as mayflies.

Ocularium A raised tubercle with a pair of simple eyes, found on the carapace of harvestmen.

Ovipositor Egg-laying organ, sometimes concealed, but often long and sting-like, as in some ichneumon wasps, or sword-like, as in bush-crickets.

Palps or pedipalps Usually quite short, segmented sensory organs, near the mouth of many invertebrates. In male spiders, they are used for signalling during courtship and the transference of sperm during mating.

Parasite An organism that benefits from a close association with another organism but which gives nothing in return.

Parasitoid Predators, such as ichneumon wasps, whose larvae feed on or in their still-living hosts, eventually killing them.

Parthenogenetic The act of reproduction without fertilisation of the eggs, common in aphids and some gall wasps.

Patella The short segment on a spider's leg between the femur and tibia, equivalent to the knee.

Phoretic Small invertebrates, such as false-scorpions, that attach themselves to the legs of larger insects as a means of dispersal.

Proboscis Tubular sucking mouthparts, either rigid or held coiled beneath the head, as with butterflies and moths.

Pupa/pupae (plural) or chrysalis The stage between larva and adult, when organs and tissue reform, prior to emergence into the adult insect.

Radula The continuously growing, rasp-like tongue of slugs and snails, used for scraping plant material.

Rostrum The elongated, piercing mouthparts of bugs, and the snout of weevils and scorpionflies.

Scutellum A triangular plate at the rear of the thorax, most noticeable in the shieldbugs.

Setae Bristles or hairs.

Sex-brand A cluster of specialised scales forming dark patches on the wings of some male butterflies. These scales release chemicals, known as pheromones, which attract the females.

Spinners or spinnerets Silk-producing structures at the tip of a spider's abdomen, capable of producing up to six different types of silk.

Spiracle Breathing pore along the side of an insect's abdomen, most noticeable in caterpillars.

Tarsus/tarsi (plural) The end part of the leg, with or without segments, furnished with claws at the tip.

Thorax Section of the body behind the head, to which legs and wings may be attached.

Tibia Segment of the leg equivalent to the human shin.

Tubercle A raised protuberance.

Umbilicus Hollow opening on the axis, at the base of a snail's shell.

Ventral The undersurface or belly (opposite of dorsal).

Vestigial Poorly developed and hardly noticeable, as in 'vestigial wings' in some moths.

Top ten tips for wildlife gardening

This list was produced by the Wildlife Gardening Forum, which is composed of around 100 organisations with an interest in wildlife gardening. It was inspired by 'Let our gardens live! A manifesto for gardens, people and nature'. For more about the forum and how to support it, go to www.wlgf.org

1. Brighten your garden with flowers that provide pollen and nectar for bees, butterflies and other insects. Choose wild flowers or garden plants to offer food from spring through to autumn. Good choices include aubrieta, forget-me-not and flowering currant for spring, lavender and thyme for summer, and sedum, Michaelmas daisy and hebe for autumn.
2. Grow a variety of trees, shrubs and climbers, or a mixed hedge, to give food and shelter. Small trees that are good for blossom and berries include rowan, crab apple and hawthorn. Ivy provides shelter for nesting birds, autumn flowers for nectar and winter berries for birds and small mammals.
3. Look after mature trees in and around your garden and they'll look after the wildlife. Mature trees are more important for wildlife than any other single factor. If your garden is too small for big trees, get some planted in the neighbourhood, and protect those that are already there.
4. Add water – an upturned bin-lid is a start or, better still, dig a pond. Make sure ponds have at least one sloping side to allow creatures an easy way out. Most wildlife likes shallow water, as well as a good range of plants for a varied habitat.
5. Leave a pile of dead wood in a shady spot. Any wood will do, although big, natural logs are best. They can make a home for anything from colourful fungi to hibernating toads.
6. Build a compost heap, which will help all your garden plants and wildlife. Compost makes for healthy soil, which is good for garden plants and wildlife. Compost heaps also shelter many small creatures, and even some larger ones, like slug-eating Slow-worms.
7. Provide food and water for birds all year round. Offering a mix of food, including peanuts, sunflower hearts, seeds, kitchen scraps and fat balls, as well as natural food such as berries and seed-heads, will attract a wide range of birds.
8. Relax! Don't be too tidy. Leave some areas undisturbed. Piles of leaves and twiggy debris tucked in a hedge bottom or out-of-the-way corner will provide shelter for frogs, mice and Hedgehogs. Hollow stems can shelter hibernating insects.
9. Allow a patch of grass to grow longer. This will encourage wild flowers, provide shelter for small mammals and food for some butterfly caterpillars.
10. Garden sustainably to help protect wildlife and the environment world-wide. Use chemicals only as a last resort, avoid peat, choose wood from sustainable sources, recycle all you can and save water.

Watch and enjoy the wonderful wildlife in your garden and discover an amazing new world thriving in your own back yard.

Further reading

Wildlife gardening

Baines, C. 2016. *RHS Companion to Wildlife Gardening*. Frances Lincoln, London.

Bradbury, K. 2017. *The Wildlife Gardener.* White Owl, Barnsley.

Bradbury, K. 2019. *Wildlife Gardening For Everyone and Everything*. Bloomsbury Publishing, London.

Creeser, R. 2004. *Wildlife Friendly Plants.* Collins & Brown, London.

Cromack, D. 2018. *Nestboxes: Your Complete Guide*. British Trust for Ornithology, Thetford, Norfolk.

Packham, C. 2015. *Chris Packham's Back Garden Nature Reserve.* Bloomsbury Publishing, London.

Ryrie, C. 2003. *The Daily Telegraph Wildlife Gardening.* Cassell Illustrated, London.

Steel, J. 2016. *Making Wildlife Ponds.* Brambleby Books, Taunton.

Thomas, A. 2017. *RSPB Gardening For Wildlife*. Bloomsbury Publishing, London.

Thompson, K. 2007. *No Nettles Required: The Reassuring Truth About Wildlife Gardening*. Eden Project Books, London.

Toms, M. 2003. *The BTO/CJ Garden BirdWatch Book*. British Trust for Ornithology, Thetford, Norfolk.

General garden wildlife

Buczacki, S. 2007. *Garden Natural History* (New Naturalist Library). HarperCollins, London.

Owen, J. 2010. *Wildlife of a Garden: A Thirty-year Study.* Royal Horticultural Society, Peterborough.

Identification guides

Ball, S., & Morris, R. 2015. *Britain's Hoverflies*. Princeton University Press, Woodstock.

Brock, P. 2014. *A Comprehensive Guide to Insects of Britain & Ireland.* NatureBureau, Newbury.

Brooks, S., Cham, S., & Lewington, R. 2014. *Field Guide to the Dragonflies and Damselflies of Great Britain and Ireland.* Bloomsbury Publishing, London.

Cameron, R., & Riley, G. 2003. *Land Snails in the British Isles*. Field Studies Council, Telford.

Chinery, M. 2012. *Insects of Britain and Western Europe*. Bloomsbury Publishing, London.

Couzens, D., Swash, A., Still, R., & Dunn, J. 2017. *Britain's Mammals*. Princeton University Press, Woodstock.

Falk, S., & Lewington, R. 2015. *Field Guide to the Bees of Great Britain and Ireland.* Bloomsbury Publishing, London.

Greenhalgh, M., & Ovenden, D. 2007. *Freshwater Life.* HarperCollins, London.

Lewington, R. 2015. *Pocket Guide to the Butterflies of Great Britain and Ireland.* Bloomsbury Publishing, London.

Roy, H., Brown, P., & Lewington, R. 2018. *Field Guide to the Ladybirds of Great Britain and Ireland.* Bloomsbury Publishing, London.

Speybroeck, J., Beukema, W., Bok, B., Van Der Voort, J., & Velikov, I. 2016. *Field Guide to the Amphibians & Reptiles of Britain and Europe.* Bloomsbury Publishing, London.

Sterling, P., Parsons, M., & Lewington, R. 2012. *Field Guide to the Micro-Moths of Great Britain and Ireland.* Bloomsbury Publishing, London.

Sterry, P. 2010. *Collins Complete Guide to British Animals.* HarperCollins, London.

Svensson, L., Mullarney, K., Zetterström, D., & Grant, P. J. 2010. *Collins Bird Guide.* HarperCollins, London.

Townsend, M., Waring, P., & Lewington, R. 2007. *Concise Guide to the Moths of Great Britain and Ireland.* Bloomsbury Publishing, London.

Waring, P., Townsend, M., & Lewington, R. 2017. *Field Guide to the Moths of Great Britain and Ireland.* Bloomsbury Publishing, London.

Further resources

Amphibian and Reptile Conservation
 www.arc-trust.org
Bat Conservation Trust
 www.bats.org.uk
British Dragonfly Society
 www.british-dragonflies.org.uk
British Hedgehog Preservation Society
 www.britishhedgehogs.org.uk
British Trust for Ornithology
 www.bto.org
Buglife
 www.buglife.org.uk
Bumblebee Conservation Trust
 www.bumblebeeconservation.org
Butterfly Conservation
 www.butterfly-conservation.org
Freshwater Habitats Trust
 www.freshwaterhabitats.org.uk
Froglife
 www.froglife.org
Garden Organic
 www.gardenorganic.org.uk
Plantlife
 www.plantlife.org.uk
Royal Horticultural Society
 www.rhs.org.uk
Royal Society for the Protection of Birds
 www.rspb.org.uk
Swift Conservation
 www.swift-conservation.org
The Mammal Society
 www.mammal.org.uk
The Wildlife Trusts
 www.wildlifetrusts.org
UK Ladybird survey
 www.coleoptera.org.uk/coccinellidae/home
Wild About Gardens
 www.wildaboutgardens.org.uk
Wildlife Gardening Forum
 www.wlgf.org
Wildlife Gardening with Jenny Steel
 www.wildlife-gardening.co.uk

Photographic credits

Bloomsbury Publishing would like to thank the following for providing images and for permission to reproduce copyright material. While every effort has been made to trace and acknowledge all copyright holders, we would like to apologise for any errors or omissions and invite readers to inform us so that corrections can be made in any future editions of the book.

6 © Richard Lewington; 8 © fotoVoyager/Getty Images; 10, 13 © Richard Revels; 14 © Phil Savoie/Nature Picture Library; 17 © Richard Revels; 19 © Alex Hyde/Nature Picture Library; 21 © Andy Sands/Nature Picture Library; 22 © Richard Lewington; 23 © Peter Turner Photography/Shutterstock; 25 © Ernie Janes/Nature Picture Library; 26 © Richard Lewington; 28 © Sue Kennedy/RSPB Images; 29 © Gary K. Smith/Nature Picture Library; 31 © Richard Lewington; 34, 44 © Richard Revels; 45 © Nature Picture Library/Getty Images; 46 © Barcroft Media/Getty Images; 86 © Richard Revels; 100 © Richard Lewington; 101, 136 © Richard Revels; 137 © Martin Dohrn/Nature Picture Library; 146 © Richard Revels; 147 © Gary Chalker/Getty Images; 160 © Richard Revels; 161 Chris Mattison/Nature Picture Library; 180 © Richard Revels; 181 © Visuals Unlimited/Nature Picture Library; 192 © Laurie Campbell; 193 © Richard Revels; 204 © Richard Lewington; 205 © Laurie Campbell; 206 © Richard Revels.

Index of scientific names

Index of English names

Bold page numbers refer to the main entry with illustration opposite.